OPEN

About the Author

JOHAN NORBERG is an author, lecturer, film-maker and historian of ideas. He is a senior fellow at the Cato Institute in Washington, DC and his books have been translated into twenty-five languages. His book *Progress* was an international bestseller and an *Economist* book of the year. Norberg regularly writes for publications such as the *Wall Street Journal, Reason* and *HuffPost*. He spreads his time between his native Sweden and the US.

OPEN

The Story of Human Progress

Atlantic Books
London

First published in hardback and trade paperback in Great Britain
in 2020 by Atlantic Books, an imprint of Atlantic Books Ltd.

3   5   7   9   10   8   6   4   2

A CIP catalogue record for this book
is available from the British Library.

Hardback ISBN: 978 1 78649 716 1
Trade paperback ISBN: 978 1 78649 718 5
E-book ISBN: 978 1 78649 717 8

Printed and bound by CPI Group (UK) Ltd, Croydon, CR0 4YY

Atlantic Books
An imprint of Atlantic Books Ltd
Ormond House
26–27 Boswell Street
London
WC1N 3JZ

www.atlantic-books.co.uk

To Frida, who ensures that I stay open and never cease to learn. Whether I like it or not.

'There is a crack in everything
That's how the light gets in.'
Leonard Cohen

CONTENTS

INTRODUCTION

TRADERS AND TRIBALISTS

'If we were to apply the unmodified, uncurbed, rules of the micro-cosmos (i.e. of the small band or troop, or of, say, our families) to the macro-cosmos (our wider civilisation), as our instincts and sentimental yearnings often make us wish to do, we would destroy it. Yet if we were always to apply the rules of the extended order to our more intimate groupings, we would crush them. So we must learn to live in two sorts of world at once.'

Friedrich Hayek, 1989

Once upon a time, a forty-five-year-old, five-foot-two man died crossing the Alps between what is now Italy and Austria. Soon after, a storm descended so his body was sealed and preserved in ice, not to be found again for more than five thousand years. When German hikers in 1991 found the mummified body of Ötzi, named after the Ötztal Alps, this gave the present an extraordinary glimpse into the past: what Copper Age life was like, how people lived and what they ate. But it also revealed their cultural and economic life.

We don't know for certain why Ötzi defied the elements and tried to cross the Alps that day, over hilly and snowy terrain at 10,000 feet above sea level. But we know why he came as far as he did. Even though he seems to have walked alone, he was never entirely lonely. On his every trip, Ötzi carried the ideas, innovations and work of thousands of people. He benefited from discoveries that he had not made himself and used tools that he had not produced.

His hat was made of bearskin and his leggings and coat were made from goat. His wide, waterproof shoes, designed for walking on snow, had bearskin for soles and deer hide for the top panels. They were so complex that researchers speculate that even 5300 years ago, Europeans had specialized cobblers who made their shoes.

Ötzi carried a kit with flint, pyrite and more than a dozen different plants for making sparks and he had a fungus for medicinal purposes. He had sixty-one tattoos, which might have been related to pain-relief treatments. He also had blade blanks, arrowheads and daggers that he had not produced himself. They were probably created by flint knappers who had spent a long time perfecting their skills. The raw material was mined from three different areas in the Southalpine region, as far as 60 kilometres away. The researchers write: 'Such variability suggests an extensive provisioning network, not at all limited to the Lessini mountains, which was able to reach the local communities.'[1] The metal for his copper axe had not been obtained from ore in the Alpine region, but as far away as South Tuscany.

Interestingly the design of the tools displays influences of both southern and northern Alpine traditions – the arrowheads are typical for Northern Italy, but the end-scraper is similar to the tools of the Swiss Horgen culture. In other words, even five thousand years ago, Ötzi benefited from a highly complex division of labour stretching over considerable parts of the continent – the kind of trade that makes it possible for people to specialize and perfect something, and exchange it for the specialized goods and services of others.

Homo sapiens is a cooperative species. Compared to many other animals, we are not particularly strong or fast, we don't have armour, we can't fly and are not very good at swimming. But we have something else that gives us an overwhelming advantage: we have each other. Because of the development of language and an oversized brain that keeps track of social relations, it became possible to cooperate on a large scale, and so make use of the ideas, knowledge and labour of others. This cooperation enabled the innovations that gave us superior artificial strength, speed and armour, in the form of clothes and medicine. It even made it possible for us to fly and cross the oceans faster than anyone else in the animal kingdom.

Man is a trader by nature. We constantly exchange know-how, favours and goods with others, so that we can accomplish more than we would if we were limited to our own talents and experiences. And it doesn't take much to get us started. We are constantly on the lookout for opportunities and it's incredibly easy for us to start a new partnership or collaboration, even with strangers. The sharing of knowledge and goods made it possible for humans to survive and prosper in inhospitable climates all over the planet. This gave rise to science, which is built on the exchange, criticism, comparison and accumulation of knowledge, and to technology, which is the application of science to solve practical problems.

We observe the benefits cooperation and mobility have given us when it's suddenly shut down. The World Bank has calculated that the greatest economic damage from epidemics like swine flu, SARS or the new coronavirus do not come from mortality, morbidity, treatment and associated loss of production, but from increased fear of associating with others. Up to 90 per cent of the damage comes from aversion behaviour, which shuts down places of production, transportation, harbours and airports.[2]

We humans innovate and we imitate, rinse and repeat, until we create something special. Enlightenment ideas in the seventeenth and eighteenth centuries tore down barriers to intellectual and economic openness, which supercharged innovation and brought unprecedented prosperity. In the last two hundred years, life expectancy has increased from less than thirty years to more than seventy, and extreme poverty has been reduced from around 90 per cent of the world's population to 9 per cent today.

Present-day globalization is nothing but the extension of this cooperation across borders, all over the world, making it possible for more people than ever to make use of the ideas and work of others, no matter where they are on the planet. This has made the modern global economy possible, which has liberated almost 130,000 people from poverty every day for the last twenty-five years.

As we will see, authoritarian China is not a counter-example to the case that progress depends on openness. When China was most open it led the world in wealth, science and technology, but by shutting its ports and minds to the world five hundred years ago, the planet's richest country soon became one of its poorest. China's present comeback is the result of a new, partial opening since 1979, and it is doing spectacularly well in the areas that have been opened, and failing miserably in the ones that have not. Chinese businesses competing on world markets have lifted millions of workers out of poverty, but protected state-owned enterprises are destroying wealth in growing rust belts. When Chinese scholars work in areas the party approves of, they end up in prestigious science journals, but when they sound the alarm about a new virus or something else that embarrasses its leaders, they end up in jail. China's Communist Party wants both the benefits of openness and the certainty of control. China's future will depend on which tendency wins out in the end.

Globalization has been described as the 'Westernization' of the world. I used to think it was. When I first became interested in history, like most people, I studied it in reverse order. So I started with the present day and age, and travelled back in time to search for its roots. This gave me a distorted view of Europe's distinctiveness. Since the Enlightenment and the Industrial Revolution began in Europe, I looked for the clues to why it happened, like so many had before me. And of course, they were easy to find: the Renaissance, via Magna Carta, Roman Law and so on, back all the way to the Greek discovery of philosophy and democracy.

This is a version of what British-Ghanaian philosopher and cultural theorist Kwame Anthony Appiah has described as a 'golden nugget' theory of history.[3] Once upon a time, the Greeks dug out a golden nugget of the earth. When the Romans conquered them, they took this golden nugget and polished it. When the empire fell, the golden nugget was partitioned, and fragments ended up in different European courts, city-states and centres of learning until it began to be reassembled in the universities of Europe and the US.

I began to lose my faith in this golden nugget when I started to come across instances of renaissances in other cultures and the fact that they had their own periods of rule of law, scientific progress and rapid economic development. I discovered that Greek philosophy was in fact a common heritage with the Islamic world. And I learned that the Chinese discovered and created most of these scientific and technological wonders on their own, a long time before Westerners did. When I saw all this, I found it increasingly difficult to defend some direct lineage model of Western civilization, especially since it depended on explaining away a millennium between Rome and Renaissance as some sort of Dark-Age aberration.

There is no golden nugget in history, but there are golden ages of creativity and accomplishment. Lots of them. The historian Jack Goldstone calls them 'efflorescences': rapid and often unexpected upturns when both population and income per capita grow. What they have in common is not their location or the ethnicity or beliefs of the populations. They happened in various places, epochs and in different belief systems: in pagan Greece, the Muslim Abbasid Caliphate, Confucian China, Catholic Renaissance Italy and the Calvinist Dutch Republic. Instead, the common element is that they were open to new ideas, insights, habits, people, technologies and business models, wherever they come from.

As I will argue, the reason that the Enlightenment and the Industrial Revolution started in Western Europe was that this region of the world happened to be the most open, partly just out of luck. It has been repeated in every place that has gone through similar institutional changes. It is not the triumph of the West, it is the triumph of openness.

This is good news for the world, since it implies that this development can take place in other cultures as well. But it is bad news for us in the West, since it means that our position is not handed to us by destiny, but by certain institutions, and they can be destroyed here, just as they were once destroyed in other parts of the world, undermining history's previous efflorescences.

Openness created the modern world and propels it forwards, because the more open we are to ideas and innovations from where we don't expect them, the more progress we will make. The philosopher Karl Popper called it 'the open society'.[4] It is the society that is open-ended, because it is not an organism, with one unifying idea, collective plan or utopian goal. The government's role in an open society is to protect the search for better ideas, and people's freedom to live by their individual plans and pursue their own goals, through a system of rules applied equally to all citizens. It is the government that abstains from 'picking winners' in culture, intellectual life, civil society and family life, as well as in business and technology. Instead it gives everybody the right to experiment with new ideas and methods, and allows them to win if they fill a need, even if it threatens the incumbents. Therefore, the open society can never be finished. It is always a work in progress.

This leaves room for forms of human order that are results of human action but not of human design. The most important institutions in culture, economics and technology were not planned centrally but were consequences of cooperation and competition, experiments and trial and error. The groups that embraced the best solutions – sometimes by coincidence – succeeded, expanded and were imitated, whereas failed experiments were put out of their misery.

As the Austrian thinker and Nobel laureate Friedrich Hayek emphasized:

> Humiliating to human pride as it may be, we must recognize that the advance and even the preservation of civilization are dependent upon a maximum of opportunity for accidents to happen.[5]

Openness to experience is a psychological trait, one of the 'Big Five' in the taxonomy of personality traits, related to imagination, intellectual curiosity and preference for variety. But this book is about the openness of institutions, not of individuals. Often they are related. People who are more open to novelty are usually less likely to want to ban it. But that is not always the case. People who are disorganized risk-takers sometimes see a need for strong rules and big governments to protect them against temptation. As we've noticed from countless personal biographies, people don't necessarily become reactionary because they hate, say, sex, drugs and rock 'n' roll, but because they like it a bit too much for their own good. Likewise, many disciplined and privately conservative individuals become open and tolerant politically not despite but because of that personality. They see with their own eyes that freedom will allow them to act virtuously and do good things.

My argument is that under open institutions people will solve more problems than they create, no matter their personality traits, and it will increase the chance that the paths of people with different traits cross, and that their thoughts and work can cross-fertilize.

In programming, there is a saying that given enough eyeballs, all bugs are shallow. The same goes for a society. The more eyeballs that are allowed to look at the accumulated knowledge of mankind and our problems, and the more brains that are allowed to add to that knowledge with their own creativity, the greater the chance that bugs will be fixed.

When people don't need permission from a central authority to experiment with new ideas, technologies and business models, but are free to create and compete (even though it might hurt sensitivities and dominant groups), we see greater human progress. The world is big; the potential number of insights, combinations of ideas and solutions are limitless. The only way to use all the knowledge and test all ideas is to let everybody have a go, and to give them freedom to cooperate and exchange freely. And the good news, as Ötzi's clothes and tools reveal, is that humans are remarkably good at it.

But there is a catch. We developed this beautiful ability to cooperate harmoniously so that we could kill and steal.

In 2001, an X-ray and a CT scan revealed that Ötzi did not just get lost in the Alps or get caught out in a sudden storm. The image revealed the exact shape of an arrowhead, buried deep in Ötzi's left shoulder. There was also a cut in his skin that matched the trajectory of that arrow. Subsequently, researchers found wounds to his right hand and wrist, which suggests that he had tried to defend himself against an attacker. He also had traces of clotted blood cells in the brain, indicative of a violent blow to the head. There was DNA from the blood of three other men on his knife and arrowheads. Ötzi did not freeze to death in a snowstorm, as it was first assumed. He was killed in hand-to-hand combat.

We can only speculate on what led to this brutal end. Some

think a dispute within the tribe forced Ötzi to flee. Others speculate that their village was attacked by another tribe and Ötzi set
off to avenge them. Or perhaps he was just ambushed by strangers.
What we do know is that this was not an exceptional fate in his
time. The violent death rate among hunter-gatherers was similar
to what it is in modern societies during wartime. Until the modern era, the lives of humans were really, as the philosopher Thomas
Hobbes once wrote, nasty, brutish and short.

Those who began to cooperate did it because it gave them a
competitive advantage against other animals and against other
groups of people. Cooperation made it easier to defeat those who
didn't play well with others. And every group has to find a way to
protect themselves against those who are happy to enjoy the loot,
but who don't contribute towards it. Therefore we learned to distinguish Us from Them.

As we will learn, our ability to form new partnerships and alliances is so strong that we become loyal to new groups in an instant,
even if they are formed on an arbitrary basis, and we start to assume
that those in our group are smarter, better and more moral than
others.

We are not just traders, we are also tribalists. We cooperate, but
to defeat others. Both attributes are integral parts of our nature,
but they push in opposite directions. One lets us find positive-
sum games, where we find new opportunities, new relationships
and new exchanges that are mutually beneficial. The other primes
us to be wary of zero-sum games, where we think others can only
benefit at our expense. This drives a desire to defeat others and
block exchange and mobility.

This is the battle between 'open and closed', so much discussed
in the context of populism, nationalism, Trump and Brexit. It is
not being fought between two different groups, between globalists
and nationalists, or anywheres and somewheres. Rather, it is being
fought within all of us, all the time.

When we feel threatened we want to escape in the security of our tribe and circle the wagons, and this makes us more conformist and more approving of strong leaders. Amazingly, even small threats to our sense of order and control – like answering questions about our attitudes without having washed our hands, or having to do so in a messy room – make us more judgmental and less tolerant.

What then about when we fear that our culture, our lifestyle or our whole society is under threat, from pandemics, immigrants, foreign countries or treacherous elites? When the whole world looks untidy? This is the state in which we find ourselves after the financial crisis and the migration crisis, with growing geopolitical tensions, where political liberation after the Arab Spring is no longer associated with stability and democratization, but with chaos and bloodshed. When the iconic image of our time is no longer the fall of the Berlin Wall, but the collapse of the twin towers of the World Trade Center in New York. And that is without mentioning potential looming disaster from climate change.

In the past, the great efflorescences in history – those major episodes of openness and progress – petered out because of what has been called Cardwell's Law, after the technology historian Donald S. Cardwell.[6] Innovation always faces resistance from groups that think they stand to lose from it, be they old political or religious elites, businesses with old technologies, workers with outmoded skills, nostalgic romantics or old folks who feel anxious because people just don't do things the way they used to. They have an incentive to stop changes with bans, regulations, monopolies, the burning of boats or the building of walls. And when the rest of us panic about the world we let them have their way. And this is how every period of openness and innovation in history was ended, except one: the one that we are in right now. An open world, if we can keep it.

The COVID-19 pandemic illustrates what can happen and

what is at stake. International trade and mobility have not only enriched the world, they have also made it possible for microorganisms to hitch a ride. Historically, rulers have used such great plagues to extend control over their populations, pull up the drawbridges and attack scapegoats, like Jews, foreigners or witches.

As a new coronavirus pandemic haunts the world, it is not difficult to imagine how it could be a decisive turning point, away from openness. Companies are forced to re-evaluate international supply chains, natives become suspicious of outsiders and global travel, and governments grant themselves new powers. At the time of writing, no government has yet 'postponed' an election because of the coronavirus, but such things have happened before in history. Panic changes politics in a nationalist direction, such as with bans on the export of drugs and medical equipment. And while that seems like a way to protect citizens, it forces other countries to do the same and results in shortages for everybody. Several bans on food export during the global price crisis of 2010–11 were intended to secure local supplies but ended up accounting for 40 per cent of the increase in the world prices of wheat and almost a quarter of the increase in prices of maize.[7]

So even though the world often moves in a nationalist direction during crises, these are the times when we most urgently need international agreements to forgo beggar-thy-neighbour policies. We rarely think of it this way, but globalization is actually our best chance to fight pandemics in the first place, since wealth, communication technology and open science have made our response to new diseases faster than ever, as science writer Ron Bailey has noted.[8]

Hospitals, researchers, health authorities and drug companies everywhere can now supply each other with instant information and coordinate efforts to analyse and combat the problem. After having tried to conceal the outbreak for weeks, China announced that it had found a new coronavirus on 2 January 2020. Using technologies developed on the other side of the globe, Chinese scientists could read the complete genome of the virus and publish it on a new global hub for medical research, on 10 January. Just six days later, German researchers had used this information to develop and release a diagnostic test to detect new infections. And when someone reveals the mechanism of the virus, others immediately get to work to find its weaknesses. Then researchers and artificial intelligence all over the world begin to explore possible drugs and vaccines that can attack it at just those points.

After just one and a half months of work, a US biotech company could send a brand-new vaccine to authorities for clinical trials. On 2 April, just three months after China admitted a new virus was on the loose, America's National Library of Medicine listed 282 potential drugs and vaccines against the new virus and were already recruiting patients or proposing to do that.

In a poorer and more closed world, without mass transportation, microorganisms travelled more slowly but they travelled freely, recurring for hundreds of years, until they had picked almost all of us off one by one. Today our response is also global, and therefore mankind has for the first time a fighting chance. This is a remarkable achievement, and we neglect it at our own peril.

This book is both a prequel and a sequel to my 2016 book *Progress: Ten Reasons to Look Forward to the Future*. That book was an attempt to document the amazing and surprisingly little-known development that has taken place in the modern world. But I never did much more than hint at the reasons *why* we suddenly made more progress in the last two hundred years than in the previous twenty thousand. This is my story about how openness made progress possible.

At the same time, I go further and examine the uncertain future of progress, by looking at the forces threatening it in the past, today and in the future, and which might yet overthrow it. I wrote

Progress just as populists and nationalists were dealing their first blows against an open world order, to remind ourselves of what is at stake. This time I take a closer look at why it is so tempting to close our horizons.

In the first half of the book, I will look at how free trade, migration, free thought and open societies made the modern world – how openness is a natural outcome when individuals try to improve their own lives, and the fact that it ends up improving the whole society and ourselves in many more ways than we give it credit for.

It turns out that almost all of the things that we hold dear, and that many now assume are being threatened by openness, were once *created* by openness. This is the dilemma for the cultural protectionist: he always defends something that former protectionists were not successful enough to prevent.

My case partly rests on an examination of global history, outlining how the Enlightenment, Industrial Revolution and the first open societies got their start in Western Europe, but not *because* it was Western Europe. European rulers tried, just like other rulers, to block openness and progress because they wanted to defend stability and order and to pick the pockets of the people. Luckily, they were not very good at it, and this opened up space for cosmopolitan Enlightenment thinkers and the revolution that is the modern world.

Global history is the genre of history that tries to correct for how national history tries to compartmentalize the human experience for patriotic purposes. Global history also looks at the borderlands and the connections, the cross-fertilization between cultures that changed them all, often simultaneously. It is interested in how Europeans learned Greek philosophy in conquered Muslim libraries, picked up scientific ideas in China and lost their certainty about the universe by finding strange things on new continents.

Because of the recent globalization backlash, some think global history is over before it really got going. Nothing could be further from the truth. It is more important than ever to understand the world, including the backlash, which is global in its nature. It was inspired by transnational events like the financial crisis and the migration crisis, and even nativists constantly travel across borders to inspire one another. The Brexit referendum gave an injection of energy to the Trump movement, and Trump's election energized populists all over Europe – agitators and parties who claim that there is one true, united people whose general will is blocked by a corrupt elite. So did money and media assistance from Putin's Russia, which is eager to show that Western liberalism is obsolete. Meanwhile Western anti-liberals look to Putin as a source of inspiration because he 'is standing up for traditional institutions', as Steve Bannon puts it.[9]

We can't live without openness, but the question is whether we can live with it. In the second half of the book, I examine why openness is always under threat, historically and right now. I will argue that the modern world was not intended, it almost happened by accident. It happened because there were too many gaps in the control of princes, priests and guilds to stop people's creativity entirely. It was embraced more broadly because it was allowed to survive so long that its consequences became apparent in the strength of societies and in the living standards of people. Is that a sufficient recipe for long-term sustainability?

I combine lessons from history with insights from evolutionary psychology to explore how uncomfortable we are with this openness. We all have psychological predispositions that push us towards tribalism, authoritarianism and nostalgia, especially when we feel threatened, by recessions, foreigners or pandemics. Our tendency to divide the world into us and them is reinforced whenever we think that the world is a zero-sum game and that we can't mutually benefit from production, mobility and trade. We are uncomfortable with a seemingly chaotic present and an uncertain future, creating an opportunity for demagogues who promise to restore order and make America, Russia, India, China or Europe great again.

I will look at how a series of crises and threats, most crucially the financial crisis, has created a sense that we are under attack and that we must protect ourselves at all costs. That is when our genetic fight-or-flight default tells us to search out enemies and fight them, or to flee into the group, behind tariffs and walls. Our human nature created this modern world and all its wonders, but it also contains the potential to tear it all down.

I will also focus on the most serious counterarguments against openness, namely worries about how it undermines communities and livelihoods, and how it creates inequality and environmental destruction. I will argue that these problems are indeed real and serious, but that the only way to deal with them, and continue to make progress, is more openness. Liberty does not give us certainty and control, but it does something more important: it leaves room for the unforeseeable and unpredictable, and that is the only place from which we can expect progress and solutions to our problems.

The main thing we have to fear is the risk that fear of these problems will lead us to turn our backs on openness. That would deprive us of the means to handle the challenges, and it might very well up-end what we have already accomplished. When looking at present living standards, health, wealth, literacy and liberty in a historical context, there is no doubt that we live in a golden age. But history is littered with golden ages that did not last.

Tom G. Palmer, one of the foremost classical liberal thinkers of our age, recently warned that:

A spectre is haunting the world: the spectre of radical anti-libertarian movements, each grappling with the others like scorpions in a bottle and all competing to see which can dismantle the institutions of liberty the fastest. Some are ensconced in the universities and other elite centers, and some draw their strength from populist anger. The leftist and the rightist versions of the common antilibertarian cause are, moreover, interconnected, with each fueling the other. [...]

Those who prefer constitutionalism to dictatorship, free markets to cronyist or socialist statism, free trade to autarchy, toleration to oppression, and social harmony to irreconcilable antagonism need to wake up, because our cause and the prosperity and peace it engenders are in grave danger.[10]

In danger *again*, I might add. The evolution that turned you and me into collaborative traders also turned us into status-seeking tribalists, worried about the advance of everybody else. This is the reason why open societies throughout history have suddenly, and sometimes seemingly without warning, slipped back into group warfare, nationalism and protectionism. Even war.

History does not repeat itself, but human nature does.

I

OPEN

1

OPEN EXCHANGE

'We are all caught in an inescapable network of mutuality, tied into a single garment of destiny [...] before you finish eating breakfast in the morning, you've depended on more than half the world.'

Martin Luther King, 1967

In July 2017, US president Donald Trump was editing an upcoming speech with his staff secretary. In the margin he scribbled three words indicating what he wanted to emphasize in the speech, and which also summed up his America First worldview: 'TRADE IS BAD'.[1]

In the view of Trump, and many of the new populists of the Right and the Left in ascendance around the world, free trade is the worst foreign import of them all. It is something forced upon the innocent people of [insert country where you happen to live] by powerful foreigners who want to destroy our industry by drowning us in cheap goods. It's a plot from the Chinese, the WTO, the EU to force shoddy and possibly hazardous imports on us. Ironically, in Europe, for a long time many critics talked of globalization as a US plot. Some called it 'Americanization'.

Soon after I read about Trump's scribbled words, a friend sent me a message from his children's school about a problem with snack boxes. Apparently, the children had started trading food with one another. And rice cakes in the boxes created bigger problems than anything else because children at school had started using them to pay for other goods and even to buy help and services. The school wanted the parents' help to stop the kids from being free traders. The children had realized that by bartering they could get something to eat that they preferred to what they already had, so after an exchange both thought they had a better snack box than before. They even developed a medium of exchange – rice cakes – that they realized they could use to extend the market.

Trade is not imposed on us from abroad. A market is not a place or even an economic system. It is what people *do* wherever they are, in all eras, even children, as long as they are not stopped from doing it by governments – or parents.

After having reviewed the historical evidence, the British journalist and science writer Matt Ridley concludes:

> There is no known human tribe that does not trade. Western explorers, from Christopher Columbus to Captain Cook, ran into many confusions and misunderstandings when they made first contact with isolated peoples. But the principle of trading was not one of them, because the people they met in every case already had a notion of swapping things. Within hours or days of meeting a new tribe, every explorer is bartering.[2]

Why do we trade? The economist Charles Wheelan once asked us to imagine the best machine possible.[3] It would turn soybeans into computers. That would be fantastic for farmers. They could do what they are good at, and still get the computers they needed to control their irrigation system. And even better, the same machine could turn books into clothing. I could pop in five copies of this book and out would come a new shirt. Amazingly, the machine could also be programmed to turn furniture into cars, medical assistance into electricity, aircraft into financial services, and sparkling water into wine. And it could transform these things the other way around as well. In fact, it could turn anything you already had into anything you wanted.

The machine would work in poor countries too, where people would put things they are able to produce even without lots of capital and education into the machine – beef or textiles, say – and out the other end they would get high-tech medicine and infrastructure. The best way of making poor countries rich would obviously be to give them access to such a machine.

It sounds like magic, but in fact, this machine already exists. It's called *trade*. It can be set up anywhere, and it runs on nothing but human imagination and on keeping protectionists (or parents) away. It's not a foreign plot, it is the fastest way to prosper more from what you produce yourself, and the only way for poor countries to get rich and for rich countries to get richer.

Mankind has, thought the Scottish philosopher and economist Adam Smith, 'a disposition to truck, barter and exchange'.[4] Wherever we look in history, people exchange – favours, ideas, goods and services. And the deeper archaeologists dig, the further back they push the evidence of human exchange. It goes thousands of years back in history and, according to some recent, astonishing findings, trade is as old as mankind itself.

Homo mercator

The first fossils of *Homo sapiens* are around 300,000 years old. So are the first, recently discovered, signs of long-distance trade.[5] Olorgesailie, the now-dry basin of an ancient Kenyan lake, is a treasure trove for archaeologists. Over the years they have found much there, but nothing as fascinating as the carefully shaped and specialized tools, spear tips, scrapers and awls that are more than 300,000 years old. It's not just their age that is remarkable, but the material they are made of: obsidian. This black volcanic glass has been much valued because it is easily fractured to produce razor-sharp cutting tools and weapons.

Obsidian is also much valued by archaeologists and historians because it is only produced in a few volcanic sites, so its presence elsewhere reveals patterns of mobility and exchange. Amazingly, none of these volcanic sites are close to Olorgesailie. In fact, the obsidian probably came from sources up to 88 kilometres away, if you take the shortcut over mountains. The researchers deem it highly unlikely that the people of Olorgesailie commuted there, and assume instead that they were part of long-distance trade networks, exchanging other goods and resources for the obsidian they wanted. This interpretation was supported by the fact that they also used colourful rocks for dyes, which had also been imported from far away.

Truck, barter and exchange – 300,000 years ago.

Humans have always cooperated. Early humans did not just exchange obsidian and tools, but also know-how, favours and loyalty. They cooperated in child-rearing, defence, hunting and gathering. Most importantly, this cooperation also extends to other humans who are not family, unrelated individuals in the tribe, and to owners of obsidian on the other side of the mountain, in constantly shifting relationships. It is not simple kin selection but reciprocity, exchange for the sake of mutual benefit. As one description of Inuit culture has it: 'The best place for him to store his surplus is in someone else's stomach, because sooner or later he will want his gift repaid.'[6]

We love to reciprocate, to the extent that we feel bad when we don't get the chance to repay kindness with kindness (or malice with malice). Producers of free online goods have been surprised to find that people want to pay, even if they don't have to, as soon as they create a smooth payment solution. This is why the bazaar salesman always gives you coffee, so that you will feel that at least you owe him a proper look at his goods. This is also why you have to think twice before you accept a very expensive gift from someone who is not your partner.[7]

Cooperation and exchange were so essential to human beings that it is hard to explain what came first: trade or *Homo sapiens*. And I mean that in a literal sense. Humans shaped trade but trade also shaped the humans we became. This is the key to understanding how humans managed to take over the world and to inhabit all sorts of climates even though we have few environment-specific genetic adaptations.

Evolutionary psychologist Steven Pinker thinks that *Homo sapiens'* peculiarities can be explained by the knowledge-using and socially interdependent 'cognitive niche' we inhabit. A couple of hundred thousand years ago, we simultaneously developed three unique traits: intelligence, language and cooperation. These are mutually reinforcing: incremental improvements in one of them make the other two more valuable, and thus change the social and physical environment – and with it evolutionary pressures for additional adaptations.[8]

Intelligence makes it possible to learn and store information and skills. A grammatically advanced language allows us to communicate this to others so they can build on our experiences and don't have to make the same mistakes or to reinvent the wheel. This gives us both the means and incentives to cooperate with others – and not just our kin. Open-ended communication allows us to share know-how at little cost to ourselves and to coordinate behaviour. Intelligence makes it possible to negotiate, sometimes implicitly, deals about favours and goods to be transferred at separate times. The moment humans started benefiting from mutually advantageous collaboration it enhanced the value of intelligence

and language dramatically, and this made more advanced cooperation possible, and so on.

But what pushed our ancestors onto this particular evolutionary
path from the beginning? There is a convincing hypothesis – to me
at least – that explains it by taking us back to the moment when
the first chimp-like creatures left the trees and became bipedal six
or seven million years ago: 'the throwing hypothesis'. Why we ever
left the trees has been a matter of controversy since Darwin's days.
Chimps are well protected in their trees but, being slow and small,
they are easy prey for lions, leopards and sabre-toothed tigers on
the ground. Now we have learned that some pretty rough tectonic
activity created the East River Rift Valley and changed the climate.
This dried out the rainforests to the east of the valley and replaced
it with savannah. 'So it turns out we didn't leave the trees after all,'
writes psychologist William von Hippel, outlining the hypothesis,
'the trees left us'.[9]

Thrown into a hostile and confusing environment, these
chimpish creatures had to find a new way to make a living in the
midst of big predators. Over the next three million years, most
of them certainly failed, but some of them came up with a way
of using hands no longer needed for locomotion, which helped
them to survive on the grasslands, changed them physically and
mentally and turned them into our ancestors. The solution was
stone-throwing.

In the remains of Lucy, the world's most famous *Australopithecus afarensis*, we can observe that some important anatomical
changes had taken place at least 3.2 million years ago. She had
a more mobile hand and wrist than chimpanzees, more flexibility in her upper arm, a more horizontally oriented shoulder, and
the hip and the bottom of her rib cage are further apart. All of
them perfectly adapted for throwing stones with force and precision. Even with such excellent joints and muscles, Lucy would not
stand much of a chance against a lion, but if she coordinated her

defence with other *Australopithecus*, they could unleash a shower of stones that would cut the big cat into pieces. They must soon have realized that they could hunt in the same fashion. With the invention of cooperation, our ancestors who used to be easy prey took their place at the top of the food chain.

This was our 'social leap', as von Hippel calls it. Individuals who learned to cooperate in stone-throwing quickly outbred individuals who committed to the old strategy of 'every chimpish chap for himself'. This would have led evolution to favour changes that made us better at cooperating, for example a large brain to understand others and manage social challenges.

If you want evidence of mankind's unique sociability, look in the mirror. Chimpanzees and the other apes have brown sclera (the part of the eye that surrounds the cornea), to hide their gaze from other chimpanzees. Chimpanzees are primarily rivals and don't want other members of their group to know that they have spotted a potential partner or tasty snack because someone else might steal the idea and get there first. Humans, on the other hand, have developed white sclera so that we broadcast the direction of our gaze to our entire group, which suggests that we benefited more from sharing information than keeping it secret. When we notice a threat, we want others to know and help to strengthen our defence. If we spot a prey animal, we want others to know so they can help us catch it.

Humans can share intentions and understand that others have the same idea. Chimpanzees can't and they don't collaborate unless it suits them. They sometimes seem to hunt monkeys as a group, but as explained by an expert on chimpanzee cognition, Michael Tomasello, it is more like a wild scramble where every chimp is trying to do what is best for him at every stage in a chaotic scene. They don't even try to communicate and the whole group does not join in. Some just sit by and wait for the others to do the work, and then fight with them over the spoils.[10]

Cultural evolution

Our social ability set the stage for a new form of evolution. 'Cultural evolution,' wrote philosopher Karl Popper, 'continues genetic evolution by other means.'[11] If one wolf is better at hunting because of a mutation that gives it better smell, say, the species has to wait for it and its descendants to procreate more successfully and for the other wolves to be pushed aside. If a human being comes up with a better way of hunting – for example, by making a better spear – others just imitate it. This is why genetic evolution works at glacial speed, while cultural evolution takes place in the blink of an eye – you watch and just do it.

If you have ever played 'rock paper scissors', you may have noticed that sometimes a stressed player accidentally reveals his choice a split-second too early, thereby giving the other player a great advantage, since it is now easy to pick a superior choice. Yet, surprisingly, that is rarely what happens; instead, it results in more draws – a rock is matched with a rock and a stone with a stone. Unconsciously, we tend to imitate others, even if it happens to be to our disadvantage.[12] Similarly, experiments in game theory show that the less time people have to make a decision, the more we cooperate. It comes naturally to us.

One-year-olds have no idea about the strange world they have been born into, so they rely on cultural learning constantly. Studies find that, when faced with a novel situation or toy, children consistently look more often at their parent to see if they signal approval or fear. More surprisingly, when infants are in a room with their mother and a stranger and an unfamiliar object, they reference the stranger more than their mother, probably because their mother is also likely to be new to the situation and is judged less qualified by the one-year-old. (Yes, they grow up so fast, don't they?)[13]

Children stay close to their older siblings or cousins, adults hang around their most accomplished peers, and we all hang around those who seem to be in the know. Perhaps it is a side effect of our readiness to pick up traits from those who seem most competent and successful among us that we are also quick to pick up their particular hairstyle, profanities and brand of breakfast cereals as well. And unfortunately, when a celebrity takes their own life, there is a spike in suicides using the same kind of method. Copying others is just in our nature.

If one individual has a better method, the whole tribe soon has it, and if a group or village stumbles upon a behaviour that makes it more successful, it soon catches on elsewhere. This is because we have a look around while engaging in long-distance trade or during conflict. Even with the primitive means of travel that the ancients had at their disposal, it is amazing how quickly methods and technologies – burial rituals, painted ceramics, new crops and weapons – appeared in villages hundreds of kilometres away soon after having been introduced.

The more people there are, the greater the chance that someone will come up with a useful idea or technology, so innovation depends on the size of the interconnected population. This means that a guaranteed way to hold a society back is to hold people down. When a large group of people are stopped from pursuing knowledge or contributing to production, a society voluntarily limits the ideas, creativity and labour it has access to. Most societies throughout most of history have discriminated against women, thereby in effect halving the ability to make progress. Mary Wollstonecraft, one of the pioneers of women's rights, explained in 1792 that gender equality was not just about human rights, but also about not wasting the ability of half of mankind. Many had talked about women's virtues, but the only way to 'render their private virtue a public benefit' was for all respectable positions to be opened up to them. 'How many women thus waste life away the prey of discontent, who might have practised as physicians, regulated a farm, managed a shop, and stood erect, supported by their own industry,' Wollstonecraft asked.[14]

During humanity's early years, cultural evolution was self-reinforcing. The more successful solutions people found, the more the population grew, and that resulted in more innovations. Researchers have suggested that the sudden development of sophisticated tool-making, art and culture in western Eurasia about 45,000 years ago can be explained by population density. At last this region had enough people sufficiently close to regularly transfer skills and knowledge between groups. Then they showed that the population density was similar in Africa and the Middle East when 'modern' human behaviour appeared there. So it's not our genes that set us apart from one another, it's our proximity to more genes belonging to other people.[15]

Charles Darwin explained that: 'primeval man practised a division of labour; each man did not manufacture his own tools or rude pottery, but certain individuals appear to have devoted themselves to such work, no doubt receiving in exchange the produce of the chase'.[16] If I am better at producing tools and you are better at hunting, we each specialize in our *competitive advantage*, so both you and I get better tools and more food than we would if we had to do both. And if we do that we will probably both invest more time and energy in becoming even better at our particular task.

We can also both benefit from exchange even if you have better skills in both areas, because you are probably slightly better at one thing than the other. Imagine that Bob and Dave need knives and a rabbit to serve their friends dinner. Let's say that Bob would only need two hours to produce a knife and one hour to bag a rabbit, whereas Dave needs three hours for the knife and since he is a lousy hunter it would take him six hours to catch the rabbit. Bob is better at both things, but he is much better at hunting than Dave and just slightly better at manufacturing. If both spent the same amount of time focused on their *comparative advantage*, Bob would spend his three hours catching three rabbits, and Dave would spend his nine hours manufacturing three knives. Then they share. Without having worked harder or longer than before, they increased their total production from two knives and two rabbits, to three knives and three rabbits. So they can now offer their friends a more generous dinner, or make do with the old production level and just head for an earlier fermented drink by the campfire.

In real life, people soon discovered they could use the surplus product to exchange for some obsidian and stone pigment from other tribes. And further gains would be realized.

Trade is not only about goods and services; it is also about knowledge. In very primitive hunter-gatherer societies and subsistence agriculture most people do roughly similar things and have broadly the same knowledge about nature and farming methods. The amount of information every individual holds in such a culture is incredibly impressive – about plants and animals, what you can and cannot eat, which farming methods to use and so on – but the total body of know-how in such a culture is incredibly limited because everyone holds very similar information. People stay desperately poor because they are all Renaissance men.

As division of labour becomes more complex, this all changes. We learn more about our particular task and we improve our skills. One person learns everything about how to create tools, another about how to fish, a third about wheat, a fourth about autoimmune diseases and a fifth about how to service the cable connection. Suddenly the total body of knowledge grows explosively, and we can benefit from it by using the tools, food, medicine and technical skill that others have created, even though we never learned it ourselves. As Friedrich Hayek explained: 'civilisation rests on the fact that we all benefit from knowledge that we do *not* possess'.[17]

Such constant cooperation and exchange give us better access to the services and goods we need, so long as we can trust that others will be there to scratch our backs if we have scratched theirs. One classic study showed that chimpanzees are more willing to share food with chimps who have recently groomed them, and more likely to respond aggressively to requests for food from chimps who had not recently groomed them.[18] But chimps have not taken this to the next level by systematically keeping track of free riders and helpers in the larger group, to administer rewards and punishments. The strange thing is not that some of them sit idly by as the others hunt monkeys, but that those slackers are just as likely to grab a mouthful of the prey as those who were hunting it.[19] The distribution principle is 'from each according to his whim, to each according to what he can steal from others'.

For any advanced cooperation to function there has to be a way to systematically reward cooperation and punish cheating. To do this in large groups of non-kin it takes an impressive prefrontal cortex with the ability to recognize others, remember their actions and judge their behaviour. We couldn't do all this without gossiping about friends, neighbours and colleagues all the time – and this takes a certain kind of intelligence: ours. In this way, the accumulated evidence of early man's ability to exchange gives us a convincing answer to a great Stone Age whodunnit.

Who killed the Neanderthals?

The Neanderthals had survived for more than 200,000 years in Europe when *Homo sapiens* first spread over the continent perhaps 50,000 years ago. Then, within just a few thousand years, the Neanderthals were gone. They didn't go extinct, as we used to think. They interbred with humans and part of them lives on in us, but increasingly the offspring survived in human settlements and the classic Neanderthal disappeared. Why?

This question has eluded scientists for decades. Neanderthals were stronger and they even had a bigger brain than *Homo sapiens* did, whatever that is supposed to entail. We do know, though, that being hairy does not mean being stupid, as newspaper cartoons might have us believe; it just means they were better adapted to the cold European climate in which they had lived for so long. Many theories about mankind's advantages were suggested, but few have survived the advance of archaeology.

One persuasive factor is that *Homo sapiens* were free traders.[20] Neanderthal groups lived in smaller and more isolated groups that did not venture far from home. In contrast, as we know, remains of even the earliest human dwellings in Europe show stone tools made of materials from far away and seashell jewellery inland. Neanderthal tools have been found close to their sites of origin. They did not have long-lasting, long-distance trade links with other Neanderthal groups and, in the instances when raw materials were transported, it was only over short distances.

Neanderthals did not even seem to have much of a division of labour within the group. Their living arrangements were unorganized with no sign of them being divided according to different functions. They did not leave behind any bone needles, which does not just suggest that they only had crudely assembled apparel and tents, but also that no part of the group stayed behind and specialized in domestic tasks when others hunted. The Neanderthals seemed not to have relied on subsistence food sources like nuts, seeds and berries or even small game. They went for the highest reward, large game, and it seems like the whole group was involved, including women and children.

Homo sapiens, on the other hand, had an advanced division of labour. They exchanged raw materials over long distances. Their living spaces were more complex and divided according to different functions. They had a more varied diet, including small animals, nuts, seeds and berries, which seems to be the result of a division of labour where men more often hunted larger game while women and children collected and prepared subsistence food sources. We assume this not just from the evidence of present-day hunter-gatherers but also from the fact that men were often buried with spear- and arrowheads whereas women were buried with grinding tools.

This approach gave humans many advantages. It gave them a greater supply of resources and of food, and helped them when big game was scarce. Their tailored clothes and tents protected them better from the cold, and children got a safer environment. But most of all, division of labour meant they constantly made progress. They exchanged ideas and knowledge within the group and between groups. As individuals specialized in different areas, they gathered more information and came up with more innovations, by chance or intent, and when one group came up with innovations, travelling bands of early humans made sure they spread rapidly to other groups.

One example is control of fire, one of the most important innovations in history. It helped us against the elements and predators, and perhaps it also grew our brains since cooked food releases more nutrients and calories than raw food.[21] It also saved us a lot of time. Chimpanzees spend around six hours every day just chewing food to make it digestible. Such a diet must have been a detriment to communication (after all, it's impolite to talk with your mouth full). Fire also bound the community together in another way. The day was extended, as foragers could now gather in small groups around fires when work was no longer possible. The topics of discussion during the day, about immediate concerns and needs, gave way to conversation and story-telling. It was a way of sharing important information and building trust within the band.

We know that Neanderthals used fire, but archaeologists who have excavated their caves have found a strange pattern: there is plenty of evidence of fires during warm periods, but few during cold periods, when they would have been most useful. This indicates that most Neanderthal groups did not know how to make fires, and only collected it from lightning strikes, which are more common when it is warm, and when they had drier fuel to make it last.[22] In contrast, when one *Homo sapiens* stumbled on the idea to use pyrites and stone to produce fire, it soon spread far and wide. Groups that did not pick up the idea could head over to another band and borrow some fire if their own was extinguished by a storm.

In the long run, it meant that *Homo sapiens'* knowledge and technology improved constantly, whereas the Neanderthals' stood still. This was all it took for human populations to constantly multiply and move into new areas, and for the Neanderthals to be forced to retreat, step by step, little by little over thousands of years. The rest, as they say, is prehistory.

The morality of trade

Trade has a tendency to expand both within society and across borders as a group starts engaging in it, not just because trade creates wealth but also because it changes behaviour and values in a way that makes more exchange and cooperation likely.

In *The Communist Manifesto*, Marx and Engels accused market exchange of having:

> left remaining no other nexus between man and man than naked self-interest, than callous 'cash payment'. [...] It has resolved personal worth into exchange value, and in place of the numberless indefeasible chartered freedoms, has set up that single, unconscionable freedom – Free Trade. [...] naked, shameless, direct, brutal exploitation.[23]

It's easy to think of examples of ruthlessness in markets, and most of us have experienced it ourselves, but it's also easy to think of

examples of ruthlessness in politics, in the bar and in the schoolyard. So the interesting question is what overall effect trade
has on our norms and our behaviour – and on our potential for
ruthlessness.

One way to explore people's attitude to fairness is to play 'the
ultimatum game'. It is an economic experiment with real money,
where a player is given some cash and then asked to give a portion
of it to an anonymous player. The other player then has to decide
whether or not to accept the offer. If the recipient doesn't, neither
player gets any money at all. Both Marxists and neoclassical business schools would have us think that the first player would always
propose a minimum to the recipient, who would always accept
because almost nothing is better than nothing. Since the game is
not repeated between the same players, there is no need to be generous to the recipient or to 'punish' a stingy first player by rejecting
the offer so that they will be more generous next time.

However, decades of experiments have shown conclusively
that people are not like *Homo economicus*. They do not act this way
anywhere. On the contrary, in rich countries the most common
proposal is to share alike, and recipients usually reject offers of
less than 30 per cent. Consider an intriguing set of experiments
in fifteen small-scale communities at different stages of development, from hunter-gatherers to farming communities. It turns out
that how they play the game is not related to gender, age, education or ethnicity, but to how much use they make of markets.
Perhaps surprisingly, the more people depend on market exchange
in their daily lives, the *more* willing they are to make generous
offers and also to punish ungenerous offers at a cost to themselves.
The market attitude is to be generous, whereas people in non-
market societies 'display relatively little concern with fairness or
punishing unfairness', concludes the research team. On average
the most market-integrated societies offered twice the share of the
least integrated.[24]

This seemed so counter-intuitive to many that the researchers went back into the field to see if the results could be replicated. They also added two more games, 'the dictator game', where the second player can't reject the offer, and the 'third-party punishment game', where a spectator can give up cash to punish the first player for an ungenerous offer. The result was repeated. The more people are used to bargaining, trade and seeking profit in their everyday lives, the less ruthless they are.

The researchers' interpretation is that the evolution of societal complexity is not just an extension of our local behaviour to friends and family. They suggest it involves the selective spread of the norms that are best facilitated by large-scale exchange and interaction. People in non-market societies also have norms about fairness, of course, but these relate to family and friends, not to strangers or anonymous others. On the other hand, those who regularly trade have default norms that include a certain generosity and openness, which makes it possible for them to extend this cooperation because generally people are more willing to trade with those who are not ruthless and unfair.

It's not just that the generous trade more, but that those who trade also become more generous. Even within communities that rely on trade, the distance to market is important. The closer people live to markets, and so the more they trade, the greater their willingness to cooperate with strangers (though perhaps not to engage in small talk on the metro). And when researchers unconsciously remind subjects of markets, those subjects become more trusting and invest more money with strangers. There is a strong connection between the biggest cities where much of trade happens and the inhabitants' open attitudes to globalization and foreigners. Open economies stimulate open-mindedness. Regular exchange seems to accustom us to the idea that interaction with others is mutually beneficial, and prompts us to show some consideration for others' interests. Those who are not used to it treat such encounters as something threatening or just an opportunity to pursue maximum short-term gain. Incredibly, the morality of trade seems to develop a sense of fairness that survives even in a game rigged to encourage ruthless materialism.

This does not mean that the benefits of trade are distributed equally. It is still possible for some to gain much more than others because of their skills, hard work or just plain luck. Sometimes how highly something is valued changes dramatically because of external factors. For example, if better education, new communication technologies and freer trade makes it possible for two billion fairly unskilled poor people to enter the global labour market, it means there is suddenly less demand for unskilled workers and more demand for highly skilled workers, thereby increasing inequality between these groups. We will look more at inequality later, but here we focus not on what trade does to our wallets, but to that thing behind it: our hearts.

As we saw, Marx and Engels thought free trade left us with nothing but 'naked, shameless, direct, brutal exploitation', but after having organized behavioural games around the world, the former Marxist economist Herbert Gintis concluded that it is the other way around: 'I would say societies that use markets extensively develop a culture of cooperation, fairness, and respect for the individual.'[25]

Joseph Henrich, who has led much of this research, says they have searched all over the world for *Homo economicus*, the protagonist of classical economics, who only cares about monetary gain, and eventually they located a group that approximates him. They do not care that other players receive equitable pay-offs even when the costs to themselves are low, and they don't reject unfair offers or punish stingy players. But you will probably not meet them in the marketplace, although we did encounter them earlier in the chapter. They are chimpanzees.[26]

Everything begins in Mesopotamia

For a long time, historians downplayed the role of trade in early civilizations. This misunderstanding was based on the fact that official documents were better preserved than receipts between merchants. Temples, palaces and pyramids survived the wear and tear of time, whereas commercial structures of wood and clay perished.

In 1944 the economic historian Karl Polanyi wrote *The Great Transformation*, arguing that markets based on supply and demand and the profit motive are new and alien to the human experience. However, just two years later, the American scholar Samuel Noah Kramer started to publish his translations of ancient clay tablets, which would transform our view of the earliest civilization in Mesopotamia, the rich agricultural land between the rivers Euphrates and Tigris (the name Mesopotamia is Greek for 'between rivers').

Sumer is the first known civilization in this region, and among the Sumerians, writing appeared around 3000 BC. Since they wrote in a cuneiform script on tough clay tablets rather than papyrus that would have rotted, many are left intact. Many an archaeologist and art historian has been disappointed to find that the earliest form of literature was a tedious documentation of ownership, transactions and prices of goods, land and labour. (One claimed that 90 per cent is rubbish.)[27] Organized commerce is as old as recorded history and settled civilization.

Who is the first person in history that we know the name of? When you ask people, most of them guess a prophet or a conqueror. They are all wrong. The first person we know by name was probably an accountant. On a clay tablet from around 3400–3000 BC, we learn that 29,086 measures of barley have been received over the course of thirty-seven months, signed 'Kushim'. Of course, Kushim could have been a job title – we know very little about what was going on five thousand years ago – but there is also a real chance that it was his real name. As historian Yuval Noah Harari speculates: 'When Kushim's neighbours called out to him, they might really have shouted "Kushim!"'[28]

Similarly, the first written reference to King Solomon's temple is a clay inscription from the seventh century BC, and it was not a religious reference or a line of prayer. It was a receipt of money the temple had received.[29]

It's not just that trade was the first activity mankind wrote about; trade was the reason that mankind started to write anything in the first place.[30] The first clay objects to have been hardened by fire were small tokens of various geometrical form and sometimes shaped like animals, created in the Middle East in 8000–4300 BC. After having spent many years studying more than ten thousand tokens, the archaeologist Denise Schmandt-Besserat understood that they were an early accounting system, a way of keeping track of goods. Cones represented grain, ovoids were jars of oil, and cylinders were domestic animals. As trade increased between villages people needed to record goods in a way that was understood by people who did not speak the same language. It seems like the cuneiform script began as a way to record these tokens, and as this more universal system of writing became more developed it removed the need for tokens altogether. Only then did writing also start to be used to record myths, religion, politics and poetry. During the late second millennium *The Epic of Gilgamesh* was written in this region, the first great work of literature that has survived.

Numbers likely arose because of trade too. At first, the Mesopotamians had a symbol for 'three sheep' and a different one for 'three cows', but they did not have a symbol for 'three' itself. And since numbers were used to count your possessions, they saw no need for zero as a number. With time, the numbers came to be understood in a more abstract way, just like the cuneiform developed from the pictographic system of the tokens.

In the Sumerian mythology, each city had been built by a god or goddess to provide them with food, water and security. The temple was therefore at the centre of each city, and always a monumental architectural achievement. Five thousand years ago, the biggest city, Uruk (in modern-day Iraq), had around 50,000 inhabitants, surrounded by 10 kilometres of city walls of mud brick. Towering above everything was the ziggurat, a temple formed as a step pyramid with a flat top, which was visible from a long distance because of the level landscape. The Tower of Babel in the Bible probably refers to such a construction, the sixth-century BC, 91-metre ziggurat in Babylon, which also was one of the biggest cities in Mesopotamia.

The city was not just the cause of greater cooperation, it was also its effect. Often we assume that people crammed into cities because they needed security against roving bandits and other tribes. But there are ancient cities that never built city walls, and some of them only built walls a long time after the city was established. Uruk was established around 3200 BC, but the walls were not erected until around 2900 BC.

It seems that cities developed for another reason. Agriculture had prospered in Mesopotamia for thousands of years, partly because the rivers flooded the area regularly. But by 3800 BC a change in climate had resulted in cooler and drier conditions. Rain fell less often, but it also meant that the swampy south became available for farming crops like wheat, barley and dates. The water was still there, and irrigation systems could make it possible to store floodwater until the crops needed it, but it took large groups of people in cooperation to build them. People started to congregate in cities to feed themselves better, and by doing so they also made it possible for more of them to do things that were not related to food production.

The American-Canadian writer Jane Jacobs explained that, unlike what we've been led to believe, agriculture was not the start of civilization, cities were. It was the density of urban clusters – 'sustained, interdependent, creative city economies' – that made all sorts of creativity and innovation possible, including better agriculture.[31]

The development of cities supercharged mankind's division of labour. This is where people met face to face, and could specialize in various tasks, develop their skills, and invest more time, energy and resources in coming up with new ideas and better methods. As a result, they became more productive and in doing so made the whole city more prosperous and dynamic itself. As we know today, in a city that is twice the size of another, the average worker produces 5–10 per cent more than in the smaller city. By measuring regional patterns of innovation and US population size, we find that a city that is ten times larger than another is seventeen times more innovative, and one that is fifty times bigger is 130 times more innovative.[32]

More efficient farmers could feed not just priests and scribes, but also bakers and brewers, spinners and weavers, metalworkers, brickmakers, jewellers, barbers, gardeners and artists – and they could hold slaves. And these could in their turn provide the farmers with clothes, tools, weapons, buildings and entertainment that they could never have produced on their own. This is why these early Mesopotamian cities record the first instances of advanced medicine, music, libraries, maps, mathematics, chemistry, botany and zoology.

Many wonder why early humans gave up what they assume to be a convenient forager lifestyle for back-breaking work on the farm, to produce monotonous food that is bad for our bodies and teeth. It's a reasonable question, but firstly, it was obviously not a sudden decision with all long-term consequences fully understood. Secondly, the evidence is that most hunter-gatherers jump at the chance of abandoning their lifestyle as soon as they find a richer and safer alternative. Midway through his book on what we can learn from traditional societies, Jared Diamond shares a story about an American friend who travelled halfway around the world to meet a newly discovered band of New Guinea forest hunter-gatherers. Once he arrived he found that half of them had already moved to an Indonesian village and put on T-shirts. 'Rice to eat, and no more mosquitoes!' they explained.[33]

The traditional understanding has it backwards. It was not that the need for security made us build the first cities, but that cities created so much wealth that they needed walls to protect it. In many Mesopotamian city-states there were two authority figures. The first was the *en*, a high priest or priestess who was in charge of the temple, both the community's link with the divine and spiritual, but also responsible for more mundane matters. The temples functioned like economic corporations with their own workshops, trade relationships and hundreds of workers and slaves. We are used to thinking about how a temple can be cleansed of merchants and money changers, but at the dawn of civilization the temple was something similar to a state-owned company, with coercive power. The high priest was a CEO, organizing labour and distributing the income. In Sumerian and Akkadian the same word is used both for 'priest' and 'accountant'. Today, it's easier to tell the difference.

The other authority figure in the city was the *lugal*, the 'great man', the commander who oversaw defence and relations with outsiders. With time, the *lugal* became more important in the cities, and the function slowly transformed into that of a king. At the same time, the role of the *en* shrank, becoming more of a ceremonial role.[34] This is just what we would expect if cities started as vehicles for social and economic cooperation, and became so successful that they had to defend their wealth and territory against other cities.

Without international trade, the Mesopotamian cultures of the fourth to first millennia BC – the Sumerians, Assyrians,

Akkadians and Babylonians – could not have survived. They had the right conditions to produce food, but they did not have the resources they needed for construction and tools. Archaeologist David Wengrow even talks about the first city as 'the first global village' because it was dependent on innovations in an area extending from the Cilician Gates, overlooking the Mediterranean, to the Gulf of Oman on the Arabian Sea.[35]

The first settled civilizations were dependent on the regular exchange of agricultural surplus for timber, metals, granite and marble from Syria and Anatolia, and later the Persian Gulf and western India. In fact, it might be that one incentive to invent productive, specialized agriculture was to create a surplus to exchange for the resources they needed (and wanted). Trade encourages economies of scale, where even small villages and countries can specialize in production that is too large for the domestic market.

The importance of Mesopotamian trade is revealed by the city of Dilmun, in today's Bahrain. This was, according to historian of trade William J. Bernstein, 'an ancient equivalent of Las Vegas' with a large population in relatively barren surroundings, that survived because of food imports and a strategic position – it was a trading post for copper from what today is Oman. Traders were called *alik-Dilmun* ('go-getters of Dilmun') because they regularly sent large shipments of grain, fish and wool to Dilmun and came back with copper, all facilitated by outside investors who expected a decent return on capital.

Soon the Mesopotamians realized that they could mix copper with tin, which melted at a lower temperature and did not bubble and was therefore easily cast. The new alloy was bronze and became the standard material for tools, utensils and weapons. But since Mesopotamians had no tin, they had to import it all the way from sources in central Asia and northern Europe via multiple land routes. As Bernstein points out, we know about this metal trade because metals do not decompose. However, along the same route there must have also 'existed a similar long-range barter for other valuable materials, such as linen, frankincense, myrrh, tigers, ostrich feathers, and a thousand other sights, sounds, and smells now lost to history'.[36]

In many respects, Mesopotamian cities had command economies. To begin with, the temple and later the king controlled the land and basic farming and forced the citizens, not just the slaves, to work. But even at the outset, there was some space for free markets. We have ample records of the grain and bread that rulers took and handed out, but people also obtained clothes, furniture and kitchen utensils, which suggests a role for more unrestrained commerce.[37]

The Sumerian sign for 'market' was a 'Y', which symbolizes that the marketplace was at a juncture of traffic routes. Sumerian merchants first worked as agents for the government and temple officials, but with time they accumulated capital, became independent and experimented with new business models. By 2000 BC, long-range trade was in private hands.

The globalists who created the classical world

The great globalists of the classical world – in fact, the people who arguably created the classical world itself – were the Phoenicians. This Semitic-speaking people came from the east coast of the Mediterranean, in present-day Lebanon. They connected the ancient Mesopotamian and Egyptian civilizations with the new Mediterranean cultures (the Greeks, Etruscans and Romans), and made it possible for ideas, people and goods to move from one corner to the other. 'They went not for conquest, as the Babylonians and Assyrians did,' reports archaeologist James B. Pritchard. 'Profit rather than plunder was their policy.'[38]

Around 1200 BC nearly all the major cities of the ancient world were sacked and destroyed by the 'sea peoples', a motley assortment

of pirates who probably came from various places in the Mediterranean. There is a lack of consensus among academics, but these
pirates probably wreaked so much havoc because of a combination of drought, earthquakes, the plague and new, deadlier swords
and javelins. This so-called 'Late Bronze-Age Collapse' destroyed
the old trade routes and took a horrible human toll. It resulted
in a small dark age in Greece and many other places, but it also
opened up opportunities for groups that would otherwise have
been stifled by powerful emperors and temples. The Phoenicians
would take advantage and end up ruling the waves for a thousand
years.

Both their trading credentials and work ethic are revealed in
their very name. 'Phoenicia' was the Greek term for one of their
major exports, a reddish-purple dye that did not fade with time
and could only be extracted by crushing the shells of large quantities of sea snails. Apparently, it took as many as twelve thousand
snails to yield just 1.4 grams of pure dye, enough to colour the
trim of a single garment.[39] Naturally, it would soon become the
colour that Roman emperors preferred for their togas, as they had
to wear whatever was most impressive and expensive.

The Phoenicians were also the first great seafarers, fearless and
persistent, who came up with a series of innovations and improvements that made it possible to sail the open seas. They used their
cedar wood to build wide merchant ships with a rounded bottom
to make room for more cargo. Their ships also featured a novelty
that has been compared in importance to the wheel for land transport: the keel, the wooden blade that descends into the sea and
keeps ships upright. The Phoenicians also pioneered standardized
shipbuilding, dry docks, artificial harbours, cartography and maritime law. They learned how to sail by the North Star, which the
Greeks came to call 'the Phoenician Star' – a name that stuck until
the nineteenth century.

By the middle of the second millennium BC the Phoenicians

started transporting their much sought-after cedar wood down the Euphrates to lower Mesopotamia. The wood was used by King Solomon for his temple and for the roof of the Temple of Artemis at Ephesus, one of the Seven Wonders of the World. From western India they brought hardwood, minerals and precious stones. This laid the ground for an elaborate trading network throughout the Mediterranean and the Persian Gulf, with a series of Phoenician city-states in North Africa and the western Mediterranean, like Carthage in modern Tunisia. Some of their cities became incredibly wealthy. The island city of Tyre has been described as a miniature Manhattan, with tall buildings and impressive economic clout.[40]

The Phoenicians did not just export and import; they also became middlemen who conducted trade on behalf of other cultures. This gave them the opportunity to learn and use the thoughts and technologies of one group and improve on them with ideas from another. As a result, they became known as skilled craftsmen and as a conduit of ideas and resources, everything from ironwork to fine music. This ancient form of globalization gave a tremendous boost to the industrial and scientific forces of the known world.

Since the Phoenicians wanted to communicate with all kinds of people, they developed a new alphabet that replaced the incredibly complex pictographic Egyptian hieroglyphs and Sumerian cuneiform. It was a simple twenty-two-letter phonetic code that was easy to learn and use, no longer requiring professional scribes and thereby democratizing both writing and business. The Greeks imported the alphabet, but added vowels, which the Phoenicians lacked. This in turn became the basis for the Latin alphabet, used by the Romans, and by you as you read this book.

This was the open, classical world that the great Greco-Roman essayist Plutarch had in mind when he praised the sea:

This element, therefore, when our life was savage and unsociable, linked it together and made it complete, redressing defects by mutual assistance and exchange and so bringing about cooperation and friendship [...] if there were no sea, man would be the most savage and destitute of all creatures. But as it is, the sea brought the Greeks the vine from India, from Greece transmitted the use of grain across the sea, from Phoenicia imported letters as a memorial against forgetfulness, thus preventing the greater part of mankind from being wineless, grainless and unlettered.[41]

Some grew incredibly wealthy on this trade while others remained desperately poor. Often it upset old patterns of trade, and many people who had previously prospered got hurt. The ensuing inequality bred resentment and hostility among those who felt left behind. Old Testament prophets often railed against cosmopolitan elites who prospered due to trade links. In the eighth century BC, Isaiah criticized those who 'clasp hands with foreigners' and Zephaniah warned that Yahweh would punish the traders and 'all who dress themselves in foreign attire'.[42]

The Phoenicians' strength came from their productivity and trade, not from their military strength, and in the end their city-states were destroyed by the likes of Nebuchadnezzar and the Romans, but they left a legacy that still persists today. The Phoenicians did not just teach the Greeks everything from architecture and glass-blowing to sport festivals and financial innovations, they also inspired them to follow in their footsteps, as traders and colonists. As the Phoenicians established cities in North Africa and the western Mediterranean, the Greeks started doing the same in southern Europe and the eastern Mediterranean. And the Romans famously proclaimed themselves the cultural heir of the Greeks.

All roads lead to Rome

The Greeks and Romans did not have the same fondness for commerce as the Middle Easterners, partly because they considered themselves superior. Often trade was seen as a necessary evil, a dirty task for slaves and foreigners. But with the exception of the Spartans, the Greeks soon learned that it brought prosperity and so they started to imitate their Middle Eastern neighbours.

The agora, the assembly space in Greek cities, took on an increasingly commercial flavour from about 700 BC. In the fourth century the comic poet Eubulus provided a witty list of everything for sale in the agora of Athens: 'figs, witnesses to summonses, bunches of grapes, turnips, pears, apples, givers of evidence, roses, medlars, porridge, honeycombs, chickpeas, lawsuits, beestings-pudding, myrtle berries, allotment machines, irises, lamps, water-clocks, laws, and indictments'.[43] There was even an 'Agora of the Kerkopes', a black market for stolen goods.

The Romans considered plundering of the provinces both a quicker and more glorious way to get rich than trade but, as was the case with many empires, the Romans' unification of enormous areas also gave new opportunities for migrants, travellers and traders. Outsiders suffered from the Romans' brutal wars, but many citizens benefited from peace within – and from Roman law and currency. Remarkably, few of the early Roman cities were walled. And even when they built walls, like the 118-kilometre Hadrian's Wall in Britannia, the purpose was not to prevent movement but to control it. Along the wall, there was a small fort with a gateway approximately every Roman mile, through which people, goods and livestock passed. By the first century BC, Rome had conquered the entire Mediterranean coastline, and since 90 per cent of its people lived within 15 kilometres of the sea, it meant that cheap water transport was possible almost everywhere.[44] If you had to go by land there was also an incredible

80,000 kilometres of paved roads. All roads did indeed lead to Rome.

Larger vessels than ever shipped soldiers and slaves but also economic treasure. The large number of shipwrecks in the Mediterranean from this period has led scholars to wonder whether the same volume of trade was reached again before the nineteenth century. Technological breakthroughs that emerged anywhere in the Middle East, North Africa, the European Continent or Britain rapidly spread to other parts of the empire. Even in humble villages on the outskirts, high-quality imported Roman pottery has been found, and there were sophisticated markets in clothing, footwear and tools.[45]

In the mid-second century AD, the Greek orator Aelius Aristides gave an account of Rome as an open civilization:

> So many merchant ships arrive here, conveying every kind of goods from every people every hour and every day, that the city is like a factory common to the whole earth. [...] So everything comes together here – trade, seafaring, farming, the scourings of the mines, all the crafts that exist or have existed, all that is produced and grown. Whatever one does not see here is not a thing which has existed or exists.[46]

In effect, the Roman Empire both created and was built by an early version of globalization. Monte Testaccio, by one of the old ports on the river Tiber, was built by it in a literal sense. This 35-metre-high hill, thought to be much higher in ancient times, is made up of around 53 million discarded amphorae. It is the result of Rome's vast imports of olive oil, which the empire's citizens used not just for food but also to wash with and burn in their lamps. When the oil was unloaded from ships, it was decanted into bulk containers and the amphorae, made in Spain, Libya and Tunisia, were thrown away, creating a hill covering an area of 20,000 square metres. This mountain of waste was not just a powerful symbol of the extent of exchange in the classical world, it was also an early harbinger of the environmental consequences of increasing globalization and consumption, a topic we will return to in chapter 8.

As a result of this unprecedented international division of labour, intellectuals began to develop ideas about a utopian, universal economy where mutual economic gain was associated with a cosmopolitan brotherhood of man. Sometime before the year 65 AD Seneca wrote about how 'the wind has made communication possible between all peoples and has joined nations which are separated geographically', and the fourth-century pagan Libanius explained it poetically:

> God did not bestow all products upon all parts of the earth, but distributed His gifts over different regions, to the end that men might cultivate a social relationship because one would have need of the help of another. And so He called commerce into being, that all men might be able to have common enjoyment of the fruits of the earth, no matter where produced.[47]

By drilling deep in the ice core, researchers can create a record of atmospheric pollutants thousands of years back. This is useful to economic historians since most lead emissions were the result of silver processing and can be seen as an indicator of economic activity. It turns out that levels began to rise around 900 BC, as the Phoenicians began to connect the Mediterranean, and then it accelerated and peaked in the first and second centuries during Pax Romana. As the Roman Empire fell into decline, levels plunged and would not reach their former heights for five hundred years.[48] The empire could not uphold security and infrastructure so trade networks disintegrated and the internal division of labour unravelled between 400 and 600 AD. It was like the Late Bronze-Age

Collapse all over again, and many professions disappeared as cities shrank. The fashionable opinion nowadays is that there was no real Dark Age, and as a reaction to traditional historians' obsession with compartmentalizing epochs, modern historians have rightly emphasized the forgotten continuity between them. But the archaeological record is pretty straightforward.

Archaeologist and historian Bryan Ward-Perkins has shown that the fall of Rome can be traced in almost any measure of living standards, whether of peasants, kings or saints. Material sophistication and mass production disappeared. Where they once built in stones and bricks, they now had to build in wood, with earthen floors. Where once even buildings for storage and animals had tiled roofs, soon only bishops and kings did. We find few coins from this period and the number of literate people declined dramatically. In some remote provinces, writing disappeared entirely. The universal economy collapsed.[49] It can rightly be called a Dark Age, a phenomenon that has been repeated in several guises and scales throughout history when openness has given way to separation and isolation.

A lesson of two islands

More than ten thousand years ago, gradually rising sea levels began to cut Tasmania off from Australia. Soon a 200-kilometre stretch of unpredictable sea made contact impossible. The Tasmanians never saw their friends to the north again, and for five hundred generations their culture developed in total isolation from the rest of humanity.

When European colonialists came to Tasmania for the first time at the end of the eighteenth century they thought the inhabitants were so much more primitive than the mainland aborigines that they assumed they belonged to a different race. The aborigines north of the Bass Strait had hundreds of specialized tools, including complex fishing gear, boomerangs, sewn bark canoes, string bags and wooden bowls for drinking. The Tasmanians had nothing of this. They had no durable boats and paddles and no advanced weapons or tools, like fishhooks, fish traps, nets, bird snares, barbed spears or boomerangs. They only used a primitive club, a one-piece spear and rocks for hunting. Worse, they had no bone tools, so no needles to sew skins into clothing. In the biting winter cold, they had to make do with a one-piece kangaroo skin over their shoulders, and by spreading grease over their skin.[50]

When archaeologist Rhys Jones described this technological decline, he controversially speculated about 'a squeezing of intellectuality [...] a slow strangulation of the mind'.[51] But it was not related to the mind or brains of the Tasmanians. They were the same as the people north of the Bass Strait. The problem was that they had lost access to the brains of others. A small population, around four thousand people, isolated from the rest of the world could not uphold the division of labour that made innovation possible. If someone in a larger population to the north came up with the boomerang it could quickly spread over the mainland, but on an isolated island, there were fewer innovators and fewer innovations to imitate.

It gets worse. Not only did the Tasmanians not innovate, but they actually forgot many of the technologies and methods they had used ten thousand years before. Ideas and skills have to be sustained and transmitted to new generations. This is easy in large populations where you have many teachers and many learners, but in a smaller population it doesn't take many failures before you forget particular skills. Looking at the archaeological record, the frequency, variety and quality of bone tools declines from eight thousand to three thousand years ago, until they disappear completely. The population relied heavily on a fish diet as late as five thousand years ago, but then the frequency of fish bones decline, and by 3800 BC they disappear entirely, along with all the tools necessary to catch them. When the Tasmanians saw Europeans catch and eat fish, they reacted with surprise and disgust.

Tasmania is an extreme example. 'The world's longest isolation, the world's simplest technology', as Jones concluded. But a similar pattern of cultural regress can be seen wherever people are isolated for a long time. Other Pacific islands also lost useful technologies like pottery and the bow and arrow. People on some islands lost the ability to build the kind of seaworthy canoes they once arrived in. The Polar Inuit of north-west Greenland became isolated from other Inuit, and in the 1820s an epidemic killed older knowledge-able members of the group. As a result they lost the ability to make bows and arrows, fishing spears and canoes, and their snow houses did not have the long heat-saving entryways other Inuit popula-tions had. These technologies were only reintroduced by migrants in the 1860s. The population that had previously declined once again started to increase.[52]

At the southern tip of South America, 10 degrees south of southern Tasmania, there is another island group of similar size: Tierra del Fuego. The population there were also nomadic hunter-gatherers in a similar climate when Europeans met them, but their lifestyles were worlds apart. The Fuegians had bone tools and dressed in undergarments, leggings, moccasins of sealskin and capes of seal, otter and guanaco sewn together. They used baited fish lines, bird snares, slings, specialized nets and bows and arrows, with fine bone-tipped arrows that were sanded and polished. They used four specialized, barbed spears, including one with a detacha-ble harpoon with a lead line. They also had sewn bark canoes with efficient paddles, compared to the unreliable rafts used by Tasma-nians that had to be propelled by women swimming alongside, pulling them forwards.[53]

This tale of two islands is really a tale of openness. The Fuegians were at least twice as numerous as the Tasmanians, so they could uphold more complex specialization, but more importantly they sometimes used their canoes to cross the much narrower Strait of Magellan and trade with mainland South America. Some of their stylistic forms and technological processes show a clear influence of northern cultures. This contact meant that Fuegians were constantly reminded of old skills and processes, and picked up new innovations from a much bigger population, which the Tasmanians could not do.

So are you a Fuegian or a Tasmanian? It's difficult to find universal laws in human history, but this is as close as it gets: cities and regions open to contact and exchange prosper, whereas closed regions stagnate. Since innovation depends on the size of the interconnected population, cities and countries that make it easy for people to travel, trade and communicate with others create impressive wealth and are fertile ground for new ideas and innovations.

The most rapid economic and technological progress has always taken place in cultures that opened up and engaged in deep and long-distance commercial ties with others: bands of trading cities, like the Phoenicians and the Hanseatic League in the late Middle Ages; city-states like Athens, Venice, Singapore and Hong Kong; countries like the Dutch Republic, Great Britain, the US and Japan after the Meiji Restoration; the Muslim world before the Mongol invasions; India under Ashoka the Great and after the reforms of the 1990s; and China during the Song dynasty and after Mao's death.

Nineteenth-century Europe is another example. As steamships and railroads reduced the cost of transporting goods, countries also began to give their citizens greater freedom to trade. Britain led the way in 1846, as it abolished the Corn Laws that had increased the price of bread for the hungry masses by enforcing trade restrictions on imported food. In 1860, Richard Cobden, who had led the fight against the tariffs, negotiated an Anglo–French trade treaty that had a most-favoured-nations clause, which meant that any trade opening given to one country had to be extended to all other members. Other major European countries joined it and import tariffs were slashed, greatly facilitating specialization and industrialization all over Europe.

At the same time, there have always been states that voluntarily turned themselves into Tasmanias because elites thought foreign influences and social mobility would threaten their position, or because of popular anger with wealthy elites, associated with foreign trade. Unlike other Greek city-states, the militaristic Spartans banned trade and relied instead on conquering and enslaving the producers they needed (which resulted in slaves soon vastly outnumbering their masters). China banned foreign trade under the Ming dynasty, as did Japan under the Tokugawa Shoguns. In modern times, communist states like Albania and North Korea have isolated themselves from the rest of the world.

None of these places became quite like ancient Tasmania. The domestic population was always big enough to sustain a division of labour, and – even if contact with the rest of the world was limited to invasions, government barter, kidnappings and espionage – they did know the world was there and they preyed on the innovations taking place elsewhere. And yet, in every case it resulted in something similar to the Late Bronze-Age Collapse and the fall of the Roman Empire: stagnation and falling living standards.

Often the protectionist backlash was a response to increased imports that helped consumers but hurt producers and workers in affected industries. The Great Depression is the classic example. Just as free trade started to make the West rich, the forces opposing it gathered momentum. Open trade combined with cheaper transportation and the invention of refrigeration made it possible for cheap American grain and meat to reach hungry Europeans, and for cheaper European manufacturing goods to enter American homes. European farmers and American capitalists responded by trying to block competition. Before World War I this did not hurt trade much since falling shipping costs more than made up for the new tariffs. But as these gains were exhausted, trade barriers began to bite.

On 23 October 1929, news broke that the free-trade coalition in Congress was breaking apart and that the US would switch to protectionism. The next day, the New York Stock Exchange collapsed after a long boom. Several tariffs were imposed and in June 1930 President Hoover signed the comprehensive Smoot-Hawley tariff, raising tariffs on 890 imports. It did not hit the national economy at first, but regions dependent on trade soon started to collapse, as did banks. Other countries were badly damaged, spurring nationalist sentiments, and they naturally retaliated with their own tariffs. Between 1929 and 1931 world trade declined by an incredible 25 per cent. The trade war helped to turn a national recession into a global depression, and in country after country nationalist politicians and dictators grabbed power.

The new battle over trade

The present era of globalization is often considered as something unique in history, but at its root it is a continuation of the truck, barter and exchange that humans have always kept themselves busy with. It is just that more people are involved and we have come up with ever better ways of reducing distance. Where once camels and the bireme galley made it possible to go where no trader had gone before, we now have jet planes, haulage trucks and container shipping. To pass on information, a twenty-first-century BC king of Ur built a 'donkey express' with the first inns for tired messengers, and the Aztecs relayed runners with messages tucked into batons.[54] Now we turn texts and pictures into digital signals, sending them to the other side of the globe in an instant, sometimes with a digital signature to close a deal. The principle is the same. We have always wanted to talk, travel and trade; we just find increasingly better ways of doing so.

The objective is always the same: overcoming the distance between us and what we want. Studies show that just the proximity to large markets and productive workers has a massive effect on our standards. One analysis came to the conclusion that if we could supply Zimbabwe with a coastline, it would raise its GDP per capita by 24 per cent. If we could move the whole country to Central Europe, it would increase by 80 per cent.[55] And that is without any institutional changes. If we could somehow lose the tyrannical ZANU-PF party in the move, we would increase GDP even more.

After the Great Depression and World War II, Western policy-makers traced many of their mistakes to the economic nationalism that hurt the global economy and poisoned international relations. As the English-American philosopher and activist Thomas Paine had warned 140 years earlier, like blood, trade cannot be taken from any of the parts without being taken from the whole mass in circulation, and when the ability of any nation to buy is destroyed it involves the seller: 'Could the government [...] destroy the commerce of all other nations, she would most effectually ruin her own.'[56]

Under American leadership, the West rebuilt the open economic order, dismantled tariffs and created a system of rules, stopping countries from arbitrarily blocking trade. Since the US was the last major industrialized country standing after the war, its businesses and workers did not fear competition as they used to. By the early 1950s, most pre-war trade barriers had already been dismantled, and a rapid increase in trade helped Europe to quickly get back on its feet.

The world embraced an open, global order as many communist and military dictatorships fell in the 1980s – and as China and India began to open up their closed economies to the world. Combined with container shipping and the digital revolution, this made global supply chains possible. If the transportation cost is small enough and the coordination ability is large enough, it is possible for more companies and countries to participate in the building of just one product, as every component is produced where it makes the most economic sense.

Today we have deeper, faster and cheaper connections than ever, but there are also many more of us. Two hundred years ago there were one billion people on the planet. Now there are more than seven billion, and more than half of them have an internet connection, so more people than ever can access and exchange information. This has been accompanied by the greatest social and economic progress the world has ever seen. Since 1990, the level of global hunger has declined by 40 per cent, and levels of illiteracy and child mortality by half. Over the same period, even though the world population increased by two billion, the number of extremely poor declined on average by almost 130,000 people every day.[57]

But these rapid advances have been accompanied by a new controversy over trade, which is threatening to rip globalization apart and create new geopolitical tensions. The benefits from trade come to us through creative destruction. We benefit from trading with a hunter because we stop our own hunting and instead specialize in producing arrows. The US benefits from importing shoes from China because Americans get cheaper shoes and can stop having capital and people employed in shoe manufacturing. We destroy old ways of doing things but for a creative purpose: to get the things we want at a lower cost, and to employ capital and labour in sectors where we can produce more. An increase in a country's foreign trade by ten percentage points is associated with an increase in productivity between 1.4 and 9.6 per cent.[58]

This creative destruction is, of course, also what condemns free trade in the eyes of many people. Competition from imports hurts particular sectors, and results in the dislocation of workers. In his inaugural address in 2017, US president Donald Trump echoed the protectionists of the 1920s in saying that free trade had resulted in 'the ravages of other countries making our products, stealing our companies, and destroying our jobs'.[59] The election of Trump has been widely interpreted as a reaction to the loss of US manufacturing jobs and the collapse of the American Rust Belt, just as similar dislocation in other parts of the world has resulted in protectionist reactions there.

The backlash against trade partly comes from a sense that others have cheated. Countries like China benefit from paying lip service to the principles of free trade while often acting in protectionist ways. There is some truth to this. For example, China has for a long time forced Western companies wanting a presence in China to surrender intellectual property, and many patents and copyrights are misappropriated. This is destructive. One way to combat it is agreements like the Trans-Pacific Partnership (abandoned by Trump), which establishes international rules that up-and-coming countries like China might be likely to adapt to.

But let's not forget that America (and all other countries) did exactly the same thing at a similar level of development. In eighteenth-century America, both private companies and government officials smuggled European inventions and bribed artisans to reveal their secrets (despite harsh punishments at home for those who did).[60] 'Yankee', after all, was originally a derisive term for smugglers. What changed was that Americans became more inventive themselves, and started to demand protection of intellectual property rights back home. This is happening in China as well. In the US-China Business Council's member surveys since 2011, between 40 and 50 per cent of American businesses say that China's protection of intellectual property rights has improved in the past year, *every year*. The share who thinks it deteriorated is in the very low single digits every year. Forced technology transfers is a concern, but only ranks as 24 out of 27 top challenges US companies face in China.[61]

China also has more trade barriers than rich countries. This is a serious problem especially for the Chinese. It means that their citizens are denied access to better and cheaper goods from other places, and this reduces the productivity specialization creates, and the purchasing power that would have created a demand for new goods and services. It would be beneficial for everyone if the Chinese (and others) dismantled their trade barriers, and that is one reason why multilateral trade deals make sense, but the fact that the Chinese government makes it difficult for their companies and citizens to buy the best is not a reason for us to punish our own citizens in the same way. As the economist and politician William Beveridge pointed out in 1931, if other countries have bad harbours that are inaccessible to our ships it is bad, but it would be even worse if we responded by throwing rocks in our own harbours.[62]

The meaningless trade balance

While these are serious concerns, '[n]othing, however, can be more absurd than this whole doctrine of the balance of trade', as the founder of classical economics, Adam Smith, told his mercantilist contemporaries. They thought exports were good and imports bad, and that it was a problem if we bought more from a certain place than they bought from us. Smith's point was that you derive the benefit of trade from the goods and services you receive, not the ones you produce, just like the material benefit from work is not the effort you exert, but the goods and services this work buys you. If you can work a little less to receive the salary you want, that is a gain not a loss. As Smith wrote, 'trade which, without force or constraint, is naturally and regularly carried on between any two places is always advantageous, though not always equally so, to both'. I have a negative trade balance with my local bookshop and a positive trade balance with my publisher, but all three of us benefit from each of those exchanges or they would not take place.

The absurdity of the idea that imports hurt becomes clear if we imagine it applied to non-national boundaries – for example, if London were to try to prevent imports of goods from Birmingham. Or if we imagine how, within London, Bromley would do better without cheap imports from Barnet, and that Hackney should stop exposing itself to competition from Harrow. In fact, if we take the idea seriously, the Thompsons on Shoreditch High Street would benefit from producing everything they need themselves, rather than letting the Wilsons around the corner on Redchurch Street take some of their jobs by selling them sweaters. The trade balance is meaningless as long as everyone benefits from each exchange.

If an economy consistently buys more than it sells, it is not because other countries are cheating, but because of macroeconomic factors, such as its citizens and government save little and foreign investment is high. Countries with high savings rates, like Germany and China, typically run trade surpluses. Countries like the US – with low savings, large budget deficits and much foreign investment – tend to have trade deficits, no matter which trade policies others adhere to.

The economic gains from free trade are mind-blowingly large. A study from the Peterson Institute for International Economics suggests that the US economy is annually around $1000 billion bigger than it would have been without post-war trade liberalization – that is $10,000 per US household. The study assumes that the cost to displaced workers from lost wages and lower wages once re-employed is $50 billion annually. This means that the benefit–cost ratio is 20:1 – that is, the gains from free trade are twenty times greater than losses.[63]

We constantly talk about the death of the American middle class, and blame it on trade, but the real story is brighter. It is true that the share of middle-income households – those mak-ing between $35,000 and $100,000 a year (in 2018 dollars) – has declined from 54 to 42 per cent in 1968–2018. But that is not because they are moving down, since the low-income share declined from 36 to 28 per cent. It was because they moved into the high-income bracket – a share that increased from less than 10 to more than 30 per cent.[64]

Between 1970 and 2019 average hourly earnings of production and non-supervisory employees have increased by no more than 5 per cent adjusted for inflation. That is miserable. However, employ-ers pay an increasing share of the compensation in non-monetary benefits, like health and life insurance, retirement pensions, paid vacation and other leave. One reason is that employees often reject positions without such benefits; another is that there are often tax advantages. Total compensation, including these benefits, has increased not by 5 per cent since 1970, but 66 per cent.[65] That's more healthy, even though it is obviously not shared equally and some workers don't get such benefits at all.

A reason why trade is often so unpopular is that we see the costs more clearly, report it and link it to trade. Think about a local factory closure. The benefit is spread out in time and geography. Perhaps it comes in the form of you paying less for goods and food than before, and since that increased your purchasing power you can now buy technology, healthcare, entertainment and holidays you couldn't before, and more people get employment in those sec-tors. Few people make a mental association between such benefits and free trade, and no news outlets report it. Concentrated losses and dispersed gains is a recipe for an eternal disconnect between the consequences of free trade and its popularity.

The '1' in the 20:1 benefit–cost ratio is not just a number, it represents real flesh-and-blood people who lose jobs – and when they do that, they don't just lose an income, some also lose an identity and a community. The backlash against trade is often

understood as a reaction to an economy that is no longer working for a wide proportion of the workforce. The benefits go to the
elites, whereas many others experience job losses or wage stagnation. In some regions that have been built around particular
manufacturing industries, like the Rust Belt, deindustrialization
has resulted in not just an economic collapse but also a cultural
one. When you are in the midst of it, it isn't much of a comfort
that the rest of the world is making progress. As the saying goes,
when you are unemployed, the unemployment rate is not 4.5 per
cent, but 100 per cent.

But this popular narrative is oversimplified, and it is an example of how easy it is to blame trade and foreigners for problems
that are much more complex. Since the 2008 financial crisis, there
has been severe dislocation and many regions have been seriously
hurt, but trade has not always been the culprit. In many instances,
the lack of it has.

Many who complain only look at direct head-on competition
from China. One refrigerator bought from China results in one
not bought from a US refrigerator company, say. But that's just
one aspect of trade, and not the major one. Most trade is in inter-
mediate goods, inputs and supplies companies need to produce.
Sometimes we buy a refrigerator from China, but more often, a
refrigerator producer in the US buys cables and light bulbs from
China to produce a better and cheaper refrigerator. Often this
boosts production and employment in the US. One study shows
that if we account for the whole supply chain, the net effect of
trade with China is *more* American jobs. The average US region
sees a net job increase of 1.3 per cent a year relative to a hypothetical region with no trade with China.[66]

It is a mistake to blame deindustrialization on trade, because
the West is producing more manufactured goods than ever before.
As the economist Donald Boudreaux points out, today American
factories produce 11 per cent more than they did when China

joined the World Trade Organization in 2001, and 45 per cent more than when NAFTA was launched in 1994.[67] US industrial capacity today is twice as big as it was in 1984 when a TV commercial for Ronald Reagan declared that, 'It is morning again in America' and that more Americans go to work than ever before.

Today even more people go to work every morning, but fewer of them head for the mill and the docks after breakfast than they used to, because technological changes have automated many of those jobs. Between 2000 and 2010 almost six million US factory jobs were lost, but manufacturing actually expanded – so much that America would have needed three million more factory workers if productivity had been constant. Machines and smarter production meant that much more could be done by fewer people. One study showed that only around 12 per cent of those manufacturing jobs were lost due to foreign trade – 88 per cent were lost because of higher productivity.[68]

So the Chinese did not take our manufacturing jobs, our robots did. And if we were to 'get those factories back', we would not get the old jobs back because in the modern factory you don't see hundreds of workers with wrenches any more, it's more like five people with a bank of computers. The main difference would be that the cost of living would increase, especially for low- and middle-income households, that consume a relatively large proportion of their income on internationally traded goods, clothes, food and home electronics, and only a small proportion on restaurant visits and real estate. According to a study in *The Quarterly Journal of Economics*, the 10 per cent richest American households would lose less than 10 per cent of their purchasing power if there were no international trade. The poorest 10 per cent, however, would lose almost 70 per cent.[69]

The world of work is always changing – if it's not trade, it's technology, robots or consumer habits. No matter why workers face dislocation, the only way to create new and better jobs is to be open to new and better business models and innovations that create new jobs, and to invest in the education that helps the displaced take advantage of those new opportunities. Instead of throwing the shipwrecked a life vest, we should help them onto a seaworthy ship.

Businesses and jobs will be lost then just like they would if we imposed tariffs, but now from a position of strength, where we have the technology and the purchasing power to replace them. If you want things to stay the same, you have to change.

Why the Rust Belt rusted

The Rust Belt is a case in point – the region of industrial decline in the Midwest and Great Lakes region in the US. Why did it rust in the first place? The American Rust Belt lost more manufacturing jobs before 1980 than it did after that. In 1950, this region accounted for more than half of all US manufacturing jobs, but in the ensuing thirty years its share fell by roughly a third, which shows that it was not just part of a general decline in manufacturing jobs. After 1985 – before NAFTA and before Chinese imports – its employment share actually stabilized, at a much lower level. Contrary to the now-popular narrative, the villain was not globalization but complacency.

After World War II and the devastation it brought Europe, a few Rust Belt companies in cars, steel and plastic, like General Motors and US Steel, had a globally dominant position. The problem was that they used this position to avoid the restructuring that would have kept them competitive in the long run. They were the world leaders and successfully lobbied state and federal governments to protect them from competition and anti-trust rules, so why bother making painful changes to make the businesses more fit? The only pressure came from aggressive trade unions like United Steelworkers and United Auto Workers. Most south-eastern states had had 'right to work' laws in place since the 1950s, which limited the power of trade unions, but the Rust Belt didn't. Threatening industrial action, they forced up wages and demanded very specified contracts that hindered restructuring and flexibility in the deployment of labour. On average, Rust Belt workers had 12 per cent higher wages and non-wage benefits than similar workers in other US regions. The firms could afford it, since their average mark-up was over 30 per cent.[70]

For a little while, these workers had a good deal. But it also meant that these jobs moved. Not to Japan or China, but to more competitive US states before there was any foreign competition to talk of. In January 1990, before NAFTA and before the World Trade Organization even existed, 975,000 Americans worked in automotive manufacturing, according to the US Bureau of Labor Statistics. In January 2020, that figure was 996,500. And their average hourly wage has increased by 70 per cent. It's just that those jobs are not in the same states now as they were in 1990.[71]

The Rust Belt started rusting almost from the start. Michael Treschow, a Swedish businessman who led the manufacturer Atlas Copco in the 1990s, describes the shock of working for the company in the US in the late 1970s and early 1980s. America was supposed to be the spearhead of the capitalist world, but seeing these outdated, mismanaged companies in declining areas was, in his recollection, a 'horror experience'. Large factories looked almost like museums of industrial history. One of the companies Atlas Copco bought – a producer of pneumatic tools in Utica, New York – still transmitted power to the machines with line shafts and leather belts, a practice abandoned in Sweden decades earlier. This and very hostile trade unions forced even optimistic Swedes to give up and move to the American South.

Far from being an example of the dangers of trade and competition, the Rust Belt is a warning of what happens when you ignore trade and competition. One researcher concludes that the

Rust Belt 'shows that the longer that lack of competition within an industry exists, the weaker the industry ultimately becomes'.[72]

None of this is meant to suggest that job losses are easy on those who experience them, but it does show that they can't be avoided with protectionist quick fixes. In fact, such fixes are radically counterproductive. Again, trade is a machine that converts whatever you are good at producing into whatever you need. The ones who suffer the most if we destroy it, or pour sand in the wheels, are ourselves.

A tariff on tyres might save a job, but at the cost of local consumers who have to pay more for tyres, which might result in a lost job in sales of tyres. And since tyre consumers now lose purchasing power, they can't spend as much on other things – for example, on restaurant visits, so perhaps a job is lost there too. The people who had those jobs are made of flesh and blood too. This is not just theory but the results of President Obama's tyre tariffs in 2009. They are estimated to have led to the loss of three American jobs for every job saved (before retaliation from other countries) – and the same mistakes are now being repeated many times over.[73]

If rich countries were to re-embrace protectionism in a big way, supply chains would collapse and businesses would scramble to find all the low-skilled labour needed to produce everything they need back home. There is, however, a tried-and-tested way to stop such a severe labour shortage and a cost explosion that would destroy competitiveness, but it is even more controversial than free trade: large-scale immigration.

As the political scientist Margaret Peters concludes, based on her research of the US experience of trade and immigration: 'Just as you can't have your cake and eat it too, you can't slam the door shut to low-skill labor while also slamming it shut to imports of the goods and services an abundant supply of low-skill labor makes possible.'[74] Well, you *can*, it you are willing to pay the price of much lower purchasing power and more poverty. If not, you can stop imports from a global workforce only if you import the global workforce. Every time trade barriers have been high, businesses have lobbied hard for more immigration. America could survive its nineteenth-century protectionism only because it had open borders.

In the case of more closed borders, foreign labour would not just feel the pull, but also a monumental push. Rapidly developing countries have built their swift progress on international trade and on being part of extended supply chains. A new protectionist world order would make armies of unemployed lose the belief in a better future back home, so they would join the millions already desperate to escape to richer countries in Europe and North America.

2

OPEN DOORS

'Thanks to each wave of new arrivals to this land of opportunity, we're a nation forever young, forever bursting with energy and new ideas, and always on the cutting edge, always leading the world to the next frontier.'

Ronald Reagan, 1989

If there is one policy that is even more beneficial than free trade, it is free immigration. The productivity of workers differs around the world, because in order to produce efficiently, you have to team up with complementary workers, machines and infrastructure. It also takes good institutions, like the rule of law and open markets. This is lacking in poor countries. This means there is an incredible wage gap between rich and poor countries, even for equally skilled workers. According to some estimates, two-thirds of the average person's material wealth is determined by where in the world they happen to work.

If people were allowed to move to the place where their labour is paid the best, the gains to world income would be astronomical. According to a back-of-the-envelope calculation, world GDP could increase by around $80 trillion, in effect doubling world GDP, and those gains would be accrued *every year*.

Abolishing all barriers to goods and services would increase global GDP by a couple of percentage points – nothing to be sniffed at – but abolishing barriers to people would increase it by 60–150 per cent, according to several different estimates. And even partial eliminations of barriers to labour mobility could increase global wealth by trillions. This is why economists talk about 'trillion-dollar bills on the sidewalk' when they refer to the simple policy of allowing people to go and work where they want to go and work.[1] (This, by the way, does not mean abolition of the nation state or no border checks to keep suspect elements out.)

It's not as easy as that, of course. Imported car parts and sneakers don't get to vote in the election, they don't speak a foreign language and they can't take up hospital beds or claim welfare. When we import a pair of hands, they are attached to a human being and a culture. And yet, it is startling that no policy in today's world could be more controversial than picking up trillion-dollar bills on the sidewalk, especially since new cultures often inject energy into our own, and it helps people to escape poverty and hopelessness, flee persecution and to be with their loved ones.

Since most of the gains of migration accrue to the migrant themselves (in higher wages), one way of reducing opposition to more migration would be to tax them at a higher rate. It would be grossly unfair, but at least it might be better than forcing them to pay thousands of dollars to smugglers to get into our labour market. Perhaps we would be more welcoming to foreigners if the benefits weren't just dissolved in the great unknowable of a government budget, but instead if all natives got an annual 'immigration bonus', reducing their tax by a couple of hundred dollars?

But supposedly we have to protect the traditional Western culture and our people. That is the counterargument from a new nationalist movement that wants to reduce even the migration that takes place today. According to this narrative, we need to be saved from clashes with other cultures, ideas and languages – from foreigners and citizens of nowhere who don't have the same feelings as we do about the homeland, our identity and traditions. But had we thought like this from the start, we would not have a Western culture to defend in the first place.

What we now think of as Western civilization is a combination of a philosophical heritage from the Greeks, religions from the Middle East, creatively interpreted by Romans in what is now Turkey, and scientific ideas borrowed from the Arabs and the Chinese. We got our alphabets from the Phoenicians, and our numbers are called 'Arabic numerals' because we learned them from mathematicians in Baghdad, who got them from the Indians.

For popular understanding, we often treat historical civilizations as sealed-off entities that might evolve, split and die, but never really meet and cross-breed. 'East is East, and West is West, and never the twain shall meet,' as the Rudyard Kipling's poem has it. For nationalists who want their cultures pure and unadulterated, this is a key part of their worldview. But it is ahistorical. Considering how separate ancient Mesopotamian and Egyptian cultures are sometimes treated, isn't it a remarkable coincidence that cult statues in both cultures were made of similar materials, exotic to them both? The most important statues had the blue of lapis lazuli in hair, eyes and eyebrows, which both cultures imported from as far away as Afghanistan and Pakistan. The gods underwent a rite before offerings that was called 'Opening of the mouth' in both cultures. The gods fed on the smoke from roasted meat, infused with incense, and in both cultures they were kind enough to leave the meaty parts for human consumption.[2]

Sometimes cultural borrowing took place incrementally over long periods, like when a new method for grinding wild plants into flour and roasting meats spread over much of western Asia more than 20,000 years ago, and methods of boiling cereals and stewing fish and other meats spread through North Africa. Sometimes it was more like a whirlwind, like Japan after the Meiji Restoration in 1868, when the Japanese understood that if they did not throw their doors open to foreign technology, they would be dominated by Western colonialists. In just a few decades, this traditional society started to build railroads, shipyards, textile mills, mines, steel foundries, telegraph lines and street lights. Consumers started buying watches, canned goods, mass-manufactured clothes and even sported Western-style moustaches, beards, haircuts and hats. Japan industrialized at breakneck speed and reduced extreme poverty from 80 to almost 20 per cent in just half a century.

The French sociologist Marcel Mauss insisted that societies live by borrowing from each other, so the history of civilization is in fact 'the history of the circulation between societies of the various goods and achievements of each'. We tend to neglect this fact, because these societies 'define themselves rather by the refusal of borrowing than by its acceptance'. That is understandable. If you and I are similar in all regards but for the fact that you say tomayto and I say tomahto, this one difference will be more visible than all our similarities and we might define ourselves by it.

Those who had patience with Kipling and read the third and fourth lines as well, already knew this:

> But there is neither East nor West, Border, nor Breed, nor
> Birth,
> When two strong men stand face to face, though they come
> from the ends of the earth!

Cultural appropriation

Some on the Left, especially at American colleges, mirror the nationalists' quest for cultural purity by rejecting the West's 'cultural appropriation' of expressions and styles from other cultures, because it is seen as denigrating, sometimes colonial. A majority culture shouldn't copy particular elements of a minority culture without respecting its wider context. But this neglects that those cultures also often took their inspiration, and sometimes the most important elements, from others as well.

When a new Swedish minister of culture was presented in 2019, the greatest controversy was stirred by her dreadlocks. 'What do you say to those who are offended by your hair?' Swedish public radio asked her. The critics thought it distasteful that she, a white woman, had stolen her hairstyle from Bob Marley and other Jamaican blacks. But where did the Catholic Bob Marley pick it up? He started wearing dreads after having converted to Rastafari, a creative combination of pan-Africanism, the Hebrew Bible and Christian clergymen who thought that the Ethiopian emperor Haile Selassie was the second coming of Christ. They picked up the idea about dreadlocks from Nazirites, radical Jews who took a vow described in Numbers 6:1–21 that they would not drink wine or cut their hair – like Samson, whose strength was in his hair. So Amanda Lind did not steal her hairstyle. At most, she can be accused of handling stolen goods.

Certainly there are those who dress up like minorities to mock them. But the problem is not that they 'appropriate', rather that they are scoundrels. To borrow, steal and remix is not colonialism – it is culture. As we saw in the last chapter, humans are imitators by nature. Just look at Lind's more conventionally dressed ministerial colleagues. The style of their suits was developed during the seventeenth century after eastern European and Muslim models. The shirts are from the Middle East and we got the neckties from Parisians who were intrigued by the small, knotted neckerchiefs of Croat mercenaries during the Thirty Years War ('cravat'). Their side-parting haircuts are stolen from Roman soldiers, and became popular because the British imposed a tax on hair powder in 1795, making it expensive to wear wigs.

The same goes for most 'pure', traditional and national styles when you take a closer look at them. The Mexican sombrero came with the Spanish, and in its turn it inspired the cowboy hat. Cowboys themselves, by the way, were just an American version of Spain's vaquero style of cattle herding, and many cowboys were originally of Mexican descent. As many as one in four cowboys were African-American (we don't know they were, because western films became popular during the segregation era).

Jeans combine workwear from Genoa (*Gênes* in French) and fabric from Nîmes (*de Nîmes*). The Japanese kimono came from China, and the Chinese cheongsam dress, which regularly causes an appropriation uproar at US proms, is ironically inspired by Western fashion. In the 1930s, conservative Chinese complained that women began to dress like French women when they wore them.

Culture is mongrelization, as the British Indian author Salman Rushdie has written, it is 'hybridity, impurity, intermingling, the transformation that comes of new and unexpected combinations of human beings, cultures, ideas, politics, movies, songs [...] Melange, hotchpotch, a bit of this and a bit of that is how newness enters the world.'[3] Everything we do is a blend of ideas, impulses and traditions from all corners of the world.

We are all mongrels

And so are we. When scientists analysed the DNA of our old friend Ötzi the iceman, they found that his maternal lineage originated in the Eastern Alps but his paternal DNA came from far, far away. It was actually more similar to ancient farmers in Sweden and Bulgaria, which raises the possibility that Ötzi's parents came from different parts of Europe and had a fling in the Alps.

The classic, white West European is a mixed breed, a combination of several different waves of immigration. First there were the hunter-gatherers who ended up here after a long journey from

Africa, such as 'Cheddar Man', from Cheddar Gorge, Somerset, England, whose ancestors walked across the ancient land bridge Doggerland into Britain 11,000 years ago, and stayed there. This makes him the oldest known Briton with a direct connection to today's population. Analysis of his nuclear DNA in 2018 showed that this man, who had always been portrayed as white, probably had a very dark brown to black skin colour, dark, curly hair and blue eyes. This came as a surprise to most people, even though analysis of other hunter-gatherers in Europe also pointed to dark skin and blue or green eyes. Apparently, white West Europeans' pale skin is not due to anything more racially significant than not eating enough oily fish and other sources of vitamin D after the advent of farming. Then the pale pigment spread rapidly on northern latitudes, since it absorbs more sunlight.

Two major waves of immigration later changed the continent and the complexion of Europeans. Firstly, farming spread quickly in Europe in the early Neolithic period, around 6000 BC, and changed the whole make-up of the continent. While archaeologists used to think this happened because of cultural transmission, modern DNA tests have revealed that migration was the cause. As farmers multiplied in Anatolia, present-day Turkey, many of them moved north into southern Europe in search of new, fertile land. They cleared the forests, grew the land with innovative technologies and started to interbreed with the native hunter-gatherers. One of them was probably the father of Ötzi. Around 5000 BC these migrant farmers had reached northern Germany. By then they had transformed the whole culture and the genetic make-up of Europe from bands of hunter-gatherers to a continent of farmers. After having hesitated for more than a thousand years, for some reason that still confounds us Swedes, they even defied the cold and the deep forests of Scandinavia as well.

The second wave occurred during the early Bronze Age, around 3000–2500 BC, and it came from the East. On the Russian and

Ukrainian steppes, above the Caspian and Black Seas, there was a population named the Yamnaya after one of their then-peculiar habits: they buried their dead in individual pits. They were pastoralists who rode horses to herd cattle across the grasslands. Perhaps as a result of climate change that made the steppes colder and drier, they started moving into Eastern and Central Europe in waves five thousand years ago. Eventually they reached Germany and Scandinavia, searching for new pastures. They brought new technologies, the horse and the wheel, and a new Indo-European language, ancestral to most European languages.

The Yamnaya people looked different from the old Europeans: they were taller and had lighter skin. They also had a mutation that was very beneficial for a culture with cattle and other livestock: they were able to digest lactose in milk. In populations that do not descend from them this ability disappears after childhood. If you are lactose tolerant, it is probably because of this steppe population.

Europe was the original melting pot. My own DNA test reveals I am a quite typical north European mixture of African hunter-gatherer, Middle Eastern farmer and pastoralist from the Eurasian Steppes. I also found out that I am 0.9 per cent Denisovan and 2.4 per cent Neanderthal. And, just as my wife always suspected, the latter is slightly above average.

Mankind has always been on the move. We have always searched for a better climate, richer soil or a mate. We have always tried to escape hunger, troublesome neighbours and violence. Sometimes we have moved on just for adventure. Modern humans emerged in Africa and started to move out between 70,000 and 60,000 years ago. The first successful emigrants probably crossed the Bab-el-Mandeb Strait on the Red Sea into Yemen. It was an impressive effort, made easier by the sea level being almost 100 metres lower during this ice age. They moved along the coasts of Arabia, India and South East Asia, and while it was previously assumed that these early humans stayed close to the coasts, recent findings suggest they roamed freely over Asia. Within just a few millennia of having left Africa, the first humans had made it all the way to Australia, in a daring and mysterious ocean crossing that still puzzles scholars today.

Another group migrated to the Middle East and southern Central Asia, and from here humans started to move into Europe some 40,000 years ago, where they met and interbred with the Neanderthal descendants of the *Homo erectus* who had moved into Eurasia almost two million years ago. Neanderthal DNA in modern Africans show that some Europeans moved back there. Another group hunted big animals like the mammoth in northeast Asia and began to follow it over the Bering land bridge between Siberia and Alaska around 15,000 years ago, and so discovered America. A thousand years later they had reached the tip of South America. So in just 50,000 years a brand new species, *Homo sapiens*, had populated the whole world, through explorers and adventurers, the brave and the curious, the hungry and the desperate. Along the way, we picked up the best ideas from those we met: languages, writing, what we can eat and how to process it safely, how to control fire and make weapons and tools.

We are all descendants of these migrations. Many of us still think in racial categories that eighteenth-century Europeans invented to try to understand differences and to legitimize colonial domination. Since these categories were based on visual observation and subjective impressions, even the proponents of such theories could never really agree whether there were three races or hundreds.

Now, with the progress of the science of genetics, we know that there is as much diversity within racial groups as there is across them. In 2018, an official document from the American Society of Human Genetics, the primary professional organization for experts in human genetics, made it clear that the concept of biological races are 'bogus claims' based on 'discredited or distorted genetic concepts'. As a result of mixing in the great historical melting pot, most genetic variation is distributed as a gradient, which 'challenges the traditional concept of different races of humans as biologically separate and distinct' and renders ideas about racial purity 'scientifically meaningless'.[4]

Resisting disease

New ideas and methods were not the only things that crossed borders as people started to move around the world – so did bacteria and viruses. Early globalization killed millions by exposing people to pathogens to which they had no earlier exposure. In the second century, Romans and Chinese picked up the Antonine Plague (probably smallpox or measles), which is said to have caused two thousand deaths a day in Rome, a city of a million inhabitants. Less than four centuries later, the Plague of Justinian devastated cities all around the Mediterranean. In the mid-fourteenth century, the Black Death killed perhaps a third of the Eurasian population. When conquistadores descended upon American cities in the 1500s, they found that their microorganisms had moved even faster and already done the terrible job for them. A century after Columbus, 90 per cent of the Mexican population had perished. As late as 1918, the Spanish flu killed as many as 50 to 100 million people.

But these plagues are also a brutal reminder that only more openness can solve problems that openness creates. Innovation and information across borders have given us the chance to keep up with the pace of microorganisms, and increasingly to overtake them. We respond faster than ever to new diseases today because researchers, health authorities and drug companies cooperate internationally and trade knowledge and coordinate treatment protocols and therapeutics.

Counter-intuitively, pandemics might be less lethal to begin with, thanks to our constant mobility. New diseases often evolve from an earlier, related strain, and if you have been exposed to a previous version you are likely to have developed some resistance against the new, deadlier strain. You are less likely to get it, and if you do, you are less likely to die from it. Some of the worst outbreaks in history affected populations that had been isolated for a very long time before being exposed to a pathogen.

A team of researchers modelled the impact of varying travel rates on the probability of a major epidemic, and found that frequent contact between populations can lead to widespread immunity. In a more connected world, low-virulence strains are more common while high-virulence strains are less likely and potentially smaller. Mobility functions 'like a natural vaccination'. The researchers speculate that many outbreaks in the last century could have been as severe as the Spanish flu had it not been for mass air travel.[5]

Hunter-gatherer groups had their own way of resisting disease. They routinely split up when the group had grown too large or there was a conflict. The genetic difference between individuals in small groups of hunter-gatherers shows that early humans avoided inbreeding, with its associated risk of diseases if both parents share a genetic weakness. As individuals reached puberty, they routinely left their own group in search of partners, sometimes in elaborate ceremonies between the groups. Originally, they can't have had any idea why they should avoid inbreeding, but some individuals developed a certain wanderlust, left the group and mated more successfully. This gave a clear reproductive benefit to the 'anywheres' in a population, who had an inexplicable urge to wander off when they reached sexual maturity, whereas the 'somewheres' stayed, teamed up with a relative and matched dangerous genes to the misfortune of the next generation.

Researchers have found vast differences in the DNA of hunter-gatherers buried at the same time, even between two children buried head to head in the same grave. They conclude that as early as 34,000 years ago, 'low levels of within-band relatedness, complex family residence patterns, relatively high individual mobility and multilevel social networks were already in place'.[6]

The major waves of migration did not end because we settled down and became farmers. The new cities were created by large-scale mobility from rural areas to towns and cities, and they became so productive because they were meeting places where merchants, missionaries and migrants from different groups and cultures met and exchanged ideas, goods and insults. 'Great cities are not like towns, only larger,' wrote the urban prophet Jane Jacobs, they differ in many ways, 'and one of them is that cities are, by definition, full of strangers.'[7]

Because of this, cities became crucibles of thought, as Thomas Mann called them. They stood a greater chance of developing useful innovations and were more likely to give individuals opportunities to live the kind of life they wanted. The risk of being the only gay in the village is bigger if your village is just a tiny band or tribe. As Peter Watson writes in his great work on thought and invention in human history:

> The city is the cradle of culture, the birthplace of nearly all our most cherished ideas. [...] Cities have been the forcing houses of ideas, of thought, of innovation, in almost all the ways that have pushed life forward.[8]

When ideas have sex

Just like a mix of genes results in more healthy offspring, the constant mixing of different perspectives, know-how and technologies made groups stronger. The moment someone comes up with a new method, we copy it. But in order for us to have something to imitate, someone has to innovate, leading to better ideas, methods and technologies. Those innovations rarely come from new ingredients – we still have the same atoms that we had a million years ago – but from new recipes. As the British science writer Matt Ridley memorably put it, progress is made 'when ideas have sex with each other'.[9] It's the combinations that have revolutionized our world: theory *and* practice, iron *and* carbon, wheel *and* axle, needle *and* thread, moveable types *and* pressure, hardware *and* software, the mobile phone *and* the internet (and, as a frequent traveller, I should add suitcases *and* wheels).

There are far too many possibilities to test them all, but the way to maximize our chances is to allow as many people as possible to test their ideas and experiment with their solutions. The more open we are to other perspectives and ideas, the greater our chance of finding a new set of skills or a new solution that improves our lives. Openness is not an altruistic attitude that we generously concede to others, it is long-term selfishness.

I recently learned that one of the most accomplished astronomers of our era is Aida Berges. I had never heard of her before, but she has classified 40,000 galaxies on her own and has detected 10 per cent of all known hyper-fast stars – stars whose velocity deviate substantially from the normal velocity of stars. One reason I had never heard of her is that she does not work in any observatory and does not even have an education in astronomy. She is a housewife from Puerto Rico with two children. Through the Galaxy Zoo online platform, where scientists have published photos of the starry sky, 200,000 amateur astronomers have helped to classify more than 150 million galaxies.[10] Who could have guessed that one of the best would turn out to be a housewife in Puerto Rico? No one. No government would have planned for it, and no research group would have included her in its team. It was only by having an open platform, where everybody was allowed to test their skills, that we were able to find much-needed talent when it hid from sight. For the same reason, openness to workers and thinkers from other places makes us so much stronger because the chance that we will find someone who improves our way of doing things or comes up with useful innovations increases when more people are allowed to try their luck.

The economist Julian Simon was a pioneer in arguing that progress was possible and poverty would decrease just as 1970s and 1980s doomsayers and environmentalists claimed that overpopulation would result in hunger and the end of resources. He thought immigration 'is as close to an everybody-wins government policy as can be'.[11] His argument was not just the trillion-dollar bills we get with a larger workforce and higher productivity; he also thought it would create brand-new value through innovation – something that followed from his belief that human beings are 'the ultimate resource'. He wrote:

Knowledge stems from human minds. Minds matter economically as much as, or more than, mouths or hands. In the long run, the most important economic effect of immigrants is their contribution to our stock of useful knowledge. And this contribution is large enough in the long run to dominate all the other benefits and costs of immigration.

Immigrants affect productivity and technology partly in their special role as immigrants by stimulating both natives and immigrants to invent new ideas that are some combination of the transported ideas and the ideas that are already present in the country of immigration. They also carry ideas and practices from one society to another, thereby inducing natives to adopt the transported ideas.[12]

Immigrants made up 24 per cent of bachelor's degrees and 47 per cent of doctorates in the American science and engineering workforce in the 2000 Census, even though they only made up 12 per cent of the workforce.[13] US data shows that around 40 per cent of Fortune 500 companies have been started by immigrants or children of immigrants, as have more than half of all 'unicorns' – start-ups valued at more than \$1 billion. Immigrants are three times more likely than natives to file a patent or win a Nobel Prize or an Academy Award.[14] The son of an Arab Muslim from Homs, Syria, who spent time in jail for pan-Arab activism, can go on to change the world of technology, as proven by Steve Jobs.

And while this gives the impression that only highly skilled immigrants benefit the economy, low-skilled immigrants also contribute to the specialization that makes everybody more productive. Many take jobs that natives spurn, like picking vegetables or caring for the elderly. Some Americans might not have been able to start a company or win a Nobel Prize had it not been for the relief provided by a maid, cleaner or gardener who had migrated from another country. A larger share of low-skilled immigrants has the effect of increasing labour-market participation of native women.

Tucker Carlson is a host on Fox News, famed for his nationalist rhetoric. In a typical segment he mocked the ideals of diversity: 'Is diversity our strength? The less we have in common the stronger we are? Is that true of families? Is it true in neighbourhoods or businesses?' Carlson asked rhetorically, consciously jumbling comparative advantages with estrangement. 'Of course not. Then why is it true of America? Nobody knows.'[15]

Well, somebody does know. Carlson would not have to go further than to his own bosses at Fox News' parent company. 'Different backgrounds and characteristics,' declares its annual report, 'bring innovative viewpoints and merit to the creation of our content and products.' Further, 'an exchange of diverse perspectives will drive creative innovation and inspire authentic stories that resonate'.[16]

Granted, there is always some corporate mumbo-jumbo in such reports, but the advantages of broadening your horizons are well documented. The American psychologist Charlan Nemeth has spent decades studying all sorts of groups, and whether it be companies, juries or airplane crews, we tend to follow the majority simply because it is the majority. But she has also found that a single dissenting opinion or another sort of perspective on the issue opens the minds of the others. People start searching for more information, consider more options, become more creative and make better decisions.

In one of many of Nemeth's experiments, subjects were tested in anagram solutions. When they received feedback that the majority had used a specific strategy, they switched to this one to the detriment of other solutions. Those who were exposed to a minority viewpoint, on the other hand, were more open to different strategies and found more correct words.[17]

Groups are better at solving problems if they are diverse. Those groups also have more friction. There is a greater risk that someone will question the assumptions or object to a quick solution, and this makes the whole process less smooth and comfortable. But this is precisely why we need it. Groups that are too similar are easily afflicted with group thinking – objections are not raised, alternatives are not explored and the group mainly looks for information that confirms what they already thought. People often self-censor so that they don't come to be seen as troublesome or used as scapegoats if anything goes wrong.

An interesting implication is that we benefit more from cooperation and exchange when somebody's experiences and knowledge differ from our own, making it more likely that they will contribute something we would not be able to do ourselves. 'Strangers instinctively question things that natives take for granted. They stimulate new perspectives because, simply, many things strike them as odd or stupid,' as technology writer G. Pascal Zachary puts it.[18] Those who leave the places where they grew up and move to new unfamiliar regions are on average more ambitious and creative than others. But even without this selection, just by going to a new place you learn to see things from different vantage points and confront old problems with fresh eyes.

It is important to explain what this argument for diversity is not. It's not the kind of exoticism where immigrant groups are supposed to exhibit their culture in a museum version of diversity where they dress up in folk costumes and sing traditional songs. That is not a version of diversity that creates bridges between cultures. And neither does it excuse the failed form of integration where large immigrant groups cluster in a few areas, far from natives and far from the labour market, and some never learn the local language. The benefit comes from migrants who participate in society, and when people from different backgrounds get the chance to meet and blend and question each other's perspective on things.

Empires of diversity

In September 2019, Stefan Molyneux, a white supremacist with a large following, took to Twitter with his killer argument against politically correct platitudes about diversity: 'If diversity is such a strength, you would imagine that at least one ancient culture would have used it to conquer the world.'

OK, challenge accepted:

The Persians.

And the Macedonians.

The Romans, of course, but that goes without saying.

The Tang Chinese.

And even more so, the Mongols.

The Ottomans!

And later on, the Dutch.

The British, naturally.

And if you count cultural conquest, the Americans in our day and age.

In fact, a phenomenon that never ceases to amaze the historians is the tiny group that manages to suddenly step out of obscurity, expand dramatically and build an empire that extended over much of the known world. The only reason why they could do that was their openness to diversity. They drew on ideas and technologies from many different tribes and people, and so defeated those who were limited to more local knowledge. Metaphorically speaking, they were better at finding just the astronomer they needed even if she happened to be a housewife in Puerto Rico.

As Amy Chua writes in her sweeping history of the rise and fall of hyperpowers:

> For all their enormous differences, every single hyperpower in history – every society that could even arguably be described as having achieved global hegemony – was, at least by the standards of its time, extraordinarily pluralistic and tolerant during its rise to pre-eminence. Indeed in every case tolerance was indispensable to the achievement of hegemony.[19]

She claims this can even be said for modern China. We forget this because we rightly focus on China's oppression of ethnic groups like Uyghurs and Tibetans. But in doing that, we tend to see the Chinese as one big, homogenous Han collective. We forget that what is now thought of as Chinese has been built over millennia by the merging of a multitude of ethnicities with different religions, customs and traditions. There are hundreds of varieties of the Chinese language, many not understood by speakers of other varieties. However, as long as this modern Chinese identity is not open to the non-Chinese, it is much less open than ancient empires were.

The strategic tolerance of historical civilizations should not be confused with modern concepts of tolerance and minority rights. Ancient emperors rarely came close to any concept of human rights, they practised slavery and were astonishingly brutal against anyone who stood in the way of dominance. They didn't embrace diversity because they were politically correct, but because of a hard-nosed realization that they would accomplish more and get access to more knowledge if they allowed more people to contribute. And people who feel like they could live according to their own beliefs and traditions also make for more loyal subjects.

The first of the great empires was the Achaemenid Persian Empire, founded in the sixth century B C. With its roots in present-day Iran, it conquered the ancient Middle Eastern civilizations and at its peak stretched from the Balkans to the Indus Valley, ruling almost a third of the world's population. The key to its rapid expansion was its strategic tolerance. Previous conquerors like the Assyrians razed subjected cities, demolished their temples and often killed whole civilian populations. Achaemenid Persian emperors like Cyrus and Darius, however, removed the ruler but left the local social structure intact, and allowed the subjects to keep their old customs. Instead of devoting resources to impose their own gods and traditions on the unwilling, the Persians harnessed different skills and ideas from various ethnic groups. Persia thrived not because the Persians were superior themselves, but because they understood that they benefited from Phoenician explorers, Greek scientists, Egyptian doctors and Babylonian astronomers. Their palaces were so impressive because they incorporated architectural styles from the Assyrians, Babylonians and Egyptians. Combined with an advanced system of roads and communications, translations of inscriptions into several languages and eventually a standard currency, it became an empire of commerce and cultural exchange.

This openness was manifested when Cyrus conquered Babylon

in 539 BC – a city then so big that news of the conquest took days to reach some neighbourhoods, according to Herodotus. Cyrus presented himself as the liberator of the Babylonians, and amazingly he claimed that he triumphed on behalf of the Babylonians' own god, Marduk. In 1879, an ancient clay cylinder was discovered in the ruins of Babylon (now Iraq), with a declaration in cuneiform script. It turned out to be Cyrus' own press release about the conquest. It has anachronistically been described as the first declaration of human rights, but it is really a magnificent description of strategic tolerance. Cyrus explains that the previous king oppressed his people and interfered with their religion. This apparently offended Marduk, who ordered Cyrus to invade and bring peace to Babylon. Rather than sacking the city, he claims to have restored the old cult sanctuaries and temples and repatriated people who had been forcibly displaced. We don't know how much of this is propaganda, but it resembles much of what we know about the great Achaemenid emperors. Many think it confirms the biblical story of the Babylonian captivity, which tells that Cyrus allowed the captive Judeans to return to Jerusalem, and even rebuilt their temple and returned 5400 articles of gold and silver that had been stolen from them.

In the fourth century BC the Persian Empire turned more despotic and less tolerant, perhaps as a response to increasingly hostile surroundings. When Emperor Artaxerxes retook Egypt in 343 BC, he looted the temples, suppressed the local religions and imposed confiscatory taxes. The idea was no longer to make subjects rich and happy enough to be loyal, but to weaken them so much that they could not revolt. But it only bred resentment. This created an opening for a new conqueror who made strategic tolerance personal, Alexander the Great of Macedonia. The Greeks already had some understanding of cosmopolitanism, which we can see in their myths. Their greatest hero, Hercules, was not just of divine ancestry but also of Egyptian ancestry. So was Perseus, who killed Medusa. He would go on to marry an African princess, Andromeda, and their ancestors founded the centre of Greek civilization, Mycenae.

Alexander would build on this heritage with huge success. As he invaded Anatolia, Persia, Egypt and India in quick succession, he did not just preserve local structures and rebuild temples. He even adopted many customs of the defeated himself. He dressed in their clothes, sacrificed to their gods and let himself be instated as Pharaoh over Egypt. In an extravagant Persian mass wedding in 324 BC, Alexander and around ninety of his officers married local brides from prominent families. Alexander himself married daughters of two previous Persian emperors.

Sometimes this behaviour offended other Greeks, but Alexander did not do it because he was becoming 'barbarianized', but because it was his way to 'Hellenise' the barbarians. His openness made it tempting for local elites to switch allegiances, welcome Alexander, and so make it possible for them to remain in power. Alexander preserved so much of the old Persian structure that some scholars have talked about him as 'the last of the Achaemenids'.[20] This also made it possible for Alexander to draw on the strengths of all different groups, especially in his efficient and cosmopolitan military. Greeks, Phoenicians, Cypriots and Egyptians steered his massive navy, and his cavalry included Persians, Bactrians, Parthians and many others.

Alexander died suddenly, aged thirty-two, and his empire began to unravel almost immediately as his generals turned on each another. And in a stunning illustration of how difficult it is to uphold the kind of strategic openness that Alexander personified, all but one of his officers divorced the wives they had taken during the Persian mass wedding. The only exception was his general Seleucus, who founded a new empire in the old Persian heartlands. His wife, Apama, became the queen.

The brief and extensive meeting between Greek civilization

and many indigenous cultures in Europe, North Africa and Western Asia would live on. It was a creative brew that gave rise to new
art, philosophy and science, and Greek as a kind of lingua franca.
It is known as the Hellenistic period and had a profound impact
on the next major empire on the world stage to perfect the art of
strategic tolerance, the Roman Empire.

Becoming Roman

One of the founding myths of Rome is the story about how
Romulus fought and befriended the Sabines, and quickly gave
up his own small, round shield for the long, oblong shields of
the Sabines when it proved better. As the French Enlightenment
thinker Montesquieu explained:

> it should be noted that the main reason for the Romans becom-
> ing masters of the world was that, having fought successively
> against all peoples, they always gave up their own practices as
> soon as they found better ones.[21]

Like the Achaemenids and Alexander, the militant Romans could
be vicious against enemies but were also quick to accept defeated
regions as new provinces, kept the local authority structure intact
and maintained local traditions. Local gods were incorporated
in the Roman pantheon (which they had borrowed from the
Greeks), often as an aspect of an older god. The Celtic deity Lugh
was linked to Mercury, and when Roman soldiers arrived in the
Libyan desert they placed a representation of the local god Gholia
alongside the Roman gods in their camp. It's difficult to imagine a
more cosmopolitan deity than the Egyptian goddess Isis. According to the philosopher Apuleius, the Athenians called her Pallas
Athena, the Cretans Diana, the Sicilians Proserpina, the Phrygians
Pessinuntia, the Elusians Ceres and so on. So everybody could still

praise whomever they praised before – with the exception of Jews and especially Christians, who posed a particular conundrum with their monotheism.

The Romans did not even have to be familiar with the gods in a particular place to tolerate them. When Publius Servius invaded the city of Isaura Palaia in southern Galatia in AD 67, he publicly praised 'whichever' gods protected the city.[22] As the great historian of Rome's decline and fall, Edward Gibbon wrote:

> The various modes of worship, which prevailed in the Roman world, were all considered by the people, as equally true; by the philosopher, as equally false; and by the magistrate, as equally useful. And thus toleration produced not only mutual indulgence, but even religious concord.[23]

A difference from previous empires was that in Rome, there was no limit to how far foreigners and immigrants could go. In a speech before the Senate in AD 48, the emperor Claudius explained that cities like Sparta and Athens declined because they always considered the conquered foreign and suspicious:

> But our founder Romulus' wisdom made him on several occasions both fight against and naturalize a people on the same day! We have had strangers as kings: granting high offices on sons of freedmen is not a rarity...[24]

This was Claudius' successful argument for letting the defeated Gauls stand for public office, command legions, govern provinces and be admitted to the Senate itself. This was a way of turning outsiders into assets. As Claudius pointed out, if someone proved his ability, especially by rising through the military ranks, he could rise to the highest echelons of power.

Many of the great emperors were born far from Rome. Trajan,

remembered by the Romans as their most competent emperor, was born close to Seville in Spain, and so was his successor, Hadrian. The next emperor, Antoninus Pius, came from a family of Gallic origins. The family of his successor, Marcus Aurelius, came from southern Spain. Next his son ruled, and after him, Pertinax, the son of a freed slave. His successor had a father from Milan and a North African mother, and his successor, Septimius Severus, was born in North Africa. Many of the most prominent cultural figures in Rome were also outsiders. The stoic philosopher Seneca was from Spain, the poet Virgil from Cisalpine Gaul and the historian Tacitus probably from southern France.

This cosmopolitanism worked because 'Roman' rapidly ceased to be an ethnicity, and evolved into a cultural and political identity, just like 'American' today can refer to people of any nationality who come to the US and sign up to its ideals. Anyone who thought and acted like a Roman was a Roman. One tool of assimilation was the promise of Roman citizenship. As a Roman citizen you also had rights to vote, stand for office, appeal to courts and to acquire and transfer property. To people around the Mediterranean it was a much sought-after status.

After the Social War (91–88 BC), when several cities revolted, Rome extended citizenship and civil rights to other tribes who spoke Italic. Members of other groups could become citizens as a gift, by willingly surrendering to Roman troops or by showing loyalty to Rome, especially through commendable service in the army. In 212, Emperor Caracalla declared that all men who were not slaves throughout the Roman Empire were citizens.

This Roman identity depended on cultural assimilation. People from all over the empire were moulded into Romans. When in Rome, do as the Romans do, as the saying goes. There were limits to Roman tolerance, though, such as the wearing of trousers. Like many before and after them, Romans focused on outward appearance when they decided what was civilized and what was primitive. The wearing of trousers was considered barbaric by the toga-wearing Romans, and associated with the supposed innate aggressiveness of the Gauls and Germanic peoples. When Claudius argued for tolerance against Gauls, he explained, 'They are all right, they no longer wear trousers.'[25]

But not even in this area could the Romans help themselves from embracing useful innovations from others. As their armies moved north they discovered that leggings could be more practical than tunics. Soon Roman soldiers wore trousers, and the fashion spread to the civilian population. By 397, the emperor thought the use of trousers so dangerously widespread that he implemented an official trouser ban. The wearing of trousers in the city could condemn the taboo-breaker to perpetual exile. Not even that stopped trousers from becoming the required dress at the court of Constantinople just a century later, by then the only Roman court.[26] And in one of history's many ironic twists, the wearing of trousers eventually came to be seen as an important distinction between civilized Europeans and naked savages.

A long time before that, the Roman army itself was becoming barbarized.[27] In popular retellings Rome is often seen as a cautionary tale about immigration, since barbarians eventually managed to overwhelm the empire from within. That really doesn't make any sense. The western Roman Empire survived for more than five hundred years, which makes it one of the longest-lasting empires in history. And it would never have grown or survived as long as it did without an orderly integration of foreigners. That goes for much of the talent that sustained the administration at the height of its power, but even more so as it began to wane, after the economy had become more feudal and the empire was running out of conquests and spoils to fund it. As the pressure on the empire grew on all sides in the third century, it made peace with Vandals, Goths and Franks on the condition that they provided troops for the depleted Roman army and sometimes contributed in other ways. In some areas the terms 'Goth' and 'soldier' were used inter-changeably. This might have been the only way to afford an army of that size. Barbarians could rapidly advance to important posi-tions in the military.

Trouble ensued after the year 376, when thousands of Goths sought refuge on the south bank of the Danube, fleeing the on-slaught of the Huns. Unlike other refugees and defeated enemies, these Goths were allowed to keep their arms and their leaders – in itself a sign of the Romans' weakness – and they quickly over-whelmed the empire. The Goth refugees soon starved, and when they did not receive the food they had been promised, many sup-posedly had to sell their children to survive. When the Romans kidnapped their leader to facilitate a relocation, the Goths rebelled. In a battle in 378 the Goths defeated a Roman army and killed the emperor. After a peace treaty, the Goths became a state within the state, sometimes raiding Rome, sometimes fighting for it (against the Hun, for example, which remained a threat for almost a century). An unstable relationship for an already rapidly declining empire, it led to the sacking of Rome in 410.

By then, Rome's effective combination of tolerance and assimi-lation had already been undermined by its embrace of Christianity in the early fourth century. The Christians had at times been per-secuted because they only accepted one god and did not declare their loyalty to Rome. But when Christianity became the estab-lished religion, it started to repress all other religions – not just paganism, Manichaeism and Judaism, but even alternative ver-sions of Christianity.

This new intolerance dissolved the glue that held the empire and all its different groups together. It led to vicious conflicts and at times civil war between Christians and pagans, who saw their old gods being banned and their temples torn down. Perse-cuted groups allied themselves with Rome's enemies, and at times even saw barbarian invaders as liberators from the new Christian tyranny. After the fall of Western Rome, the East Roman Byzantines forced pagans and Jews to convert with the threat of torture and massacres. The same Montesquieu who argued that openness was the key to Rome's rise, thought this intolerance was the beginning of the downfall:

> Just as the old Romans strengthened their empire by permitting every kind of religion in it, so was it subsequently reduced to nothing by amputating, one after the other, the sects which were not dominant.[28]

For Europe, a dark age of intolerance ensued. As rulers and armies started to claim that they ruled and conquered in the name of the one true god, religious dissent became a crime against him and no compromise was possible. During the Crusade against Cathars, who believed in two deities, Christians might have killed as many as a million people in the early thirteenth century. 'Kill them all for the Lord knoweth them that are His,' as the inquisitor Arnaud Amalric is supposed to have told his Crusaders in 1209 when he learned that there were also Catholics in the Cathar stronghold of Béziers. Five years earlier, the Fourth Crusade had shocked Europe by sacking the world's largest Christian city, Constantinople, massacring civilians and raping even nuns. For long periods, the Chinese, Ottoman and even the Mongol empires were much more tolerant than Europeans.

Mongol tolerance

As Béziers and Constantinople fell, Genghis Khan had in just a few decades set about building history's largest land empire. Like the Crusaders, he was a vicious warlord, sparing no enemy or anyone in their family, but unlike them he did not try to impose one belief. It's not how we think of him nowadays, but Genghis Khan's policies within the empire would today open him up to accusations of being a politically correct, latte-drinking virtue signaller. The Mongols practised religious freedom and ethnic tolerance and in the place of kinship and tribal loyalty they put meritocratic standards. He preferred to promote the unknown, competent camel boy or cowherd of another faith than a less competent tribal peer. This was not because he was woke, but because he had to in order to find the best fighters, engineers and administrators for an empire created from scratch.

As the anthropologist Jack Weatherford writes about the Mongols: 'Because they had no system of their own to impose on their subjects, they were willing to adopt and combine systems from everywhere [...] They searched for what worked best; and when they found it, they spread it to other countries.'[29]

The Mongols' openness gave them an advantage over other rulers, who often exiled the competent and skilled if they interpreted the prevailing religion in a somewhat different way. Of the perhaps 150,000 Mongol horsemen who invaded Europe in 1241, only around a third were ethnic Mongols. They attacked with the combined material, intellectual and technological resources of northern China, Central Asia, Russia and Persia. Wherever they went, they brought the best Chinese engineers who built the portable towers, catapults and other weapons of attack on site when they needed them.

In a skirmish with the enemy outside Vienna, Habsburg soldiers were surprised that the Mongol officer they had captured turned out to be a middle-aged, literate Englishman. After his ideas had forced him to flee England as he faced excommunication from the Church, he had sought refuge among the more tolerant Mongols.[30] And in a sad illustration of the state of tolerance in Europe, as they failed to defeat the Mongols, Christian mobs instead named the Jews as scapegoats, and burned down their quarters and massacred them, from York to Rome. The only reason Europe wasn't overrun by the Mongol army was that their emperor, Genghis' son Ögedei Khan, had died, and they turned back home to fight over succession.

When a French monk, William of Rubruck, arrived on a diplomatic mission to the Mongol capital Karakorum in 1253 he found that all religions were already practised there, including Christianity. The Mongols were curious about his certainty that he knew the one true way, and decided to stage a competition that sounds like something out of a Monty Python sketch. The emperor asked religious scholars to debate before three judges, a Christian, a Muslim and a Buddhist, as well as a large audience. The only rule was that they couldn't offend or attack the others. In several rounds, with shifting alliances, they debated God's nature, good and evil and reincarnation. After each round they drank fermented mare's milk to prepare for the next one:

> Finally, as the effects of the alcohol became stronger, the Christians gave up trying to persuade anyone with logical arguments, and resorted to singing. The Muslims, who did not sing, responded by loudly reciting the Koran in an effort to drown out the Christians, and the Buddhists retreated into silent meditation. At the end of the debate, unable to convert or kill one another, they concluded the way most Mongol celebrations concluded, with everyone simply too drunk to continue.[31]

If that sounds brutish, we should keep in mind how such disagreements were solved in other parts of the world. At the same time Rubruck's sponsor, King Louis IX, burned hundreds of Hebrew books, and Christian priests travelled around to arrest and torture suspected heretics.

So it was in no way a foregone conclusion that Europe would eventually come to be seen as the home of enlightenment and tolerance. This was the region that almost tore itself apart over religious disputes. Again and again, Europeans killed each other to see who had the better god. This was seen most destructively during the Thirty Years War (1618–48). Great powers often attacked and expelled minorities, especially Jews. Starting on the eve of St Bartholomew Day's in 1572, around 10,000 Huguenots were massacred in France.

How the Spanish Empire was lost

As Spanish kings reconquered Muslim land on the Iberian peninsula, they often acknowledged and accepted their contribution. But the religious establishment grew increasingly nervous about the new country's diversity and the idea was planted that only 'purity of blood' could give it unity and strength. After 1480, the Spanish Inquisition specifically targeted and tortured converts suspected of still being secret Jews and Muslims.

Following the fall of Granada, the last refuge of the Muslims, the triumphant Ferdinand of Aragon and Isabella of Castile gave Jews four months to convert to Christianity or leave Spain. Some 200,000 Jews converted and as many as 100,000 might have been expelled. They were forced to leave all their gold and silver behind, but took much of Spain's cultural capital and entrepreneurial ability with them. In 1502 Isabella forced the same brutal choice on Muslims in Castile, and other parts of Spain soon followed.

Wave after wave of persecution ensued. Starting in 1609, a quarter of a million Moriscos – Muslim converts and their descendants – were expelled. As whole towns were deserted and skilled agricultural workers disappeared, Spain's eastern coast collapsed economically. Combined with the discovery of America and religiously motivated war, this search for purity was supposed to bring glory to Spain, but in fact it destroyed the foundations of its wealth and culture. During the sixteenth and seventeenth centuries, Spain defaulted on its debts – the closest we come to state bankruptcy – no fewer than nine times. Urbanization went into reverse and Spain's real GDP per capita was actually lower in 1750 than it had been in 1500.[32]

King Ferdinand may have understood the harm he was doing to his country. In a letter to the Duke of Aranda he wrote that the Inquisition had persuaded him to expel the Jews, 'which we now do, because of our debts and obligations to the said Holy Office: and we do so despite the great harm to ourselves, seeking and preferring the salvation of our souls above our own profit and that of individuals'.[33]

The contrast with contemporary rivals was stark. The Ottoman Sultan Bayezid II threatened his governors with death if they did not welcome the Jews who had been expelled from Spain. They and the exiled Moriscos played an important role in introducing new ideas and technologies to the Ottoman Empire. Bayezid II gloated that through the expulsions, the Spanish king 'impoverished Spain and enriched Turkey'.[34] The Muslim Mughal Akbar I reigned for fifty years over an ethnically and religiously diverse empire on the Indian subcontinent. In a letter to Spain's King Philip II in 1582, he pointed out that those who only follow their own traditions uncritically exclude themselves from the possibility of ascertaining the truth: 'Therefore we associate at convenient seasons with learned men of all religions, thus deriving profit from their exquisite discourses and exalted aspirations.'

Simultaneously, a small, reluctant part of the Spanish Empire reacted fiercely to the despotism and Inquisitions, and was to fight its way out of it and create a cosmopolitan economic superpower – the Dutch Republic, the predecessor of the Netherlands. The provinces of the Low Countries had free markets and were used to their own laws and customs. So, when Spain's Philip II tried to take direct control of them in the 1550s with high taxes and the persecution of protestants, they rebelled. It didn't make it easier for the bankrupt emperor to win their hearts and minds that his unpaid troops ran riot, raping and slaughtering indiscriminately. In 1581, the northern provinces, which were to become the Netherlands, declared their independence from Spain, though the fight would continue for a long time yet.

The republic they created was unlike anything that had been seen in Europe. It had no established state church, and despite the Calvinist majority, Catholics, Jews, Lutherans and other minorities got the right to worship and print their own texts. Borders were thrown open to people from all origins. The republic was too diverse to impose one belief, but there was also an imperative to attract immigrants to grow the economy. Dutch cities became havens for groups oppressed elsewhere: Huguenots from France, Protestants from Habsburg regions, Sephardic Jews from Spain, Ashkenazi Jews from Germany and Poland, Quakers and Pilgrims from England.

These immigrants helped the Dutch to surge to dominance in several industries in a very short time, from diamonds and silk-weaving to tobacco-spinning and chocolate-making. In seafaring and textiles, immigrants made up more than half of the workers. By tapping into the new citizens' international networks, the region became a centre of global trade and finance. Dutch merchants used new financial instruments to share risk and allowed even small investors to participate, which made for very liquid capital markets. Stronger property rights than in other countries facilitated investment and commerce, and women were also more empowered. A visiting German noted that, 'Dutch women, even young, unmarried women, were free to come and go, unaccompanied and unchaperoned, to work, conduct business, and engage in conversation almost like men.'[35]

The rich, vibrant cities also created a golden age of culture, producing famous names such as Rembrandt and Vermeer. Wealthy

merchants and art markets took the place of the Church and aristocrats as patrons of the arts. Scenes of everyday life and other
secular subjects became popular in painting. Free-thinkers from
the whole continent thrived in the cosmopolitan cities. This is
where the French Catholic philosopher Descartes lived and published his works, and where John Locke went into exile from
Stuart England. Spinoza, whose family had fled the Portuguese
Inquisition, was too radical for his own Jewish community but not
for the republic.

This diversity and creativity turned it into the richest country on earth.[36] In 1500, Dutch GDP per capita was almost half
of Spain, in 1600 it was rapidly catching up, and soon it surged
ahead. The Dutch Republic was also about to become a global
power. In a desperate effort to stop them, Spain blocked their ships
from all Iberian ports in 1598. The intention was to block them
from making use of colonial markets, but the Dutch responded by
sailing directly to those markets themselves. In 1602, merchants
sponsored by the government started the world's first listed public company, the Dutch East India Company. Around half of the
biggest investors were refugees from Spain. Soon the Dutch drove
out the Portuguese from Malacca and Sri Lanka, and challenged
Spain in the Caribbean and northern South America.

As a new colonial power, however, the Dutch showed that their
ideals about freedom and openness only applied domestically. A
Dutch force with Japanese mercenaries exterminated almost the
whole population of the Banda Islands, east of Java, when the
Dutch wanted to monopolize their spice trade in 1621, and eventually replaced them with slaves and convicts.

Innovations in shipbuilding made the new trade empire possible. In the 1590s, the Dutch developed the 'fluyt', a ship with
a very large cargo space and a flat bottom and shallow draught
that made it easier to navigate shallow ports and rivers. To build
it they used a new wind-driven sawmill that reduced the time to

cut sixty beams from 120 days to four or five days. These highly innovative techniques made it possible for the Dutch to build better ships more quickly than other countries and at half the cost.[37] By 1670, the Dutch fleet was bigger than the combined fleets of Spain, Portugal, France, England and Germany – countries with a combined population of around 50 million people. This wasn't bad for a population of just 1.5 million people – a third of them recent immigrants. In the 1670s this tiny country managed to resist a simultaneous French and English invasion.

With greater wealth, imported skills, as well as creativity and innovation in warfare, the Dutch eventually got Spain and other powers to recognize their de facto independence. One important factor was that they could fund their war effort better thanks to more advanced financial markets, whereas the Spanish – who had expelled this talent – had to borrow from other rulers at higher interest rates. In 1648 the Dutch Republic was formally recognized as an independent country, after what has been called the Eighty Years War. What used to be a small waterlogged periphery of tiny city-states, with few natural resources and no army, had managed to bring Europe's greatest power to its knees.

The melting pot

The Dutch example would become important to the Industrial Revolution and global economy, since others imitated its successful policy of tolerance. Despite the discrimination of Catholics, Britain became a remarkably open country, especially after the Glorious Revolution of 1688 put the Dutch leader William of Orange on the British throne. Many of the skilled artisans and financial experts who kick-started the Industrial Revolution were immigrants, Huguenots and Jews. The union between Scotland and England in 1707 made for a productive cross-fertilization of ideas and technologies.

The colonies in America took this openness one step further, after they broke free from Britain in 1776, to become not just a nation full of immigrants but a nation *of* immigrants. One precondition was an absolute freedom of religion. In the radical Constitution of 1789 the Americans refrained from instituting a national Church. In fact, God and Christianity is nowhere to be found in the Constitution. The only mention is a rejection of religious tests as a condition for holding public office. Critics were outraged, claiming that delegates had for the first time in history removed religion from public life. Many worried that Catholics, Jews, Muslims and, even worse, Quakers would now be eligible. One delegate to the North Carolina convention warned that with this Constitution the Pope of Rome could be elected president.[38]

Many Americans did not appreciate the new openness. The first colonies, often founded by puritans and others who thought that only they possessed 'the truth' were not tolerant. Most people lived in cities or states with established churches. Religious dissenters had often been blocked from voting and sometimes expelled from the colony. Those who returned risked capital punishment. But in the 1700s the immigrant population increased and, with it, religious diversity. The religious revival of the 1730s known as the Great Awakening further challenged established churches, and merchants championed tolerance. This meant the revolutionary army fielded against the British was very diverse, and it seemed strange to many that those who fought for the new country would be discriminated by it. And the inescapable fact was that America was physically vast, and the first census of 1790 recorded only 3,227,000 inhabitants – fewer than Ireland. The new country needed skilled workmen but also cheap, unskilled labour to clear the land and build the cities.

Another reason for the open institutions was that the Founding Fathers believed in individual rights and political equality, with the obvious exception of the enslavement of African Americans and the treatment of native Americans. Considering they were steeped in Enlightenment ideals, it is shocking that so many of them accepted these original sins of the American republic, or at least rarely protested loudly against them. On keeping the country open, however, they were united. And many of them had their own immigrant story to tell. Eight signers of the Declaration of Independence were born in another country.[39]

One of the grievances against King George III in the Declaration was that he had prevented immigration to America and obstructed laws of naturalization. Thomas Jefferson, its principal author, talked about 'a right, which nature has given to all men, of departing from the country in which chance, not choice, has placed them, of going in quest of new habitations, and of there establishing new societies', and thought it 'fortunate for the United States to have become the asylum for so many virtuous patriots of different denominations'.[40] The first president, George Washington, stated that, 'The bosom of America is open to receive not only the opulent and respectable stranger, but the oppressed and persecuted of all nations and religions.'[41]

The first act of naturalization restricted citizenship to white persons, but even then it was one of the world's most liberal ones, requiring only two years of residency to acquire citizenship, and applied no restrictions on religion, skill or wealth. When the Federalists, who believed in a powerful central government, were in charge they extended the time while the more libertarian Jeffersonians reduced it. After 1802, five years of residency was the norm.

Tench Coxe, a merchant and member of the Continental Congress from Philadelphia, celebrated that America would now be 'an asylum of religious liberty', and predicted that this tolerance would give America the same economic vitality and success that it had given the Dutch.[42] Another supporter of this openness, the politician William Vans Murray, predicted that because of this diversity America 'will be the great philosophical theater of the world'.[43]

Immigrants poured into the US especially after 1840, tempted by the promise of rich farmland and individual freedom. Protestants from Britain, Germany and Scandinavia were now joined by Irish Catholics escaping hunger, and intellectuals and activists from all over the world who fled persecution. After the beginning of the Californian gold rush in 1848, thousands of Chinese migrated to the West Coast. By the end of the century the railroads had opened up new lands for development and steam-powered ships had reduced transportation costs. Between 1880 and 1920 the US received almost 24 million migrants. By then, an increasing share arrived from southern and eastern Europe, for example Italians and Poles. At the beginning of the twentieth century, almost 15 per cent of the population was foreign-born, and virtually all Americans descended from immigrants just a few generations back.

This contributed to a population explosion in the US, from 3.9 million in 1790 to 100 million around the time of World War I, after which the US began to impose substantial immigration controls on Europeans for the first time. A series of laws had already banned Chinese, Japanese, other Asians and African immigrants. A system of national-origins quotas gave preference to Northern and Western Europeans, barred Asians but kept the door for Latin Americans open. In 1968 this quota system was replaced with preferences based on family relationships and job skills, which once again resulted in an increase in Asian migrants.

America was also blessed by the intolerance and hatred of other cultures, which forced many exceptional minds to make the journey there. None was uglier and more self-destructive than Nazi Germany. When Hitler purged German universities of Jews it was like bombing his own armoury of knowledge and science. The dismissed represented not only 16 per cent of all Germany's physicists, chemists and mathematicians, but as much as 50 per cent of all the citations to papers published before 1933. Eleven of the dismissed scholars were past or future Nobel Prize winners.[44]

Hitler even insisted that Fritz Haber, the pioneer behind synthetic nitrogen fertilizer, be persecuted, despite his conversion to Christianity. One of Haber's prominent colleagues pleaded to Hitler to spare Haber and told him that these purges would set Germany back a hundred years in physics and chemistry. Hitler retorted: 'If Jews are so important to physics and chemistry, then we'll just have to work one hundred years without physics and chemistry.'[45]

The list of thinkers who escaped Hitler reads like a Who's Who of the scientific world: Fritz Haber, Albert Einstein, John von Neumann, Niels Bohr, Edward Teller, Erwin Schrödinger, and many more. Most of them escaped to the US, which was safe and far away. 'It was the most significant influx of ability of which there is any record,' wrote the novelist and chemist C. P. Snow. 'The refugees made [the US], in a very short time, the world's dominant force in pure science.'[46]

It was an incalculable loss to Germany, not least in terms of military capability. The scientists who could have given Hitler research, technologies and perhaps even the nuclear bomb he sought were exiled. Instead, they helped the US to get it. In 1942, the first human-created nuclear reaction was performed by an American team led by Enrico Fermi, who had fled fascist Italy when it implemented race laws. From then on, the US effort to produce nuclear weapons accelerated, and refugees from countries like Germany, Austria, Hungary and Italy played important roles. The many immigrants who worked on the Manhattan Project made it a peculiarly international team for a top-secret military venture.

Just like the Spanish King Ferdinand admitting that his policies of exclusion hurt his country, the Nazi regime eventually
came around to the same conclusion. In July 1942, as the tide of
battle was turning, Hermann Göring warned his science council
that many insights and technologies could be 'extremely valuable and… would take us very far. But we cannot exploit it, simply
because the man is married to a Jewess or because he is a half-
Jew.' As the more dogmatic Nazis around the conference table
shook their heads, Göring insisted that Jewish researchers had
abilities 'we need and which would absolutely take us a step forward at this moment. In this situation it would be madness to say:
He has to go!'[47] But if the National Socialists specialised in anything, it was madness.

Unlike most other receiving countries, and despite its history
of slavery and Jim Crow laws, the US managed to create a uniquely
open national identity that migrants could join and be a part of,
no matter their origin. In Europe we often talk about second-
generation immigrants and even third-generation immigrants,
whereas they would more often be known as first-generation
Americans in the US. This, in combination with the freedom and
the possibilities the US offered, helped it to remain a magnet for
the best and the brightest all over the world. And that helped it to
achieve and maintain leadership in science, technology, business
and the arts.

Not fit for our society?

Few of those who now fear immigration deny the benefits we
derived from these previous waves of immigrants. More often
they say that they were the good immigrants who built strong
communities, strengthened our economy and created important
companies. Present immigrants are allegedly different; they will
not fit in; they have the wrong religion and will never learn the

language; they work less and are more often dependent on welfare and crime. Instead of strengthening our society, they are undermining it. But interestingly, this is what we also said about previous waves of immigrants when they were new to our society and before they had had a chance to integrate and prove their worth and ability.

Even in that country of immigrants, the US, large groups, often majorities, thought the next wave of immigrants would destroy everything that previous immigrants had created, as Peter Schrag has documented in his book *Not Fit for Our Society*. Even those Founding Fathers who embraced open borders were worried that the immigrants who came after the English would not be able to adapt. In 1751, the great cosmopolitan Benjamin Franklin warned that Pennsylvania was becoming 'a country of aliens'. The large number of German immigrants meant they would never learn the English language or American customs. They will 'Germanize us instead of our Anglifying them'. (And revealing a surprising limit of his knowledge of foreigners, he also wrote that Germans and Swedes were of a somewhat suspect 'swarthy Complexion'.)[48] In 1781, Thomas Jefferson worried that Europeans from monarchies 'bring with them the principles of the governments they leave'. And if they were able to throw them off, it would be 'in exchange for an unbounded licentiousness, passing, as is usual, from one extreme to another'.[49]

This is a common concern in every era, and with some justification. If people come from countries with broken and oppressive institutions, perhaps they will recreate those here? But it ignores the self-selection of people who migrate. Often those who leave a country are those least sympathetic to the system of government there, the ones yearning to breathe freely. Look at your friends and relatives: who do you think would be the first to move to the other side of the planet if your country suffered from war or oppression? It is more likely that those who leave home would be those with the least fear of moving to the unfamiliar and living alongside people with different languages, ideas and religions. On average, the most tolerant and flexible migrate, while more of the die-hard traditionalists stay home. Furthermore, their experience of living in a new, freer country changes most migrants' attitudes even more in a libertarian direction. People have a status quo bias, and if something works well they are more open to doing more of the same.

It did not take long for Americans to conclude that Germans and Scandinavians did not end the republican experiment but helped to sustain it. And soon they were seen as model citizens, especially compared to the new dangerous immigrants, the Irish, who were described as poor, lazy, drunkards, criminals and – worst of all – Catholics. They were loyal to Rome not to liberty, and voted as their priests told them. 'The strange, cruel monster of Rome can never amalgamate with the fair and beautiful form of America,' exclaimed one tract, 'Liberty and Despotism are two eternal opposites.'[50] The arrival of Italians and Poles met with the same resistance.

Had natives back then known that six of the eight judges on the present US Supreme Court had been raised as Roman Catholics (and the remaining two Jews), they would surely have concluded that we live in a tragic future where despotism has won. Had they known that the Irish would by 2020 have captured the vice presidency (Mike Pence), the Senate (Mitch McConnell), the House Republicans (Kevin McCarthy), and were represented among former and present advisors to the president (Steve Bannon, Kellyanne Conway), they would probably have assumed that there had been a hostile takeover of the Republican party by anti-American globalists.

Anti-Irish sentiment back then were so strong that it spawned a briefly successful political party, the 'Know-Nothings', so named because its early adherents refused to answer questions about the party. In the mid-1850s, forty-three of the 234 members of the House of Representatives were Know-Nothings, and they held several governor and mayoral offices before it broke apart over the issue of slavery.

As the Irish fought bravely in the Civil War, started working, raised families and built communities, they came to be seen as a normal part of society. At least they were Christians, compared to the conniving Jews and immoral Chinese. An Irish immigrant and Labour leader from California, Denis Kearney, rallied successfully against the Chinese, ending all his speeches with, 'And whatever happens, the Chinese must go!' In the 1870s and 1880s, a series of laws even temporarily stopped Chinese immigration altogether.

Attitudes against Jews hardened as more of them arrived from Eastern Europe. Now Jews could be rejected by prestigious New York clubs, with the excuse that it was nothing personal, '[i]t was purely racial'.[51] In the 1920s quotas reduced their numbers, and not even Nazi terror changed it. Most infamously, the German liner laden with Jewish refugees, the SS *St Louis*, was sent back to Europe in June 1939, where more than two hundred of them were killed during the Holocaust.

The pseudoscience of eugenics had scared Americans into thinking Jews imported worse 'biological material'. Around World War I, mental tests had supposedly revealed that Italian and Polish (often Jewish) immigrants had an IQ that was roughly 15 points lower than Anglo-Saxons. The conclusion was that intelligence was restricted to north-western Europeans, and immigration ran the risk of turning America into a country of imbeciles. However, in their obsession with biology, they had ignored how education, nutrition and living in a culture of technology raise IQ for every-body (a phenomenon known as the Flynn effect). Fifty years later the Italians had caught up with the average on IQ tests, and the Poles had passed it by nine points![52]

Eventually, of course, Jews and Chinese and Europeans in

general came to be seen as decent and hard-working citizens who strengthened America – at least compared to Mexicans. When I began to inform myself about US attitudes to immigration in the early 2000s, the influx from the south was the great scare, exemplified by Samuel Huntington's 2004 book *Who Are We?* Americans I spoke to said the US used to be a great melting pot but the Hispanics were different and threatened to bifurcate the country. They were more numerous, more geographically concentrated and also stayed more in touch with their homeland so they would never learn English. They were also more criminal and with their history they would not learn liberty or be as patriotic as previous immigrants.

Two decades later, we have learned that Hispanic immigrants are *less* likely to commit crime than US natives and, adjusted for age and education, US-born Hispanics are *more* patriotic than other Americans. In fact, US citizens born in other countries are more likely than natives to say that the US is better than other countries, that they are proud to be Americans, and to express trust in the three branches of government.[53] I agree with many American conservatives that the country needs more patriots. The best way to get them is often to import them.

As for language, only 5 per cent in the fourth generation of Mexican immigrants speak Spanish very well, even in Southern California where the concentration is the largest. Linguists conclude that, 'Spanish appears to draw its last breath in the third generation', not that different from previous immigrant groups.[54]

The data suggests we underestimate the pace of assimilation because those who integrate the fastest are the least likely to identify with their ethnic origin. Polls about language, education, work, income and religion only catch those who self-identify as, for example, Hispanics. They miss the 17 per cent in the second generation who have stopped self-identifying as Hispanics, 27 per cent in the third generation and a majority (56 per cent) in the fourth generation. Only those who identify the most with the region their ancestors come from are still in the data at that time, so obviously we think that immigrants are worse at assimilating than they are.[55]

In 2017, the Republican congressman Steve King said: 'We can't restore our civilization with somebody else's babies.' But that is the genius of America. Ever since its founding it has been built on and carried forward by somebody else's babies and, as Ronald Reagan said in his last speech as president: 'We lead the world because, unique among nations, we draw our people – our strength – from every country and every corner of the world. And by doing so we continuously renew and enrich our nation.'[56] Steve King, of German and Irish ancestry, happens to be an example himself of how somebody else's babies can become a part of the country, and even advance to its highest ranks (admittedly, in this case, also proving that immigration does not necessary strengthen America every single time).

Previous immigrants – good. Present immigrants – bad. That is, until they also become previous immigrants. This pattern repeats itself again and again, in most places. It is not exclusive to the US. There is a classic Israeli comedy sketch from a 1970s comic troupe called Lul. Successive waves of Jewish immigrants – Poles, Russians, Germans, Yemenites – reach the shores of Israel only to be mocked by the Jews already there, who say they don't fit in. But as soon as each group makes itself at home, it joins the other onlookers to hurl abuse at the next wave of Jews reaching the promised land.

People who move to another country are often met with suspicion and fear because they are different and we still don't know how they will turn out. But then they start working, start businesses, fall in love, raise families and in the second or third generation they are seen as good examples of what immigrants should be like, compared to a new immigrant group that has not

yet had time to do all this. We are always standing in the midst of
an unpredictable process, so the past is seen in a forgiving light,
whereas the future always seems uncertain.

Another one of these regular shifts is underway, and soon we
will see Hispanic immigrants as benevolent, at least compared
to the next group – Muslims, who are supposed to be poor and
criminal and more loyal to a backwards religion than to Western freedom, so integration will be hopeless. Does that sound
familiar? As the migration scholar Aristide Zolberg pointed out:
'Everything now said about the unsuitability of Muslims for life
in a liberal democracy was once said about the Irish in the US.'[57]

Is this time different?

Some Westerners are very keen on telling Muslims how bigoted
and fundamentalist they should be according to their religion.
This is often based on caricatures or selective readings. But it also
ignores the speed with which values change. If you take a snapshot of the world today, you notice that emancipative values, like
freedom of choice and equal rights, are much more common in
the Western world than in Asia, Africa and Latin America. But a
snapshot misses changes in direction. All cultures are embracing
more emancipative values as their populations become richer and
better educated. An analysis of World Values Survey data shows
that young Middle Easterners, in the world's most traditional
societies, are now similar in their values to the young in the most
liberal Western countries in the late 1960s and early 1970s, when
their parents thought that their nihilism and narcissism (and
'whatever they call music nowadays') was ruining everything that
was holy and pure.[58]

And again, it ignores how the most open-minded often self-
select to migrate, and how meeting with more open and democratic
cultures accelerates this process (for most, if not for everybody). A

majority of American Muslims think there is more than one way to interpret Islam and that the traditional understandings should be updated. They are slightly more likely than others to say that religion is important in their lives, but when asked about what is essential to being a Muslim, more of them answer 'working for justice' and 'protect the environment' than following the Koran. Compared to the US public as a whole, Muslims are more likely to say that it is never justifiable to kill civilians for political or religious reasons.[59]

The same pattern holds in Europe where the younger generations of Muslim immigrants are more relaxed and also have more diverse friendship groups. Muslim immigrants in Western Europe do not seem to differ much from natives when it comes to their religious activity, and polls show they mostly identify with their new country and have trust in democratic institutions.[60] In 2016, 93 per cent of British Muslims said they felt they belonged to Britain, with more than half saying they felt this 'strongly'. While you might wish that more than 64 per cent of them were satisfied with the way democracy works in Britain, that is almost 20 percentage points more than the share of the British public who were satisfied with British democracy. They are also more likely than non-Muslims to trust parliament and other democratic institutions.[61]

The major difference between Muslim immigrants and natives is that they are more similar to the minority of Christian conservatives on issues like gender equality, gay marriage, sex outside of marriage, abortion and pornography. But these attitudes change the longer they live in a more liberal society. Attitudes to homosexuality reveal how quickly this can happen. In 2007 just 27 per cent of US Muslims said that homosexuality should be accepted by society. Ten years later, this had almost doubled, to 52 per cent. This means that US Muslims are now more tolerant than the average American was in 2006 (five years after Baptist preachers Jerry

Falwell and Pat Robertson had blamed 9/11 on God's vengeance on gays and lesbians).

A World Values Survey of Middle Eastern immigrants to Sweden shows that they hold less emancipatory views, such as tolerance and gender equality, than native Swedes but more than people do in the countries they came from. They are somewhere halfway between origin and destination, and close to the views of citizens of Catholic south European countries. The longer they have been in Sweden, the more 'Swedish' their values become.[62]

Muslim immigrants become more liberal all the time, and the youngest group is the most liberal. This is just what we should expect if they follow the same pattern as other immigrant groups. It does not mean this progression is automatic or that there is no risk it will go into reverse. It just means these fears – sometimes borrowed almost verbatim from the agitation against previous immigrant groups – are not supported by evidence.

Immigration, especially from different races and cultures, often stirs suspicion and even fear, and that is natural. Newcomers are different and they behave differently. That is exactly why we need them to constantly re-energize and regenerate our populations. But at the same time, it is not strange that we are suspicious of that which is different, until we understand what it is. However, it does not reflect an inevitably adversarial relationship between natives and migrants. On the contrary, areas with more immigrants are on average also more pro-immigration. Urban, cosmopolitan centres are more open, while rural areas and smaller cities more sceptical. In the US, you find the most anti-immigrant votes in areas with fewer immigrants and ethnic minorities. In Europe, most scepticism is concentrated in Eastern European countries that have received almost no asylum seekers, rather than in Sweden and Germany, where most of them go. Within Germany you find the most hostility in the East, where you find fewer immigrants and less of an open tradition.

The simple fact is that we get used to change. We learn that people are not as dangerous as we thought, and we start seeing them not as immigrants but as neighbours, doctors, teachers and waiters. We get used to diversity. However, it's harder to get used to quick changes. A rapid increase of minority groups in previously non-diverse regions triggers suspicion and opposition to immigration – not necessarily because someone changes opinion, but because the issue becomes more salient. Those who were already sceptical become more sceptical. Backlashes against immigration are more related to the speed of changes than to its levels.[63]

That is probably a good thing, because most people have no real idea about the levels. They generally overestimate the number of immigrants in their country by a factor of two or three. The British, Germans and French think they make up 25–26 per cent of their populations when the correct answer is 12–13 per cent. Swedes think immigrants make up 25 per cent of the population, an overestimation by 9 percentage points. Americans guess they are 33 per cent – 19 percentage points more than the reality![64]

The fear of increases is one reason why it is a mistake to try to force immigration on countries that don't feel ready for it. It would not be unreasonable to think that Central and Eastern European countries could accept some share of the refugees who make it to Europe, but it is difficult to think of a policy that would do more to spur anti-immigrant and anti-EU sentiments in these countries than being forced by rich EU countries to accept refugees that they have no tradition of admitting and are not interested in welcoming.

Change has to come from within these countries, for example as economic realities spark a new discussion about the benefits of immigration. Interestingly, some Eastern European countries that are strongly anti-immigration in rhetoric also have the most need for immigrants because of large-scale emigration and low birth rates. Without more immigrants they suffer labour shortages, and an economic model based on cheap labour-intensive production is at risk. This is why Poland has silently opened its doors to workers from the East. In a way, you can even say this nominally anti-immigrant country is the most immigrant-friendly in Europe, since it hands out more first residence permits than any other EU country, especially to Ukrainians. Not because the government likes immigrants, but because it needs them.

What they do to our jobs

The recurrent hostility to immigrants is dominated by two major concerns: what they do to our jobs and what they do to our culture. Just as with international trade, the problem is that some natives do inevitably lose out. There might be trillion-dollar bills waiting on the sidewalk for society as a whole, but for some individuals an already meagre wage is threatened. Even though more workers help us increase production and reduce the cost of living, workers with less education and less skilled jobs often find they are in the sectors that attract recent arrivals. Already being in a difficult situation with low pay and suddenly finding yourself competing against people who have just arrived in the country causes understandable resentment.

How much do you think they have to lose? The most respected economist who is critical of immigration is George Borjas at Harvard. According to his estimate, the wages of native-born US high school dropouts are 1.7 per cent lower than they would have been without the influx of immigrants in 1990–2010. And there are few dropouts. More than 90 per cent of Americans are in education categories where wages *increased* because of immigration, even according to Borjas. This is a pessimistic estimate, and Borjas admits he is a lonely voice among economists ('What I don't understand is why people don't agree with me').[65]

This number is interesting because it is much smaller than most laymen would guess. The reason is simple: more potential workers does not mean more unemployment or less demand for jobs, or else a large country like the US would always have a much higher unemployment rate than a smaller country like France or South Africa. It means that you get a more advanced division of labour and more demand for other kinds of jobs. Immigrants might move into labour-intensive jobs where they don't need perfect language skills. When those who used to do these jobs face competition, they often move into niches where they make more of a unique contribution, sometimes managing these new arrivals who don't have the right skills yet, and aspects of the job that involve more communication. Since these new arrivals consume as well as produce, they also increase the demand for other kinds of jobs in the economy.

One IMF study of rich countries estimates that an increase in the migration share by one percentage point raises GDP per capita in the long run by roughly 2 per cent, mainly because it increases labour productivity since a more diverse workforce can accomplish more and help each other to specialize. Both the bottom 90 per cent and the top 10 per cent of native income earners benefit. Low- and medium-skilled immigration benefit both groups equally, whereas much more of the benefit goes to the top 10 per cent when the share of high-skilled immigrants grows – interestingly, the one kind of immigration that many of the new nationalists approve of more.[66]

Studies of the fiscal impact of immigration on host governments throw up small effects, and they depend very much on labour participation and the structure of the welfare state. On average, immigrants appear to have a minor positive net effect for host governments.[67] But a decent average can hide great successes and a few fiascos. Bad policy can make a mockery of an open policy. Giving an opportunity to people who are ready and willing to work, and also sheltering those who face persecution in their home country is not the same as regularly admitting large numbers of refugees into a country with generous benefits and discouraging work. If refugees aren't integrated, there is a risk that they end up concentrated in troubled pockets, without means of supporting themselves and the skills they need for social mobility.

Collective bargaining in Sweden has created de facto minimum wages at more than 70 per cent of the median wage in most industries. That worked well when we all had the same education, similar skills and were on our third job. But for those who have just arrived in Sweden, lacking contacts, higher education and the Swedish language, it is a second, more impenetrable border. If your productivity is less than 70 per cent of the median Swede, you are priced out of the market and will never get the kind of jobs that would increase your experience and skills and your productivity. *The Economist* has described the reception that Sweden gives its many refugees as almost designed to stir resentment: 'showering refugees with benefits while making it hard for them to work'.[68]

In Britain, the public perception is that the many EU migrants since 2000 have been a drain on public resources. The evidence suggests otherwise. Just as Britain was about to revoke free movement for EU citizens, the Migration Advisory Committee, commissioned by the Home Secretary, presented its analysis of the impacts of EU migration. In 2016–17, European migrants made a net contribution to the British public finances of £4.7 billion, since they work more and are less likely to receive benefits. As a comparison, the UK-born population were a net drain over the same time, by more than £41 billion. Obviously immigrants use public services too, but they also share the cost of fixed expenditures, thereby reducing the financial burden for natives.[69] A single year does not reflect the lifetime fiscal impact, since most migrants are young and will cost more as they grow old. And yet the same report estimates that the typical EU arrival in 2016 will make a lifetime net contribution of £78,000 to the British government.

American data shows that immigrants on average use means-tested public benefits at a much lower rate than comparable natives. If natives used Medicaid as little as immigrants did, the system would cost 42 per cent less.[70]

What they do to our culture

Some like immigration, some don't. Some are uncomfortable with heterogeneity and think that it changes the neighbourhood too fast; others think it makes it more interesting and creates more choice. Given these differences, the question is how immigration affects our society in the aggregate.

Fear of crime has always been close to the top of the list of concerns about immigrants, and that remains the case. But actually, US data shows that immigration reduces crime. Legal immigrants are only a third as likely to be incarcerated as US natives, and illegal immigrants are only slightly more than half as likely.[71]

The dominant narrative in Europe is that immigration is a certain cause of crime. But we also pay more attention to crime when the perpetrator is different from us, and we draw general conclusions based on a few, visible gangs without considering the context. On 17 February 2012, the *Daily Mail* ran the headline '"Immigrant Crimewave" Warning: Foreign Nationals Were Accused of a QUARTER of All Crimes in London'. However, foreign nationals make up around 40 per cent of London's population, so it seems like they are over-represented mainly in headlines. Britons think that 34 per cent of prisoners are immigrants. In reality 12 per cent are, in line with their share of the population.[72]

Research shows this is a complex issue with many local variations. Immigrants are often younger and poorer and in some regions more likely to be unemployed. If refugees find it difficult to bring their family, they are more often male. All these circumstances are statistically associated with more crime and, all else being equal, should lead to an increase in crime. But in some cases, immigrants are over-represented in crime statistics without there being an overall increase in crime, suggesting there is a replacement effect. The bottom rungs of, say, inner-city gangs are filled with new, poor immigrants, as natives or previous waves of migrants move up in society and out of crime.

A UK study showed a link between increased property crime and more asylum seekers, but not with wider immigration, and neither had an effect on violent crime. A study of sixteen West European countries showed that an increase in immigration is associated with more crime, but this is because a larger share of immigrants moves to poorer regions with more crime and adapts to the local crime levels. Within regions, more immigration did not increase crime. The strongest link was that the larger the share of immigrants in a population, the more people feared crime, which can explain why this narrative is getting stronger in the popular mind.[73]

Of course a single immigrant who hurts people is one too many, and vetting potential security threats and stopping criminals from entering the country is an important part of every policy of openness (another reason why legal points of entry are necessary, so we know who is here). However, if we are to judge diverse groups of millions of migrants according to a few bad apples, we also have to include the many migrant heroes in the analysis, like the migrant from Colombia who saved a Miami police officer from being gunned downed by driving his van into the line of fire and pulling him to safety. Or the Polish chef who fought off a terrorist on London Bridge with a narwhal tusk in 2019. Not to mention all the migrants who populate our law enforcement and health services. Generalizations go both ways.

Crime is not the only fear about immigration. A common concern is that too much diversity threatens the social fabric of society, which would be a high price to pay for inviting new groups. The political scientist Robert Putnam, a pioneer in the study of social capital, has famously argued that diversity can be a threat to social cohesion. A large study of American communities led him to conclude that diversity does not produce angry ethnic tribalists, but it does 'bring out the turtle in all of us'. He meant that people in ethnically diverse areas 'hunker down', they volunteer less, register to vote less, distrust their neighbours and leaders more, and instead of joining bowling clubs, they huddle unhappily in front of the television (Putnam's old nemesis).[74]

The result is often used to contest the value of diverse, cosmopolitan societies but – contrary to its omnipresence in media – the effect is small. According to Putnam's own calculations, many other things affect trust more than diversity, often much more, but for some reason they don't figure as prominently in the debate. It's not just obvious ones like poverty and crime, but also education, home ownership, population density and even average commute time. If social capital is really the reason why you argue against immigration, you should agitate even more passionately for smarter and faster city technologies and AI to optimize traffic flows to reduce commuter times.

In a review of ninety papers on diversity and trust all over the world, the researchers found a pattern that supports just one half of the turtle theory: in heterogenous areas we are less likely to trust or have contact with our neighbours, although interestingly this does not spill over to generalized trust, informal help or voluntary work. And in fact, diversity is positively related to interethnic contact and trust.[75] This is also Putnam's own conclusion:

> over the long run, as we get to know one another, and as we begin to see things that we have in common with people who don't look like us, this allergy to diversity tends to diminish and to go away.[76]

One thought-provoking paper looked at a version of this turtle effect. A Harvard political scientist asked rail commuters in a
mostly white Boston neighbourhood about attitudes to immigration and integration. Then he put two Mexican nationals on commuter trains, speaking Spanish to one another. All it took was three
days of exposure to Spanish-speakers to get commuters to report
much more exclusionary attitudes to Mexican immigration.[77]

This paper has been picked up by nativists to prove that we
are inherently segregationist. What they neglected was that the
researcher also asked people about their attitudes after ten days
of exposure to the Spanish-speakers. Exclusionary attitudes did
not continue to grow, they started declining again as, after just
another seven days, the commuters started getting used to diversity. This is also what the recruited Mexicans told the researcher:
they reported that commuters had started smiling at them and
even engaging in small talk.

So immigration probably has some negative effects on culture,
especially as it picks up speed and we suddenly cross paths with
strange, new groups. In a larger, more diverse place, you are less
likely to interact with or even understand your neighbours. It's
perfectly understandable why some people prefer a more locally
friendly place where they know the people next door rather than
a bustling, dynamic metropolis where no one speaks to others on
the bus. But that's the price for living in a more creative and prosperous society, and most people are willing to pay it, at least if
their own migratory patterns are to be believed. And if we get over
this initial reaction, we'll get used to it.

Without new people and the ideas they bring, the society that
does remain becomes dull and sclerotic. A more homogenous culture may be marginally more sociable, but it will be outperformed.
As some Eastern European countries and many Western towns
have found, those cultures may even die out, as the young move
away for the chances and the creativity of more diverse places.

People from far away are essential idea-transporters. Though their existence can cause tensions, migrants, merchants and cosmopolitans are the engine of world history. The meeting and interaction of cultures and the mixing of ideas and beliefs across borders opened minds and created our classical civilizations. As we will now see, it even created the Renaissance and the Enlightenment.

3

OPEN MINDS

'In the case of any person whose judgment is really deserving of confidence, how has it become so? Because he has kept his mind open to criticism of his opinions and conduct.'

John Stuart Mill, 1859

Have you heard the story of how a typo won World War II? It goes something like this: joining the Natural History Museum in London in 1926, Geoffrey Tandy was its first cryptogamist, which meant he specialized in non-flowering, spore-reproducing plants like seaweeds, mosses and ferns. When Tandy enlisted as a volunteer in the Royal Navy Reserve in 1939, the Ministry of Defence got a bit more excited about him than he thought warranted. To his surprise, he was immediately sent to Bletchley Park, where the best minds in Britain were hard at work trying to crack the code of Nazi Germany's Enigma machine.

Apparently, the ministry had assumed that Tandy, the cryptogamist, was a *cryptogrammist*, specialized in encrypted texts and therefore the ideal man to help Alan Turing and the others to crack codes. They really had no use for a seaweed specialist. But since the Bletchley operation was top secret, the army thought it best that Tandy stayed there until the end of the war, contributing little to the war effort. They couldn't have been more wrong.

One day in 1941, codebooks from a German U-boat arrived at Bletchley Park. It could have been the lucky break they needed to break the codes, they thought, but unfortunately the documents were sodden and beyond salvage. If only they had someone at Bletchley who was specialized in preserving and preparing wet specimens. If only they had a cryptogamist among all those cryptogrammists. Because of a typo, they were in luck. Tandy knew exactly how to dry the paper safely, and a call to the museum elicited a supply of the tools he needed. The documents were saved and their cryptic clues could be revealed by Turing and others more specialized in those tasks. Thanks to Geoffrey Tandy, the Allies could learn about German plans and communications and hasten the end of the war.

Or so the story goes, according to the Natural History Museum.[1] There are reasons to doubt some parts of it. Deciphering as a science was basically invented during this period, so the chance of the army thinking they would have just come across a highly educated specialist they had never heard of seems slim. When the war broke out, the British had to build intelligence from scratch, and they recruited people from all corners of society. Tandy's education and skills in language, keeping records and doing analytic work makes him seem like the kind of person who would be very much in demand. No typo was needed to create an interest in him. And he did not waste his time doing crosswords; in fact, he led a bureau that tried to make sense of technical jargon in foreign documents.

But no one has questioned that Tandy's expertise in preserving marine specimens suddenly took on a new and surprising significance. And this, rather than a potential misspelling, is the real story of Bletchley Park. The facility was so successful not despite but because it was filled with experts from a multitude of different fields, each looking at the problems of other disciplines with their own eyes and tools, and therefore increasing their chance of creating new combinations and insights. They came from fields like mathematics, geometry, statistics, chemistry, linguistics, literature – and spore-reproducing plants.

Though top secret, Bletchley Park was the scene for an amazing demonstration of the power of open science. A modern version is InnoCentive, a platform for open innovation where participants can present difficult scientific and technological problems that frustrate them, and pledge a reward to the person who can solve them. It could be an electronics company struggling with a tweak to its manufacturing process or NASA needing help to predict solar eruptions. To date, almost 400,000 people from more than 190 countries have contributed, and the platform has awarded more than $20 million to successful solutions.

What is fascinating is that the success rate is around 75 per cent. Complex problems that have confounded experts in an organization for years can be solved quickly when the rest of the world has a look. The takeaway is that you might be the smartest guys or gals in the room, but your room is small. By opening up the process, you can suddenly benefit from the knowledge and creativity of people you would otherwise only have met by chance (i.e. probably not at all).

Even more interesting is that this designed serendipity reveals that new insights often come straight out of left field. A study of InnoCentive found: 'The further the focal problem was from the solvers' field of expertise, the more likely they were to solve it.'[2] Again, it is all about surprises and combinations. A person from a distant field can look at an old problem with fresh eyes, and apply ideas and methods that are novel in this context but well understood by him. A chemical problem was not solved by a chemist but by a molecular biologist, and a toxicological quandary was solved by a researcher in protein crystallography. The problem of separating spill oil from water when frozen was solved by an outsider who used his expertise in the cement industry. NASA's challenge was not solved by an astronomer but by a retired radio engineer using his knowledge in plasma physics.

Mankind has made so much progress because we innovate and we imitate. Just stumbling across new ideas and imitating whatever we see is a recipe for very slow progress. It takes a long time until trial and error sorts out the wheat from the chaff. But we can speed this process up by creating systems and platforms where we search for new knowledge systematically, expose it to criticism, integrate the result into our body of knowledge, and apply it to our ways of doing things. Being open to other points of view and learning from other perspectives – whether from friends, foes, cryptogamists or even (horror) colleagues – is integral to intellectual progress. Our confirmation bias always traps us in a very limited view of the world, but free speech, peer review and cognitive dissonance set us free.

The birth of science

The philosopher Karl Popper wrote that 'science must begin with myths, and with the criticism of myths'.[3] Mankind has always had myths. We have always developed stories about gods to explain the origin of the universe, disasters and thunder and lightning. But it took free minds and an inquisitive spirit to criticize those myths and to reject the idea that arbitrary interventions by gods and spirits explain the world.

As far as we know, the search for other causes first began in ancient Greece, in the cosmopolitan trading centres on the Ionian coast in the sixth century BC. On the island of Miletus, a group of thinkers – Thales, Anaximander and Anaximenes – started to explain the world, matter and living things without any reference to supernatural forces. They described the world as an orderly place, governed by impersonal and natural laws that can be discovered and described. A century later, Hippocrates explained that disease was not a punishment from the gods, as previously thought, but always had a physical cause.

The Greeks did not create something from nothing. They inherited technologies and observations from the Egyptians and Babylonians, but the revolutionary aspect was that they did not just continue recording experiences, they tried to understand them by formulating theories. These could be supported and rejected by reference to empirical evidence, which meant they could be criticized and improved upon in an open debate. Through curiosity and criticism, the Greeks quickly arrived at increasingly better theories that could explain more of the world around them.

In other words, the Ionians invented science and philosophy, which were basically the same back then. But why did it happen there and then?

The Austrian physicist Erwin Schrödinger (yes, the one with the cat) saw three causes behind the Ionian enlightenment. The first one was that the region did not belong to a big powerful state or empire, but consisted of small, independent city-states or island-states, and so gave people a relative freedom to behave and think differently. Secondly, the Ionians were seafarers and traders, interposed between the East and the West and, as Schrödinger pointed out, 'Mercantile exchange has always and everywhere been, and still is, the principal vehicle for an exchange of ideas.' The third reason was that these communities were not 'priest-ridden'. They did not, like Egyptians and Babylonians, have a centralized religion or a privileged priestly caste who could establish orthodoxies and punish those who thought differently. And they certainly did not have rulers who claimed to be gods.[4]

To this we can add the fact that Greek philosophers had a fairly literate audience. The Greeks had imported the Phoenician alphabet during the early eighth century BC, and by the sixth century, literacy was relatively widespread. Myths and theories could be written down and could therefore also be examined, challenged and shared in a new way. In popular plays like Aristophanes' *The Clouds*, philosophers debated whether thunder and lightning were caused by the gods or the clouds.

Schrödinger's conditions – pluralism, trade, tolerance – aren't exclusive to the Ionian enlightenment, but they just about sum up every episode of sustained intellectual innovation in history. Trade and migration make it possible for different ideas and traditions to meet and enrich each other. 'Perhaps the most powerful cause of the breakdown of the closed society was the development of sea-communications and commerce,' wrote Karl Popper.[5] They provide the thinker and scientist with ingredients. But if there is already a set menu stopping you from combining the ingredients in new ways to create new dishes, these innovations are not of much use. So we also need a certain degree of freedom and, specifically, the absence of a rigid intellectual monopoly that establishes dogmas and bans curiosity and dissent.

In all these regards, ancient Greece provided a remarkably hospitable environment for independent thought, and it occurred during a period that has become known as the Axial Age from around the eighth century BC. People began to ask new questions about the world and morality, in an era of growing wealth and increasing contacts between different parts of the world: Greece with Persia and Egypt; China with India and South East Asia; the Middle East at the crossroads of different cultures. Philosophers and prophets tried to come up with systems of morality that were universal and did not just apply to their own group. Buddha in India, Confucius and Lao-Tzu in China and the prophets of the Bible were contemporaries of the early Greek philosophers. Ancient rituals and animal sacrifices were replaced by moral codes.

The criticism that Xenophanes of Colophon (in the sixth and fifth centuries B C) levelled against the gods in popular religion is an illustrative example of how the Greeks took their ideas further than everybody else. Xenophanes observed that Greek gods look like Greek men and women, dress like them, talk like them, and behave in all sorts of embarrassing, human ways. He then pointed out that Ethiopian gods look like Ethiopians and Thracian gods like Thracians. This convinced him that humans create gods in their own image:

> If cattle, horses and lions had hands, and could draw with those hands and accomplish the works of men, horses would draw the forms of gods as like horses, and cattle like cattle, and each would make their bodies as each had themselves.[6]

Here is the wisdom of the seafarers. 'Close contact with other tribes is liable to undermine the feeling of necessity with which tribal institutions are viewed,' as Popper observed.[7] By comparing their own ideas with other cultures, the Greeks got a useful, critical distance to their own traditions, which is more difficult if you are brought up in a vast empire, hearing only about the one true way. Aristotle compared the constitutions of 158 Greek cities before he developed his own theory about the best political system.

The Greeks lived in rivalling city-states with much contact and a common language, so debates could be intense both within and between them. This facilitated a rational and critical examination of received wisdom. It is telling that Socrates' search for the truth always starts with expressing ignorance about a subject and challenging what others took for granted about it. Once you have different theories that aren't compatible, you need common standards for discussion and evidence in order to compare and evaluate. This forced philosophers like Plato and Aristotle to think deeply about the nature of knowledge and what makes a belief justified.

In the fourth century, Aristotle, an immigrant from Macedonia, became the first person to define the laws of logic, by which we can structure our information and accumulate knowledge. And rather than just speculate, he used it to collect and understand information about the natural world as one of the world's first empirical scientists.

For the first time in human history, as far as we know, these factors created a culture that saw intellectual innovation as a virtue. In ancient Babylonian and Egyptian texts, we have no examples of writers attacking the received wisdom and claiming originality, whereas the Greeks did it all the time. As Aristotle pointed out, when contradicting his teacher Plato in the *Nicomachean Ethics*:

> it would appear desirable, and indeed it would seem to be obligatory, especially for a philosopher, to sacrifice even one's closest personal ties in defence of the truth. Both are dear to us, yet 'tis our duty to prefer the truth.[8]

And significantly, even though Xenophanes attacked popular religion, he was not persecuted for his dissent. In his satirical plays, Aristophanes ridiculed gods and politicians – and even their war efforts. A wide diversity of opinion was tolerated, and often considered a public good, especially in proto-democratic Athens during its golden age in the fifth century BC.

In his funeral oration, where the Athenian statesman Pericles famously said (according to Thucydides) that, 'We throw open our city to the world', he also argued that good ideas are not useful to the city if they can only be expressed in private: 'Instead of looking upon discussion as a stumbling-block in the way of action, we think it an indispensable preliminary to any wise action at all.'[9]

The trial and death of Socrates in 399 BC illustrates the limits of free speech even in Athens. Dissidents and provocateurs were also killed in all previous civilizations, though. What set Athens apart was that the limits were much less restrictive and allowed for an amazing variety of thoughts, theories and opinions. In its golden age, this tiny city-state of perhaps 300,000 people became the home of philosophers, playwrights and historians that are still towering figures in the history of ideas and literature – people like Socrates, Plato, Aristotle, Aeschylus, Aristophanes, Euripides, Herodotus, Thucydides, Xenophon. It is difficult to find even a single thinker of a similar stature from Athens' authoritarian rival Sparta.

The darkening age

Many in the West have tried to tell the story of the modern world as the fulfilment of European destiny – some sort of steady advance from Athens to Rome, and onwards to the Renaissance, the scientific and Industrial Revolution, until suddenly here we are with modernity and indoor plumbing. It is understandable. Since ancient Greek thought was so revolutionary, and since it took place where East met West, any civilization that made the final leap to wealth and freedom could think of Athens as the great predecessor. But the narrative is not just simplified; it is false. Science and progress do not follow a simple trajectory. Sometimes it is halted, sometimes it is reversed. There is no straight line between Athens and the West. On the contrary, the links were severed, the legacy destroyed and no significant scientific progress occurred in Europe for more than a thousand years. In fact, many scientific discoveries and technological advances were forgotten after the fall of Rome, while they were in fact kept alive and further developed in the Arab world and in China.

The reason was that Schrödinger's enlightenment conditions went into reverse in the West. Most fatefully, tolerance of unorthodox questions and innovative answers was wrecked by a reimposition of fundamentalist dogma. This time regression came in the form of Christianity. This seems strange to those who think Christian culture explains the rise of the West. Since they were all Christians back then, the few enlightened souls who fought against Christian mystics and despots were also Christians, and it is possible to create a narrative with them as protagonists. But if history teaches us anything, it is that any religion can halt progress as long as it establishes a monopoly on thought and punishes the unorthodox. As the historian Jack Goldstone concluded after looking at episodes of rapid scientific and economic development on different continents:

> In fact, we can identify an important element of religion that does appear to accompany such periods. This is not the characteristic of any particular religion, but rather the existence of many religions, under conditions of pluralism and toleration. By contrast, the passing of such efflorescences are almost always marked by the return or imposition of a crushing official religious orthodoxy.[10]

One of the foremost problems with philosophers, according to the Church Father Augustine (354–430 AD), was that they disagreed with one another. Writing about Athens ('this demon-worshipping city'), he complained its rulers had never 'taken care to judge between all these and other well-nigh innumerable dissensions of the philosophers, approving and accepting some, and disapproving and rejecting others… Even if some true things were said in it, yet falsehoods were uttered with the same licence.'[11]

Believing that ideas about life and death and good and evil were commands by God, Augustine wanted them imposed on everyone, by force, for their own good. After Emperor Constantine made Christianity an official religion of the Roman Empire in 313, this became state policy and pagan religions were suppressed.

Constantine himself banned books by heretics and imposed a death penalty for hiding copies. Soon the old temples were closed and anyone found worshipping images was punished by death. Fearing torture and execution, some pagans burned their own books before they were used against them as proof of heresy.

As Catherine Nixey shows in gruesome detail in her book *The Darkening Age: The Christian Destruction of the Classical World*, bands of zealous Christians rarely waited for officials to act, they started destroying temples and statues in rampages that resembled more recent terrorist acts by Islamic fundamentalists in the Middle East. In 392 AD, the Bishop of Alexandria led a Christian mob to the Temple of Serapis, one of the architectural wonders of the ancient world, and reduced it to rubble. The tens of thousands of books it housed, the remnants of the great library of Alexandria, were destroyed or lost, never to be seen again. Many intellectuals fled an increasingly dangerous city. One day in March 415 AD, a rabble of Christians blocked the daily ride of the famous pagan mathematician and astronomer Hypatia, dragged her to a church, stripped her naked and flayed her skin with broken pieces of pottery.

Finally, in 529, the emperor Justinian declared that anyone who refused baptism would be exiled, and some seventy thousand people were said to have been forcibly baptized in Asia Minor alone. He also declared that those who suffered from 'the insanity of paganism' would no longer be allowed to teach. After nine hundred years of philosophizing, Plato's Academy in Athens was closed. In 532, the seven last philosophers of the Academy left Athens to seek refuge with the Persian king.[12]

Much learning and literature was simply lost to the world during 'the Great Vanishing' that ensued, partly the result of an active campaign against pagan texts. Epicurus probably wrote hundreds of books and essays; apart from a few letters and a list of maxims, nothing has survived. At the end of the fifth century an ambitious literary editor compiled an anthology of the best prose and poetry of the ancient world. Out of 1430 quotations, 1115 are from works that have been lost.[13] The writings 'of the Greeks have all perished and are obliterated', cheered the early Church Father John Chrysostom.[14]

What was started by bans and vandalism was completed by simple neglect, ignorance and actual forgetfulness. The division of the Roman Empire into a Latin West and a Greek East in the fourth century deprived most Europeans of Greek learning, and disintegration of the western part accelerated the decline. Climate and pests ruined books. Since Europeans did not know how to make paper, they wrote on animal skin. This parchment was expensive, so old works were often scrubbed away and overwritten. It's similar to the BBC's bulk-erasing machine that was used to systematically wipe out 1960s and 1970s television shows to reuse video cassettes instead of buying new ones. The difference is that what was lost was not episodes of *Doctor Who* but our classical heritage. Around 90 per cent of all classical literature is estimated to have been lost.[15]

In his history of Western philosophy, Anthony Gottlieb paints a disturbing picture of how science went into reverse as it became subservient to religion:

By the year 1000, medicine, physics, astronomy, biology and indeed all branches of theoretical knowledge except theology had virtually collapsed. Even the few relatively educated men, holed up in monasteries, knew markedly less than many Greeks had done eight centuries earlier. Most of classical literature, including Roman literature, was largely unknown, except to a handful of monks. The few mathematical jottings to be found are for the most part downright stupid. In short Christianity was colossally ignorant.[16]

Islam was Europe's teacher

In the tenth century, the great Arab historian Al-Masudi, gave a damning verdict on Christian culture, in the same way some Westerners now write off Arab culture:

> In the time of the Hellenes and during the early days of the Rum [...] the sciences were honoured and enjoyed universal respect. From an already solid and grandiose foundation, they were raised to greater heights every day, until the Christian religion made its appearance among the Rum; this was a fatal blow to the edifice of learning; its traces disappeared and its pathways were effaced.[17]

Europe did not impress; the greatest mathematicians, astronomers and physicists were now to be found in the Islamic world. Between the eighth and twelfth centuries the sophistication of the Islamic world made it the heir of classical civilization. The cause of its superiority was that now it was the most open and cosmopolitan civilization, stretching from Spain and North Africa, across Iraq and Persia, and all the way to India. It benefited from the mixing of the new faith with older Roman, Greek, Jewish, Persian and Hindu traditions. A civilization of travellers and traders, it had the opportunity and incentive to learn from other cultures, past and present.

Baghdad, the vibrant capital of the Abbasid Caliphate, was enriched by merchants and craftsmen who spoke Arabic, Persian, Indian, Turkish, Armenian and Kurdish and were free to explore and debate ideas.[18] Scholars from all these backgrounds met at Baghdad's House of Wisdom, where translations of the world's literature were collected. The Muslim cities that were also Jewish and Christian had vast libraries filled with books of paper – the production of which they had learned from the Chinese. And their rulers often paid scholars to travel to other countries to find new books. They created the first centres for higher education, often seen as a precursor to universities, like Al-Karaouine in Morocco, founded by a woman from a merchant family in 859. This is where Pope Sylvester II studied, who is credited with introducing Arabic numerals (originally from India) to Europe – the kind of numbers that say how far you are through this book. 'Islam was Europe's teacher,' as Harvard historian David Landes wrote.[19]

Crucially, the Islamic world kept Greek philosophy and science alive, when it was forgotten or persecuted in the West. Beginning in the eighth century the classical Greek philosophical and scientific texts were translated into Arabic, including Aristotle.[20] These were used as a foundation for impressive advances in astronomy, mathematics, medicine, chemistry, physics and optics. The Iraqi mathematician Al-Khwarizmi invented modern algebra to facilitate practical work in law, economics and engineering. The Persian astronomer Omar Khayyam managed to measure the length of the year as 365.2421986 days and devised a solar calendar in 1079 that was more precise than the Gregorian calendar adopted in Europe more than five hundred years later. The Arab geographer Muhammad al-Idrisi produced the most accurate map of the world that anyone had yet seen.

Some innovative thinkers used the same methods of reason and logic to study religion, even claiming that the Koran had to be examined critically. The philosopher-physician Ibn Rushd (1126–98) from Cordoba in Muslim Spain, famous under his Latinized name Averroes, was the most important of them. He was the greatest authority on Aristotle of his time and his extensive comments on the Greek thinker had such importance for the survival of ancient philosophy that Raphael chose to include him in the pantheon of philosophers in the fresco *The School of Athens* in the Vatican Palace (he is the one in a green robe and a turban, looking over the shoulder of Pythagoras).

Ibn Rushd claimed God had created a logical universe of cause and effect that could be understood with scientific methods. Indeed, it had to be. If a religious revelation contradicted science it had to be reinterpreted or understood metaphorically. Such ideas were always controversial and provoked the religious establishment. Independent thinkers like Ibn Rushd depended on the protection of enlightened rulers – and, as judge and court physician of the Almohad Caliphate, he had it. This protection could just as easily be withdrawn, though, and it was by the next caliph. In 1195, Ibn Rushd was banished in disgrace to a small village close to his home of Cordoba. Many of his books were burned and permanently lost.

This was a long time coming. The Islamic world had begun to fracture, and with that its philosophy became less self-assured and more inward-looking. There was a series of revolts against the Abbasid Caliphate, and the empire was broken up into several feuding parts. In the eleventh century, Muslim Spain began to slowly disintegrate because of civil war and the Christian invasion. Partly as a result of this insecurity, the tradition of tolerance receded and the education system became more conservative. Establishments that focused on religious study started to replace institutions of scientific inquiry. Scholars used to have secular professions, but now they gained full-time employment at these madrasas, as long as they stuck to the orthodoxy. Graduates were rewarded with important government jobs. A quantitative analysis shows that the number of books on scientific subjects in the Muslim world began to drop sharply in specific regions at the time when madrasas expanded.[21]

At the same time the foreign threats were getting more destructive. In the thirteenth century, the Muslim world found itself squeezed by Christian Crusaders from the north, and Mongol invaders from the east. In just half a century, more than half of their dominions were lost. Cordoba, the centre of learning in

Islamic Spain, fell in 1236 as the Christian Reconquista gathered pace, and in 1248 the economic metropolis of Seville also fell.

Much worse was to come. It has been said that the Islamic Golden Age ended on 13 February 1258, one of the bloodiest days in human history. After a twelve-day siege, a Mongol army breached the walls of Baghdad, the intellectual capital of the Muslim world. Mongol troops entered the city, massacred the population of men, women and children, and destroyed mosques, hospitals, schools and all thirty-six libraries. It is said the waters of Tigris turned black from the ink of all the books thrown into it, and red from all the scientists and philosophers killed.

Yet this was not the final blow. A century later, the Black Death depopulated the Islamic world, and in 1400–02 the Turco-Mongol emperor Timur's brutal invasion brought even more destruction to the region. Such disasters took an immense human and economic toll and many regions did not recover. But they also reinforced the conservative religious reaction, which claimed secular philosophy had led their culture astray and demanded a return to what they took to be traditional Islam. The influence grew of thinkers like Al-Ghazali (1058–11) who rejected Greek philosophy and claimed science could never understand a world governed by the will of God. Only religion and revelation would do. Augustine had defended compulsion in Christian religion by saying that it was just like 'one who pulls a boy's hair in order to prevent him from provoking serpents by clapping his hands at them'.[22] Like him, Al-Ghazali saw dissenters like children, and said that barring them from studying dangerous ideas was just like: 'the boy is barred from the bank of the river so that he does not fall in'.[23]

A rebirth

As with Rome, the twin scourges of domestic fundamentalism and barbarian invasions ruined a great, open civilization. But

once again, science and philosophy were thrown a lifeline, one
that would help usher in the European Renaissance and Enlightenment. The great Catholic historian of liberty, Lord Acton,
described Europe's Dark Ages thus:

> Western Europe lay under the grasp of masters, the ablest of
> whom could not write their names. The faculty of reasoning,
> of accurate observation, became extinct for 500 years, and even
> the sciences most needful for society, medicine and geometry,
> fell into decay, until the teachers of the West went to school at
> the feet of Arabian masters.[24]

No treasure in conquered Spain meant more for medieval Europe
than all the manuscripts by Arab, Jewish, Greek, Persian and
Indian authors that lined the shelves of Muslim libraries. European scholars marvelled at the breadth of the intellectual heritage
and scientific findings they discovered. In 1085, the important city
of Toledo fell into Christian hands, and for a while, before Spain
expelled the Jews and Muslims, scholars from all traditions met
there, interpreted and debated. Many Christian scholars learned
Arabic to understand and translate books. 'Muslim learning,
having seeped into the Christian West for decades from Andalu-
sia, commenced a torrential outflow. It was a process mimicking
osmosis at first and later, a conveyor belt,' writes American historian David Levering Lewis.[25]

The Europe that laid its hands on this wealth of learning was
in better shape to receive it than it had been for a long time. It was
in the middle of a period of relative political stability and population growth. Trade had expanded and with it came urbanization
and a growing demand for education. Between 1150 and 1215 the
first universities were established in Paris, Oxford, Cambridge,
Bologna and Salamanca, and they began to debate and circulate
the new imports. Almost all of what we regard as new European

findings in mathematics, physics, chemistry and medicine in the sixteenth and seventeenth centuries were based on the earlier Islamic development of ideas from many different civilizations. The roots of modern science were global, not European.[26]

A central role would be played by the newly discovered works of Aristotle, on everything from metaphysics and epistemology to ethics and politics. Latin Christendom already had access to some of Aristotle's ideas about formal logic, but that often resulted in sterile abstractions. Now they also found his ideas about how logic could be used to observe the world and acquire empirical ideas that could be compared, criticized and accumulated. More than that, they realized this master of logic had in fact done more than anyone else to study and explain the natural world, from stars, motion and geological change to the embryological development of hound sharks. Aristotle had gathered and systematized massive amounts of biological data, much of it based on the two years he spent studying the zoology of Lesbos. To European thinkers at the time, it must have felt like finding the Rosetta Stone, with which it was suddenly possible to translate the natural world.

Cicero described Aristotle's literary style as 'a river of gold'. We will never be able to step into this river because all Aristotle's works intended for the public have been lost. What survived are probably lecture notes never intended for publication – more technical manuals than rivers of gold – but the intellectual power of their contents was enough to shake the medieval world. It was an impressive and well-integrated system, albeit one created by a pagan philosopher without a Christian god. It was tempting but dangerous. Just like in the Islamic world, religious authorities feared the rational method would undermine their power.

From the University of Paris, the intellectual centre of Christian Europe, reports soon came that Aristotle inevitably meant trouble. Students were said to be intoxicated with the new ideas and grew bold. Christian doctrines that could not be proven by reason and logic were criticized fiercely, even revelations and sacraments. And worst of all, some clerics also found the new ideas convincing. In 1210, the teaching and reading of Aristotle's *Physics* and *Metaphysics* was banned, even in private, on pain of excommunication from the Church. But many kept reading Aristotle in private, and some did so openly in defiance. The atmosphere was getting hostile. In 1215, the books were once more condemned, and in 1231 Pope Gregory IX banned them again until they had been examined and purged of errors with thick, black ink. But the fact that the bans had to be reiterated shows that the previous ones had not been effective. The traditionalists fought a losing battle against the enthusiastic new Aristotelians. If students couldn't read the books at the university, they did so elsewhere. In 1225, the chancellor of the University of Paris complained about the havoc the new pagan philosophy had wreaked on his city: 'The torrents have destroyed nearly all our city; pouring themselves out upon the great sea of doctrine, they have disturbed its waves, hitherto so pure and calm.'[27]

And it turned out that Aristotle could be useful. Some opponents of Greek philosophy realized they had to learn its methods of structuring knowledge to be able to argue with their opponents. He was also useful in the Church's brutal struggle against Cathar heretics. The Cathars believed in two forces, one good and one evil, who had created the physical world. By using Aristotle's treasure trove of data about the biological world, the Church could give specific examples of the unity and beauty of nature, as proof that there was only one good god.

If the Church couldn't defeat Aristotle's ideas, it had to harness them. This dangerous new power source must be brought under the Church's control. The most ambitious and important attempt at reconciling Aristotle with Christianity was done by the young Thomas (1225–74) from the city of Aquinas, close to Naples, who was so brilliant that he was said to be able to dictate several works to different secretaries at the same time. He was deeply influenced by what Ibn Rushd (whom he referred to as 'the Commentator') had done with Islam, and made it his life's work to do the same for Christianity.

Rejecting the earlier Christian idea of the world as a vale of tears and men as ignorant sinners, Thomas Aquinas outlined an idea about a rational and beautiful universe. It was a good home for human beings, who do not just suffer and wait for life after death but can create a good life here and now. According to Thomas, man can attain knowledge about the world through the evidence of the senses and reason and logic, without any divine grace or illumination. And religious truths could either be proven rationally or cover areas that reason couldn't tell us anything about. There could be no contradiction between reason and faith, since both had been given to us from God.

This was in effect the Renaissance foot in the medieval door, since it supplied reason and empirical research with its own domain, and gave latitude to curious philosophers and scientists to explore the world empirically. Thomas had not intended it, but he put faith on the defensive. Since revelation only covers the areas that reason doesn't, it meant faith would retreat into a steadily shrinking domain as a scientific mindset managed to chart an increasingly large territory. And as secular thinkers grew bolder, some began to point out contradictions between faith and reason, and would start to tear apart Thomas' harmonious unity.

Religious authorities fought back, just as they had done in the Islamic world. In 1272 the civil war between Aristotelians and traditionalists in Paris led to the splintering of the liberal arts into two faculties, each with its own rules, teachers and students. After three years the papal legate ended the schism in favour of the conservatives, and the radical Aristotelians led by Siger of Brabant fled the city, only to be summoned by the Inquisition of France. In March 1277, after a request from the Pope, the Bishop of Paris issued a list of 219 errors made by Aristotle, Ibn Rushd, Thomas Aquinas and more radical Aristotelians. Anyone who reached these conclusions, taught or even listened to them would be excommunicated from the Church. Eleven days later, the Archbishop of Canterbury, regent of the University of Oxford, issued his own condemnation of Aristotelian errors, and more investigations were started. Siger of Brabant was murdered under suspicious circumstances just a few years later. A secretary was said to have gone mad and killed him with a pen (enemies said he had done so much damage with his own pen that he deserved it), but there was no investigation into his murder.

Unlike in the rapidly disintegrating Islamic world, European wealth was now growing and cities expanding. More secular centres of learning emerged, and the Church and the religious orders had become richer and were now more open to a message that rejected the asceticism of the early Christians. And there was too much competition between different European universities and cities for the authorities to suppress inconvenient ideas in the long run. As early as 1229, the University of Toulouse published an advertising circular that promised students no restrictions on the teaching of Aristotle. The new University of Padua had no theological institution until 1361 and only a small one thereafter, so the Greek philosopher could be freely studied. The mighty city of Venice protected controversial Paduan scholars from papal prosecution.

When Franciscan friars attacked the Aristotelians they faced opposition from the increasingly influential Dominican order. In 1228 the Dominicans had themselves banned its members from studying the Greek philosophers, only allowing them to 'inspect them briefly'.[28] But the brilliant Thomas was a Dominican, and they had started to consider him their greatest intellectual champion. When he was being attacked, they responded by banning any member of the order to criticize Thomas publicly.

In 1323, Aquinas was canonized. Two years later, the bishop retracted the Parisian condemnation as far as it involved Thomas. Meanwhile, translations of Aristotle and Ibn Rushd continued to pour into more urbanized and better-educated societies. The genie was out of the bottle.[29] One consequence was a new, passionate curiosity about all the wonders of the natural world. The Aristotelian Albertus Magnus was a pioneer in the empirical research of botany, zoology and minerals. He claimed that: 'it is [the task] of natural science not simply to accept what we are told but to inquire into the causes of natural things'.[30]

In important intellectual circles the established idea that everything had already been revealed by God began to be challenged by a new thirst for knowledge, even a modest idea of progress. In a sermon in Pisa in 1306, Fra Giordano said: 'But not all [the arts] have been found; we shall never see an end of finding them [...] and new ones are being found all the time.'[31]

No further proof is needed of the fact that all ideas can stifle progress if they are turned into orthodoxy than the fact that in the hands of religious and political authorities, even Aristotelian ideas could fossilize and suppress new ideas. European universities that had banned Aristotle's books now made them obligatory, and the Church turned some of his hypotheses about physics and the universe into dogmas that were not to be questioned. In the thirteenth century, Aristotle was considered blasphemy at the University of Oxford; a century later, the same university had a rule that bachelors and masters of art who do not follow his philosophy were to be fined five shillings for every point of divergence from Aristotle.[32]

For example, Aristotle thought the only change in the heavens was circular motion, an idea that suited the Church's division of perfect heaven and turbulent earth, which it enforced as orthodoxy. When the Church refused – at least proverbially – to look through the new telescopes that revealed moons around Jupiter and other things that were not supposed to be there according to theory, it conveniently forgot Aristotle's insistence that all theories, including his own, have to face 'the test of the facts of life, and if it harmonizes with the facts we must accept it, but if it clashes with them we must suppose it to be mere theory'.[33] However, this created a growing gap between the Church and an increasingly secular intelligentsia. The study of nature at Italian universities had become more practical and even experimental, and now it delivered blow after blow to the traditional worldview. Discoveries of sunspots and supernovas revealed that the heavens were in motion all the time. Planets turned out to travel in elliptical not circular orbits. The astronomers Copernicus and Galileo – both with a link to the University of Padua – even removed earth from the centre of the universe. Since reason and empirical study had already been given a prominent role, an avalanche of new facts created a major credibility problem for conservative forces.

Gutenberg's printing press spread the word about new ideas and discoveries. In 1500, some ten million books were in circulation and a growing share of the population was literate. After 1500, the European mind was opened up even more because of the great voyages of discovery, prompted by attempts to find trade routes with Asia. 'In that hemisphere I saw things incompatible with the opinions of philosophers,' wrote Amerigo Vespucci about the continent that would be named after him. Europeans found new insights, strange plants and unknown creatures.[34] After contact with India and China was established, startled sailors and traders brought home more advanced science, novel products and techniques. Those who disseminated news about these strange places gained a more prominent role in the public debate, and since they were often the ones most interested in novelty, this changed the balance of the culture from tradition to innovation. Having sailed to Goa in 1534 to serve as physician, Garcia de Orta concluded that eyewitnesses accounts from journeys were more important than speculation: 'you can get more knowledge now from the Portuguese in one day than was known to the Romans after a hundred years'.[35]

It is telling that Francis Bacon's fictional scientific utopia *New Atlantis* from 1626 has twelve fellows called 'Merchants of Light' with the sole purpose of setting sail to foreign countries and gathering new knowledge. And increasing commerce led to a new emphasis on understanding, describing, measuring and pricing objects and products. Accurate information about worldly things became a necessary pursuit for traders.[36]

In the sixteenth century, Iberian scholastics became trailblazers in economics and international law when they combined Aristotelianism and Renaissance humanism to grapple with the new discoveries about astronomy and new continents. The School of Salamanca (named after the most influential university), with Francisco de Vitoria as the leading name, pioneered the cause of human rights by defending native Americans against Spanish and Portuguese enslavement and enforced conversion, arguing that they might be different and not Christian, but they have rationality and free will and therefore right to life, liberty and property. Some of the Spanish scholastics expanded this into a proto-liberal idea of individual rights and free markets and thought that the king's role was limited to protecting those rights. To the horror of traditionalists, radicals like the Jesuit priests and writers Francisco Suarez and Juan de Mariana considered the king an employee of the people, and if he violated them, they had the right to rebel.[37]

The ideas of the Salamanca school would eventually have an impact in Protestant countries as well, through natural law thinkers like the Dutch diplomat and jurist Hugo Grotius and the German political philosopher Samuel Pufendorf, who were influenced by them and integrated their ideas into their own systems of thought.

An orthodox backlash

By 1700, Europe had gone some way to emerging from its dark ages but it was still no more advanced than Asia. Average incomes and productivity in most of Asia were higher than in Europe. And even though Europeans were becoming more literate, they were still not as literate or educated as the Chinese. But Europe had something else: by now, Europe was finally more open than other civilizations. This fact would change the course of world history.

Between the late 1500s and the mid-1600s, during a period of cooling (the 'little ice age'), parallel cycles of population growth and price increases on food prompted a series of rebellions, civil wars and state breakdowns in Europe, the Middle East and Asia. The European Reformation unleashed religious conflict and the Thirty Years War, and Charles I lost his head during the English Civil War. The Ottoman Empire faced rebellions and Sultan Osman II was executed in 1622 after a military uprising. In China, the Ming dynasty was overthrown by the Manchus who set up the Qing dynasty in Beijing in 1644. Meanwhile the Mughal Empire in India started to disintegrate.

Faced with these devastating crises, rulers rearranged structures to preserve social order and their own power. The biggest long-term effect came from the now-familiar conclusion that social and religious modernization had made them weak. Many assumed the upheavals had come upon them because they had abandoned traditional beliefs. Now came a fierce reaction.[38] The religious elite in the Ottoman Empire blamed its leaders for having abandoned traditional beliefs, and argued for a 'circle of virtue' in which pious rulers and obedient subjects knew their place and faithfully followed a conservative interpretation of Sunni Islam. After 1650, the dominant ambition was to discover how things had been done in the past and follow that example. The Ottoman's tolerant tradition was abandoned, and they began to heap scorn on the outside world and on domestic innovation. Neighbouring Safavid Persians had recently started to enforce Shia Islam, and exiled or killed Sunni clergy. The Mughal emperors in India also reversed their policies of tolerance and razed Sikh and Hindu temples.

Meanwhile, the conquering Manchus who were searching for ways to justify their new rule over China, imposed a rigid Confucian state orthodoxy, pure of Buddhist and Taoist influence. Stronger hierarchies were established, innovations eschewed and independent intellectual life quashed. The old literature was purged of dangerous ideas and modifications, and memorization of classics texts became the requirement for official positions. The government started persecuting intellectuals for what they wrote or read during what has been called the 'literary inquisition'. Houses were searched for forbidden books and scholars suspected of being anti-Qing could be sentenced to execution, exile or forced labour. It was primarily aimed at political rather than intellectual dissidents, but it did long-term damage to opportunities for education.[39] Just like in the other new conformist regimes, the pace of science and innovation collapsed.

At first Europe was no different. Elites reacted to the crises of the seventeenth century just as they did in the Middle East and Asia: by enforcing political authority and intellectual orthodoxy. What made Europe different was that they failed. Protestant reformers wanted to return to what they saw as a more pure, traditional form of Christianity that they thought Rome had betrayed. Luther did not want religious tolerance where Protestantism was established and advocated the death penalty for blasphemy. Calvin's Geneva was a police state, where church attendance was obligatory and heretics were tortured and burned at the stake. Even the open Netherlands buckled under pressure from the Calvinist church during these difficult years, and in 1656 Cartesian teachings were banned by the States of Holland. The same year, the Jewish community of Amsterdam excommunicated Spinoza, and after his death his books were banned.

Trying to reimpose its authority, the Catholic Church also became more repressive during its counter-reformation. The Roman Inquisition began to seek out heretics more aggressively. Thinkers and writers like Giordano Bruno, Lucilio Vanini and Ferrante Pallavicino were executed. Copernicus was denounced by both Calvin and Luther for his account of how the earth revolved around the sun. In 1616, seventy-three years after Copernicus' death, Rome caught up with him and banned his work. In 1633 the Inquisition famously forced Galileo to recant his heliocentrism, threatening him with torture. He spent the rest of his life under house arrest. Some great scientists, like Thomas Harriot, who made important astronomical breakthroughs, kept their discoveries secret since they 'preferred life to fame'.[40]

High-profile cases like this restricted free inquiry in Italy, and in Spain and Portugal where there were also inquisitions. When the young English poet and free-speech advocate John Milton visited Galileo in Florence in 1638, he wrote that repression and self-censorship 'had dampened the glory of Italian wits'.[41] Work continued in other areas, but scholars became increasingly conscious of the boundaries of acceptability. The counter-reformation was strongest in Spain, where there was a strong reassertion of traditional authority, sometimes combined with an aggressive national chauvinism. Spanish universities that had been world-leading under the Salamanca school now fell under the control of rigid Catholic ideology, their spirit of curiosity crushed.

With a traditionalist reaction setting in at French universities as well, and with Austria and Germany in ruins after the Thirty Years War, this was, says science historian Floris Cohen, the moment when Europe could have suffered from 'a loss of momentum such as might then have become the first step in a process of decay, petrifaction, and ultimate extinction'.[42]

The European exception

However, there was a glimmer of hope. Even though the traditionalists reacted in Europe just as they had in the Middle East and Asia, they faced more difficult obstacles: political, religious, ethnic and linguistic divisions, city walls, autonomous universities and an abundance of different religious denominations. Their power ambitions were not smaller, but they came up against important geographical limits in the form of Europe's peninsulas, forested landscape, riverine marshes and mountain ranges.

As the Scottish philosopher David Hume explained in 1742: 'EUROPE is at present a copy at large, of what GREECE was formerly a pattern in miniature' and: 'The emulation, which naturally arises among those neighbouring and independent states, is an obvious source of improvement: But what I would chiefly insist on is the stop which such limited territories give both to *power* and to *authority*.'[43]

What Hume meant was that Europe, just like ancient Greece, was in a sweet spot. It was too divided for any one ruler or elite to impose an orthodoxy over the whole continent, as had happened in China, but at the same time it was connected by mutual exchange so territories could constantly learn from one another. By the late 1700s, Qing China measured around 14.7 million square kilometres. The two biggest western European powers, France and the Austrian Dominions, were smaller than 0.7 million.[44] Mountain ranges divide Spain from France and separate Italy from northern Europe. Dutch rivers and Swiss mountains raised the cost of invasions.

At the beginning of the sixteenth century, there were around five hundred more or less independent political units in Europe. Some of these jurisdictions let oppression and persecution run wild, but only at the risk that others would supersede them. What's more, the danger that all of them would make the same mistake or that they would be able to coordinate repression was small. Even when big states came to dominate, shifting alliances successfully opposed dominance by a single power.

Countries like Spain and the Netherlands had local and regional authorities with a large degree of independence. Western Europe also had many autonomous cities that experimented with self-government. Some like Basel were open to refugees, which made it difficult for despots everywhere. The powerful city-state of Venice refused to send dissidents to Rome when the Pope requested it. To this can be added semi-autonomous universities and academies.

At the same time, Europe was connected by commerce, intellectual networks and language: namely Latin for the elites. There was a certain cultural unity on the divided continent that made the Anglo-Irish politician and philosopher Edmund Burke proclaim: 'No European can feel himself a complete exile in any country on the continent.'[45] The royals constantly vilified, undermined and attacked each other, and yet they also inter-married, invited one another's traders and intellectuals, and stored away their ill-gotten gains in each other's vaults (mostly Amsterdam's and London's because they had more faith in amoral merchants than in their own ilk). When the Pope switched to the Gregorian calendar in 1582, the whole of Europe eventually adopted it, even Britain in 1752. In the end, assuring the smooth flow of correspondence and exchange was more important than disrespecting your rivals.

This created an emergency exit for intellectuals that did not exist on other continents. Every country suppressed something, but by moving to the one most hospitable to their particular heresies, freethinkers always found an outlet. Thinkers like Erasmus and John Comenius constantly moved to places that were least offended by their activities. Hobbes wrote *Leviathan* while exiled in Paris, and Locke wrote his major works as a refugee in Amsterdam. The Dutch natural law thinker Hugo Grotius escaped from the Netherlands to Paris to be able to write in freedom. The French philosopher Descartes moved in the opposite direction, for the same reason. Voltaire settled down in Ferney in 1758, right by the Swiss border, to facilitate an easy escape if he angered French authorities, but just outside of Geneva in order to avoid a Calvinist ban on theatrical performances.

The fate of Christian Wolff is a great example. In 1723, Friedrich Wilhelm I of Prussia had been convinced by Pietists that Wolff's ideas were dangerous to religion and society, and the king ordered the philosopher to leave his realm within forty-eight hours or be hanged. Wolff left the same day, and in a centralized empire that would have been the end of it. But within days, Wolff had secured a professorship at the nearby University of Marburg (in modern Germany) with attached promises that he would not be censored. There he attracted increasing fame and, when Friedrich Wilhelm died in 1740, Wolff was welcomed back to Prussia.

Even when thinkers and writers did not cross borders, their books did. Just two years after the ban on Galileo's *Dialogue*, it had been smuggled out of Italy and published in the cosmopolitan border town of Strasbourg. Independent-minded Catholics could be published in Protestant countries and vice versa, and whatever both sides censored always had Amsterdam. Printing houses all over Europe made it impossible to keep any book away from the readers for very long. Spinoza, banned by both Calvinists and Catholics, could nonetheless be read everywhere, in Latin, French, English and Dutch. Many dangerous editions were designed for illegal distribution and bore a false printer's name and place of publication. The printers were important in other ways as well, supplying authors with an income and providing refugees with shelter and meeting spaces.

At the end of the eighteenth century, the Qianlong Emperor burned the great Chinese encyclopaedia on technical and economic issues, *Tiangong Kaiwu*, and it was gone. Meanwhile in

France, Diderot and d'Alembert edited their own *Encyclopédie*, and managed to provoke the powers that be. The Catholic Church put it on its index of prohibited books and the French king banned it completely. But with the help of a personal stipend from Catherine II of Russia and Swiss publishers, Diderot persisted and the wild success of these bestselling volumes disseminated Enlightenment ideas elsewhere in the continent.

Jealous emulation

David Hume had talked about the 'jealous emulation' of European neighbours. Whenever someone came up with something that improved its economy or defences, it was imitated by the others. Kings and dukes competed to provide patronage and therefore also refuge to the most successful scientists and writers, partly for the prestige it gave them, but also because they needed them for commercial and military purposes. Every realm needed its mathematicians, map-makers, engineers, artisans, armorers and sailors. Those who persecuted innovators – and many did – fell behind those who didn't. Between 1000 and 1800, those regions ruled by an absolutist leader saw their total urban population decline by 100,000 people per century compared with more liberal regions.[46] Leaders who could see beyond origin and religion were rewarded with innovations, wealth and a growing population.

In 1784, the Prussian philosopher Immanuel Kant credited this rivalry and emulation with facilitating the advent of the Enlightenment:

Now the States are already involved in the present day in such close relations with each other, that none of them can pause or slacken in its internal civilisation without losing power and influence in relation to the rest [...] Hence the restrictions on personal liberty of action are always more and more removed, and universal liberty even in Religion comes to be conceded. And thus it is that, notwithstanding the intrusion of many a delusion and caprice, the spirit of Enlightenment gradually arises as a great Good which the human race must derive even from the selfish purposes of aggrandisement on the part of its rulers, if they understand what is for their own advantage.[47]

An important factor was the role of the church as a unified force separate from the government, unlike the Christian Orthodox Church in Russia and the Byzantine Empire. The papacy always worked hard to stop any ruler from attaining power over them, for example by appointing bishops. It secured support from cities in Italy and Germany to limit the strength of the Holy Roman Emperor, and so both exploited and deepened Europe's political fragmentation. Then the Reformation created even more division and undermined authority generally. The unintended consequence of the Protestant condonation of a personal relationship with God, independent of prelates, was to limit the role of churches generally.

The alternative to open debate and research has always been to yield to authority, but after the Reformation you had to ask 'which authority?' Many concluded that you could not support your views by reference to any authority but sense and reason. This complex backdrop made it easier for innovative thoughts to survive somewhere in Europe, until it had proved its worth and was picked up by more regions. By the mid-eighteenth century, even in absolutist monarchies, the suppression of dissent had become more of a ritualized formality than a dangerous threat.[48]

The jealous emulation meant that Europeans became accustomed to imitating rivals and even people they distrusted and disliked. That was crucial when they came into contact with the Arab, Indian and Asian cultures and couldn't get enough of their novel ideas and methods. In contrast, Chinese scholars often tried to get authorities to accept learning from the West by convincing them that it had Chinese origins and could therefore be considered legitimate. Europeans had no such qualms, and even named innovations after the place where they learned them. They calculated with 'Arabic numerals', ate 'turkey' (from America, but associated with Turkish merchants) on 'Chinaware', decorated with Persian rugs and used a lacquerware technique called 'Japanning'.

The access to new ideas, methods and discoveries spurred the imagination to new heights. The late seventeenth century saw the growth of learned societies, communities and 'invisible colleges', where philosophers and scientists met. In 1660, the Royal Society was founded in London, with its motto *'Nullius in verba'*, meaning 'take nobody's word for it'. They demanded evidence, and showed the ancient thinkers as little respect as the ancients had shown those preceding them. Unlike the French Royal Academy of Sciences, founded six years later, the society was open to anyone who contributed new useful insights and inventions, not just professional scientists.

Many were inspired by Francis Bacon's vision of how experimental science would create useful technologies if the knowledge was coordinated and made widely accessible. This was new. Ancient thinkers thought of science as a goal in itself, and that fields such as farming, ironworking, shipbuilding and textiles were beneath them and better left to slaves. Most of the time, artisans simply reproduced old methods, and only occasionally, often by accident, came up with new ideas. Now intellectuals started thinking about how they could apply science to make great leaps in technology and commerce.

More than five hundred years earlier, Arab scientists like Ibn al-Haytham in optics and Jabir Ibn Hayyan in chemistry had already insisted that experiments were needed to test hypotheses and create useful knowledge, but post-Baconian scientists took this further in building new instruments, conducting more experiments and building bridges between scientists and industrialists, philosophers and craftsmen. With new telescopes, microscopes, thermometers, barometers, chronographs and vacuum pumps, which they often built themselves, they uncovered more of nature's secrets than ever before.

The Republic of Letters

Tying philosophers and scientists together was the remarkable Republic of Letters, 'the main institution behind the meteoric takeoff of useful knowledge in Europe during the Scientific Revolution and the Enlightenment', according to the Dutch-American-Israeli historian Joel Mokyr, who has documented its importance.[49] The Republic of Letters was a spontaneously organized institution, consisting of intellectuals who corresponded on philosophy, politics and science. It was not set up by anyone, it was not designed, and none of the participants could even have dreamed of the importance it would come to have.

It started with a small group of like-minded thinkers who wanted to share and test new ideas and stay up to date with what the others were doing, but their principles of free entry and contestability – similar to those of the Royal Society – turned it into a growing community of great importance to the Enlightenment and for technological advances in textiles, steel, electricity, medicine and countless other fields. This virtual republic had perhaps 1200 members all over Europe in the late 1600s, and 12,000 a century later.

It was a cosmopolitan group, made up of people of all countries and denominations, constantly interacting and influencing one another via a new continent-wide postal system developed for the needs of finance and trade. One of the founders, John Wilkins, said that its purpose was to 'repair the ruins of Babel' and in this it worked splendidly. People of different religions stayed in close touch about scientific matters, even fundamentalists who despised the convictions of the others. While countries' armies killed each other on the battlefields, intellectuals from both sides continued to exchange their best ideas. 'The philosopher of one country sees not an enemy in the philosophy of another; he takes his seat in the temple of science, and asks not who sits beside him,' wrote Thomas Paine.[50]

With a constant exchange of letters, books and papers, these Enlightenment thinkers ignored religious taboos and escaped government censorship. They only accepted evidence and logic as authority, and this authority could be wielded by anyone, not just by traditional authorities with power, ancestry or wealth. Apparently, the examination the participants exposed themselves to could be fierce. The French philosopher Pierre Bayle, who had escaped to Rotterdam, explained its ethos:

> This commonwealth is a State extremely Free. The Empire of Truth and Reason is only acknowledged in it; and under their protection an innocent War is waged against any one what-ever. Friends ought to be on their Guard, there, against their Friends, Fathers against Children [...] Every body, there, is both Sovereign and under every-body's Jurisdiction.[51]

No one escaped critique and revision. Not even the greatest scientist of the age, Isaac Newton. He had claimed it was impossible to correct chromatic distortion in lenses, which results in a mismatch so colours do not combine as they should. Others challenged Newton's conclusion. In an almost perfect example of the open science ideals of the Enlightenment era, the Royal Society did not turn to religious authorities or ancient books to settle the matter, but to John Dollond, the son of Huguenot refugees and a silk-weaver who had taught himself optics. At first, Dollond trusted the words of Newton, but eventually, a series of experiments with different types of glass convinced Dollond that the great man was wrong, and in 1758 he built a telescope that corrected for the aberration. Later, the self-taught optician ordered a portrait of himself, with a copy of Newton's great book, and a bookmark indicating the page where he had made the mistake.[52]

A Dutch mathematician and physicist, Nicolaas Hartsoeker, who did not hesitate to criticize Newton, saw this mutual contestability as the lifeblood of the new sciences:

> I very humbly beg of all whose opinions I have attacked, perhaps with too much liberty, not to take it in a bad way, since I have most often done this only to invite them to do the same to mine [...] this philosophical war will likely cost a bit of ink but there will be no spilling of blood.[53]

The corresponding Enlightenment thinkers circulated what they found correct, improved what they found promising and attacked what they found faulty, because they wanted to improve the world and their own reputation in the hope of achieving fame, fortune and patronage. For the first time, the authority of ideas replaced ideas of authority. By doing so, they established a tradition of criticism, which is something very unusual in the history of the world. A tradition is by definition a behaviour passed on by previous generations. The extraordinary achievement by the Republic of Letters and other Enlightenment thinkers was that they managed to turn the challenge of tradition into a new tradition.

Dogmatic slumber

Research is a collaborative and cosmopolitan venture as well as a competitive one. Today, a single academic paper can look a bit like the Republic of Letters. Between 2014 and 2018, there were 1315 papers listed in the Web of Science citation index by more than a thousand co-authors. There were forty-nine papers during this time that were co-authored by scientists from more than sixty countries, and nearly two-thirds of these had authors from more than eighty countries.[54]

The Enlightenment tradition lives on in systems of free speech, independent media, universities and academic journals, and that is why we need systems of schooling that are independent of the ruling political majority. These are systems we have created to handle our confirmation bias. We all pay more attention to data points that support what we already think. If we are left to our own devices, a wealth of information might very well just make us even more convinced of what we already thought. And that goes for experts and scholars as well.

Over two decades, the American psychologist Philip Tetlock elicited 82,361 forecasts from 284 individuals whose job it is to comment and advise on trends about the world, economics, politics and major events. He found that the experts were not much better than informed non-experts. There was even some evidence that they had a harder time adjusting to new information. The 'fatal tendency of mankind to leave off thinking about a thing when it is no longer doubtful, is the cause of half their errors', as John Stuart Mill wrote in *On Liberty*.[55] They didn't even excel in their own field of expertise because they often had their own pet forecast – you know, that kind of prediction that will always be proven right around the next corner. Tetlock exemplifies this point with the biologist and environmentalist Paul Ehrlich, who argued in 1968 that overpopulation would soon lead to global famine. Instead, chronic undernourishment steadily declined. Ehrlich just reacted by postponing doomsday a little bit every time he returned to the subject, like a religious fanatic keeps postponing doomsday when it fails to appear at the right time. Meanwhile hunger continued to decline. Today it is around a third of what it was when Ehrlich wrote.[56]

This is a problem that can't be solved by knowledge alone. The more you know, the more data points and theories you can use to support your own preconceived ideas. So how can we awake from our dogmatic slumber? By forcing ourselves to listen to our enemies, who have an equally strong confirmation bias but hold the opposite beliefs. 'Love your enemies' might sound a bit over the top but it's definitely true that we should listen to our enemies; otherwise we shut ourselves off from important information.

Look at how we try to find truth in a courtroom. It is not by looking at all the available evidence and trying to make up our mind. It is by giving a prosecutor the task of looking at the evidence and making the strongest possible case for a defendant's guilt, and by letting a lawyer look at the evidence and construct the most likely case for his innocence, and then allowing them both to contest the other's point of view. We create an adversarial system where two groups look at the world from opposite sides, so that we are more likely to get closer to the real story.

Our opponents help us understand the world better than we otherwise would. We can't take systems like that for granted. It is counter-intuitive to celebrate the presence of people who think differently, and many think that science should answer to public opinion or political preferences. It is very easy for any system of knowledge to harden into an orthodoxy, and for outsiders to be considered traitors. As became evident with Aristotelianism during the Middle Ages, even the best ideas can become destructive and lose their ability to advance knowledge if allowed to stifle the opposition. More recently, the idea – often embraced because it was thought to imply equality – that human consciousness is a blank slate became academic orthodoxy. This led many social scientists to reject findings in evolutionary biology and behavioural psychology out of hand.

This is more rule than exception in authoritarian and totalitarian countries, which is why they fail to create thriving scientific ecosystems even when they spend massive amounts on research. If Soviet's leading agronomist, Trofim Lysenko, said that genes do not exist and that any acquired characteristics are inherited, dissenting scientists were silenced or killed, crop yields collapsed and biology and agronomy were set back half a century. Nikolai Vavilov, one of the most promising young Soviet biologists in the 1930s, was confronted by Lysenko for basing his work on Darwin and not Marx and Engels: 'you wrote that […] evolution must be viewed as a process of simplification. Yet in chapter four of the history of the party it says that evolution is [an] increase in complexity.' Vavilov was soon arrested, accused of destroying Soviet agriculture and died of malnutrition in prison aged fifty-five.[57]

After Mao, China's Communist Party has tried to avoid such mistakes by softening up its claims to hold the scientific truth, and has instead consciously revived the ancient Chinese ideal to 'seek truth from facts'. In certain areas, this has given more room for scientists, but the very structure of a dictatorship creates a fear to think or say anything controversial, and this introduces a constant tension. We don't know yet which promising avenues Chinese scientists and intellectuals dare not pursue out of risk of compromising themselves, but we already see the destructive effects of the system whenever the unexpected happens.

When the viral respiratory disease SARS appeared in southern China in November 2002, the government kept it secret for months, delaying both its own and the world's response. You would think it had learned the lesson. But history repeated itself with the new coronavirus. Chinese authorities could have stopped it from becoming a global pandemic if they had acted the moment the first cases were discovered, but instead they instinctively silenced whistle-blowers and denied human-to-human transmission. Medical professionals who sounded the alarm about the outbreak were detained by the police. State-run media did not mention the risks for weeks, but warned netizens not to spread rumours about it. The Wuhan Health Commission even seemed to have denied the existence of new cases during a week-long Communist Party conclave, so as not to embarrass the bosses. Ten minutes past midnight when the conclave had ended, the bad news was revealed.

In a rare statement, China's highest court actually admonished the police for silencing doctors: 'If society had at the time believed those "rumors", and wore masks, used disinfectant and avoided going to the wildlife market as if there were a SARS outbreak, perhaps it would've meant we could better control the coronavirus today.' And it added that there was only one way to stop hearsay: 'Rumors end when there is openness.'[58]

But if authoritarians really wanted openness, they would not be authoritarian.

The necessary bright spark

We have to be vigilant in democratic countries as well. The social psychologist Jonathan Haidt is worried that American universities are at risk, since many treat the campus less as a vehicle for objective research and truth-finding, and more as a battlefield for a wider culture war. A strong inflow of progressives and social liberals that started in the 1970s has reproduced itself to the extent that students and scholars of other persuasions are now less attracted by this environment and are sometimes being discriminated against. Almost 38 per cent of academic psychologists – who have studied bias and discrimination more than others – say they would avoid hiring a qualified person if they knew he or she was conservative. One in four would discriminate against a conservative in reviewing their grant applications.[59]

This is dangerous. Much of the science behind the benefits of openness that I use for this book is conducted by scholars who like openness. That is why they study it and why they frame the questions in the way they do. And that's fine. But I would not be able to trust that research if there were no people on the other side who took a long hard look at the same data and pointed out weaknesses and mistakes. Those who worry more about the problems and risks associated with an open world are more motivated to do that. The more universities are populated by people with similar worldviews and political beliefs, the less useful it will be, even to those who share their viewpoint.

A Gallup poll in 2018 found that 61 per cent of US students thought the climate on campus 'prevents some people from saying things they believe because others might find them offensive'. And students who identify as Democrats and Independents are actually more likely to think so than Republicans. Another part of the study might explain why. It found that 37 per cent of students think it can be acceptable to shout down controversial speakers and as many as 10 per cent of students think it can be acceptable to use violence to prevent someone from speaking.[60]

On some campuses necessary work against discrimination of minority groups has turned into a contest about who can turn the most innocent difference of opinion into evidence of hate and oppression. Having another understanding of the economy or of affirmative action can be enough to be attacked. This is not strange. Such purging of dissent always happens when a homogenous group establishes an orthodoxy. But if universities want to continue to be a place for open inquiry, they must make sure not to play along. 'Both teachers and learners go to sleep at their post as soon as there is no enemy in the field,' John Stuart Mill observed.[61]

Fortunately, some universities are beginning to take a stand, some by embracing the 'Chicago principles' of free speech, declaring that 'concerns about civility and mutual respect can never be used as a justification for closing off discussion of ideas, however offensive or disagreeable those ideas may be to some members of our community'. Their view is that the role of a university is not to make people comfortable but to make people think.

This statement was first signed by the University of Chicago. It has some proud traditions in that regard. As Robert M. Hutchins, president of the university, responded when critics wanted him to stop the Communist Party leader from speaking in 1932 after being invited by a student organization: 'I am convinced that [the] cure lies through open discussion rather than through inhibition.' Conservatives insinuated that Hutchins defended an open campus only because he was personally into 'pink ideas' (just as some college protesters today accuse defendants of free speech of being closet racists), but he made it clear that disagreement is the whole point of the academy: 'The answer… is that free inquiry is indispensable to the good life, that universities exist for the sake of such inquiry, that without it they cease to be universities.'[62]

It is easier to spend time with and listen to people who already think like you do, and it is tempting to look for intellectual purity. In the presence of outsiders we sometimes hunker down, Robert Putnam-style. But most great achievements come about when people are led outside their intellectual comfort zones and have to think in new ways. 'Truth has ever originated from the conflict of the mind with mind; it is the bright spark that emanates from the collision of opposing ideas,' as Mill's friend and contemporary Herbert Spencer put it.[63]

The mixing of people and ideas gave us the Renaissance and the Enlightenment and the Industrial Revolution. The Republic of Letters was a momentous example of what can happen when people meet across borders, but we also saw this mixing across professional borders within societies during this period, as bridges were being built between formal sciences, practical work and commercial skill.

Bacon had called for cooperation between savants and fabricants – those who knew things and those who made things – and soon philosophers visited mechanical workshops and craftsmen studied scientific papers. Intellectuals and innovators began to meet in coffee shops where people gathered to hear the latest news and gossip, read newspapers, debate ideas and test theories. In England they were sometimes called 'penny universities' since anyone could join the discussion and listen to the latest hypothesis for just the price of a coffee. 'Gentry, tradesmen, all are welcome hither, and may without affront sit down together', in the words of a contemporary rhyme. Coffee houses were the internet of the Enlightenment era, as the British science and technology writer Tom Standage points out, and just like the internet, they were disorganized and often uncomfortable, and anything could happen. Luckily.[64]

Strong legal, cultural and mental barriers used to separate philosophers, scientists, engineers, artisans and entrepreneurs. The idea that an engineer would work for a businessman or that a craftsman would share ideas with a scientist over a cup of coffee would have seemed unbelievable or even shameful to previous generations and other cultures. But during the Enlightenment these barriers were breaking down because they now had a common goal: to understand and improve the world, and make a buck.

When this fluid mixing of thinkers and tinkerers was combined with political and economic openness, the result was the modern world.

4

OPEN SOCIETIES

'Economic development requires "a million mutinies".'
Robert Lucas, borrowing a book title by V. S. Naipaul

When open minds, open exchange and open doors come together for a sustained period of time, the result is discoveries and achievements that facilitate new discoveries and achievements. If this positive circle is not cut short by authorities or disasters, the result is a quantum leap in technology and living standards.

The great fact of economic history is what economist and historian Deirdre McCloskey has called 'The Great Enrichment'. Starting in the early 1800s, for the first time in world history, the efflorescence was not stopped. Growth did not peter out. It just kept growing and growing. Wealth doubled, and then it doubled again, and again and again and again. In the most advanced economies, the average income (adjusted for inflation and purchasing power) has increased since 1800 from around $3 a day to roughly $100, according to McCloskey. So the goods and services available for the average person have increased by at least a factor of 30 – or nearly 3000 per cent.[1] In fact it has increased by twice that amount if we were to measure the value of our spare time as the wealth we are willing to forego to get it, since the average employed individual today works less than half as many hours per year as they used to, and even more than that if we consider that we start working later in life, retire earlier and live longer after retirement.

Trade and migration on their own are good at creating static gains. Division of labour helps us move from a lower level of production to a higher one, and exchange of goods, services, ideas and technology helps us spread rapid dynamic gains once they appear as well, but they can't give us an extra 3000 per cent by themselves. That can only happen when you start using a combine harvester instead of harvesting and threshing manually, move your cargo from a sailing ship to a container vessel, replace muscles with coal, nuclear and solar, shovels with tunnel-boring machines, the donkey express with a mobile phone, abacuses with spreadsheets, oil lamps and candlelight with electric light, and eyes, ears and brains with sensors, barcodes and algorithms. In short, it can only happen when open exchange, doors and minds are combined and reinforce each other.

You can observe it in your everyday life and how it has changed beyond recognition from your ancestors two centuries ago, because of scientific knowledge, technological progress, organizational innovation and economic growth. You can see it in the fact that you are not desperately poor – in 1800 around 90 per cent of the global population lived in extreme poverty. Today more than 90 per cent are not extremely poor. You are not illiterate (or if so, you wasted good money on this book) but in 1800, only 12 per cent of the world could read and write. Today that is roughly the share that can't read and write. And you are most certainly not dead, but there is a great probability that you would have been back then. In 1800, almost every second child died before their fifth birthday, and giving birth was as dangerous to a woman as playing a game of Russian roulette with a six-shooter. Today, child mortality is below 4 per cent and global maternal mortality stands at 0.2 per cent. Global life expectancy has increased from twenty-nine years to over seventy-two.[2]

Are you over thirty? Then express some gratitude to the British because that's where it all started, in the 1700s, when openness in different dimensions began to come together, creating a society not from a hierarchical blueprint, but from the ongoing actions of a growing number of people from all parts of society. This meant the culture and the economy continued to grow, change and surprise even its rulers. The result was the Industrial Revolution. And then the US inherited this openness and used it to achieve even greater wonders.

That does not mean that the great enrichment is a Western or a Protestant legacy, as some would have it. Golden ages of creativity and accomplishment have appeared in many eras and many cultures, such as pagan Greece, the Muslim Abbasid Caliphate, Confucian China, Catholic Renaissance Italy and the Calvinist Dutch Republic. The common denominator is that they were, compared to other contemporary cultures, more open, with more trade and contacts that led to a mixing of cultures and ideas.[3] The difference from the British experience was that their openness did not last. It was snuffed out by invaders, tyrants or reactionary backlashes.

The Chinese should have been first

The Industrial Revolution and the start of the open society could very well have happened in China, under the Song dynasty (960–1279). A thousand years ago, when Europe was considered so much of a backwater that much of it was not even worth raiding, the Chinese already navigated with the nautical compass, read books printed with moveable type and fought with gunpowder – the three inventions that Karl Marx, writing in the 1860s, credited with having ushered in Western capitalism. Historian Stephen Davies writes: 'in the key areas of economy, government, social structure, and intellectual life and scientific investigation, Song China was as close to modernity as eighteenth century Europe'.[4]

The first Song emperor Taizu fought hard to unite China after a period of unrest and xenophobia, but when he had done so, he wanted to make sure there would be no return to chaos and warlordism. He invited his military officers to a banquet where he gave a speech convincing them it was time for them to retire. He explained that peace would only come if they were all released from service, returned home and lived on generous retirement benefits. History (or at least Song propaganda) records that the surprised officers all accepted, and so China came under civilian rule and focused on domestic development rather than military expansion. It was a period of relatively limited government where the absolutism of previous eras gave way to a more rule-bound system. The emperor even instituted a council of ministers headed by a prime minister, and the bureaucracy was made more professionalized and meritocratic.

The Song dynasty revived the cosmopolitan traditions of the Tang dynasty (618–907). Muslim traders, Indian monks, Persians and Jews were welcomed back. The first emperor appointed an Arab Muslim as chief astronomer. Cities were filled with merchants and scientists from every corner of the world, and became melting pots of cultures and ideas. To raise the level of knowledge the government compiled encyclopaedias and anthologies with everything from fiction stories and political essays to findings in mathematics, medicine and farming for an increasingly literate population. Scholars were free to explore new knowledge and do research. China became the place where the best talent and the craziest ideas met and instigated rapid innovation and growth. Foreign goods inspired craftsmen to experiment with new techniques, and Chinese artists and poets adopted novel ideas and styles.

They imported superior varieties of rice from Vietnam and the windmill from the Middle East. Scientists and scholars thrived and made advances in mathematics, astronomy, medicine and metallurgy. Woodblock printing spread learning, and in the 1040s Bi Sheng, a commoner, invented ceramic moveable types for printing, fastened on an iron plate, removed and fastened again in a new pattern for the next print. With this method hundreds and sometimes thousands of copies of text were printed quickly and relatively cheaply.

City folk were fed by innovative farmers who over a short period had doubled output and were turning 'into a class of adaptable, rational, profit-oriented, petty entrepreneurs' because of secure property rights and free trade.[5] Instead of controlling commerce and forcing people to work, the enlightened rulers allowed people and goods to flow freely.

In an early blueprint for the US Homestead Acts, individuals who opened up new lands and farmed it got a permanent right to that land, and also the right to sell. The area of cultivated land grew dramatically and would not be surpassed until the modern era. Farmers also constantly adapted new and higher-yielding crop varieties. Increased efficiency made many agricultural workers redundant, who moved to cities and manufacturing sectors. Tea traders who did not want to assume the risk and burden of carrying large amounts of coins came up with the idea of exchanging them for promissory notes, which could be converted back to cash when they arrived home. They had just invented paper money, which greatly facilitated trade, especially in rural areas.

Internal controls of movement were relaxed to create the largest integrated market in the world. Since the Chinese had recently lost access to the Silk Road, naval commerce grew in importance, and the merchant fleet was second to none. Financial innovation kept them afloat with the arrival of joint stock companies that separated owners and managers. Leaders proclaimed: 'Profits from maritime commerce are very great. If properly managed, they can amount to millions. Is this not better than taxing people?'[6]

An impressive system of roads was built that got crops, fruits, vegetables, timber and paper to harbours, where they were loaded onto large ships based on Persian, Arab and South East Asian designs. The pound lock was invented to raise and lower boats between stretches of water of different levels of rivers and canals, greatly helping connect the Yellow River and the Yangtze. Ocean-going ships could have up to six masts, watertight compartments and a crew of as many as a thousand men. The result was a wealth explosion and a population explosion – more than doubling a population that had been fairly stable at around 50 million for half a millennium.

Old traditions and hereditary privileges had been undermined by a high degree of international trade and domestic urbanization. With this came a radical new culture of individualism, an emphasis on self-discovery and self-improvement.[7] People from different backgrounds were competing with innovations and technologies unlike anything the world had ever seen.

Song China was the world's most advanced civilization, based on open trade, open doors and open minds. And it was ready to take the next step, into the modern world. It was close to unleashing an industrial revolution, half a millennium before it was even a glint in James Watt's eye.

The Chinese cleared whole forests to smelt ores into iron in gigantic foundries, and when this led to a shortage of wood, some innovative businessmen discovered how they could find and use power stored as coal. According to tax returns, by the late eleventh century, iron output in China was almost as much as the whole of Europe produced in 1700. They also experimented with textile machines, powered by pedals and watermills, which made it possible to mass-produce fabrics. Marvelling at one of these inventions, Mark Elvin, a scholar of Chinese history, speculates:

> if the line of advance which it represented had been followed a little further, then medieval China would have had a true industrial revolution in the production of textiles over four hundred years before the West.[8]

The fall of Song

This was not to be, however. And not because the Chinese lacked the materials, the energy sources or the scientific knowledge. There came a time of devastating war, but ideas and knowledge do not disappear, so China could have bounced back. More troubling was how China reacted to this time of war and uncertainty: by renouncing its openness and cosmopolitan character.

In 1127, the Song lost northern China to invading Jurchen troops and moved the capital to modern Hangzhou, creating a much-reduced state now known as Southern Song. The same fundamentals of openness and commerce applied, though, and they were even intensified. Entrepreneurs learned how to use the dirtier coal at disposal there, and discovered how to extract copper from the by-products of ironworking. Soon Song once again had a flourishing culture and economy. As the saying went in the capital: 'vegetables from the east, water from the west, wood from the south, and rice from the north'.[9]

In 1235, the Mongols started to attack Southern Song, but because of major naval innovations, like paddlewheel-powered battleships and onboard catapults that hurled gunpowder and incendiary bombs, the Chinese held the line and for a time even pushed the Mongols back. But the Mongols persisted, and in 1279 it was over when the last of the Song navy was defeated at Yamen.

In a final act of defiance, the Song elite refused to surrender and opted for suicide. The last Song emperor, only seven years old, died in the arms of his councillor, as they jumped off Mount Ya into the sea below.

However, Genghis' grandson Kublai Khan was not just China's conqueror but also its pupil. Once the Mongols saw that openness had made the country phenomenally rich, they abandoned the idea of depopulating China's agricultural land and using it as grazing ground for the horses. Instead, Kublai Khan's new China preserved Song's scientific and technological legacy and combined it with new methods and expertise that Mongols picked up in the rest of Eurasia, now once again reconnected through the Silk Road. International trade expanded under a Pax Mongolica.

Kublai Khan recruited Uighurs, Persians, Central Asians and Europeans as governors and ministers. Arab and Greek scientists produced advanced maps and astronomical tables. Merchants, artisans and workers from all over the world and from all religions thronged the streets. Muslim doctors understood surgery, but the Chinese had better knowledge of internal organs, so together they could make greater advances. This was the China that so impressed the Venetian explorer Marco Polo, who was himself appointed an official in the city of Yangzhou. China was so far ahead of Europe that many thought all his talk of a sophisticated civilization created by barbarians was a fable (and not just the bits that obviously were).

Not even the Mongols could resist the bubonic plague, though. It didn't just kill millions, it also destroyed international trade and much of its wealth. A series of revolts against the Mongol court ended with the establishment of the ethnically Han Chinese Ming dynasty in 1368. Despite a few bursts of creativity, this was the beginning of the end of China's great cosmopolitan era. The humiliation of having been conquered by foreigners made the new rulers xenophobic. The destruction of the Song dynasty was said to be the weakness and disorder created by its openness and commerce (which seems unfair considering the Mongols' winning streak everywhere, and that the reason Song held out longer than most was its innovations). So the new rulers dismantled checks and balances on its power, built massive walls to keep foreigners out and started trade wars with neighbours.

The new Ming dynasty portrayed itself as the opposite of the dynamic, bustling Song China. Here was instead a stable, paternalistic society that gently guided (with purges, censorship and spies) duty-bound scholars, self-sufficient farmers and obedient traders who only dealt with locally produced goods. They did not need innovations, and when they came upon mechanical clocks and other similar devices in the old dynasty's palace, they destroyed them. They banned private involvement in astronomy, and had to stop readjusting the calendar when the people occupying the now-hereditary positions did not know how to do it. The Ming even decreed that citizens should restore clothes and headwear to what they had been in the good old days, five hundred years earlier.

The first Ming emperor claimed that few people ever had to travel more than 13 kilometres from home, so internal controls on movement were reintroduced. Private overseas trade was banned on pain of death, and ships, docks and ports were sabotaged. Foreign languages and customs were prohibited, and religious freedom abandoned. Several times silver coins were banned to make commerce more difficult. By 1500, subjects were no longer allowed to leave the country. It was, in effect 'an anti-modern revolution', with the goal of reimposing a stable, traditionalist society from the top.[10]

From 1644 Manchu rule made it even worse, as we saw in the last chapter. Being outsiders, a small population of nomads from the steppe who had captured an ancient civilization, they justified their rule as true Chinese with a more rigid, traditionalist interpretation of Confucian ideology. Under their Qing dynasty, tightly controlled scholars were assigned the task of 'purifying' classical texts by eliminating dangerous modifications and innovations. So only under a foreign Manchu dynasty did China become an orthodox Confucian state, abandoning its traditions of openness.

Soon the Qing succeeded in deceiving Europeans that China had remained traditional and unchanged for centuries (the Chinese 'have become stationary – have remained so for thousands of years,' wrote John Stuart Mill in 1859).[11] Despite major improvements in areas like agriculture under their rule, they had a principled hostility to trade and innovation. They expropriated private property and in 1661 forced the whole population of the previously dynamic southern coast to move almost 30 kilometres inland.

Neither Ming nor Qing succeeded entirely in their nostalgic counter-revolutions. The Chinese always found ways of evading controls and re-establishing trade, but the dynamic, innovative society did not survive. The nativist backlash was the beginning of a long decline that would turn the world's most advanced civilization into a miserably poor country, attacked and humiliated by more powerful European powers in the nineteenth century. China would only return to the world scene when its economy was once again opened up to the world in the late twentieth century.

The reason that China's progress was so fragile was that the Chinese government was so strong. The country was centralized with an all-powerful emperor and an efficient bureaucracy. When an emperor embraced openness and trade, the result was impressive, but when an emperor decided against it, it all came tumbling down.

A British request for trade in 1793 was famously rejected with the claim that the Chinese already had everything and do not 'have the slightest need of your country's manufactures'. Lord Amherst was sent all the way back home in 1816 because he refused to kowtow – kneel and bow so low that your head touches the ground – to the emperor. (A millennium earlier, an Arab delegation had refused in the same way to the Tang emperor, but he had just acknowledged that, 'Court etiquette is not the same in all countries', and welcomed them anyway.)[12] At that time, the emperor was still close to the truth, but it was spectacularly ill-timed, because Europe was just about to take off.

Zheng He vs Columbus

The most sensational illustration of the stark reversal of Europe's and China's fortunes was the switching of places during the Age of Discovery. China should have been the country that discovered the New World. When Ming emperors banned private sea trade, they did not stop trade. Instead it was transferred into government hands, enriching government officials. Between 1405 and 1433, the emperor sent a gigantic fleet on seven voyages to project power and wealth around the Indian Ocean and create a system of tributary states. Under the command of the Muslim eunuch Zheng He, around 250 vessels carrying almost 30,000 men sailed to South East and South Asia, Arabia and East Africa. Decades before Columbus was born, they travelled much further than he would, on much larger vessels. Zheng's flagship might have measured as much as 135 metres, compared to Columbus' tiny Santa Maria of only about 20 metres.

But China's maritime adventure was curtailed by a single decision. One day, the emperor decided that it was enough. In 1433 the voyages ceased and three years later, the construction of seagoing ships was made illegal. The greatest fleet the world had ever seen rotted. Some remaining ships seem to have been burned. When some courtiers revived the idea of sailing the seas decades later, the records of the voyages were destroyed by civil servants to prevent people from getting any ideas.

There are many theories about why China abandoned the oceans. Some think it was an ideological decision, a reflection of the new, insular mentality under the Ming. Contact with the outside world was politically and socially destabilizing. Others think it was just too expensive, when they also had to use massive resources to rebuild the Great Wall. A third hypothesis is that it was the outcome of a power struggle between the eunuch faction at court, which led the voyages, and the Confucian scholar-bureaucrats, who denounced their globalist ambitions. But it doesn't really matter why; what's important is that they could do it. A single decision by a single person (or at least, by the young emperor's powerful advisors) could turn a whole civilization inwards.

In Europe the Genoese mariner Christopher Columbus was also snubbed by the powerful. He could not find anyone to fund his attempt to search for a westward route to Asia anywhere in his own Italy, so he asked the Portuguese king, who turned him down. As did the dukes of Medina-Sidonia and Medinaceli, and the kings of England and France. He spent twenty frustrating years looking for a royal patron. Had this been China, it would have been the end of the story. But in a fragmented Europe he could keep looking, and in the end, the Spanish court agreed to sponsor him. In 1492, he was on his way.

When somebody is successful in a more open, competitive system, they are imitated. When Columbus found the New World, it was a Sputnik moment for the other European powers. The Portuguese who had turned Columbus down now also quickly set sail for America. The Pope was not interested in a chaotic scramble for territory, so he tried to structure the dawning age of discovery by dividing the globe into a western Spanish half and an eastern Portuguese half. But the King of France demanded to see where in Adam's (of Adam and Eve fame) bequeathing this provision had been made. Protestant powers like England and the Netherlands ignored His Holiness completely.

Luddites in power

This was the crucial difference between the West and China. Not that Western rulers were smarter, more benevolent or more open to innovation. They thought very much like Emperor Francis I of Austria-Hungary, who declared to an assembly of teachers in 1821 that if anyone 'comes with new ideas, he can go, or I will remove him'.[13] They were just as likely as the Chinese rulers to try to impose 'order and stability', and stifle dissent and innovation that threatened the established order. They were just not very good at it.

Attacks on creative destruction that sound like they are straight out of the Ming or Qing handbook proliferated in Europe. Queen Elizabeth denied William Lee a patent for his pioneering knitting machine in 1589 with the argument that it would eliminate jobs. The Privy Council banned a needle-making machine in 1623 and ordered all the needles made with it destroyed. In 1632, Charles I prohibited the casting of brass buckles, claiming that six casters would take the jobs of six hundred workers.[14] In 1704, Denis Papin built the first version of a steam-powered boat, but the maiden voyage broke the monopoly of the boatmen's guild, and in Fulda they attacked Papin and smashed his steam engine to pieces. In German cities, automatic looms were banned in 1685, and the emperor of Austria-Hungary banned factories in Vienna. Since he also opposed steam locomotives, the first railway line in the empire had to use horse-drawn carriages.

The economic historian Sheilagh Ogilvie has studied the activities of European guilds, the cartels of workers that were given monopoly within a city, and the power to regulate who could produce what and how, with whom and at what prices. The conclusion is that over a five-hundred-year period, 'opposition to innovation was not just an incidental aspect of guild's activities, but central to

their incentives as privileged interest groups'.[15] It happened everywhere and in all sectors, as soon as an innovation was thought to
threaten business interests.

Before the Industrial Revolution, all the great episodes of
progress and open inquiry were ended. Those with social status,
formal skills, tacit knowledge, special equipment, natural resources
or any kind of privileged position tied to a specific way of doing
and producing things, always sensed a lethal danger whenever
someone introduced new technologies or organizational forms
that threatened it. Therefore, they had an incentive to take control
of the political process and stop it, or at least slow it down. And
they succeeded in doing that every time, except once, and that was
enough to change the world.

In the previous chapter, we saw how attempts by European
rulers to root out scientific innovation and intellectual dissent
floundered because those thinkers could escape and take their theories and knowledge with them. Similarly, these elites fought hard
to control economic change but faced the same problem. Persecuted innovators and entrepreneurs could pack up their machines
and business models and go and enrich the neighbours instead. So
the wisest of rulers realized it was better to endure some eccentrics and troublemakers than to see them go away and make their
arch-rivals rich and powerful.

Papin's misfortune in Fulda did not stop the British from experimenting with steam engines. The multi-shuttle ribbon frame
(used for weaving) was banned in most of Europe but spread in
the Netherlands after 1604. French innovators escaped to the
seigneurial enclave of Saint-Sever to introduce new technologies banned elsewhere. In the 1780s, this tiny village had twenty
large-scale cotton-spinning factories, fifty mills for manufacturing, dyeing and finishing cotton cloth, and twenty-three ceramic
workshops. Ecclesiastical jurisdictions were also used as free zones,
like Saint-Seurin and Saint-André, which were so notorious that

the guilds of nearby Bordeaux pejoratively referred to their inhabitants as 'novateurs' (innovators).[16]

Lord Acton thought Europe's blessings came from the unique battle between Church and state over who would get to control the people:

> To that conflict of four hundred years we owe the rise of civil liberty. If the Church had continued to buttress the thrones of the Kings whom it anointed, or if the struggle had terminated speedily in an undivided victory, all Europe would have sunk down under a Byzantine or Muscovite despotism. For the aim of both contending parties was absolute authority. But although liberty was not the end for which they strove, it was the means by which the temporal and the spiritual power called the nations to their aid.[17]

In other words, the only way to gain allies in the struggle for total power was to grant them some freedom from power. Many Europeans found their freedom by playing despots off against one another. When the Holy Roman Emperor wanted to control the Italian city-states in the twelfth and thirteenth centuries, they formed the Lombard League to keep him out, and got the support of the Pope. When the Pope objected to trade with the Muslim world, Venice engaged in it anyway by obtaining trade concessions from the emperor in Constantinople. Sometimes whole populations in border areas shifted their allegiance to the jurisdiction that taxed them the least.[18]

The civil war

The British got to modernity first. Again, we must avoid the temptation to read history in reverse and overemphasize the libertarian aspects of British history that would somehow make it predetermined that it was the British who would abolish slavery and monopolies, embrace free trade and free speech, and become the first country to industrialize. In the early seventeenth century England was – just like its neighbours (with the exception of the Dutch) – all about royal absolutism, censorship and a mercantilist command economy controlled by guilds and monopolies that blocked creative innovation and destruction. When the Marxist historian Christopher Hill described the lack of competition in this era, he asked us to picture:

> a man living in a house built with monopoly bricks, with windows (if any) of monopoly glass; heated by monopoly coal (in Ireland monopoly timber), burning in a grate made of monopoly iron. His walls were lined with monopoly tapestries. He slept on monopoly feathers, did his hair with monopoly brushes and combs. He washed himself with monopoly soap, his clothes in monopoly starch. He dressed in monopoly lace, monopoly line, monopoly leather, monopoly gold thread.[19]

Hill's list of monopolies just keeps going, including hats, belts, buttons, dyes, butter, salmon, lobster, salt, pepper, vinegar, glasses, bottles, wines, spirits, beer, tobacco, pens, paper, books and golf balls, and many, many other items. In 1621, there were seven hundred such monopolies in England, granted by the court in exchange for favours and bribes.

Monarchs in European countries at the time fought fervently with parliaments over taxation and monopolies. The difference was that in the long run, the English royals were far less successful. While the Spanish Crown prospered from an overseas empire, forced labour and gold and silver, the English kings and queens did not succeed in monopolizing trade with America, so independent traders got rich, rather than the court and its loyalists. England was increasingly defined by what Karl Popper has called 'the worst danger to the closed society – commerce, and a new class engaged in trade and seafaring'.[20]

The power struggle between the king and parliament spiralled into the English Civil War of 1642–51. It ended in regicide, a dictatorship under Cromwell and eventual restoration of the Stuart monarchy, yet still opened minds to the idea that something else was possible. During the Civil War, for the first time, a consistent set of libertarian ideas was espoused by a movement called 'Levellers', started by urban radicals like John Lilburne and Richard Overton and strong in independent congregations, tradesmen, artisans and shopkeepers. The Levellers outlined a philosophy about self-ownership. All rights resided in the individual so parliaments and kings were their servants and constrained by their rights. A legitimate government would 'open the press', abolish control over religion (since 'divine truths need no human help to support them'), declare all hereditary privileges and exemptions 'void and null', and 'would have freed all trade and merchandising from all monopolising'.[21]

The Levellers were crushed by Cromwell, and their last pamphlet is signed 'prisoners in the Tower of London, 1 May 1649'. But they set off a spark that would start many fires. Logically, the idea that you own yourself is the first freedom, from which all others follow. But historically, it was discovered last, after people had been given a certain freedom to expand their individual spheres and reveal that we are all different, with our own, separate lives, and have to use our individual rationality to search for truth and flourish.

Many Leveller ideas would eventually make it into the classical liberal ideology that would transform Britain and America, albeit in a more moderate form (it took a few centuries to digest the Leveller demand for worker franchise, for example). Standing on the scaffold, sentenced for treason, the last words of the Leveller Richard Rumbold, were: 'I am sure there was no man born marked by God above another; for none comes into the world with a saddle on his back, neither any booted and spurred to ride him.'[22] More than a century later, American founders like Thomas Jefferson quoted these words, defending their own revolution.

In the decades after the Civil War, the relatively open and rapidly urbanizing English economy created more independent wealth. These new mercantile groups began to think of England as a dynamic, commercial society, in contrast to the old ideal of a landed aristocracy ruled by the king, who formally owned all property. These thinkers drew not just on Leveller inspiration and their own experiences, but also the eye-opening contrast between Spain and the Dutch Republic. The old consensus had been that land and natural resources created wealth, but Spain had it all and was now on the brink of ruin, while the Dutch had neither and was now the richest country on the planet, just by giving their citizens freedom to innovate and trade. One English observer found that Dutch lands did not produce:

> grain, wine, oil, timber, metal, stone, wool, hemp, pitch, nor, almost any other commodity of use; and yet we find, there is hardly a nation in the world which enjoys all of these things in greater affluence.[23]

Now the English also wanted to go Dutch. Josiah Child, the most widely read economic writer of the time, argued: 'if we intend to have the trade of the world we must imitate the Dutch'.[24] In 1685, a prominent writer on economics, Carew Reynell, explained that, 'England is properly a nation of trade' and 'the chief things that promote trade and make it flourish are that it be free, naturaliza-tion [immigration], populacy [a large population], comprehension [toleration], freedom from arrests, certainty of property and free-dom from arbitrary power'.[25]

Around this time appeared a political party hostile to royal absolutism and sympathetic to economic liberalization, which contemporaries considered an attempt to revive the Leveller movement.[26] It was the Whig Party, led by Lord Shaftesbury. An important character in that story was Shaftesbury's personal physician, John Locke, whom he convinced to write more about politics and who would go on to become the founding father of classical liberalism.

According to the emerging Whig ideology, the economy was not a zero-sum game. Wealth was not just taken from others, but created and therefore potentially infinite. Trade could make both parties richer at the same time. Exiled in the Dutch Republic, John Locke wrote that land in itself did not represent much value; 99 per cent of it came from human labour and technology used to work the land. To Locke, this showed 'how much numbers of men are to be preferd to largenesse of dominions'.[27] War and possessions did not make a country great, only an industrious population did, and it needed freedom. Locke thought it would take a revolution to get it.

The Glorious Revolution

The final blow against royal absolutism came in 1688, with the Glorious Revolution. King James II was increasingly seen as a despot and intent on imposing Catholicism on the people. But many Catholics were also hostile, since the king claimed that he was sovereign and not even the Pope could limit his power. This time the revolt against a Stuart king was less violent than the Civil War but the consequences were more momentous, creating – according to Daron Acemoglu and James Robinson in their history of long-term institutional change – 'the world's first set of inclusive political institutions'.[28]

The Glorious Revolution was not just a revolution but an outright Dutch invasion, albeit one that parliament encouraged because of its fear of an increasingly autocratic king and a possible Catholic restoration. The Dutch were eager to stop an alliance between England and France that could have destroyed them. In November 1688, the Dutch stadtholder (de facto head of state), William of Orange, both nephew and son-in-law of King James, invaded England with a fleet four times bigger than the Spanish armada. Almost 500 ships with perhaps 20,000 men; Dutch soldiers, foreign mercenaries and English rebels. In many towns people rose up and joined them, and many royalist officers defected. As they approached London, they faced little resistance. James fled to France, and William and his wife Mary, James' daughter, were made joint monarchs.

Many of the liberal Dutch attitudes, policies and innovations that we looked at in chapter 2 were now transplanted into England, or Great Britain as it would be known after the union with Scotland in 1707. Onboard Mary's ship to England was John Locke. In Dutch exile, he had written *Two Treatises of Government*, a neo-Leveller call for revolution against despots. In his telling, governments are created only to protect the freedom of its citizens and must therefore be limited and restrained. A king who does not protect his citizens' rights to life, liberty and property, but instead encroaches on them, 'unkings' himself. Now Locke could safely publish the book and see some of its ideas realized.

William and Mary could take the throne only after having promised to uphold a Bill of Rights and respect parliament's authority, just like *Two Treatises* demanded. This was the moment when Britain became a constitutional monarchy with rule of law. Even though parliament did not become much more inclusive, the right to petition it was universal and those petitions were taken seriously. Royals stopped interfering with legal decisions. Judges were appointed for life and could not be removed for political reasons.

English law now applied to all citizens, and lords could lose in court even against a commoner. To understand how radical a departure from convention this was, we must remind ourselves that many Europeans were basically outlaws (in the classical sense, outside the law) in any dispute with the aristocracy. As late as the eighteenth century, the Margrave of Ansbach could impress his mistress with his marksmanship by shooting a tiler from the castle tower and the Duke of Mecklenburg could capriciously kill one of his high-ranking advisors because he wanted to bed his (now) widow.[29]

Acemoglu and Robinson point to the rule of law as a consequence of the nature of the revolution. This was not one elite replacing another, but a broad coalition of the gentry, merchants and manufacturers and both Whigs and Tories, who rose up against the king, 'With many parties at the table sharing power, it was natural to have laws and constraints apply to all of them, lest one party start amassing too much power and ultimately undermine the very foundations of pluralism.'[30]

Many of the old arbitrary interventions in the economy were abolished, and the government started protecting property rights, including intellectual property rights. (In 1710, at last, authors got the copyright to their books, thank you.) For us moderns who suffer under the reliable, regular taking of taxes, it might be difficult to understand the importance of ending arbitrary taxation, but forced loans and outright confiscation that rulers used to resort to ruined any incentive to invest and work for long-term results. Who would sacrifice short-term consumption for a possible future gain when the English king could just seize £130,000 in bullion that merchants had stored in the Tower for safety, as he did in 1640? Or if the dictator rewarded soldiers by allowing them to 'pay themselves' by rampaging through urban, commercial areas, robbing banks, breaking into shops and stealing everything they could carry away, as Zaire's Mobutu Sese Seko did several times in the late twentieth century.[31]

The vision of a more mobile, innovative, growing Britain could be seen in the swift decision to replace the hearth tax, which punished manufacturers who depended on fire and heating, with a land tax. Another element was a new financial industry that gave Britain deep capital markets and a declining cost of capital, which funded many hopeful innovators and entrepreneurs (as well as costly wars with France).

Of course, the new dominant business interests also wanted to use the government to protect their own industries. But since the major players were a more diverse group than before, often with opposite ambitions, it was difficult for any commercial elite to coordinate its anti-competitive ambitions. Any attempt at monopoly or protection faced devastating protests from others.

Open exchange

What made Britain and the countries that followed in its footsteps open was that there was no longer a controlling hierarchy, no overarching plan, no road that everybody had to walk. There was suddenly room for the unexpected. An important reason for Britain's superiority during the early Industrial Revolution was that the government did not tell people with important skills where to go. On the continent, engineers were supposed to serve in the military, civil service or in teaching, to make the country powerful. In Britain they generally had to turn to the private sector for employment, so they set about designing better clocks, mills, lighthouses and spinning machines instead.[32]

People with learning and ideas had other outlets than universities and churches. As literacy grew, so did the newspaper industry, often giving a voice to those discontented with the establishment, which facilitated further change. Novelists started writing directly for a mass audience. Authors increasingly experimented with realism, dealing with people's everyday lives and social issues, even in historical novels. Sensitive topics like poverty, racism and women's roles were suddenly discussed in popular literature.

It was as if the new institutions were rigged for surprises. Rule of law gave entrepreneurs predictability in long-term pursuits. In the absence of monopolies they were free to compete with new ideas and products even if that threatened traditional interests, and they then got to profit if they succeeded. Resources belonged to the owner of the land, so mineral riches and coal for the furnaces and engines were happily dug up, unlike on the continent, where they belonged to the Crown. Arbitrary taxation was banned and property rights protected.[33]

Banks now channelled money to the most promising ideas, and new turnpike roads and canals were built by private interests where businesses needed them. There was a new patent system that held out the promise of major rewards for innovation. Crucially, unlike the French and Dutch patent system, the British did not give government officials the task to evaluate an invention's contribution to society. The right to an innovation was to be protected whether bureaucrats liked it or not. In the terminology of the economist and historian Deirdre McCloskey, innovations were no longer supposed to be tested by experts but by trade, which is the difference between trying to predict the future and being open to surprises. A substantial and growing middle class of consumers started to steer the direction of the economy. 'The English have the wit to make things for the people, rather than for the rich,' observed the French politician Charles de Biencourt.[34]

A few spectacular intellectual property rights successes, like James Watt's steam engine, goaded many would-be innovators to try their luck, and so benefited the economy immeasurably.[35] They helped create the concept of the professional inventor who spent all his time tinkering and experimenting to solve mankind's problems.

When we talk about the Industrial Revolution we think about

steam power and textile machines, but this was an era of belief in progress more broadly. People from all walks of life started to take a more careful look at their own activities and see if they could think of a way to improve it. The number of British patents for agricultural tools rose from perhaps five or six per decade before 1760 to eighty per decade in the 1830s.[36]

Urban craft guilds started to lose their power to reject new competitors, new methods and machines. New trades and rural areas were not covered by guilds in Britain (unlike in Germany, Austria, Spain and Italy), so entrepreneurs could generally find a haven to experiment with new ideas and factories. Dockyard towns, country towns and industrializing new towns in the Midlands and the north had free entry and competition. Sometimes it was enough for entrepreneurs to move to the suburbs to escape guild control, as when London businesses moved to suburbs like Whitechapel and Spitalfields. Soon officials refused to enforce the guild system altogether. By the mid-eighteenth century, control had in effect broken down, while the much stronger guilds in southern Europe remained in control for another century. In Austria, Hungary and Portugal compulsory business organizations weren't abolished until the 1870s and 1880s.

There were protests from those who faced competition in Britain as well. Especially in the west of England, wool workers violently attacked jennies, flying shuttles and gig mills, but the result was that they destroyed their own industrial base and chased the industry out to Yorkshire. And parliament consistently refused to legislate against creative destruction. A resolution by the Justices of the Peace in Preston reflects the attitude of the authorities: 'if a total stop were put by the legislature to their erection in Britain [to the new machines], it would only tend to their establishment in foreign countries, to the detriment of the trade in Britain'.[37]

It is easy to overemphasize the break with the past that the Glorious Revolution represented. Many of the changes had started before 1688, and many others would have to wait a long time. Catholic emancipation would only take its first, modest steps a century later, and the idea that human rights applied to the female half of humanity was still a long way off. The victory for free trade, with the abolition of the Corn Laws that benefited landowners at the expense of the hungry, would take more than 150 years. And even though they talked about rule of law, property rights and free speech, the British still enslaved, robbed and silenced colonial subjects. Nonetheless, compared to what had come before (not just in Britain, but all over the world), the changes were substantial and the country had been set on a new path that would make subsequent steps towards a more open society come more naturally.

Perhaps the most important change in post-1688 Britain was the one in attitudes, one that would facilitate and inspire many of the later changes. The victory for urban and commercial values provided traders and manufacturers with a major boost of self-esteem and the sense that they were creating a new world. No longer did they feel they had to aspire to the old culture and estates of the aristocracy. Instead, the aristocracy began to feel like they should aspire to be more bourgeois. This was the real revolution – a growing group that did not desire to become aristocrats.[38]

The new middle classes with all their purchasing power were becoming a more important group than the landed classes. Samuel Johnson complained that the emerging capitalism broke down social barriers. The shoe-shiner had traditionally shown great deference to his social betters on whom he relied, but he now started to treat everybody alike as they were all customers rather than superiors or inferiors. As the society of contract started to replace the society of status, many defenders of the status quo warned that tradesmen and workers were becoming 'impertinent' and 'saucy'.[39]

This is the theme of a brilliant trilogy of books by Deirdre McCloskey. Her argument – based on an impressive display of data and examples from statistics, history, sociology, psychology, art and literature – is that the cause of the great enrichment in the last two hundred years is not capital accumulation or institutional change. Those are just consequences of the major change in what we think of commerce and social mobility. Starting in the Dutch Republic and then Britain, bourgeois pursuits – that were once seen as, at best, a necessary evil to fund a hierarchical society with aristocratic lifestyles for the mighty – were revalued and started to be seen as desirable or even honourable in themselves.

This helps us understand how the British could rapidly modernize even though many old restrictions were still on the books. In the new commercial culture, the British just ignored and evaded laws they saw as arcane and immoral. For example, internal trade and regulations of markets in labour and land were in the hands of local magistrates. They had the power to intervene forcefully in people's lives had they wanted to, but in practice they usually abstained, creating a de facto laissez-faire policy.[40]

Banks often sidestepped interest rate ceilings that would have forced them to restrict lending to only the most creditworthy, by treating loans as overdrafts on the account or by dramatically over-charging for things like postal fees. The Navigation Acts, which restricted trade with the colonies to English ships, were evaded not just by traders but through deliberate neglect by officials who found the regulations stupid. When trade was banned or suffered under heavy tariffs, smugglers kept the oceans open and gave con-sumers access to the creativity of others, like cheaper and more colourful clothes, for example.

Adam Smith (who would go on to take a role as Commissioner of Customs!) defended smuggling as a legitimate activity. Usu-ally it was done by an 'excellent citizen' who had just happened to do something the law unjustly punished. It was so common that Smith even wrote that those who pretend to have any scru-ple about buying smuggled goods were obviously hypocritical, and 'instead of gaining credit with anybody, serve only to expose the person who affects to practise them, to the suspicion of being a greater knave than most of his neighbours'.[41]

Open doors

Britain's doors were also thrown open to the human resources it needed. Along with William and Mary came many Huguenots and Jews who were essential for Britain's ensuing economic rise. Just like Spain before it, France learned that it hurt itself and benefited neighbours by revoking freedom of religion. Only slightly exaggerating, the Duke of Saint-Simon wrote in his memoirs that the attack on Huguenots had 'without the least pretext of necessity, depopulated a quarter of the kingdom, ruined its commerce and weakened it in all parts'.[42]

With the help of their knowledge and networks, London soon took over the role as the world's financial centre from Amsterdam. The Huguenots' skills in many areas of manufacturing gave Britain a flying start in early industrialization. The most important was clock- and instrument-making, which elevated the fine arts of mechanics and the value of precision. Many inventors during this era started out as humble makers of clocks and instruments.

People of other ethnicities and religions were given citizenship with full rights, with the exception of standing for public office and attending the old universities. But these exceptions drove them towards the business and financial sectors. A declaration of the City of London's loyalty with King George II reveals the extent of immigrants among important merchants. Of 542 signatories, at least a third were of non-British descent, over a hundred were Huguenot, forty Jewish and thirty-seven Dutch. A similar declaration on the accession of George III in 1760 showed comparable proportions.[43]

As Voltaire famously described the spirit of tolerant commerce while visiting London in the 1720s:

Go into the London Stock Exchange – a more respectable place than many a court – and you will see representatives from all nations gathered together for the utility of men. Here Jew, Mohammedan and Christian deal with each other as though they were all of the same faith, and only apply the word infidel to people who go bankrupt. Here the Presbytarian trusts the Anabaptist and the Anglican accepts a promise from the Quaker. On leaving these peaceful and free assemblies some go to the Synagogue and others for a drink, this one goes to be baptized in a great bath in the name of the Father, Son and Holy Ghost, that one has his son's foreskin cut and has some Hebrew words he doesn't understand mumbled over the child, others go to their church and await the inspiration of God with their hats on, and everybody is happy.[44]

The union between England and Scotland was another injection of energy. Not only were the most important thinkers and interpreters of the era Scottish, like David Hume and Adam Smith, but so were many of the innovators. Often Scots and English combined their ideas and ambitions to unleash innovation. The prime mover of the era, the steam engine, was the combined effort of the Scottish inventor James Watt (an instrument maker) and the English industrialist Matthew Boulton, who funded the efforts and induced Watt to move to Birmingham to create a commercially viable version that would transform the economy. Scotland was also a leading iron producer, and it was a Scot, James Beaumont Neilson, who came up with one of the most important innovations, hot-blast iron smelting.

In the colonies, the British and other European powers conquered, subjected and discriminated against local populations.[45] Back home, though, a commercial society was replacing feudal control, and in business it turned out to be more important what you could accomplish and offer than who you were and where you came from. Even though individuals were often prejudiced, their aggregate decisions in open, competitive markets were more colour-blind by necessity. The person who excludes potential financiers, partners and customers because they are of another religion loses to those who don't.

Open minds

In his great work on the Industrial Revolution in Britain, Joel Mokyr points to two cultural attitudes that facilitated the revolution, and both were attitudes of openness.[46] The first was the now-familiar willingness to borrow from others, which had been inspired by encounters with older and more advanced civilizations in Asia and the Middle East. The British were ceaselessly curious about ideas from other places and became famous for applying, adapting and tweaking already existing technologies. The slogan 'Not invented here' was for all practical purposes replaced by 'Stolen with pride'. Daniel Defoe, of *Robinson Crusoe* fame, went so far as to claim that 'in almost all the great Things, we are now Masters of, and in which we so much exceed all our Neighbouring Nations, are really founded upon the Inventions of others'.[47]

The second was the willingness to deviate from the accepted wisdom of previous generations. Cultures that regarded the canon or the words of their fathers as sacrosanct, squashed innovation. 'It is the exception, the deviant, the aberration that is agent of change', which sounds a bit like a 1990s Apple advert for 'Think different'. In most previous cultures aberration was seen as apostasy. But as a result of the Republic of Letters and other Enlightenment thinkers, a tradition of criticism had emerged. For a brief moment in time, in a small part of the world, it was not the defenders of tradition who got the most social prestige, but the thinkers, engineers and innovators who questioned everything and thought it could be done better.

In the eighteenth century, the British had opened its mind to Enlightenment science, its harbours to trade and its doors to talent from all places. Compared to all societies that had come before, the British now had a greater freedom to explore strange new knowledge and experiment with new technologies – combined with the insight that they would make a decent profit if successful. Most importantly, if someone else came up with a better way of doing something, they too could try their luck and were allowed to defeat the incumbent if more people liked their idea, technology or product. Combined with an open culture where thinkers and tinkerers, and innovators and industrialists constantly compared notes and collaborated and competed, Britain progressed from the traditional occasional innovation at widely spaced intervals, to what the historian of technology A. P. Usher calls 'continuously emergent *novelty*'.[48]

Thomas Newcomen got his idea of a steam engine that exploited vacuum and atmospheric pressure from the scientists at the Royal Society, but it would not have come about without his experiences of flooded mines and his skills as an ironmonger. The brewer James Prescott Joule was inspired by the scientist John Dalton to experiment with electrical motors to produce ale. This led Joule to discover the law of conservation of energy. His findings were first resisted and his papers rejected, but eventually the curious brewer convinced the scientists. The derived unit of energy, the joule, is named after him.

Mankind has always stumbled upon better ways of doing things and, because of our propensity to imitate, they have spread quickly in mobile societies, but until around 1750 those technologies had very narrow epistemic bases. In other words, we had little understanding of what we were actually doing, and that made it difficult to keep improving it. It was, in Mokyr's words, a world of:

engineering without mechanics, iron-making without metal-lurgy, farming without soil science, mining without geology, water-power without hydraulics, dye-making without organic chemistry, and medical practice without microbiology and immunology.[49]

During this industrial enlightenment, people systematized what was learned in workshops, mines and experiments. By apply-ing that science to technology it became possible to consciously manipulate materials, machines and methods, debug and improve and adapt them to changing circumstances and new uses. 'The age is running mad after innovation; and all the business of the world is to be done in a new way,' complained Samuel Johnson.[50]

This culture was reinforced when it had proof of concept. Peo-ple were not just sold a new narrative, they saw that it worked – not just in large and noisy steam engines that gave men the power of giants, but just as importantly in cheap and comfortable underwear for the first time in history. Balloons gave people the ability to defy gravity, but there were also better nails and screws. Railways and steamships made it possible to cross huge distances, and inoculation saved people from smallpox.

People could see it in their own living standards. The Indus-trial Revolution is often described as a time of terrible poverty and awful working conditions. Compared to our times, that is definitely the case, but this conclusion conveniently ignores the much more horrifying living standards in rural areas and non-industrialized towns that made an escape to a factory town seem like the best hope for millions. It was in Dickens' dirty Lon-don that real wages for workers doubled in less than a century for the first time anywhere. In 1900, the industrialized areas of Europe were more than three times richer than non-industrialized south-ern Europe.[51] If capitalism and industrialism meant shameless exploitation, the only thing worse than being exploited was not being exploited at all, and they created the resources to combat the nasty social side effects of development. As Deirdre McCloskey writes:

> Modern economic growth has led to more, not less refinement, for hundreds of millions who would otherwise have been poor and ignorant – as were, for example, most of your ancestors and mine. Here are you and I, learnedly discussing the merits and demerits of capitalism. Which of your or my ancestors would have the leisure or education of a Colquhoun or a Coleridge to do that?[52]

Previously cultures had been defined by the landed and hereditary classes and, at best, its ideas and expressions trickled slowly down to the lower classes. Greater freedoms, literacy and purchasing power gave new classes more self-confidence and a chance to steer cultural demand. Increasingly they read novels, bought newspapers, went to the theatre and looked at new forms of art and decoration. New fashions started in the growing middle classes in cities and trickled up to the traditional elite – and this elite has not stopped complaining about mass culture since.

It was a time for innovation in the arts as well. In dizzyingly quick succession Romanticism was followed by Realism, Neo-Classicism, Naturalism, Expressionism and Symbolism. There was also a breakdown in traditional distinctions, both between genres and intended audience. British music-hall and American vaudeville became wildly popular after the 1850s with their combination of song, satire and comic acts for an audience who could eat and drink during performances. The same themes were later incorporated into the new motion-picture industry. Art magazines were published with colour lithographs and soon photographs. New styles like Art Nouveau combined fine arts and applied arts, and many of the artists had the ambition to mass-produce furniture, metalwork, glass art and ceramics to democratize design and put it into people's homes.

With increasing wealth also came more leisure. Urban populations assembled in restaurants and cafes, and got access to parks and museums. Taking the train to the beach became a favourite pastime, even for factory workers. Team sports, like football, gained standardized rules and were increasingly played in schools. Britain and other rapidly industrializing countries also saw a tremendous growth in civil society organizations and associations. People came together for entertainment, mutual assistance and to advocate for women's rights, against slavery and other social issues.

One of the most transformative changes was the cultural approval of romantic love. Previously marriage had been considered a political or financial institution, and therefore arranged by older relatives. Marrying for love was seen as a selfish betrayal of the family, which needed a supply of manpower and useful in-laws in the struggle for survival. The American historian Stephanie Coontz described how this changed after the advent of Enlightenment ideas and the market economy with its wage labour, which made children less dependent on their parents. Suddenly personal choice was seen as desirable and practicable, and individuals were encouraged to marry for love. 'For the first time in five thousand years, marriage came to be seen as a private relationship between two individuals rather than one link in a larger system.'[53]

The American revolution

What made the world safe for progress was the fact that Britain's openness was transmitted by its colonists over the Atlantic to America. There it would be used to create the most powerful country on earth, one with a lasting effect on the ideas and political systems of countries around the world.

This new world was never hospitable to old ideas. The English elites didn't even manage to establish hierarchical colonies with enforced labour after the Spanish model. When the royally chartered Virginia Company founded Jamestown in 1607, they quickly found there was no gold to steal and they could not force the dispersed native groups to work for them. Plan B, which was to force the English settlers to work for subsistence ratios, also failed because too many escaped to live with the natives or to try their own luck (even though this was punishable by death). When all else failed, the only way to create viable colonies was to give settlers freedom. In 1618, they were freed from their contracts, received a title to a plot of land and market incentives to invest, build and produce.

Again and again, English elites tried to create authoritarian communities abroad with lords and subjects, but every time it broke down when settlers demanded economic freedom and a voice in governing the colony. The settlers who got their freedom did not necessarily believe in freedom for others more than the conquistadores or the Virginia Company. Many of them instituted their own system of coercion by importing slaves from Africa and took any opportunity to push native Americans off their land. But the mode of colonization was to have a profound influence on the political traditions of North America. Starting in Jamestown, the English colonies created general assemblies based on a franchise of all male property holders. As Acemoglu and Robinson wrote: 'It was the start of democracy in the United States.'[54]

In 1776, the settlers in America eventually made their own revolution against the British. It was for many of the same reasons, inspired by the same kind of ideas. The pioneer historian who unlocked the secrets of the revolutionary atmosphere of ideas was Caroline Robbins, who made the same journey as the colonists once did. In 1926, she became the first woman to earn a PhD in history from the University of London, but moved to

Bryn Mawr College in the US, so she was well placed to trace the intellectual connections between the two continents. In her 1959 work *The Eighteenth-Century Commonwealthman* Robbins showed that, in order to understand the revolution of 1776, we have to understand the English Civil War and the ideas swirling around afterwards. She followed generations of pamphleteers and dissenters, and documented that they were in an ongoing, long-lasting dialogue with the radicalism of the Civil War era and Lockean Whiggism. They carried ideals like free thought, religious liberty and equality before the law over the Atlantic and stirred up revolutionary fervour. The old British resentment at being governed by a distant despotic king took on a heightened, almost feverish character when this king was on the other side of an ocean.

The American Declaration of Independence reads a bit like an executive summary (or at least a poetic summary) of Locke's *Two Treatises*, and Thomas Jefferson called Locke's book 'perfect'. He considered Locke, Newton and Bacon the three greatest men to have ever lived.[55] In a study of pre-revolutionary America, Bernard Bailyn finds that Locke was invoked by writers all the time, 'as if he could be relied on to support anything the writers happened to be arguing'. Locke could only be matched in influence by the 144 widely distributed essays called *Cato's Letters*, written by the radical Lockeans John Trenchard and Thomas Gordon.[56]

There is no better proof of the global influence of the American revolution than the fact that the French king Louis XVI came to regret supporting the American colonies against Britain. That was all power politics to him, but the consequence was that the world saw that simple settlers could govern themselves better than a powerful monarch could. Suddenly the idea of an open society was not just a dream. The restless French masses adopted that lesson and attempted to follow it themselves in 1789, with less success.

A perfect rage

While Britain was industrializing, America was still an agrarian economy, and not a very relevant one to world affairs – a small population far away from the world's economic and political centre. But, to an even larger extent than Britain, the economy and culture of the US was open. While the British had to avoid, evade and dilute old hierarchies, the Americans could start anew without them. This was a country without kings, aristocrats, state church or even remnants of guilds and feudalism. The Declaration of Independence did not state that the goal of government was faith, order and tradition, but each individual's life, liberty and pursuit of happiness.

The Constitution turned the country into a unified common market without internal tariffs and borders. Migration was open and people came from all corners of the world, bringing their ideas and skills, and were allowed to experiment with them in new organizations and business ventures spanning the whole continent. New steamboats on the extensive river system opened the West, and in record time, railways were built to bind the continent together. By 1905, fully 14 per cent of the world's railway mileage passed through a single US city, Chicago. Immigrants started to settle a land abundant in resources that had lain dormant. Between the end of the Civil War and the start of World War I, the new Americans brought 400 million acres of virgin land under cultivation – a quantity almost twice the size of Western Europe.[57]

Many technologies were imported wholesale. Samuel Slater became known as the 'Father of the American Industrial Revolution' by Americans but as 'Slater the Traitor' by the English because he memorized industrial designs as an apprentice in a cotton mill in England before escaping to New York in 1789, which textile workers were not allowed to do. There, Slater replicated the machines and founded a series of spinning mills.

With a sense for business and a belief in the ability to move from rags to riches, innovation also became a folk activity. People in small-town attics and in crop fields got creative even in humble pursuits. The number of patents for horseshoes leapt from fewer than five annually before 1840 to an amazing thirty or forty every year in 1890–1910. Since the US government set the patent fee at only 5 per cent of what the British government charged, it was possible for a much larger share of the population to participate.[58]

Oliver Evans, a country boy from Newport, Delaware, invented a high-pressure steam engine for factories and steamboats and created the world's first automatic production line, half a century before Henry Ford was born. It is typical of the times that Henry David Thoreau, now remembered as a transcendentalist poet and for his reflections on the simple life by Walden, was also an inventor and a leading producer of pencils, based on his idea of using graphite with clay as a binder.

'Young America,' declared Abraham Lincoln, 'has a great passion – a perfect rage – for the "new".' Lincoln, who himself was awarded a patent for a device to lift boats over shoals, thought that if Americans could endure anything old 'it is only old whiskey and old tobacco'.[59]

Quicker than other countries, the Americans turned steel, oil, electricity and the internal combustion engine into consumer goods for the common man. America soon caught up with its old colonial master Britain in technology, wealth and power, and then surpassed it. In 1800, the British economy was more than twice as large as the American one. A hundred years later, despite rapid growth in the UK, the American economy was more than twice as large as the British, and about to take over its global political role.

The humanitarian revolution

Other countries also started growing rapidly as they picked up open values and institutions similar to those in Britain and the US, and the technologies and business management practices these had made possible. This was the start of the Great Enrichment. It did much more than make us rich and save us from early deaths. It started a revolution in our moral sentiments, for the better. Many assume that the defining feature of the free market is the profit motive but, as Max Weber wrote, the impulse to acquisition has in itself nothing to do with capitalism, it:

> has existed among waiters, physicians, coachmen, artists, prostitutes, dishonest officials, soldiers, nobles, crusaders, gamblers, and beggars. One may say that it has been common to all sorts and conditions of men at all times and in all countries of the earth.[60]

What makes the free market different is that you can only make money by giving someone something they value more than the money it costs them. It was revolutionary. Other individuals and groups are no longer our enemies, and if we stop them from stealing our money and exploiting privilege and monopoly, the insights, work and projects of others do not threaten us. On the contrary, it creates a bigger pool of people, ideas, technologies, goods and services that can help us improve our lives and increase our productivity if we are open to it. If we do not have to restrain the enlightened self-interest of others, then we don't have to constantly control them and discriminate against them to protect ourselves. It means other countries are not by nature our adversaries and war is not inevitable. The advancement of other groups does not necessarily take something away from us, and we don't have to keep them down or out to protect ourselves. It's not dog eat dog; it's live and let live.

This was the worldview that inspired and facilitated the great classical liberal breakthroughs of the nineteenth century, the beginnings of democracy with a free press where different interests were allowed to compete in the political process. Barriers that had blocked and discriminated against other ethnic and religious groups also slowly began to be lifted. Women, who were all but considered men's property in most countries in 1800, slowly started to get rights to education, to work, to own, to inherit, and eventually to vote and stand for office. And this unleashed another economic revolution that would become more visible in the twentieth century, since the emancipation of women opened up societies to the ideas and energy of the other half of the population.

The most definitive achievement came in the ugliest sphere. In 1800, slavery was practised in almost all countries (or at least their colonies), just as it had been practised for ten thousand years. Slavery was so established that many who opposed slavery, like Washington and Jefferson, owned slaves, and it happened that slaves who were freed or rebelled got slaves of their own. But just a hundred years later, slavery had been abolished in most countries, after a tireless campaign from an abolitionist movement on both sides of the Atlantic. The British even established the West Africa Squadron to suppress the slave trade between 1808 and 1867. At its peak, it made up a sixth of the whole Royal Navy.

In an increasingly open society, where Anglo-American law began to accept obligations only in relation to consent, slavery started to seem like an anachronistic anomaly. The starting point of the classical liberals who began to set the agenda was self-ownership and voluntary exchange of ideas. 'Some propose that the social world of persons begin with a command, and some propose that it begins with an exchange,' wrote David M. Levy, who has brought this forgotten part of our history to life.[61] When liberal economists like Adam Smith attacked slave traders for being 'the refuse of the jails of Europe [...] whose levity, brutality, and baseness, so justly expose them to the contempt of the vanquished',[62] they actually had to fight the leading men of arts and literature who thought that natural hierarchies were somehow more dignified than supply and demand.

You might have used the phrase 'dismal science' to describe economics, but you might not know that it was coined by the celebrated traditionalist writer and historian Thomas Carlyle because he despised how market exchange undermined the white man's natural place at the top of creation. Carlyle thought the economists' ideal of 'letting men alone', even men of other races, made for a dreary, dismal world where people didn't know their rightful place. He preferred a hierarchical order where the black man is '*compelled* to work as he was fit, and to *do* the Maker's will who had constructed him'.[63] And this retrograde battle was supported by luminaries like John Ruskin and Charles Dickens.

Likewise, the historian Thomas Haskell argued that the new humanitarianism after 1750 was partly the result of a new way of perceiving human relations fostered by the market. He focused on the Quakers, who were both prominent business pioneers and leading campaigners for abolition and other humanitarian causes. Frequent market relations with strangers encouraged colour-blindness and a cosmopolitan sense that we are all individuals and therefore also responsible for how our actions affect others.[64]

Scholars who are more hostile to capitalism complain that emancipation and humanitarianism were just the result of bourgeois class interest. Friedrich Engels admitted that trade 'has an aspect wherein it pays homage to morality and humanity'. Since cooperation is lucrative, capitalism has brought about more peaceful habits and the fraternization of peoples. However, Engels still rejected it all because the bourgeoisie didn't do it for pure humanity but for profit. 'The more friendly, the more advantageous,' he wrote, and found it a hypocritical way of misusing morality for immoral purposes.[65] Viewed from a less moralistic perspective, a system of rules for production and exchange that makes even the immoral act moral does not seem like the bane of humanity, but more like its blessing.

The glorious failures of Europe

So, at last, we had a new world, 3000 per cent richer and infinitely better because, instead of the divine right of kings, we had individual rights. They may have been often honoured only in the breach, but they were at least widely honoured for the first time in history. It was a positive spiral. The more freedoms people got and the more open societies were to the participation of women, minorities and migrants, the more talent was unleashed.

This revolution started in the north-western corner of Europe, but it did not happen because these populations were somehow better or their rulers any wiser. It could have happened elsewhere – as proven by previous episodes of efflorescences – and it is not impossible anywhere, as shown by the recent wave of globalization, when countries that have opened up their economies have repeated this development: Eastern Europe, East Asia, and now even giants like China, India and Vietnam. They have been able to make the economic transition that the British pioneered, but in just a third or a fifth of the time, partly because they can leapfrog to the latest technologies, and make use of the insights and innovations already made.

Apart from a few eccentric voices, such global development is not what the prevailing establishment had in mind. They wanted order and control, just like elites in other regions, but they couldn't keep up with the ideas, skills and machines that could always move elsewhere. Those who managed to impose order, like the Spanish, lost out to those who couldn't. As the Danish-American historian Patricia Crone puts it: 'Europe failed: had it succeeded, it would have *remained* a pre-industrial society.'[66]

Indeed, the story of Europe's eventual triumph can be told as the story of its failures: the failures of kings and emperors to unify the European continent; of Church authorities to impose a single religious orthodoxy; and of monopolies and guilds to block new technologies and business models. This was not for a lack of trying.

Feudal lords in Western Europe were unable to uphold control after the bubonic plague in the fourteenth century decimated the workforce, and peasants demanded that labour markets replaced serfdom. Workers had many alternatives and independent towns to flee to. When the count of Flanders came across one of his runaway serfs on a visit to the town fair in Bruges and arrested him, city folk rushed to arms and chased the count out.[67] He had to return with a superior army to get him back, which obviously raised the cost of being a feudal lord. (This was a major difference from Eastern Europe, where landlords managed to expand holdings and deepen control of serfs after the plague.) After the Peasants' Revolt of 1381 captured London, authorities stopped imposing the Statute of Labourers, which had fixed wages, made it a crime to refuse work and move from home in search of better jobs.

The Catholic Church could not stay in charge of the continent, and none of the Protestant churches managed to take its place. The Habsburgs failed to snuff out independent-minded Dutch. Because of their example, British kings and guilds failed to control business, and those businesses failed to coordinate their monopolistic practices as they would have liked. The British could not build the hierarchical, extractive colonies in America they aspired to, and would in the end fail in preventing the colonists from declaring independence and creating a reservoir of freedom on the other side of the Atlantic.

And every time kings, oligarchs and priests failed to keep up with changes in behaviour, culture, technology, business and finance, a space opened up for experiments and surprises, and that is where the magic – the printing press, secular science, the steam engine, factories, financial markets, free trade, women's rights, abolition of serfdom – happened. Simply told, Europe failed its way to success.

In retrospect, it is easy to see that these advances, which were so fiercely contested and persecuted and only supported by a small, brave minority, made our modern world. And that openness in politics, economics and culture is the best way of assuring the continued, open-ended search for improvement. The only remaining, disturbing question is, if these institutions weren't planned or designed or even wanted – if they were in effect accidents of history, and allowed to linger because people were surprised by how well they worked – will they be able to survive in the long run?

Remember, only once in human history has a promising efflorescence not been cut short by the forces opposing openness. At least so far.

II

CLOSED

5

US AND THEM

'The "call of the tribe" – of that form of existence in which individuals enslave themselves [...] is heard time after time by nations and peoples and, even within open societies, by individuals and collectivities that struggle tirelessly to negate the culture of freedom.'

Mario Vargas Llosa

It must have been an amazing time to be alive. There was peace between the great powers. The world was racing towards more freedom, opportunities and wealth than ever before. Wars, famines and revolts seemed like a distant memory from a time when mankind was still immature and unenlightened. And every day people experienced the wonders of science and of technology. Diseases were cured, people could communicate at incredible distances and cross the world with fast means of transport. Poverty was defeated and the right to vote extended. Human rights were expanded to more groups, and justice was administered more humanely.

It was, in the words of one contemporary, tempting to look upon each completed decade as the prelude to a better one, and to conclude that we were 'on the straight and unfailing path toward the best of all worlds'.

If only.

The same forces of progress were at work in the era described above as they are today. But back then, it was not enough. Because this is how the Austrian novelist Stefan Zweig described the world before 1914, with its confident optimism about the future, right until it was smashed to bits by nationalism and militarism. In one particularly painful paragraph in *The World of Yesterday*, from which this description comes, Zweig wrote:

> I never loved that old earth more than in those last years before
> the First World War, never hoped more ardently for European
> unity, never had more faith in its future than then, when we
> thought we saw a new dawning. But in reality it was the glare
> of the approaching world conflagration.[1]

Writing in the 1930s and early 1940s, Zweig already found it difficult to describe to the young that sense of hopefulness and optimism that had animated the world just a few years before, since they had 'grown up amidst catastrophes, collapses, and crises, to which war has been a constant possibility and even a daily expectation'.

During the late nineteenth century, classical liberals warned that the colonial conquest of other peoples would come back to haunt Europe, as it created a more centralized, militaristic culture back home and replaced mutually beneficial trade with zero-sum imperial conquest abroad. In 1902, a disappointed Herbert Spencer, the British philosopher and sociologist, warned of the 're-barbarization' of the world, which would pit group against group, race against race, and nation against nation. By glorifying conquest and national superiority, 'an unceasing culture of blood-thirst' had emerged that was undoing civilization and would surely end in blood and tears.[2]

Mankind does not just create progress; from time to time we also undo it. Most of the time, we cooperate and trade peacefully, but once in a while we also start trade wars and real wars, we close borders and shut down new technologies, burn dissenters and persecute minorities. The historian Hugh Trevor-Roper invoked the witch-craze of the sixteenth and seventeenth centuries against the idea of uninterrupted development. There were witch-beliefs in the Dark Ages, of course, but the systematized persecution and the mass executions came *after* the Renaissance:

> it was not, as the prophets of progress might suppose, a lingering ancient superstition, only waiting to dissolve. It was a new explosive force, constantly and fearfully expanding with the passage of time. In those years of apparent illumination there was at least one-quarter of the sky in which darkness was positively gaining at the expense of light.[3]

The Ming dynasty turned its back on innovation and globalization; the Islamic Golden Age was quashed; the Ottomans, Persians, Mughals and Spanish ruined their empires by demolishing their foundations of openness. Europe was taken over by national socialists and communists, and tried to destroy itself twice in the twentieth century (or three times, counting the Cold War). At times, we go crazy and slit throats with industrial efficiency. Mass expulsions and massacres are commanded by despots but are put into effect by the people – even though we like to forget that afterwards, and point our finger to a single instigator. But why?

The painful truth is that the openness that has made life safer, richer and healthier than ever is awfully difficult to sustain. Openness often makes us uncomfortable, and we search for a kind of certainty and belonging that freedom does not guarantee. As I argued in Part I, mankind's ability to cooperate and exchange is the key to our success. But paradoxically this ability evolved as a tool for competition – to beat others.

Samuel Bowles, Director of the Behavioral Sciences Program at Santa Fe Institute, says:

> Warfare was sufficiently common and lethal among our ancestors to favour the evolution of what I call parochial altruism, a predisposition to be co-operative towards group members and hostile towards outsiders.[4]

Almost every example of altruism scientists have observed in the animal kingdom is an instance of individuals sacrificing themselves for genetically similar relatives. But humans care for and cooperate easily with complete strangers, we reward good deeds and punish those who violate social norms, even at a high personal cost. We are also parochial, favouring our group members over outsiders as partners and in the allocation of resources, even if they are not kin. Since both these strategies are costly, they have puzzled many evolutionary biologists. But Bowles believes parochial altruists who were willing to fight against others on behalf of their group members could have emerged and proliferated because of frequent combats. The small groups that cooperated the best were also more able to defend themselves and their resources, and it gave them the opportunity to hunt in teams and to kill competitors.[5]

After our ancestors learned they could defend themselves through collaborative stone throwing, we became the deadliest animal on the planet. No predator could ever defeat us again. The only thing that could defeat us now was *other people*. This started an intellectual arms race. The groups that were the most collaborative – those that could immediately set all their differences aside when they were threatened, and fight side by side – defeated the others. As the psychologist and neuroscientist Joshua Greene writes:

Biologically speaking, humans were designed for cooperation, but only with some people. Our moral brains evolved for cooperation within groups, and perhaps only within the context of personal relationships.[6]

Call it our original sin, but this cruel origin of some of our most impressive traits and moral attitudes still haunts us and guides us to do things in excited circumstances that shock our reflective selves into disbelief. It tempts us to constantly divide the world into Us and Them. It makes us suspicious of other groups and classes, outsiders, migrants and foreign countries, and it gives demagogues and dictators an opportunity to foment prejudice and violence against other groups, be they Jews, Muslims, argumentative women, Kulaks, Tutsis, Bosnians or gays.

Blues and reds, Rattlers and Eagles

It doesn't take differences in colour, creed or country to trigger our tribal instinct. I first learned about the power of group identification in school. In first grade I was assigned to class 1b in the Maltesholm School in Hässelby in western Stockholm. Quickly we in 1b began to think we were better and smarter than 1a, even though nothing but chance had put us where we were. We began to spread rumours (some of them not fit to print) about how bad the kids in 1a were. Most of the time this was very innocent, but a low-intensity rivalry was always there, and we always thought the best things in school – like the nicest classroom and new editions of textbooks – should go to us, and were very indignant when 1a got something we considered better. If a fight started between someone in our class and the others, we spontaneously took the side of our own classmate.

But our class was also divided in two groups, the blue and the red group, which dictated when we had maths and gymnastics and other subjects. I had been arbitrarily assigned to the blue group, and soon we came to think the blue group was the best and the red pupils were losers.

Years came and went, and as I got to know kids in the red group I realized I had things in common with some of them. But the major change came later, which united red and blue group, and 6a and 6b (because we were now getting older): a common enemy. Our school was merged with the Trollboda school, and suddenly we were supposed to go side by side with the 'Trollboda-lice', as we called them. They looked just like us and came from the same background, but they came from far away (3.2 kilometres, to be exact). We didn't know them, so obviously we sensed a threat. If a fight broke out, we would spontaneously take the side of the good, decent kids from Maltesholm, even if they belonged to the red group or 6a.

In a modest way, my experience at school bears some resemblance to one of the most famous psychology experiments about group bias and conflict. In the summer of 1954, twenty-two boys from Oklahoma City schools were sent to a camp in the Robbers Cave State Park, Oklahoma. The eleven- and twelve-year-old boys – all white, middle-class and Protestant – were separated into two groups that got to befriend each other in isolation. When the existence of the other group was revealed on the sixth day, relations quickly became hostile.

The two groups called themselves Rattlers and Eagles and soon came up with symbols that they imprinted on their shirts, and invented traditions and norms. A high-status Rattler hurt his toe without saying anything, so Rattlers decided that they were tough, and since they were tough they also took up swearing. And because the Eagles wanted to set themselves apart, they banned cursing and organized prayer sessions. The macho Rattlers saw Eagles as 'sissies' and 'babies', while the pious Eagles called the Rattlers 'bums'. Boys who deviated from their group were rapidly brought into line.

In the second week, the teams engaged in competitive activities like baseball and tug of war, and shortly things descended into regular conflict and vandalism. Fights broke out and the staff had to keep the groups separate to avoid injuries. In just two weeks, boys who were the same in most important respects had created two separate tribes with different norms, treated each other as enemies and held their noses when they were near each other. Muzafer Sherif, the social psychologist who designed the experiment, had proven his point: conflict did not require any natural differences between groups, but could be provoked between any set of groups if they were placed in a context of rivalry and struggle over limited resources. He believed only a common, overriding goal could unite the rival groups, and attempted to illustrate this in the third week.

The Robbers Cave experiment received attention all around the world. That same year, William Golding illustrated how well-educated boys could rapidly become tribal savages in his novel *Lord of the Flies*. But here was a real-life experiment showing how little it takes to get well-adjusted boys from the same background to start to hate and hurt other boys. We have a tendency to think in terms of ingroup and outgroup and act accordingly, even though differences between groups may be trivial or non-existent. Some sort of 'ethnocentrism' is a universal trait in all cultures, according to anthropologist Donald Brown.[7]

It's not that we aren't empathic enough, it's that ingroup love often turns to outgroup hate. A recent study showed that people who score highly on an empathy scale are also more negative against a political outgroup. Students prone to empathy are actually more likely than those low in empathy to be amused by reports that a student with opposite political views had been injured.[8]

In *Danube*, Italian scholar Claudio Magris explained that fascism is not the love of one's friends, family and homeland. It is to love one's friends, family and homeland, but also fail to realize that other people, in other places, who look different, love their friends, family and homeland too.[9] This is how ingroup orientation distorts our perspective.

Minimal group paradigm

Muzafer Sherif was desperate to understand why compassion within groups was matched by savagery against outsiders. As a young man he had seen the vicious ethnic warfare during the dying days of the Ottoman Empire. Armenian boys suddenly disappeared from his school, and he was almost killed when Greek soldiers occupied his city and indiscriminately killed Turks.

Another psychologist, Henri Tajfel, had also witnessed group hatred up close. A Polish Jew, he saw his whole family murdered during the Holocaust. While others had speculated that irrational emotions and authoritarian personalities could explain Nazi violence, Tajfel could not bring himself to believe it, since he had seen so many normal Germans supporting the atrocities. Instead, he thought that prejudice was the result of natural forms of social categorization that had spiralled out of control.

In a series of experiments, Tajfel and his colleagues measured ingroup bias when groups were based on irrelevant differences. These studies were intended to give a baseline for comparisons, and then the researchers could add negative stereotypes and other conditions to see what created conflict. But disappointingly, they didn't have to do that. People expressed ingroup loyalty and outgroup discrimination just by being included in a group, even though differences were trivial and they did not know who the other members were, had never met them and couldn't even hear them.

In one study, students were shown paintings by Wassily Kandinsky and Paul Klee, asked to express their preferences, and then divided into groups they were told were based on those preferences. With no contact, no dispute, no value conflict and no possibility for personal gain, the expectation was that no discrimination would take place. But when a 'Kandinsky student' was asked to allocate rewards to strangers anonymously, he preferred other Kandinskys to Klees. But worse, the students wanted to create as large a difference as possible between members of the two groups, even if it meant a lower reward for the members of their own group. The subjects didn't want to maximize the gain of the ingroup, they wanted to beat the outgroup as much as possible.[10]

In a follow-up study, they devised groups where members were aware that the grouping was completely randomized. Astonishingly, even then, subjects assigned to different groups on the basis of a coin toss showed an ingroup bias.[11] The simple fact of thinking of people as members of a group activates something within us that wants 'us' to beat 'them'. And that makes perfect sense when you consider that our tribalism evolved during a more dangerous period when beating the outgroup was more important to our survival than slow progress.[12]

This tendency is sometimes referred to as 'Vladimir's choice', after an Eastern European fable. God appears before Vladimir, a poor peasant farmer, and tells him he will grant him one wish. Before Vladimir chooses, God adds a caveat: 'Anything I give to you will be granted to your neighbour Ivan, twice over.' Vladimir frowns, contemplates, and suddenly lights up as he concocts the perfect plan: 'OK, take out one of my eyes.'[13]

We don't act like this individually, of course, which is why Vladimir's choice seems so comical. But we do collectively when we frame situations in terms of competing groups. Then we prefer maximum difference to maximum profit.

Since Tajfel's pioneering experiments, many other studies have documented our ingroup favouritism. Our ability to form new partnerships and alliances is so strong that we become loyal to arbitrary groups, and think those in our own group are smarter, better and more moral than others. We attribute bad behaviour in our group members as single instances that can be explained, but the same behaviour in an outgroup as evidence of bad character. And we experience ourselves as a group of diverse individuals, but an outgroup as a homogenous collective. We are better at remembering information that confirms our stereotypes, and when our self-esteem or the value of our group is threatened we become more positive to the ingroup and more prejudiced against outsiders.[14]

Tajfel's minimal groups revealed something even more problematic than Muzafer Sherif's ideas about 'realistic conflict theory'. Sherif suggested that discrimination and conflict had a rational basis in a real conflict about power and resources. Obviously, this can make any kind of conflict much more intense, but Tajfel showed there does not have to be any conflict there at all; it is enough for us to perceive a difference, without any basis in economics or politics.

Our insistence on loyalty to arbitrary group norms is also related to what is known as the Behavioural Immune System. We are engaging in a primitive form of preventive medicine every time we avoid someone with a runny nose, a cough or a rash. This unconscious reaction was developed long before we had any understanding of microorganisms and it is necessarily oversensitive since the consequences of missing a sign of disease could be fatal. Therefore, anyone who seems to deviate from what is normal can trigger this gut reaction of discomfort or disgust. It could be that someone has a different skin colour, another sexual orientation, alternative clothing or even a physical disability, even though they pose no disease threat at all.[15] It can even be extended to 'unnatural' technologies.

It has been shown that people who are more afraid of germs express more negative attitudes against foreigners, which is one reason why those who want to whip up hostility against minorities often compare them to animals or talk about them as dirty.

'Tremendous infectious disease is pouring across the border,' as Donald Trump has described Mexican immigration.

We know a lot about the differences and complexities within our group, but outsiders can seem like a big, threatening blob. People who are afraid of spiders think spiders are bigger than they are and move faster than they do.[16] Likewise, rival groups actually seem to be physically closer than they are, which indicates that our beliefs about the world are often related to threat perception. A fascinating study showed that New York Yankees fans thought Fenway Park, the stadium of a rival team, was closer than it really was, while non-fans did not think so. New York University affiliates thought prestigious Columbia University was closer to them than it really was, when they read a threatening comparison with Columbia, while they did not make the same mistake with a neutral university.[17] This might explain why nativists grossly exaggerate the number of immigrants in their country.

Studies show we discriminate from a very early age, before we have learned this behaviour from any societal structures. In one experiment, nine- and fourteen-month-old babies showed aggressive tribalism based on nothing more than taste in food. Researchers checked if the babies preferred green beans or crackers, and then showed them rabbit puppets with the same and the opposite food preference being alternatively helped or hurt by dog puppets in a ball game. In the next phase, the babies got to reach for one of the dog puppets. It turned out that the babies actually preferred the dog that hurt the rabbit with the opposite taste in crackers and beans, to the dog that helped that rabbit.[18]

Rooting for the clothes

None of this comes as a surprise to anyone familiar with the curious human physical activity called sports. Rarely is tribalism on more public display than during sporting competitions. Football teams are made up of a constantly changing group of players from all over the world, and sometimes the player you booed in the rival team becomes an admired part of your own, yet these football teams inspire total devotion in a substantial segment of the population. In some the sport also arouses hostility, hatred and even violence against other teams' supporters. As comedian Jerry Seinfeld put it: 'Loyalty to any one sports team is pretty hard to justify, because the players are always changing; the team could move to another city. You're actually rooting for the clothes when you get right down to it.'

In one disturbing study, male football fans' brains were scanned while they watched others receive electric shocks through electrodes on the backs of their hands. When they saw a fellow supporter in pain, regions associated with empathy were activated, but when supporters of a rival team were in pain, activity was elicited in a region associated with reward instead. It seems like they derived pleasure from the misfortune of the outgroup.[19]

A Dutch study of football violence showed that hooligan tribes were a mix of different ethnicities and of both poor, working-class and higher-income men, so there were no 'real' loyalties lurking in the background. These men risked their lives and health for team colours.[20]

That has a long history. In the Roman and Byzantine empires, aggressive factions supported chariot-racing teams. In Constantinople, the fans of the different racing teams the 'Blues' and the 'Greens' turned into something between hooligans and political parties, and often came to blows. In 532, one mass riot threatened the rule of Emperor Justinian, who supported the Blues, resulting in large parts of the city being destroyed, and perhaps thirty thousand people killed, mostly Greens.

And lest you think only sports fans are susceptible to group influence, a study of politically interested American college students should also be mentioned. Democratic students prefer a generous welfare policy and Republican students a stringent one, unless they are told that their own party supports the other policy. When told that their party endorsed it, the subjects switched position, and Democrats preferred a harsh welfare programme and Republicans a lavish one. Of course, they claimed this belief was guided by nothing but an evaluation of the objective content of the policy, but in effect they were rooting for the political label.[21]

It sounds like we are all crazy. But in fact, instinctively rooting for clothes and labels is not that surprising: we are an animal that survived and prospered because it cooperated in groups that became so large they couldn't identify one another without culturally acquired identity markers – dialect, dress, hairstyle, make-up, manner.

The human brain is not a general-purpose computer, free from input, as assumed by the thinkers who believed in the 'tabula rasa', the blank slate. Recent breakthroughs in evolutionary psychology – informed by neuropsychology, genetics and paleobiology and other sciences – have painted a new picture of the brain as a large and heterogenous network of modules, specialized to solve different problems. It's more like the internet than a computer. This is why people who have pulled over on a bridge to throw themselves to a certain death actually lock their car before they do so: it's not that they make a conscious decision that they might be coming back and want the car untouched, it is that one part of the brain deals with the automatic protection of belongings and is not always affected by even the most dramatic news from other parts. Humans have reasoning instincts that make particular inferences effortless when a cue alerts us to the fact that we face a particular problem type. It doesn't entirely dictate our behaviour, in the way that animals are commanded by their instincts, but it takes a conscious effort to revise and overrule them.

This saves us a lot of computing power, but since these evolved circuits are inherited from our ancestral environment, they sometimes lead us to solve the wrong problem at the wrong time. We still want to eat all the sugar we see, because we think that pizza and Coke are 'in bloom' only this week. Similarly, we are still more afraid of snakes and spiders than cars and cigarettes. And we still want to belong to our group, and are suspicious of others, because once upon a time it made cooperation possible. If a group of people regularly go through the efforts to hunt, gather and build shelters, they also need a way to recognize those who contributed, so that they are not exploited by freeloaders. And since other groups pose a threat to their territory and even their lives, they develop an expert ability to recognize outsiders. We pay close attention to where anyone who crosses our path fits into our social universe, and we favour people the closer they are to us.

Nastiest and nicest

This paradox suggests the answer to a number of fundamental questions about humanity: is mankind by nature good or evil? Are we the noble savages of Rousseau's impression (corrupted by modern civilization) or are we the aggressive egotists as Hobbes thought (pacified by strong governments)? Are we like chimpanzees – whose societies are based on violence and domination, and who kill chimpanzees from other groups for the simple reason that they can – or are we more like their calm and peaceful cousins bonobos, who seem fairly tolerant and often relieve social tensions with sex?

The reason we can find good arguments for both worldviews is that they each mirror one half of our nature. We are calmer than other animals in most situations, but under certain circumstances we are so aggressive that we don't hesitate to kill on a huge scale. In the words of the anthropologist Richard Wrangham, 'We can be the nastiest of species and also the nicest.'[22] We are like bonobos within our group, but easily behave like chimpanzees between groups. Peace at home and war abroad. In fact, we are much more peaceful than bonobos in everyday life (who are more violent in the wild than when observed in captivity), but with the potential to be much more aggressive than chimpanzees, who have never engaged in industrial war and planned genocide. A chimpanzee would never be able to enter a subway train and sit next to strangers without starting a fight, but then a chimpanzee would never enter a subway train with a bomb in his backpack (even if he could build one), intent on killing people for a religious or political cause.

In his book *The Goodness Paradox*, Wrangham explains that humans behave in this way because we are a self-domesticated species.[23] We are much less reactive than the great apes and our common ancestors. We don't regularly lose our temper and lash out. We don't constantly charge at each other to demand submission from the other. This is essential to sustain the mutual gain that made civilization possible. Humans regularly share food and cooperate to get more of it. In contrast, when two chimpanzees enter a room with food, normally only one of them will be fed.

But how did this come about? Peaceful relations and cooperative behaviour are better for the group and for the species in the long term, but that does not explain the transition. Evolution is not that simple. As some people became more docile, it would have made it easier for the violent to dominate them. So how did we escape their tyranny? It turns out that Charles Darwin was on to something when he wrote, in 1871, that 'Violent and quarrelsome men often come to a bloody end.'

According to Wrangham, evidence suggests those men who consistently bullied and abused others and took more than their share were quite often executed if they persisted. The evolution of language made it possible for the rest of the band to whisper about the alpha male and plan on killing him in his sleep or when he was unarmed. Often, all the men in the group stabbed the despot, to show that it was a common decision. Everybody had to be in on it so as to avoid a cycle of retaliation (even the Brutus characters who had been close to him).

The consequences for the human race were revolutionary. It removed much of the would-be bullies' reactive aggression from the gene pool, making life safer for the more docile and tolerant so that they could procreate. We became expert cooperators by removing the uncooperative. But at the same time, this process helped to make our violence more devious – the planned, deliberate attack, guided by a motive (a grievance, retaliation, material gain) rather than by sudden aggression – and turned us into experts in collaborative violence. Chimpanzees also retaliate violently when they think they have been wronged, but only humans retaliate in a group.

The reason thinkers have not been able to agree on whether the human race is violent or peaceful is that they have thought about aggression as a continuum from more to less. The key to solving the puzzle is to understand that reactive and proactive violence are two different forms of aggression. One is 'hot', the other is 'cold'.

Our 'cold', calculated violence can quickly spiral out of control even more than the reactive kind if we don't check it (through justice systems and other institutions). One reason is that we are much more aware of the pain we suffer than the pain we inflict on others. This is partly because we hear more about it. Both media and our friends and family are eager to convey news that is relevant to our group, so we always learn more about disasters that befall people who are similar to us. But we also tend to underestimate the pain we inflict ourselves. In an interesting experiment, participants took turns pressing with their right index finger on a force transducer resting on the other's left index finger. They were told to apply exactly the same force that the other participant had just used. However, they always overestimated the force the other had used, and underestimated the force they used themselves, so the force escalated quickly. After less than ten turns, the partici-pants were pushing down on each other's fingers almost twenty times harder than in the original push.[24]

If you have kids, you are familiar with this scenario. Both will say the other one hit harder. This study shows they may both actu-ally think they're telling the truth. The world of geopolitics and terrorism is far from these simple sensory perceptions, but it is easy to see how this biased awareness leads to events spiralling out of control. 'The others provoked us, right?' We just responded proportionally, and they suddenly went mad. They asked for war. It's not an eye for an eye, but two eyes for an eye, as the researchers point out.

Going back to Wrangham's theory about how humans domes-ticated themselves, the threat of being executed by your own band must have focused everybody's mind (to say the least) on how their behaviour was viewed by others. The absence of a dominant male resulted in a dominant group of adult men who reinforced adher-ence to group norms and traditions. Instead of the alpha male we got what has been called the 'tyranny of the cousins'. Wrangham observes that, once this system is in place, a few words from a sen-ior member of the group should be enough to remind anyone of the importance of conformity.

It has been suggested that this is why we are so obsessed with what others think of us and why we are so afraid of being criti-cized. We are eager to conform to the views and behaviour of our peers because conformists don't run the risk of being ostracized or killed for being out of line. As the social psychologist Jonathan Haidt writes: 'The first rule in a dense web of gossip is: be careful what you do. The second rule is: what you do matters less than what people think you did, so you'd better be able to frame your actions in a positive light.'[25] To this we can add a third rule: if you have broken group norms in a way that is undeniable, you should accept blame and show remorse. It helps if you blush.

This is necessary background when we try to understand humans' need for recognition and to belong to something bigger than ourselves, a group with common experiences or memories. Nothing is worse than the feeling of being invisible, forgotten or rejected by your group. Today it kills us more slowly through stress hormones, blood pressure and drugs, but once upon a time it killed us quickly, as we became defenceless against the elements, animals and other humans. That is why we might be willing to do horrible things to maintain group integrity. It is also why an important political trigger for tribalism today is the feeling that 'the government doesn't care about people like me'.

At the same time, it is wrong to portray us as solely collective beings. It's complicated. We want to fit in, but we also want to stand out and have our own individual lives, reaching our personal life goals. This tension is the source of many of the conflicts involved in the human condition. Many who have left the hunter-gatherer lifestyle grumble that life in the band was like something out of *Nineteen Eighty-Four* – you are being watched and judged every second, and the group can do whatever it likes with you, your relationships and possessions.[26] Remember, a dominant group of adult men is not seen as a cuddly camaraderie of cousins by most members, but a *tyranny* of cousins.

Fluid tribalism

If we have strong ingroup biases when groups are artificial, it is easy to see how much stronger this tendency becomes if we think of group differences as ancient and natural – if they are based on, say, colour, creed or country – or when symbols and clothes are not arbitrary but reflect an important part of our identity. What hope is there, then, to ever find a way to coexist peacefully in a global world?

In April 1994, masses of Tutsis sought shelter from Hutu

militias at a Benedictine convent in Sovu, Rwanda. Instead of protecting them, the mother superior, Sister Gertrude, a Hutu, called in the militants, who hacked the refugees to death with machetes and hoes. However, she did not turn over the Tutsi nuns. Their identity as Catholics was more important to her than their ethnicity. Seeing that the veils saved the lives of the nuns, a nineteen-year-old Tutsi, Aline, begged Sister Gertrude for a veil. Aline had spent time in the convent because she was considering taking her vows but, since she had not yet done so, Sister Gertrude categorized her more according to ethnicity than religion. She refused to give her a veil, and Aline was murdered. 'My daughter was killed because of a little piece of cloth,' Aline's mother said at the trial seven years later.[27]

The fact that we are wired for tribalism does not mean we are wired for any particular kind of tribal mentality. In all its awfulness, this example shows that. Had Sister Gertrude only seen ethnic groups, she would have condemned all Tutsis in the convent to a swift, brutal death. But whenever she came upon a Tutsi woman who had taken her vows, she put away one map of human groups, and read the world according to another. And this is what we do all the time, consciously or unconsciously.

As Amartya Sen writes in *Identity & Violence*: 'A Hutu laborer from Kigali may be pressured to see himself only as a Hutu and incited to kill Tutsis, and yet he is not only a Hutu, but also a Kigalian, a Rwandan, an African, a laborer and a human being.'[28] And since we contain multitudes, we always have a choice in determining what is relevant. We constantly invent and reinvent us – and them.

Skin colour and other traits associated with race might seem like a stable division by which we judge people. However, our evaluation of their meaning shifts and changes. In the late eighteenth century, European racial attitudes began to harden, and became an obsession, with terrible consequences. One reason was the need to rationalize the transatlantic slave trade and colonial projects. It was not easy to subject, enslave and sometimes exterminate whole populations while also sleeping well at night and thinking of yourself as a decent family father – unless you could convince yourself that they were some sort of inferior beings. But such views are not inevitable.

Travelling by foot, most early human hunter-gatherers would not even once in their lifetime have met a single individual who could have been reasonably described as belonging to a different 'race', no matter how you define it. Skin colour might be very important if it predicts coalitional membership in a particular country or circumstance, but the number of interracial encounters would quite simply not have been enough in our prehistory to wire our cognitive machinery for them. It is more likely that it is a placeholder for group identity when we don't know more about a person.

This has been illustrated by a fascinating experiment where students followed an argument between two mixed-race teams of basketball players, and then were subjected to a surprise memory test where they were asked to pair sentences with photos of the players who said it. The subjects were sufficiently aware of skin colour to rarely attribute a sentence from a white man to a black man. However, when the researchers introduced a marker of team membership, like different-coloured shirts, this all changes. Suddenly students forgot to care that much about race and instead focused more on team membership. Now they were better at pairing sentences with players according to which team they belonged to. The subjects had lived in a world where race is constantly observed, discussed and weaponized politically, and yet less than four minutes of exposure to another, artificial way of categorizing the social world reduced their perception of it dramatically. 'This implies that coalition, and hence race, is a volatile, dynamically updated cognitive variable, easily overwritten by new circumstances,' according to the researchers.[29] We are, in fact, just like Seinfeld's football fans, rooting for the clothes.

It seems like a new and arbitrary grouping can be encoded just as strongly as race – or even more strongly. Interestingly, the above experiment showed it is not the same case with sex. Even if you introduce different-coloured shirts, the respondents rarely attributed words from a man to a woman and vice versa. Sex was always encoded more strongly than team membership. And that makes sense evolutionarily. Few of our forager ancestors ever encountered anyone of a different skin colour so it is not a deep evolutionary category. But they met men and women every day, and they differ in ways that were more important to our ancestors.

Authorities who play on tribalism understand this. Realizing how attributes in common lead us to disregard old group divisions, leaders have often forced minorities to wear special clothes or symbols. In 1215, Pope Innocent III decided that, in order to stop spontaneous mixing, Jews and Muslims 'shall be marked off in the eyes of the public from other peoples through the character of their dress'.[30] Local laws put this into effect by forcing them, for example, to wear a turban, a cone-shaped 'Judenhut', a red Star of David or a badge over their breast, usually white or yellow. The Nazis reintroduced this idea with even more sinister motives, by forcing all Jews to wear a yellow Star of David.

The way we classify people according to context has been documented again and again. It is a widely held belief that people are better at remembering people from their own race (the 'they all look alike' effect), and it is often explained by the fact that we spend more time with people who look like ourselves and so are able to differentiate between them better. But one study suggests this has little to do with race and is actually more concerned with members of our group. Two researchers assigned people to arbitrary mixed-race groups ('Moons' and 'Suns', for example). They showed them pictures of members of both groups and then gave them a memory test. Race had no effect on how well they remembered faces; they better remembered faces belonging to their own group, even if the grouping was itself arbitrary.[31]

The exception was people who had been assigned as a 'spy'. They had been told they were members of one group, but were ultimately supposed to be loyal to the other group. The spies had a good recollection of members of both groups, simply because that was relevant to their goal. With the right motivation, we can pay attention to the outgroup as well, and see individuals rather than just the collective. E. O. Wilson, a pioneer of the evolutionary study of social behaviour, saw this as a core human trait:

> Human beings are consistent in their codes of honor but endlessly fickle with reference to whom the codes apply. The genius of human sociality is in fact the ease with which alliances are formed, broken, and reconstituted, always with strong emotional appeals to rules believed to be absolute. The important distinction is today, as it appears to have been since the Ice Age, between the ingroup and the outgroup, but the precise location of the dividing line is shifted back and forth with ease.[32]

Our oversensitive smoke detector

This elastic tribalism makes evolutionary sense for a cooperative creature. In our violent prehistory, bumping into the outgroup in a dark alley could result in being rapidly taken out of the gene pool. If the stakes are that high, our vigilance must function like a smoke detector designed to give false alarms now and then, rather than miss a threat to our lives once in a while. But as we saw in chapter 1, some of the most successful early humans travelled large distances to trade and pick up new ideas and methods. Just like we had to be worried about potential hostilities from strangers, we had to be open to new opportunities for exchange with them. While an initial alertness was of value, so was an ability to rapidly switch to a friendly stance if the stranger seemed trustworthy and possessing abilities and resources that could be of value.

We constantly categorize people, and this helps us but also sometimes deceives us. Any kind of division will make us observe a particular difference between our group and that group. However, because of our adherence to group identity, we often exaggerate difference between groups or even entirely manufacture them. One example is the study of national character. When people are asked about the stereotypes they hold about different nations, we find they are very stable across cultures. But when we give people personality tests, we find the average national results bear little resemblance to the national stereotypes. It turns out our thoughts about neighbouring countries are sometimes little better than fiction.

For example, we all know that Canadians are agreeable, whereas Americans are neurotic and pushy. Even Canadians and Americans agree, and assume that between ten and fifteen standard deviations separate them on agreeableness and neuroticism – a colossal difference – but when you look at personality tests, Canadians and Americans almost score the same on those traits. It seems we develop such stereotypes partly to establish self-identity in relation to the other. However, this sometimes creates bizarre results – according to stereotypical characteristics, Canadians are more similar to Indians than Americans, and Chinese from Hong Kong are closer to Hungarians than they are to mainland Chinese.[33]

This is good news. It means that, even though we are wired for tribalism, none of the tribal divisions we are so obsessed with today is intractable. We are not necessarily doomed to tribal warfare. The coalitions we pay attention to can and do change all the time. This is why recent immigrants are almost always seen as strange and threatening, as described in chapter 2, whereas previous immigrants now seem like model citizens. They are no longer 'them', they are now 'us'. The problem, of course, is that this new identity is often created and strengthened by contrasting ourselves with new outsiders. The Rattlers in Robbers Cave became tough and Eagles pious almost by accident, but they immediately emphasized and reproduced those norms.

New conflict lines help us forget the old, which is just another example of how malleable our coalitions are. In 1963, the Robbers Cave experiment was repeated with eleven-year-old boys (eight Christians and ten Muslims, many from fiercely religious schools) in Beirut. Conflict soon broke out between the two groups – the Blue Ghosts and the Red Genies – and after three boys had threatened one boy with a knife, the experiment was called off. No one familiar with Beirut's fractured history would be surprised, but the fighting did not take place along religious lines. The three Genies with the knife were Christians, but so was the victim. In the camp, 'Ghost/Genie' quickly replaced religion as the most important division.[34]

Our evaluations of outgroups constantly change according to circumstances, even when groups stay the same. One study of American students in 1943 found that descriptions of Chinese and Japanese had switched places. The Chinese, who had been considered sly and treacherous in the 1930s, were now seen as reserved and courteous. The Japanese, who had been seen as artistic and progressive, were now described as sly and treacherous. Russians were brave and hard-working in 1942, but considered cruel and conceited in 1948.[35]

If it is tempting to conclude that tribalism is a weakness of the common man, and that elites and intellectuals are needed to moderate it, that is a misreading of history. Even though we all share this tribalist default setting, most people are good at constantly adapting perceptions of divisions in accordance with new experiences and meetings. Often it gets really dangerous only when elites and intellectuals use our groupishness to invent or cement a particular division ideologically or 'scientifically' and make us forget its fluidity. Karl Popper thought his own profession was responsible for stoking these group conflicts:

> Why do I think that we, the intellectuals, are able to help? Simply because we, the intellectuals, have done the most terrible harm for thousands of years. Mass murder in the name of an idea, a doctrine, a theory, a religion – is all our doing, our invention: the invention of intellectuals. If only we would stop setting man against man – often with the best intentions – much would be gained.[36]

Today, the nationalist Right in Europe are keen on telling the history of the continent through the prism of conflict between Christendom and Islam in an effort to convince us that a clash of civilizations is our destiny. The Battle of Vienna in 1683 – when the united Christian armies under the Polish-Lithuanian King John III Sobieski saved Europe from the Muslim Ottoman Empire – is an important part of this founding myth. But it didn't look like that back then. Europe had more important dividing lines than Christianity/Islam. Queen Elizabeth I of England, establishing a Protestant nation, allied with the Ottoman sultan in the late sixteenth century. The Bishop of Winchester declared the pope 'a more perilous enemy unto Christ, than the Turk; and Popery more idolatrous, than Turkery'.[37] In 1683, the Ottomans were allied with the Catholic French King Louis XIV, who feared the similarly Catholic Habsburg dynasty more than he feared Muslims. The French supported a Lutheran Protestant uprising in Hungary in 1678, who sought the support and vassalage of the Ottomans, and these united forces lay siege to Vienna, while France tied up Habsburg forces on the western front.

Neither was the other side religiously united. King John III broke the siege with the help of Sunni Muslim Tatars, descendants of refugees who got asylum in Lithuania in the late fourteenth century. King John III is not just a hero of the alt-right, but also of Muslims, since he was the regent who created a lasting Muslim community in north-eastern Poland by giving land to Tatars and securing the construction of mosques.

Political tribalism

New, seemingly intractable political fault lines – like 'Red/Blue' in the US and 'Brexiteer/Remainer' in Britain – offer exhibit A for many scholars examining our political tribalism. Our political parties are not just a vehicle for fixing potholes and creating jobs, but constitute a team to support.

In the 2016 primary elections Donald Trump was the Republican candidate who adhered the least to traditional conservative orthodoxy, but he was seen by many voters as the most reliable conservative for the simple reason that he was much better than the others at expressing his distaste of Hillary Clinton and the Democrats. When US students are queried about potential roommates, they consider it more of a turn-off if they vote for the other party than if the roommate described himself as 'not at all clean and tidy'. And this is not because of love for their fellow partisans; the desire not to live with someone from the outgroup is seven times bigger than the desire to live with one from their own party.[38] In another study, 77 per cent of Americans rated members of the other main political party as less evolved humans.[39]

In Britain, only two-thirds feel attachment to a political party, but almost nine in ten identify as a Remainer or Brexiteer. Relationship counsellors say that Brexit has contributed to serious quarrels between couples, and therapists regularly meet old parents who feel resented by their children.

Social media has added another ingredient to the broth. Many assume the problem is that online you only follow those who already share your views. I don't think so. People who read news online are more likely to come across opposing views than those who read news in print, and those with the strongest views are more not less likely to seek out the other side.[40] Filter bubbles are not new. In the era when every household had a newspaper, you only heard from political opponents in the vile abstracts journalists of your tribe wrote. More than a century ago, the Swedish author August Strindberg complained that newspapers and books only gave the reader more arguments for what he already believed, and that everything that contradicted those beliefs was excluded, so 'he never gets out of his standard diving dress'.[41]

In those days the opponent was a distant danger that you mostly talked about disparagingly with your friends, not an immediate threat. Now you regularly have the experience of being confronted with your worst political enemies every time you open Twitter or Facebook. They are in your face but not of your tribe. And the fact that the opponents are close triggers much fiercer tribal reactions. Our Stone Age brains assume bad people have broken the perimeter and we must fight back. Obviously, our group mentality leads us to interpret them in the least generous terms. It is easy to assume that the worst and most ill-mannered exponent of the other side – someone you had never heard of but your friends mockingly retweet – is representative of them all. So you share his outbursts with all your friends, and thus stoke up more hostility. In contrast, the crazies on your side are obviously just embarrassing exceptions to keep quiet about, and the fact that your opponents treat them as representative of your whole group makes those opponents even more evil.

But these new divides are not just examples of our tribalism, they are also proof of how malleable our identities are. No hunter-gatherers defined themselves by their attitude to Trump or Brexit, and yet many now find it difficult to think of themselves as anything but. For many, rooting for the team is more important than what the team does. When pollsters asked in 2015 whether Americans agree with Barack Obama that universal healthcare is a good idea, 82 per cent of Democrats, and only 16 per cent of Republicans did. When asked the same question, but instead told that it is Donald Trump who supports it (which he did at the time), Democratic support dropped to 46 per cent and Republican support increased to 44 per cent.[42]

The case of Brexit is a particularly fascinating example of how our identity changes when a new divide takes the oxygen from the old ones, and people start to position themselves around it. Until recently the British didn't care much about Europe. In 2019, they called one another traitors because of their position on a subject that only a tenth of them said was important before the 2016 referendum was called. By the summer of 2019, 87 per cent identified themselves by this issue – in fact, 15 per cent *more* do that now than bothered to turn out for the referendum.[43]

We see that other tribal classifications pale in comparison when a new conflict takes on a more important meaning. Americans now dehumanize political opponents at more than twice the rate as when they evaluate other outgroups like Muslims and Mexican immigrants.[44] And while the share of British who would object to a relative marrying someone of a different religion declined from 18 to 10 per cent between 2008 and 2018, 37 per cent of Remainers would be upset if a relative married a Brexiteer.[45]

If people can become aggressively tribal about issues they cared little about just a few years before, it is both good news and bad. The good news is that no particular division is a necessary part of the human condition. The bad news is that we can easily be encouraged to start a fight, if people in power and the media constantly talk about a divide, and particularly if you feel threatened and denigrated by the other group in question. Nothing gave as much boost to the Trump campaign than Hillary Clinton's attack on 'deplorables' among his voters, and the Brexit leader Nigel Farage talks happily about how Remainers think that 'we're thick, we're stupid, we're ignorant, we're racist'.

These divisions did not come out of nowhere, of course. There were already important divides that crossed traditional political allegiances, like young/old, urban/rural and national/cosmopolitan. The Trump campaign and the Brexit referendum weaponized those identities but it was by no means a certainty that they would become so salient.

This should be a cautionary tale. The more we talk about one way of grouping people, the more likely it is that people will align themselves accordingly. This is relevant when we think about a kind of identity politics that began trickling down from the radical Left at American universities into politics, journalism and internet forums in the 1990s. This was a reaction to real injustices, institutionalized discrimination against minorities and women in the past, and continued marginalization in the present. The traditional way of coming to terms with this was to enlarge the circle of respect, to open up our systems, the professions and universities to all on equal terms, to transcend groups and focus on the content of character rather than the colour of the skin. As a reaction to the slowness of the process, some radicals started seeing this as incredibly old-fashioned. Rather than talking about the rights of individuals, they started stressing group identity and the differences between these groups. Being group-blind came to be seen as just another injustice, neglecting the unique experiences of the oppressed.

This is understandable, but it is risky if it creates the sense that institutionalized racism is inescapable and that different groups can't get along. One problem with talking about how we can never really understand other groups, and that we can only take pride in our own collective identity and fight our corner, is that we activate this sensibility in more people. Perhaps even in poor whites without a college degree, who are told they have unearned power and white privilege whenever they bring up their own problems: instead of thinking about their concerns in terms of their region, or their education and labour-market position, some will start to think of themselves in terms of their white identity.

When people read stories about how different groups meet and integrate, they express more tolerant values afterwards. But if they read stories about more separation, they become more intolerant against minorities, and become more authoritarian in other policy areas as well. As early as 2005, political psychologist Karen Stenner warned:

> all the available evidence indicates that exposure to difference, talking about difference, and applauding difference [...] are the surest ways to aggravate those who are innately intolerant, and to guarantee the increased expression of their predispositions in manifestly intolerant attitudes and behaviors.[46]

We have to talk about identities when people are discriminated against on the basis of them, and it's not possible to educate people about racism, sexism and homophobia without talking about injustices that such groups have faced in the past. But it's dangerous if the rhetoric shifts into defining these group identities as the most important thing about us, and lays blame on individuals because they happen to be born into a group that has historically been responsible for these injustices. As one American voter put it in 2016, when he decided to reluctantly vote as a 'white' (for Donald Trump): 'If you want identity politics, identity politics is what you will get.'[47]

A tribal brain in an open world

The major question this chapter raises if we wish to avoid undermining the progress outlined in the first part of this book is: how can we live in an open, cosmopolitan world if we are this tribalist?

My firm conviction is that it is precisely because we are so tribalist that we need an open, cosmopolitan world. If we did not regularly meet and communicate and exchange with individuals from other groups, they would forever remain the mysterious, dangerous outgroup, the barbarians at the gates. The ones whom we raid whenever we think we have an advantage, and who raid us when they think they do. In *The Better Angels of Our Nature*, Steven Pinker has documented how much more frequent war was in our past before we opened economies, doors and minds to outsiders. Tribes raided and killed neighbouring tribes every time they thought they had a major advantage because of numbers or surprise, because why not? One less rival. Kings and princes genuinely believed war was the natural order of things, and peace was just a brief interlude during which one rearmed for the next battle.[48]

In a closed world we look at others through binoculars. In an open world, we constantly bump into them. That is not always easy. It causes resentment and conflict, and at times fist fights. But it also lays the foundation for new connections and understanding that make peace and trust possible.

To understand how, let's return to Robbers Cave, the real-life *Lord of the Flies* experiment. Several years after the death of Muzafer Sherif, the man behind the experiment, his archives were investigated by the Australian science historian Gina Perry. She found something odd – notes about a similar but aborted experiment Sherif had attempted the year before Robbers Cave. This time the two teams, called Pythons and Panthers, were not as antagonistic as expected. When the Pythons lost a tug of war, they admitted that the Panthers were better and deserved to win, and when a biased baseball umpire gave an unfair advantage to one of the teams, that team called him out. The researchers, pretending to be camp counsellors, stole clothes, destroyed the Panthers' tent and cut down their flag in an attempt to provoke the tribal hostilities they thought lurked just beneath the surface. The boys assumed the clothes had been lost in the laundry, and helped to put the tent back up. When the Pythons swore on the Bible that they had not cut down the flag, fighting was avoided, and the boys even started to think they were being manipulated. If this was *Lord of the Flies*, it was a version where Ralph and Jack stayed friends and asked William Golding why he was trying to make them fight.

Realizing he had failed, Sherif aborted the experiment. And, cheating science, he kept silent about it, changing the conditions for a better-choreographed repeat at Robbers Cave the next summer – the one that would go on to shock the world about the savagery of innocent boys. The difference the first time around was that he had allowed the boys to mix at first, before they were separated into two groups. This had forged friendships that weren't easily broken. In Robbers Cave, he did not allow this. Initially the two groups didn't even know of the others' existence so it was easier to foster hostilities.

This experience sounds like a vindication of the 'contact hypothesis', first formulated by social psychologist Gordon Allport in 1954. This is the idea that equal status contact between individuals from different groups, especially if it is in pursuit of a common goal, reduces antagonism. Cult leaders try to isolate their followers from outside influences precisely because they don't want their own control and group loyalty ruined by contact with the outside world.

This was a very influential theory that contributed to decisions like affirmative action and bussing students to other schools to reduce segregation. A 2018 review found twenty-seven high-quality studies on the contact hypothesis, and twenty-four of them revealed positive effects on prejudice reduction.[49] However, those studies only looked at very specific situations, to fit the conditions Allport thought were needed. Allport warned that just sharing space with others would not help. (After all, has contact with the outgroup on Twitter really made you more favourable to them?) In fact, it could hurt, if a focus on diversity at school or at work results in people focusing more on their identities and separating themselves from other groups. It can even function as a tribal trigger, making everybody emphasize their separate identity. Successful contact theory is the opposite, making us ignore particular differences by creating and focusing on cross-cutting identities and goals.

This was my own experience back at school. In the blue group, we considered ourselves superior to the red group and bonded quickly. But since we met at least briefly every day, there was plenty of time to get to know the kids in the red group. I realized I shared my interest in tennis with one of the kids from the red group and we pursued that. Later on, I found out I had my listening to Alphaville and Depeche Mode in common with another red boy, and politics with a third. These new connections created new, small groups and identities that cross-cut the old, and they grew to become more important than the old ones. Recategorizing old groups into a subordinate category identity like this is a more effective way of reducing intergroup bias. My best friend today, Pär, is an old rival from the red group.

And this is, in fact, more common than sticking to and weaponizing our identities, even though we pay more attention to the latter because it is so dramatic. I focused on football hooligans above, but they are a tiny segment of all football fans. A much more common experience is that football creates new bonds between people, and they can quickly turn each other into ingroup. When I am abroad with male friends, I notice they always bond with strangers on trains and in bars over nothing more than their love of football. For some reason my love of tennis doesn't make me quite as many friends. (I guess the presence of me – the outgroup – helps them to bond even more.) In one study, Manchester United fans were reminded of their love of football. Afterwards, 22 per cent of them decided to help a stranger who tripped and shouted in pain. But as many as 70 per cent of them helped out if the person who tripped was wearing a jersey from a rival team, Liverpool. Almost as many as would help a fellow United fan (80 per cent).[50]

Historically, we have expanded the circle of people we feel empathy for by discovering that we belong to groups that overlap the old divisions. When we realize there are members of an outgroup who share an important trait with us, they don't seem that alien to us any more. It could be our religion or ideology or our taste in literature or music, or the fact of being a mother or a teacher or a Trekkie.

One summer night in New York City in 1997, a white cop beat up a black man he had arrested. Later on, at the police station, he noticed that the suspect was wearing a necklace, and on that necklace hung a crucifix. That was enough for the policeman to forget about policeman vs suspect, and white vs black. Now he only saw two Christians. The policeman told the man that he too believed in Jesus, and apologized.[51] This kind of recognition of a shared trait – repeated millions of times, in thousands of dimensions, over the history of *Homo sapiens* – has led us to expand our circle of empathy from our own family, to our band, our community, our country, and finally the entire human race. We expand 'us'.

Two things have accelerated this process in the last couple of centuries: mass communication and markets. Literacy turned the lives and travails of people in faraway lands into a part of everyday life. And it has been argued that fiction, especially after the mid-seventeenth century, was even more important. Novels and plays told from the perspective of children, women and ethnic minorities made readers laugh and cry with them, and realize that people of another gender, class or ethnicity were individuals just like them, with the same senses, affections and passions. If we prick them, they also bleed. If we tickle them, they also laugh.

Markets and trade have also always been essential in breaking down tribal barriers. As Marx and Engels pointed out, because of free markets, 'fixed, fast-frozen relations, with their train of ancient and venerable prejudices and opinions, are swept away'. Thomas Paine pointed to the same effect, but in a more positive light:

> I have been an advocate for commerce, because I am a friend to its effects. It is a pacific system, operating to cordialize mankind, by rendering nations, as well as individuals, useful to each other [...] is the greatest approach towards universal civilisation that has yet been made by any means not immediately flowing from moral principles.[52]

And yet, the tribal instincts are still part of us, and from time to time, they wreak havoc and let slip the dogs of war. Comparisons are not necessarily competitive, observes the social psychologist Marilynn Brewer, but one condition can quickly turn ingroup love into outgroup hate. That is a situation where outcomes are seen as zero-sum, when we 'cannot improve our position or sense of well-being unless the outgroup is doing less well than we are'.[53] Unfortunately that is what our Stone Age minds – and our Stone Age leaders – often try to convince us that the world is like.

6

ZERO-SUM

'You hear lots of people say that a great deal is when both sides win. That is a bunch of crap. In a great deal you win – not the other side. You crush the opponent and come away with something better for yourself.'

Donald Trump, 2007

For an eternal and omnipotent being, God's mood does seem to be a little changeable. When we first meet him in the Old Testament, the Hebrew Bible, no one would mistake him for a bleeding-heart liberal. He tells his chosen people there is really no nice way to get along with outsiders: 'You shall annihilate them – the Hittites and the Amorites, the Canaanites and the Perizzites, the Hivites and the Jebusites – as the LORD your God has commanded you, so that they cannot teach you all the abhorrent ways they worship their gods.' Cities further away can be handled in a slightly less gruesome way, by killing the men and abducting the women and children.

Yet, if we continue reading until we reach the Book of Jonah, we now find the prophet Jonah eagerly awaiting God's destruction of Nineveh, the capital of Assyria, only to find that God has changed his mind, asking Jonah, rhetorically: 'should not I spare Nineveh, that great city, wherein are more than sixscore thousand persons that cannot discern between their right hand and their left hand' (4:11). The hand metaphor is God's way of saying the Assyrians can be excused because they are confused: they just don't know the truth.

Many religious scholars, including quite a few believers too, have wondered about God's seemingly random changes in mood. Is he a God of peace or of war? To answer, we must look for clues to the changes in the circumstances facing the scripture writers. In his intriguing book *The Evolution of God*, Robert Wright argues that the depiction of God reflects whether the authors' groups were in a zero-sum relationship with other groups and nations or not. When the neighbourhood is hostile, God is full of anger against outgroups, but in times of peace – when goods cross borders instead of soldiers – his depiction becomes one of religious toleration.[1]

A zero-sum game is one in which the gains of one side are the losses of another. Football is a typical zero-sum game – every goal is a gain for one team and a loss for the other team, so you win only by defeating the other side. Within each football team, however, the game is non-zero. If your teammate scores it is a gain for you as well, so you benefit by helping each other and cooperating better.

When the Jewish people were fighting to carve out a new nation in a crowded neighbourhood they were in a zero-sum logic with others, and it doesn't get much more zero-sum than being defeated and exiled by the Babylonians. This is the era when we find an angry God, intent on vengeance and extermination. But the Jews were set free by Cyrus the Great and the ensuing Pax Persica made peaceful cooperation and exchange with neighbours possible. Nineveh, which used to be a brutal rival, was now a trading partner. In books of the Bible usually dated as post-exilic, like the Book of Jonah, we suddenly meet a God who is much more tolerant of neighbours' gods .

Robert Wright thinks we see the same transition in the New Testament. To us it seems like Jesus always had a cosmopolitan message of universal love. But that is not how he comes across in one of the gospels, the Gospel of Mark, which was written first, around four decades after Jesus' death. That's a long lag, but many people who met Jesus might still have been around, so it gave Mark less artistic licence than it gave Matthew, Luke or especially John – writing six or seven decades after the Crucifixion. In Mark, there is not much of a message of love and brotherhood. Jesus tells you to love God, but not that God loves you. There is no 'Let he who is without sin cast the first stone', no 'turn the other cheek', and no Sermon on the Mount. In fact, when a Canaanite woman asks for help to exorcize a demon from her daughter, Jesus first turns her down with the argument that he was only sent to 'the lost sheep of Israel' and, using one of his least gracious allegories, it is not right to take the children's bread and 'toss it to the dogs'.

Wright suggests the Christian message gradually took a universalist turn as it gave up the belief in instant apocalypse, and Paul started building congregations throughout the Roman Empire. The century after Jesus was one of dislocation and urbanization. Peoples and cultures from every part of the empire moved to rapidly expanding cities, and religious organizations became important meeting places for rootless migrants. For that to work, a message of interethnic brotherly love had to replace a tribal one. If you want an open church, 'there is neither Jew nor Greek' is a more constructive sentiment than comparing foreigners to dogs. This is what we see seeping into the later Gospels.

The same dynamic is apparent in Islam. On the one hand, you have many expressions of religious tolerance in the Koran, such as 'To you be your religion; to me my religion' and 'Let there be no compulsion in religion'. Allah commands that even though the infidels spout nonsense, 'thou art not to compel them', we should instead 'endure what they say with patience'. On the other hand, the Koran is full of belligerence and commands to attack infidels: 'Make ready then against them what force ye can' and 'kill them wherever you find them' (polytheists, in this case, not all infidels).

Again, this reflects the political situation at the time. At first, Muhammed – a trader by profession – was pursuing a non-zero game strategy, trying to convince other cities and believers to join him. It was a language of peace and exchange, full of praise for Christians and for the Jews, chosen, according to the Koran, by Allah, 'in our prescience, above all peoples'. The strategy failed and ended in power struggles and a war of conquest against other tribes. Once Muhammed told his followers to pray in the direction of Jerusalem; now he attacked and expelled Jewish tribes in Medina, and said that you can't take Jews and Christians as friends, 'They are but one another's friends.'

This is when the language of war commences. Taken out of context, such verses give the impression there is to be an eternal war between religions, but even here it is not their religion Muhammed holds most against them but their supposed acts of war and persecution. About thirty words after 'what force ye can', Muhammed adds: 'And if they lean to peace, lean thou also to it.' Even in the famous 'sword verse', just after stating that you should kill polytheists wherever you can, Muhammed commands that if any of the polytheists seek asylum, 'let him reach his place of safety'. He makes it clear that only polytheists waging war are to be killed, excepting those who 'in no way failed you, nor aided anyone against you'. When Pax Islamica was established, freedom of worship was granted to Christians and Jews, and soon to Buddhists and polytheists as well.

This, thinks Wright, is the answer to the question 'Is Islam [or any other religion] a religion of peace?' The answer is yes. And no. You can find versions of the Golden Rule ('Do unto others...')

in all religions, but you can also find intolerance and punishment (often eternal). In times and places of zero-sum logic, God advocates aggression and war, and people kill in his name. In times and places of non-zero relationships, God is an advocate of tolerance and trade with non-believers.

If even God is so quick to adjust his message about the world and mankind when he finds himself under threat, what kind of an effect does it have on us mere mortals?

Zero-sums make us groupish

Muzafer Sherif's interpretation of his Robbers Cave experiment was that conflict and tribalism were unleashed because the boys were playing zero-sum games. When two groups believed they were fighting over the same, scarce resources, it triggered warfare between normally well-behaved boys at a summer camp.

People who think they are in a zero-sum relationship against other groups are much more likely to make the choice of Vladimir, who asked God to take out one of his eyes because God would grant his neighbour twice what he asked. They are more likely to oppose free trade and equal rights for minority groups, and instead of pursuing equally binding rules and mutual gains in international relations, they are more concerned with trying to make other countries less well off, even if it comes at their own expense. Ironically, they often turn a non-zero-sum game into a loss for both sides. In one study, after having been asked about ethnic identification and perceived group competition, a majority of white undergraduate students were willing to sacrifice several million dollars for a predominantly white student organization in order to avoid minority organizations getting more than them.[2]

This challenges the common notion that we are aggressive egomaniacs privately who become enlightened social beings at the ballot box. On the contrary, we are often searching for win–win outcomes with others in our personal relations on the market and in civil society, since that benefits us and the community the most, but when we start thinking about ourselves as belonging to a group that is competing against another group, we are willing to sacrifice our eyes and wealth to make the others worse off.

The theologian and socialist Reinhold Niebuhr drew our attention to something similar in his book *Moral Man and Immoral Society*. Individuals 'are able to consider interests other than their own', but groups have 'less reason to guide and to check impulse, less capacity for self-transcendence, less ability to comprehend the needs of others' and are therefore less restrained in their collective egoism. This groupishness led people to seek satisfaction in the will-to-power and aggrandisement of the nation, which risked ending in war. Niebuhr's only hope was that Europe would avoid 'issuing into complete disaster'.[3] He wrote in 1932.

Zero-sum thinking does not just ruin summer camps, sometimes it ruins civilizations. In *The Moral Consequences of Growth*, Harvard economist Benjamin Friedman shows that periods of rapid economic growth in the US and Europe have been the periods when barriers to tolerance and equal rights have been lifted. When the economy is growing, jobs are multiplying and wages are increasing, established majority groups feel outgroups (women, ethnic and religious minorities, and foreigners) can get ahead without themselves losing out. However, in episodes of economic stagnation, they feel like the outgroup's progress is bought at their expense, which leads to more discrimination, hostility to immigrants and scapegoating of minorities. At times it creates a vicious circle of group warfare, violence and a breakdown of open institutions, which in turn reduces prosperity, which increases group warfare and so on.[4] After all, the surest way to win a zero-sum game is to play it against a dead adversary.

During 'the long depression' starting in the 1870s, a series of crises and panics in Europe and the US poisoned ethnic relations.

In America, the populist movement was born, which was a defence of an agrarian, small-town way of life against industrial capitalism, but also of the old way of life against immigrants who might take away jobs and drive down wages. The agitation against Chinese immigrants was fierce and resulted in the Chinese Exclusion Act of 1882, the first law that barred an entire ethnic or national group. In the 1890s, the American South began to adopt segregationist Jim Crow laws against African Americans.

In Europe, the same economic troubles gave rise to a more reactionary form of nationalism. Led by the newly unified Germany in 1879, Europe started to abandon free trade. Germany also saw its first boom in modern anti-Semitism. Anti-Jewish parties and campaign groups were started, selling a zero-sum worldview, 'Jewish department stores' supposedly destroyed independent craftsmen and exploited workers. Anti-Semitic anti-capitalism took root in the labour movements, and the German Conservative Party adopted much of the anti-Semitic agenda. The ideas also quickly spread to Italy, France and the Habsburg Empire, and even to Britain, where some liberals hypocritically exploited it in attacks on the Jewish prime minister Benjamin Disraeli.

The next serious outburst of nativism came after the 1920–21 depression. In 1921, the Ku Klux Klan was re-formed in the US, and quickly found a nationwide audience for hatred against blacks, Jews and Catholics. At its peak in the mid-1920s, the Klan probably had more than two million members. In a series of laws in the 1920s, America implemented its first general immigration controls. Meanwhile, Europe saw an upswing of anti-Semitic and fascist groups, and while the recovery of the late 1920s took some wind out of their sails, the Great Depression of the 1930s gave them a new boost, with disastrous global consequences.

There was, therefore, always a high probability that the financial crisis of 2008 and the ensuing Great Recession would unleash zero-sum thinking and a new bout of nativism. The particular scapegoat chosen differed, depending on who was at hand locally. In the US, attitudes to Mexican immigrants hardened; in Britain attitudes to Eastern European immigrants did; in much of Europe, Muslim minorities became the target of increased hostility and hate, and there was also a rise in anti-Semitism.

It's not zero-sum

Not even in times of recessions is it correct to think of the economy as zero-sum, it just feels like it. On a macro level, it is then negative-sum: we produce less value than we did yesterday. And the minorities and immigrants that we are quick to blame are often the first to suffer from the sudden dearth of jobs and incomes. And overall, the modern economy is explosively non-zero. As we've seen, this is not just a matter of a couple of per cent but 3000 per cent in two hundred years. The growth of knowledge and technology has made life dramatically better for most people in most places. It is obvious that everybody does not share in the gains to an equal degree, but the gains of one person do not necessarily come at the expense of others. As long as markets are relatively free, no deal, no purchase and no employment decision is ever made unless both parties believe they benefit more from doing it than avoiding it. If a businessman gains a reputation for deceiving or crushing business partners, others avoid him like the plague.

One of the more popular versions of zero-sum thinking is Karl Marx's interpretation of free market capitalism. Writing in the British Museum Reading Room in the mid-nineteenth century, he prophesized that the rich would get richer, but only by exploiting the workers even more, so the middle class would become proletarians, and the proletarians would soon starve. In the history of predictions, this might be the most badly timed one (with the possible exception of the 'nineteenth-century Nostradamus', Jeron Criswell King, who made the mistake of giving a precise date when London would be destroyed by a meteor and Pennsylvania would suffer from a mass outbreak of cannibalism). When Marx died in 1883, the average person in England – the most industrialized economy – was more than twice as rich as he was when Marx was born in 1818. Doubling of the material standard of living, which by earlier trends should have taken mankind more than two thousand years to achieve, took the English just half a century. By 1900, extreme poverty in England had been reduced by three quarters, to around 10 per cent.

Western workers have an income several times higher than a hundred years ago, but this did not happen because capitalists stopped 'extracting surplus labour' of workers or because of an epic struggle between 'labour and capital'. The labour share of the national income did not increase during the last hundred years – all of their unprecedented increase in income was down to the growth in the size of the pie.

Faced with this refutation of the theory, some socialists adjusted or abandoned it, but others pretended it had in fact confirmed the theory, perhaps guided by the kind of methodological trickery Marx privately admitted to in a letter to Engels in August 1857 about a recent prediction: 'It's possible that I shall make an ass of myself. But in that case one can always get out of it with a little dialectic. I have, of course, so worded my proposition as to be right either way.'[5] These Marxists claimed that this could only happen because someone, somewhere else, was being more and more harshly exploited by all classes in the capitalist economies – namely, the developing countries in the south and east. Lenin declared that Western capitalists had succeeded by 'bribing' the workers and giving them a bourgeois lifestyle, the resources for which derived from imperialism and the exploitation of other peoples.[6]

There is no doubt that colonialism took a terrible toll on poor countries, but the trouble for Lenin's rationalization is that all

continents have grown faster simultaneously. Developing countries have grown much richer *after* the advent of free markets in
the West, and it has happened at an even faster pace in recent
decades as these countries opened up their own economies and
gave their own citizens greater freedom to own, trade and start
businesses.

True, GDP per capita in Europe and the US is roughly seven
times higher than a hundred years ago, but Latin America's is six
times higher, Asia's is eight times higher and Africa's is four times
higher. And on all continents there has been a dramatic growth of
population since then, by a total of more than five billion people.
So if wealth is a zero-sum game, who did we take it all from?

Had we shared all the wealth the world had then equally, the
result would have been that we would all have been poorer than
the average Tanzanian is today. So the wealth we have today is the
result of us being able to produce more thanks to investment and
innovation, rather than a new distribution of the old.

If we have an annual growth rate around 1 per cent per capita,
it means that it takes more than seventy years to double our GDP
per capita. If we can increase it to 2 per cent annually, we would
cut that time in half. In other words, all the riches we already have
would double in roughly thirty-five years. If we consider such a
massive wealth increase it is easier to understand why a particular
change in redistribution in this year's government budget, so that
you get a little more or less, is trivial. Much more important is how
those changes affect the incentive to, say, get an education that is
more in demand on the labour market, start a business or take a
risk on a new idea. This is what increased wealth for us all in the
long run.

The George Mason economist Tyler Cowen points out that
if the US had grown one percentage point less annually between
1870 and 1990 the country would in 1990 have had the same
material standard as Mexico in 1990.[7]

All redistribution is not consumption, though. For example, public spending on mass education has given more people the abilities they need to participate in society and to develop their ideas and skills. Infrastructure projects have facilitated mobility and trade. These are large-scale investments in the future that have contributed to more total wealth. The sum is positive, not zero. And yet, we often perceive that we are in a zero-sum relationship, even though we are not.

Folk economics

Paul Rubin has examined the phenomena of 'folk economics', the worldview of people who are not trained in economics. It is the economics of wealth allocation, not production, where people mostly think of prices and profits as a way of distributing wealth, not as incentives to produce and innovate. 'The world of folk economics is a zero-sum world', and the primary economic problem is how to get a larger share of the pie for you or your group, not to grow the size of the pie.[8] Our economic instinct tells us the economy is like a game of sport: it's win/lose – whatever someone wins, someone else loses – and our primary economic objective is to be on the winning side.

In George Mason economist Bryan Caplan's provocative book *The Myth of the Rational Voter*, he looks at the areas where the assumptions of a majority of people are the furthest from the conclusion of economic scholars, and trade and immigration are among the worst. Whereas economists document enormous mutual gains, people in general think they are often zero-sum games. Caplan thinks this is related to a general anti-foreigner bias, since these myths become more powerful the further the other country is from us culturally. For example, trade with Mexico is seen as more zero-sum for Americans than for Canadians.[9]

Zero-sum is the myth that launched a thousand economic

mistakes. Almost every kind of angst the nationalist Right and the populist Left feels over the economy is based on it in one form or another. If the rich get richer, it's because they take it from us. With more immigrants, there are fewer resources left for the natives. If robots become smarter, there will be no jobs left for us. If trading partners like China and Mexico gain, it must be at our expense.

Why are we so bad at understanding that voluntary relations and an open economy are non-zero? Once again, we have to turn to our past to understand why our problematic reasoning instincts actually make sense.

If a spaceship from an alien civilization had decided to drop in on *Homo sapiens* every 10,000 years to see when we were sufficiently advanced that it might be worth making first contact, they would have had to be very, very patient. Even if they limited their sneak peeks to one every 10,000 years, they wouldn't have found much new to write home about. The captain's log might have read something like this (inspired by *Star Trek* and Joshua Greene),[10] starting 300,000 years ago:

VISIT	POPULATION	SOCIETY	COMMUNICATION	TRANSPORTATION	TECHNOLOGY
300,000 years ago	<5 million	Hunter-gatherer bands	Spoken language	Walking, endurance running	Primitive tools
290,000	<5 million	Hunter-gatherer bands	Spoken language	Walking, endurance running	Primitive tools
280,000	<5 million	Hunter-gatherer bands	Spoken language	Walking, endurance running	Primitive tools
270,000	<5 million	Hunter-gatherer bands	Spoken language	Walking, endurance running	Primitive tools
260,000	<5 million	Hunter-gatherer bands	Spoken language	Walking, endurance running	Primitive tools
250,000	<5 million	Hunter-gatherer bands	Spoken language	Walking, endurance running	Primitive tools
240,000	<5 million	Hunter-gatherer bands	Spoken language	Walking, endurance running	Primitive tools
230,000	<5 million	Hunter-gatherer bands	Spoken language	Walking, endurance running	Primitive tools

VISIT	POPULATION	SOCIETY	COMMUNICATION	TRANSPORTATION	TECHNOLOGY
220,000	<5 million	Hunter-gatherer bands	Spoken language	Walking, endurance running	Primitive tools
210,000	<5 million	Hunter-gatherer bands	Spoken language	Walking, endurance running	Primitive tools
200,000	<5 million	Hunter-gatherer bands	Spoken language	Walking, endurance running	Primitive tools
190,000	<5 million	Hunter-gatherer bands	Spoken language	Walking, endurance running	Primitive tools
180,000	<5 million	Hunter-gatherer bands	Spoken language	Walking, endurance running	Primitive tools
170,000	<5 million	Hunter-gatherer bands	Spoken language	Walking, endurance running	Primitive tools
160,000	<5 million	Hunter-gatherer bands	Spoken language	Walking, endurance running	Primitive tools
150,000	<5 million	Hunter-gatherer bands	Spoken language	Walking, endurance running	Primitive tools
140,000	<5 million	Hunter-gatherer bands	Spoken language	Walking, endurance running	Primitive tools
130,000	<5 million	Hunter-gatherer bands	Spoken language	Walking, endurance running	Primitive tools
120,000	<5 million	Hunter-gatherer bands	Spoken language	Walking, endurance running	Primitive tools
110,000	<5 million	Hunter-gatherer bands	Spoken language	Walking, endurance running	Primitive tools
100,000	<5 million	Hunter-gatherer bands	Spoken language	Walking, endurance running	Primitive tools
90,000	<5 million	Hunter-gatherer bands	Spoken language	Walking, endurance running	Primitive tools
80,000	<5 million	Hunter-gatherer bands	Spoken language	Walking, endurance running	Primitive tools
70,000	<5 million	Hunter-gatherer bands	Spoken language	Walking, endurance running	Primitive tools
60,000	<5 million	Hunter-gatherer bands	Spoken language	Walking, endurance running	Primitive tools
50,000	<5 million	Hunter-gatherer bands	Spoken language	Walking, endurance running	Primitive tools
40,000	<5 million	Hunter-gatherer bands	Spoken language	Walking, endurance running	Primitive tools
30,000	<5 million	Hunter-gatherer bands	Spoken language	Walking, endurance running	Primitive tools
20,000	<5 million	Hunter-gatherer bands	Spoken language	Walking, endurance running	Primitive tools

VISIT	POPULATION	SOCIETY	COMMUNICATION	TRANSPORTATION	TECHNOLOGY
10,000	<5 million	Hunter-gatherer bands, but also some agriculture and tiny cities. (Let's keep an eye on this planet!)	Spoken language	Walking, endurance running, primitive boats are becoming more frequent	Primitive tools
Today	>7 BILLION	Global industrialized economy, global trade, large-scale democratic governance	Near universal literacy, global communication network connected to portable, personal devices	Automobiles, trains, ocean-going ships, submarines, aeroplanes, extraterrestrial travel (have landed on their moon)	Electricity, nuclear power, personal computers, artificial intelligence, biotechnology, etc

Two things stand out from this list: the first twenty-nine visits – and the thirtieth visit. The aliens would have been forgiven for giving up on us after a couple of trips. Nothing much happened that would have impressed them during the first 290,000 years they looked at our species. Only during the thirtieth visit would our alien visitors find something to impress the superiors back home and make them think *Homo sapiens* might be on its way to becoming a warp-capable civilization. Most interesting is that almost all of the amazing breakthroughs, discoveries and innovations on display during that thirtieth visit occurred not over 10,000 years, but during the last two hundred years.

'Progress that is both rapid enough to be noticed and stable enough to continue over many generations has been achieved only once in the history of our species,' as the British physicist David Deutsch writes.[11] If our last 300,000 years were condensed into a twenty-four-hour day, the two hundred years when almost everything happened would be the last minute. The best minute ever. This is the astonishing minute where our long lifespans, our safety, our health, wealth and technology come from. But these sixty seconds are, however, not where our brains and our instincts and attitudes come from. Those emerged during the previous 86,400 seconds. And of course, our prehistory is much, much longer than the last 300,000 years.

Openness has allowed a kind of life that our old and more tribal selves have a hard time comprehending. During some 99.9 per cent of our species' existence, individual human beings did not experience progress, innovations and mutual benefits with strangers. It was, in most cases, a zero-sum game for most individuals: someone's gain was another one's loss. More for you meant less for me. If our minds developed during such circumstances, it is no wonder that they are adapted to this.

Equality matching

As we have seen, humans have always engaged in trade and a division of labour, but that doesn't mean trade has always looked the same as it does today. For most of our species' existence, daily income – food – spoiled quickly, so it had to be consumed on a daily basis. No one could save and amass great wealth. The rewards of hunting or foraging were expected to be shared, not enjoyed individually.

As some hunter-gatherers began to make the transition to a more complex economy, this egalitarian attitude clashed with a system of individual efforts and wages. Psychology professor William von Hippel tells the story of a remote aboriginal community in Australia where the manager in charge of the environmental monitoring and clean-up teams was impressed with their hard work and wanted to give them a raise. He was surprised to find them indifferent to the offer, and some even declined it. When he asked why, they explained that when they got home at the end of the working week, their relatives asked them what they had made and demanded it was shared. A higher income did not mean a larger benefit, and it even made the workers frustrated to watch others take more of their money.[12]

The kind of trade our ancestors engaged in mostly took the form of 'equality matching' – a way of matching contributions so that those who were lucky during this week's hunt helped those who weren't, in the knowledge that the roles might be reversed next week. The goods exchanged were very similar or at least easily comparable. This risk-pooling was much better for the individual than the alternative feast-or-famine cycle, but it came with the risk of being cheated next time by someone who refused to return last week's favours. This has led us to develop an uncanny ability to monitor the behaviour of others and punish shirking. We seem to have brain circuitry designed to detect cheaters in situations of exchange. When logical problems are presented as a way of detecting cheaters instead of as an abstract problem, we perform much better, no matter if we are hunter-horticulturalists in the Amazon or office workers in a paper company in Slough.[13]

Our forager ancestors used tools and weapons, and wore clothes and jewellery, but since these had to be carried around everywhere, they were limited to possessions that were easily acquired and quickly replaceable. Foragers rarely used heavy and elaborately decorated artefacts that took a long time to produce. It was a world with little capital and little surplus to invest in future rewards. It may be occasionally frustrating today to find recommended updates every time we turn on our mobile phones, but technological updates in our prehistory could take millennia. In the archaeological literature you notice how specific stone techniques are considered 'new' when they have been in place for several thousand years.

For almost all of the time that *Homo sapiens* has existed, most of us did not get to experience economic growth, long-term investment or technological innovation in our lifetimes. So why would we have developed an intuitive understanding that it is not zero-sum?

In prehistory, when someone in the band had much more than the others, it was probably not because he had a longer education or had come up with a better product, but because he had refused to reciprocate for past benefits. If a neighbouring tribe had more than you, it was not the result of their better research and development or a smarter supply chain, but because they had pushed you from the best land. With the advent of agriculture, exploitation got worse, as chiefs took as much as they could. And ever since, elites have fought over the best land, since it is the one thing they can't make more of, as estate agents point out. The harsh deal for the average person did not change until the last two hundred years of unprecedented economic growth. If someone had more than you, you had reasons to be resentful because he had probably taken it from you.

The urbanist and journalist Jane Jacobs once described the striking difference the modern market economy has made:

> The doings of craftsmen and merchants are so innocent compared with making wars, pillaging, extorting, persecuting, executing, censoring, holding prisoners for ransom, and monopolizing land at the expense of serfs, peons, or slaves – all honorable activities for people who would sooner have died than sink into trade.[14]

The upshot is that evolution has adapted us to deal more with war-making and pillaging than with craftsmen and merchants.

Our belief in the zero-sum economy resembles our fear of the dark. This seemingly irrational fear has served a very useful purpose in protecting our species. Predators prefer to hunt under the cover of darkness, and since humans used to be prey, those who got up and took a stroll in the middle of the night often ended up in the belly of a big cat. Those who felt a grinding anxiety about the dark and stayed in hiding survived and passed on their anxiety to us. We should be grateful. But since then, humans have made an incredible ascent from prey to top of the food chain; we learned to control fire and introduced electrical light, and we all got mobile phones to call for help when needed. Granted, it is still dark, and it is easy to trip up and fall down the stairs, but that is nothing compared to being eyed by hyenas and lions. And yet, we still lie there, unable to sleep, terrified about monsters under our bed or an imminent crisis at work, and not about cars, cigarettes or nuclear war, which pose real threats to our lives.

We changed the world, but our brains didn't notice. Just like we changed the economy but failed to redesign attitudes about wealth and innovation. And now we sit there, fearing capitalists, immigrants and trading partners while neglecting the greater risks that tariffs and controls would pose to our living standards.

Our hunter-gatherer ancestors traded with other groups, even long-distance, but it was in a direct, personal way with immediate, obvious benefits to both sides. We knew exactly what they contributed to our well-being, and thought that they deserved the goods we were handing over in exchange. Today, we are still very good at intuitively understanding the benefits of immediate exchange – where we buy and sell something, shake our trading partner's hand and thank each other – because we both get away with something that has more worth to us than what we gave. In large, complex economies the same logic applies, but not the same emotions because most exchanges are far distanced from such personal meetings, by many layers of unknown parties, made possible by relatively recent innovations like writing, money and credit.

The writing of this book will probably give me many cups of cappuccino at my local coffee shop, not because I give them a copy of the book in exchange for it but because of an overwhelming causal chain that involves you, the buyer of the book, but also coffee-bean producers, truckers, shippers, financial markets and even the producer of the helmets the miners wear when they dig out the iron for the steel to the chainsaws that produce the pulp for the cup my coffee is poured into.[15] The beauty of the modern, global market is that we work hard for the benefit of people we have never heard about. 'Modern competition is described as the fight of all against all, but at the same time it is the fight of all *for* all,' as the sociologist Georg Simmel put it in 1908.[16] But this complexity also means it is impossible for anyone to fully comprehend all the links in even a very simple form of exchange.

Steven Pinker believes many clashes over economics stem from this conflict between traditional, personal exchange and modern market exchange, 'one of them intuitive and universal, the other rarefied and learned'.[17] Suddenly, we can see the wealth of others but we don't understand what they have contributed to get it. Do we even know what they are doing all day? (Honestly, do you even know what your colleagues contribute?) The monitoring mechanism that almost automatically tells us if a deal is fair and if someone is shirking has a hard time functioning in a world of impersonal connections. As a result, it is no surprise that politicians and ideologues can easily make us think that another group is not really paying their fair share, or doing anything useful.

Getting innovation wrong

In our past it also made sense to be suspicious of creative individuals who tried to change ways of doing things, since innovations are always risky and most of the time they fail. People who live on the margins might not be able to afford any risk. If the tribal lands barely feed you, someone who comes up with a different way of using the seeds, and wants to rotate the crops in an unfamiliar way, might possibly succeed and then feed you all better, but why take that chance if failure equals starvation?

Even when innovation succeeded, it was impossible for most people to link its use to the risky and creative behaviour that created it. Say you just picked up your first finely shaped 'hand-axe' known to archaeologists as Acheulean. No matter how happy you are about your acquisition, it wouldn't give you an understanding of the value of innovative individuals (in this case, one or several wildly creative *Homo erectus* half a million years earlier). More likely it would just reinforce the value of imitating the neighbour who seemed happy with his specimen.

That the origins of cultural and technological innovations always seemed obscure before our time is revealed by how the ancient Babylonians looked at it. Their world saw innovation happening at warp speed compared to everything that preceded it. According to one myth, written down by Berossus (a priest and a contemporary of Alexander the Great), all these fruits of civilization were given to mankind by a fish-like creature called Oannes. 'From the time of that beast nothing further has been discovered,' concluded Berossus.[18] It is telling that the Babylonians had no memory of their Leonardos, Newtons and Edisons, but still more fascinating is the fact that even during this rapidly changing era, they did not notice enough cultural and technological innovation in their lifetimes to think anything more could be discovered.

The idea that objects have true and constant values, rather than being valuable only in relation to the preferences of consumers, is a phenomenon economists call 'the physical fallacy'. It is another result of our equality-matching brains trying to comprehend market exchange: if I shared a reindeer with the neighbour last month, I expect a reindeer feast in return today; if I don't get one, I have been cheated. But in a complex market economy, the supply and demand has probably changed since last month, and prices with them. If there is a scarcity of reindeer this week, the price is up. That is great as it stops us from running down a scarce resource and creates an incentive to save it and eat rabbits instead, or to breed more. But if we can't buy something this month at the same price as we did last month, our equality-matching brains feel like they have been cheated.

As the economist Thomas Sowell has explained, man does not create physical matter at all, so the economic benefit of a man-made object does not come from its atoms but from its form, location or availability. So those who arrange such beneficial trans-formations contribute to the value of things, 'whether his hands actually come into contact with physical objects or not'.[19]

Sowell mentions that the physical fallacy also has temporal blinders, making us think of the production process as a very short process of manual work, and everything that comes before (lenders funding the venture, managers assembling and organizing labour and machines) or after (middlemen ensuring the products end up where the consumers are) is not seen as productive. This view of the production process is arbitrary, according to Sowell, but it is just what we should expect of a hunter-gatherer mentality, where the relevant production and consumption process is exhausted by two steps: 1) hunt or gather, and 2) eat. In a complex economy you would also have to ask who funded the additive manufacturing centre and who made sure that great skin lotion ends up with the person with a desperate itch on the other side of the globe. This means lenders and middlemen do not take away anything from you but add to a positive-sum result. But since they don't seem to cause physical objects to come into being, many think of them as social parasites, and when these groups have been associated with minority groups like Jews or overseas Chinese, this hostility has sometimes exploded into scapegoating and violence.

If this reminds you of the classical critique of capitalists as exploiters, it is because Marxism is a version of the physical fal-lacy. If the only true value is created by the time the worker put in to produce a physical object, the capitalist simply steals sur-plus value to make his profit. All the work the capitalist does is ignored, from innovative business models and efficient organiza-tion to long-term investment (few workers are willing to wait for pay until the product is sold) and risk-taking (even fewer workers would agree to forgo pay if it turns out that the product doesn't sell).

In the modern, open economy our relationship with outsiders has been turned on its head. Since it is based on rule of law, property rights and voluntary exchange, people can only prosper by creating something of value to others. If a prince, nobleman or robber wanted our money in the past, they just took it from us. If a businessman wants our money, he has to offer us goods or services that we value so much that we are willing to give up our money to lay our hands on them. If another tribe got more skills and resources, it used to be dangerous because it meant they could more easily conquer us, winning the zero-sum game between us. Today, if a tribe on the other shore invents a photoelectric sensor or manages to harness power from the sun, it means we get access to smart electronic devices and unlimited energy.

Many pundits try to scare us with the fierce competition that we will face from all the engineers in India or the huge biotechnology industry in China. However, the most important benefit we can derive from such sectors is not jobs for our engineers or profits for our biotech companies, but the general increase in knowledge and technological capability they contribute to. It is difficult and costly to develop a new antibiotic, a cure for Alzheimer's disease or a way to make graphene collect the electrical current from solar cells efficiently, but once someone comes up with it, it is easy to use it everywhere to save lives and develop cheap, clean energy. For a long time, mostly a few Western institutions and companies invested heavily in solving such problems, with the rest of the world benefiting from those discoveries. Hopefully, we will see more such discoveries coming from other places in the future, so that those in the West can get a free ride once in a while as well. Globalization means that more people from more countries are developing new knowledge and technologies that benefit the whole world. The only thing that would turn this into a problem is a zero-sum mentality on either or both sides that shuts minds and borders to those insights and innovations.

Myths of trade

In no area is the zero-sum myth more prevalent than trade. When I published my book *In Defence of Global Capitalism* in 2001, it was an argument against the anti-globalists who thought free trade and multinational companies would make us in the West rich, but it would make poor countries poorer. I explained that this is not the case, that on an open market no deal is made unless both parties think that they benefit, and that poor countries would benefit tremendously from globalization. I think it's fair to say this debate is settled, not because of my book but because everybody can see the incredible rise of poor and middle-income countries like India, China, Vietnam and Bangladesh. In the last three decades more people have been lifted out of extreme poverty than ever before in human history. But people have not given up the zero-sum myth, so now I encounter the reaction that they oppose globalization because it makes the poor richer, and the rich poorer! They now think that *we* lost. 'If there's reincarnation,' economist Donald Boudreaux wrote on his Facebook page, 'in my next life I want to be a trade myth: I'll never again die.'[20]

As I've made clear, creative destruction also creates losers – the word 'destruction' is a giveaway. But for open Western countries the benefits of international trade outweigh the cost by roughly twenty to one. It doesn't get much further away from a zero-sum game than that. Yet, when asked about the effects of trade (approximated by its impact on employment), only 11 per cent of Americans thought that both the US and its trading partner benefit. Half of the respondents thought it helped the trading partner but hurt the US. And the zero-sum mentality was on prominent display: the more a person thought that trade hurt the US, the more he thought it benefited the trading partner.[21]

Those who have grown accustomed to interpreting trade as a zero-sum game find themselves unable to extend moral approval to trade even when their conscious mind entertains a scenario where trade is understood as a win–win phenomenon. Facing a choice between a trade policy that benefits both countries and one that hurts the trading partner, they prefer the latter. As the researchers conclude: 'trade is not perceived as mutual cooperation for the collective benefit; instead, it is about gaining an advantage over one's competitors'. When they see trade opportunities, they don't think comparative advantage, they think Vladimir's choice.

A popular interpretation of the recent return of protectionist ideas in the US and Europe is that globalists have forgotten the losers from free trade, and that those who fear being destroyed by international competition are now fighting back. However, Edward Mansfield and Diana Mutz at the University of Pennsylvania gathered information on industry and individual skill levels, and found that personal exposure had little effect on the attitudes towards free trade. The only potential exception is that educational attainment predicts pro-trade views, which has often been interpreted as an expression of economic self-interest.[22]

They did find something else, though, when they asked how positively whites, blacks and Hispanics feel about their own group relative to the other two, and then asked them about trade. The stronger ethnocentrism they expressed, the less they liked free trade. On the surface this does not make any sense. 'Why should how blacks feel about whites and Hispanics (or vice versa) have anything to do with trade liberalization?' Yet in another way, it makes perfect sense. The more you think in terms of us vs them, the less likely you are to think groups can engage in mutually beneficial behaviour. Mansfield and Mutz believe this finding puts the result of education in a new light because, after accounting for the effects of one's worldview, education does not have a direct effect on trade views. So it is not that more education makes you profit from free trade or makes you smart enough to realize its

global benefits. It's that education reduces ethnocentrism and
outgroup anxiety.

One poll showed that a large majority of Americans would
eliminate a thousand foreign jobs to protect a single American
job. One problem, of course, is that the trading partner might
share the same ethnocentric sentiment, and would happily sacrifice a thousand US jobs for one job back home. In the end, the
net result of this kind of 'America First' policy is a net loss of two
thousand jobs to protect two jobs.[23]

One way of getting around this mutually assured tariff destruction is to extend the size of the group making the decision. The
United Steelworkers supported Trump's steel tariffs when they
were first suggested, but changed its mind when the tariffs were
unveiled, since they were also aimed at Canadian firms, whose
workers are members of the same union. On a larger scale, the
same logic is at play when trade policy is delegated from individual European countries to the European Union. There is a pooling
of some national sovereignty involved. We Swedes sacrifice our
ability to hurt the Germans economically (and really ourselves
too), but only in return for them giving up their ability to hurt us.
In reality, it is a way to restrain national governments so that citizens and businesses can cooperate more safely.

The abundance of international agreements and treaties covering subjects like trade, arms control and cooperation on everything
from air traffic control to the environment is seen by nationalists
as a surrender to globalist elites. But it's often a way of trying to
assure mutual restraint between national governments so that we
can safely pursue mutual gains and lessen the risk of ending up
in the kind of geopolitical tit-for-tat rivalry that we have seen far
too many times in history.

Schumpeterian profits

Even though the economy is not in itself a zero-sum game, there is a common perception that the recent rise in inequality within most countries is turning it into one. There are certainly examples of this, where the wealthy got rich at the expense of others and now use their wealth to gain special privileges and political protection. But in itself, inequality is just a comparison of quantities and does not say anything about the relationship between them. Inequality can increase between two individuals who are both getting richer if they do it at different paces, which is normally the case in a dynamic economy.

In the late 1970s, China was very equal, but equally poor. Nine out of ten Chinese people lived in extreme poverty. Economic opening and ensuing growth since then have reduced the share of extremely poor to one in ten Chinese. Of course, these advances did not take place at the same rate everywhere (the greatest growth was in cities and along the coasts). Therefore inequality increased rapidly, from a Gini coefficient (a measure between 0 and 1 of a country's inequality: the closer the number is to 1, the greater the degree of inequality) of around 0.3 to almost 0.5. Anyone who sees equality as the most important value would consider this development to be a terrible setback. Those who see poverty as the big problem see it as one of the greatest advances ever made.[24]

Some get rich by stealing and some get rich by abusing a monopoly position, but on a free market the most common way of becoming rich is to give customers the goods and services they crave.

The economist and Nobel Laureate William Nordhaus has looked at what he calls 'Schumpeterian profits' in the US economy during the post-war era. These are the profits that innovators and entrepreneurs make above the normal return on investments when they engage in creative destruction – introducing new goods, technologies and methods into the economy, such as computers that replace hand calculations and barcodes that replace manual sorting. Nordhaus' conclusion is that those greedy entrepreneurs capture no more than 2.2 per cent of the social value of their innovations, despite first-mover advantage and patent protection. That 2.2 per cent makes up many of the billions and billions you read about on the Forbes list and hear socialists and populists condemn. But it is nothing compared to the almost 98 per cent that society gets, specifically consumers; in other words: all of us. In a modern economy profits are quickly competed away. Other companies imitate or innovate around the Schumpeterian companies, and soon others come up with superior goods and services.[25]

Not only is creative destruction not a zero-sum game. It creates massive amounts of wealth, and the best thing is that all of us who took no part in the effort or the risk get the lion's share of it just by going to the shop. Even though we might not think cheaper transistors and longer-lasting asphalt are particularly glamorous, anytime we get something cheaper, faster and better than before, it allows us to use more of our resources on something else that we do value: on our health, on that holiday, on independent theatre or more pyrotechnics at Rammstein concerts.

You might ask yourself why entrepreneurs get themselves deep into debt and neglect friends and family to work long hours for a tiny chance at a success that would give them no more than 2.2 per cent of the gains. Perhaps they just love their work, or they might be chronic optimists who falsely assume they have a much better chance than others of triumphing. Or perhaps that 2.2 per cent, and the tiny chance of becoming the next Jeff Bezos or Bill Gates, is sufficiently attractive to make it all worthwhile. Super-rich entrepreneurs have the same effect on the great mass of experimenters that James Watt's riches had on hopeful innovators during the Industrial Revolution.

An entrepreneur once described the market to me as a

minefield. On the other side is the new knowledge, products, services, technologies and business models that are of immense value
to society. But the path before us is strewn with dangers, general
uncertainty, technological failure, cooperation problems, changing
consumer demand, unpredictable business cycles, changing interest rates, taxes and regulation, and plain bad luck. We don't know
how to cross it safely. So the key is to send as many people as
possible over, to find the road ahead for society. Most of them will
hit a mine, but a few will make it through. It is not always fair
and it is not always the 'right' person who makes it through, but
that is not the point. The point is that this is what gets us to the
other side.

The Jeff Bezos test

Our focus on inequality in dollars and cents sometimes neglects
what is more important: what we can buy with those dollars and
cents. Amazon's Jeff Bezos might be ten million times richer than
we are, but is he really ten million times better off than we are?

Forget about dollars and cents for a minute, and think of all the
things that create the good life. Sure, Jeff Bezos can travel by private jet and doesn't have to wait in line at security, but the major
difference over the last half-century is that even broad swathes of
the population can travel internationally. And on that flight Bezos
probably doesn't have a much better mobile phone or computer
than we do. On those devices, thanks to the internet, he doesn't
have a million times better access to the world's knowledge or
entertainment than we do.

While en route, Jeff Bezos probably eats similar food to the rest
of us, since most people can now also afford exotic food, even previous luxuries like meat and fresh fruit. Traditionally, being poor
meant chronic undernourishment, and stunting was a common
result. As a result, the average British worker was 13 centimetres

shorter than a typical upper-class male two centuries ago.[26] The difference is now negligible.

Of course, Jeff Bezos can waste his money on the most exclusive clothing brands, but the major difference compared to other eras is that now even low- and middle-income households can afford comfortable clothes that are not that much poorer in quality, whereas most people used to wear itchy unwashed wool before the Industrial Revolution. Shoes of leather used to be so expensive they were sometimes mentioned in wills. Before the 1800s, most people's wardrobes were similar to that of the Indian street vendor's I once met who, while growing up, shared a total of one pair of pants and one shirt with two brothers. So if one of them went for a meal in a respectable home or establishment, the others had to stay home. Now most of us even have servants who wash our clothes – they're called washing machines.

Even though Bezos can easily afford several mansions, the rest of us don't have to settle for homes without insulation, electricity and indoor plumbing any more. Homes used to be so poor in quality that 'house breaking' by burglars was a literal activity. Typical habitations were so infested by dirt and vermin that a historian said that from a health point of view the only good thing was that they burned down easily.

Our kids have almost the same chance to learn to read and write as Bezos' kids, and to survive until retirement. Even though there are serious health differences between rich and poor, all that money doesn't give Bezos a much longer lifespan than us. Since the late nineteenth century, roughly seven eighths of the social gap in longevity has disappeared, according to the Nobel Laureate Robert Fogel.[27]

Compare this to the difference in real standards a hundred or a thousand years ago, when the kings and super-rich had horses, thousands of candles lit by servants, private tutors and a Groom of the Stool who assisted them in their toilet needs (yes, many aspects of their lives have also improved). Meanwhile, the great majority had to walk to get anywhere, scant education apart from the Bible, little lighting and no sanitation other than throwing the waste out the door – or out the window, when it was polite to warn passers-by with the shout of 'gardyloo!' (watch out for water). In fact, despite our obsession with monetary inequality, the material goods that make for a good life are much more equally distributed than they have ever been before. Ironically, one reason for this is that entrepreneurs like Jeff Bezos, Bill Gates and Sam Walton have been allowed to get super-rich from business models that make all sorts of goods, services, foods, technologies, medical devices and drugs cheaper and therefore accessible to more people than ever before.

As Joseph Schumpeter wrote:

Queen Elizabeth owned silk stockings. The capitalist achievement does not typically consist in providing more silk stockings for queens but in bringing them within reach of factory girls in return for steadily decreasing amounts of effort.[28]

Our old measures of wealth underestimate such changes because they were created to measure how many bars of iron we produce and they are not very good at capturing the value created in a modern economy with choice, variation, innovation and quality improvements. For example, our inflation measures regularly ignore the price reduction that turns new luxury technologies into something we can all afford, since goods and services are only added to our consumer price index after they have become so cheap that they are available to everyone. The personal computer entered the US consumer price index only in 1987, when you could buy a Commodore Amiga 500 for just 5 per cent of the price you would have had to pay for a IBM 5100 a decade earlier. The mobile phone started entering price baskets in the

late 1990s, when they had already come down in price by some
90 per cent from the 1984 version (which weighed 790 grams).
Super-rich individuals who spent money on these goods when
they were super expensive helped to reduce the price until the rest
of us could afford them. Sequencing a human genome cost more
than $10 million in 2005; now you can get it for less than $1000.
The first lab-grown burger cost $330,000; soon it will be down to
$5. But none of those price reductions will ever be included when
our purchasing power is measured, since they will only make it
into the indexes when their costs are already negligible.

We also have no way of measuring what we get for free. A cynic,
said Oscar Wilde, is a man who knows the price of everything and
the value of nothing. It's the same with GDP. It measures what we
pay, but it's lousy at estimating the value of things that are free or
almost free. When we replace physical goods we paid for – maps,
cameras or encyclopaedias – with free digital versions, it *reduces*
GDP and traditional productivity measures. Twenty years ago, we
took 80 billion photos a year, and we had to buy film and process
it, and it cost us fifty cents a picture. Therefore it was registered in
GDP. The two trillion photos we take today on our smartphones
cost us almost nothing, so it doesn't seem like it gives us anything
of value.

A simple way of trying to understand the real consumer surplus
in an innovative high-tech economy is to ask people what they
would pay to get something back in their lives if it didn't exist.
And apparently it is very difficult to get anyone to give up the
internet for a million dollars – something that is only included in
GDP at the sum we pay for our broadband connection. According to a 2015 poll, a third of us would rather give up sex than the
internet, which strongly suggests that 'nothing' doesn't quite cover
its contribution.[29] One such study of the consumer surplus showed
that we value the access to search engines at almost $18,000, email
at more than $8000 and digital maps at $3600 annually. If we

were to include just these three digital services in our measures of wealth, GDP per capita would be increased by roughly half![30]

To get a more accurate sense of the overall consumer surplus, we would have to do the same thing with every small invention that now costs us very little. How about anaesthesia? If there were no way to reduce the pain in the world, what would you pay to have it? If you ask someone before going into surgery you would see that the price would approach their total wealth. And yet it is rarely visible in GDP statistics.

Making it zero-sum

Not all wealth is created innocently and creatively, though. According to *The Economist*'s index of crony capitalism, a quarter of the world's billionaires derive their wealth from markets that are susceptible to monopoly or depend on government favours or licensing. This includes mining and commodities, defence, banking, tech, telecom, infrastructure, real estate and construction.[31] It doesn't rule out the possibility that they made money on heroic entrepreneurship to the benefit of consumers, of course. If a company becomes the most successful because it is the best company, and the market is so open that the company must continue to innovate to stay on top, that is great. Their position might be dependent on economies of scale and network effects, but that is not cheating if it is what helps them produce better and/or cheaper goods and services than any competitor. But we have to be eternally vigilant. The index does suggest that favourable policies towards particular businesses are often decisive and that profits are larger than they would be on a competitive market. Often these businesses use their expertise and their resources to strangle the competition and capture the regulatory process. Regulations and taxes become tailor-made for them, to the detriment of the overall economy.

There are some prominent examples of this. Big financial companies have been allowed to reduce capital buffers to a pittance, with the knowledge that they have a government safety net. In good times they win; in bad times, the taxpayers lose. This system of 'too big to fail' corresponds to an ongoing, implicit subsidy of almost 100 million dollars every day to the top eighteen US banks.[32] This has created an oversized banking system that increases risk, and many brilliant graduates who could have been innovative in other sectors go there to design new exotic securities that are little more than regulatory arbitrage.

The EU spends 41 per cent of its total budget on subsidies for farmers, major energy producers rely on government favours and handouts, and residents legislate to block new construction so as to keep the great unwashed out and property prices up. Six of the top ten richest counties in the US are in Washington, DC, which suggests that lobbying politicians for favours is a growth industry. 'When buying and selling are controlled by legislation, the first things to be bought and sold are legislators,' as P. J. O'Rourke observed.

These are examples of the 'conspiracy against the public' that Adam Smith saw people of the same trade engage in, even when they only meet for merriment and diversion. Smith explained that this is not the result of voluntary exchange, which is non-zero, but of the picking of pockets, which is zero-sum. This is his oft-misunderstood argument for free markets and free trade. It was not that businesses are always good – in that case they could be entrusted with privileges and monopolies. It was that they would be awful unless they were constantly exposed to fierce competition that would force them to innovate and lower prices.

We push people into zero-sum games whenever we create public systems that take from some to give to others. One example is Europe – a continent divided by a common currency. The Euro was supposed to create unity between European countries, but since it (implicitly at first) created a common responsibility for public debts, it has created a situation where all sides feel they are being taken advantage of by others. North Europeans are angry because they had to pay for the bailouts of profligate Euro members to the south (often, in fact, by bailing out German banks that had lent to these countries). South Europeans are angry because Brussels and Berlin take control of their public finances and tell them what they are and aren't allowed to spend on. This is a recipe for a constant tug of war that is easily exploited by nationalists on both sides.

One ad from the Swedish anti-immigrant party, the Sweden Democrats, for the 2010 election shows an old white woman faltering slowly towards the public purse to get her retirement benefits but being pushed aside by burka-clad women with babies in buggies demanding child benefits. Government services like schooling and healthcare do not seem to create this tension, but transfers between parts of the population (like generous cash benefits and housing) do. Researchers have found that welfare regimes like Scandinavia's, where immigrants are eligible for benefits just by getting to the country, have stronger and more stable support for anti-immigrant parties. Where welfare programmes are more tied to occupation and past contributions, it seems citizens don't feel they are in competition with immigrants for limited resources, and do not express the same welfare chauvinism.[33] Obviously, this effect is heightened when there is a huge inflow of refugees in a short time and public resources are overstretched.

Status is zero-sum

Unfortunately, one aspect of all human relationships has an important zero-sum aspect to it: social status. The wealth of everybody, or at least most people, can increase simultaneously, but the status of everybody cannot because it is related to one's rank within a group or in society. It is not a growing or shrinking pool of benefits created by our work and technology, but an evaluative hierarchy based on our shared cultural beliefs.

From the animal kingdom and the schoolyard we know all about *dominance*, the status we get from our ability to intimidate others. While this is not an unfamiliar way of getting others to submit in groups – or in businesses and politics, as we saw in the previous chapter – *Homo sapiens* has a tendency to get rid of its bullies. Much more common is *prestige*, the status we get from being impressive, admirable, helpful or just fun to be around. We want to be close to such people because it is useful to have the top dogs on our side. Prestige is much more conducive to mutual gains than intimidation and force, of course, but – as Kevin Simler and Robin Hanson point out in an illuminating chapter on social status – there is only so much respect to go around.[34] We can't all be considered (explicitly or implicitly) the strongest or wisest. If someone comes along who is better than me at playing football or resolving conflicts, my relative status shrinks. 'We can't all be heroes because somebody has to sit on the curb and clap as they go by,' as Will Rogers observed.

This can be witnessed in seemingly absurd competitions over who gets to sacrifice the most for the group. A big man in New Guinea once declared victory after having given more food and gifts to another tribe leader: 'I have won. I have knocked you down by giving so much.'[35] Simler and Hanson compare this to the behaviour of a small brown bird called the Arabian babbler, where the highest-ranking birds compete fiercely to do more than their fair share in feeding the others or attacking predators. Higher-ranking birds quite often push other birds off their perch to take over their guard duty, and all this results in them protecting their status, with all the benefits that entails. We – and the Arabian babblers – want to be friends and allies with those who do good things for their friends and allies, so it makes evolutionary sense to be that kind of good person. And lest you think we have moved on from this in modern society, just watch two wealthy middle-aged men squabbling over who gets to pick up the bill after a lavish dinner.

In many circles, it is considered deeply unfashionable and even unsettling to talk about status. That is partly because it seems to upset our egalitarian values, and often because we think the 'status symbols' used by other groups – flaunting expensive watches and the right shoes or knowing the latest influencer trend before others – are unbearably silly. But that is probably because we get some of our status by not caring about such superficial displays. And the same people who would never carry around an expensive designer handbag or talk about how much they bench press would not hesitate to tell you how you should prepare that rabbit ravioli they just discovered at a Tuscan vineyard, or the fact that they are reading that bleak yet surprisingly amusing Slovenian novel. Some show who they are through their consumption choices, others by telling us they don't care for shopping. Some take great pride in being popular on social media, others about not having a presence.

Status hierarchies exist in every known society, according to the anthropologist Donald Brown, and not just those based on sex, age and kinship, but also those based on individual traits. Successful hunters in traditional hunter-gatherer groups get more access to women and their offspring are treated better, for example.[36]

The higher status someone is, the more others will defer to them and treat them better. Whether we like it or not, we always evaluate people because we are looking for potential partners and associates. In order to attract the best and the most loyal ones, we display our best traits and abilities, and also our compatibility with those we like. We are always eager to let others know about the skills we have, our great taste and the things we know – naturally in a humble, self-deprecating way (because that approach happens to accrue more status in our circles).

Status is not really a zero-sum game, of course, because we don't all measure status in the same way. In driving this point home, David Friedman asks us to think about our time as students. In a way everybody was at the top of their own ladder. The few students who were passionately into drama knew they were the most important people at the university while the others were just there to provide them with an audience. Those into sports thought the same thing about themselves. Others believed themselves superior because they were into politics and considered others as potential supporters who would help their career. Some considered themselves the most important at university for the simple reason that they were the best students academically.[37] Thankfully, nature arranged matters so that we conveniently tend to value things we are good at. I can be better than you, and you can be better than me simultaneously, because we have different scales.

But, still, it's no fairy tale. Some will never find their group, and others will be at the bottom of the pecking order within their groups. Nevertheless, it points to the necessity of pluralistic societies where different groups and values coexist, and people are allowed to move to where they feel welcome and appreciated. The fragmentation of hierarchies and unified beliefs in the open society is in fact one of its greatest benefits. It allows everyone to search for the particular work they are passionate about – and even if they don't find it, they can usually gain others' respect by being the reliable parent, the good friend, the handy neighbour, the inventive cook, by arranging goth clubs, being the hard-working goalkeeper, gamemaster in the local Darkon Wargaming Club, or this year's gooseberry marmalade rookie.

In psychology professor William von Hippel's story about mankind's development he mentions that many other species have only one way to get ahead in life. If you are a male dung beetle, you must be able to roll a ball of faeces that is many times your body weight. That's the one ability that will impress a female dung beetle to mate with you and create new dung beetles that can take over the family business when you are not there any more. If you are bad at it, that's it. But for humans, the number of strategies is only limited by our imagination.[38] This was not the case in traditional society, when life for people who weren't kings and nobles was still pretty close to the dung beetle experience. But in modern, open societies we are allowed to find our own group to belong to and our individual ladder to climb.

The more open the society, the more different paths there are to status and human flourishing, and more people from different groups will get a chance to attain it. Some will find this threatening. Not just those who have problems finding their own role but also those who think they've found it, but fear this position does not guarantee the same status in the future. As new groups or previously disadvantaged ones move up in society, get better access to jobs and higher wages, this can rattle the previously dominant group. They don't have to lose in an absolute sense and their lives may improve materially, but if it improves much faster for other groups, it still can feel like a loss.

This has often been a source of discontent and dreams about 'good old days' when life was easier and we all got along – or at least, when our own group was in charge and others knew their place.

7

ANTICIPATORY ANXIETY

'The whole modern world has divided itself into Conservatives and Progressives. The business of Progressives
is to go on making mistakes. The business of Conservatives is to prevent mistakes from being corrected.'

G. K. Chesterton

If you visit Hagley Park in the West Midlands of England and
make it to the big eighteenth-century house of the Lyttelton
family, walk another half-mile to the east and you'll come upon an
exotic and impressive sight once you clear the trees.

In front of you is what seems like the ruins of a Gothic castle.
There are four corner towers, but only one is still standing, complete with battlements and an intersecting stair turret. The others
are reduced to one or two storeys and the wall connecting them
has collapsed. Just two remaining windows impress the spectator
with their tall gothic arches. Below them is a pointed doorway,
and above it three shield reliefs.

You stand there in awe, lost in thought. It is a place of history,
memory and nostalgia. You start thinking about the ancient history of which this place could speak, and wonder what spectacular
building once stood here.

The answer is none. The ruin was constructed just like this in the mid-eighteenth century, with the purpose of giving the impression that this was a place of wonder, where a magnificent castle had once been until time, nature and a few heroic or barbaric acts reduced it to a state of decay. It is a selective, artificial version of history – very much like the politics of nostalgia that comes from opponents of openness and progress. They tap into a powerful sentiment right now, when we experience a yearning for the good old days in many countries. When asked if life in their country is better or worse today than fifty years ago, 31 per cent of the British, 41 per cent of the Americans (a plurality), and 46 per cent of the French say that it is worse.[1]

Nostalgia is not new. The mock castle of Hagley Park was not extraordinary back in its day. Building ruins from scratch – 'ruin follies' – was at the height of fashion for the European aristocracy in the eighteenth century. They built shattered castles and crumbling abbeys to commemorate their real and imagined past. In 1836, Edward Hussey of Scotney Castle in Kent improved his old house by smashing it and turning it into a ruin that made for a nice view from his new house. In the late eighteenth century, another aristocrat built an extravagant six-storey tower in Désert de Retz in north-central France, made to look like the remaining column of a colossal temple. Right beside it he built a ruined Gothic temple.

The ruin craze was part of a broader reaction against the Enlightenment and its ideals of reason and progress, which came to be called Romanticism. It glorified nature, nation and history, and turned the nostalgic desire for childhood and home country from pathology to movement. Sometimes it was not a rejection of modernity but a way to create a continuity that made it easier to live with change, as industrialization and urbanization quickly changed living conditions. 'This acute awareness of tradition is a modern phenomenon that reflects a desire for custom and routine in a world characterized by constant change and innovation,' wrote Witold Rybczynski.[2]

The term 'nostalgia' was coined by the Swiss doctor Johannes Hofer in 1688. It was his word for the sad, obsessive desire of students, servants and soldiers in foreign lands to return to their home. In *The Future of Nostalgia* the scholar of comparative literature Svetlana Boym points to the curious fact that, by the end of the eighteenth century, intellectuals from different national traditions began to claim they had a special term for bittersweet homesickness that did not exist in any other language. Germans had *Heimweh*, the French *maladie du pays*, the Russians *toska* and the Polish *tesknota*. And other emerging nations also claimed that only they, because of their unique national identity, knew the true meaning of the sad, beautiful welling-up of longing. Boym 'is struck by the fact that all these untranslatable words are in fact synonyms; and all share the desire for untranslatability, the longing for uniqueness'.[3]

This was the era when governments and intellectuals began to construct national identities, especially to resist occupation during the Napoleonic Wars and rebuild afterwards. The folk songs they praised as a pure expression of the people's traditional sentiments were rewritten in new versions because the old lyrics were far too vulgar and not sufficiently patriotic. Authorities also created national languages, often by systematizing a local dialect and enforcing it on everybody through the education system. Linguistic boundaries became rigid, and many oral traditions perished. In the Holy Roman Empire of the German Nation only a quarter spoke German. Even in Prussia, which did the most to encourage poets and writers to create a common German identity to resist Napoleon, German was just one of six major languages. At the Vienna Congress 1815, Prussia was registered as a 'Slav kingdom', and Hegel talked of Brandenburg and Mecklenburg as 'Germanized Slavs'.[4] In his book *The Myth of*

Nations, the historian Patrick Geary claimed that even in a country like France, with centuries-old national boundaries and long linguistic traditions, not many more than half spoke French as their native language in 1900. Others spoke different Romance languages and dialects, and in some areas Celtic and Germanic languages.[5]

Just as the aristocrats built fake ruins, kings and poets were now erecting artificial ethnicities and nations. Some did it out of love for the homeland, but some also saw its potential as a cement for ideological collectivism. Yet, although such ruins and ethnicities are artificial, our feelings for them are real. Remember that it just takes a shared preference for Kandinsky or Klee to create a common bond with a stranger. So it's not strange that an idea of a common history and destiny unites people easily. And while the history of ethnic nationalism is, as US diplomat Dan Fried pointed out, like cheap alcohol – first it makes you drunk, then it makes you blind, then it kills you – civic forms of nationalism have inspired fights for freedom and inclusion of immigrants and minority groups too.

Nostalgia is a natural, and even important, state of mind according to psychologists. Anchoring our identity in something enduring helps us when all that is solid seems to be melting into air. Everything always changes, but we also need a sense of stability and predictability. When things change too fast, we lose our sense of control. This is probably why a yearning for the past is especially likely when we experience rapid transitions, like maturing into adulthood, ageing into retirement, dislocation, migration or rapid technological change.

People going through rough times can be helped by remembering better days in the past and the idea that joy is possible again. For dementia sufferers nostalgia can help establish some sense of personal continuity. The best way to deal with it is not leeches or opium (or execution, which a Russian general threatened nostalgic soldiers with during the War of the Polish Succession in 1733). It is a glass of wine, the favourite music from your teens and the family photo album.

As Alan Jay Levinovitz explains, it is important to make a distinction between three sorts of nostalgia: personal, historical and collective.[6] Personal nostalgia is made up of first-person memories and contributes to your own sense of identity and history. If personal nostalgia is about what life was like for you in the past, historical nostalgia is a generalization about what the past was like, often in the form of a longing for an enchanted, simple world – the good old days. Collective nostalgia is the emotional attachment to collective cultural identities: this is what my group was like or endured in the past. Just like personal nostalgia, this emotion can be a source of strength that helps you through difficult periods. The insight (or illusion) that your people or your nation endured something together can help and inspire. But it is also easily abused for political forces, who promise they can restore the greatness that has been lost. It is wrong, because we can't go back – and even if we could, we wouldn't find what we were looking for because it was never there and, in any case, would not be able to give us the solution to future problems.

When were the good old days?

In a wonderful episode of the podcast *Pessimists Archive*, Jason Feifer explored nostalgia throughout history.[7] If you want to make America great again, you have to ask yourself when America was great, he thought. The most popular answer seemed to be the 1950s. So then he asked scholars of the 1950s whether they thought that was the good old days. Definitely not. People were worried about race and class, riots in American cities and the very real threat of instant nuclear annihilation. There was anxiety about rapidly changing family life and especially the new youth cultures and mindless, consumer-oriented students on campus. American sociologists warned that rampant individualism was tearing the family apart. And by the way, in this era that we remember as tranquil, job churn was much more rapid than today. Many pointed to the 1920s as the good old days.

However, back in the 1920s, people worried about how rapid technological change was threatening our fundamental sanity – radio and recorded music gave us too much speed and too much choice. So did the automobile, which would probably ruin the morals of the young. In the *New York Times*, you could read on the front page that scientists had concluded that 'AMERICAN LIFE IS TOO FAST'.[8] The famous child psychologist John Watson warned that increasing divorce rates meant the American family would soon cease to exist. Many romanticized the calmer lifestyle of the late 1800s. Seeing how family life was changing, some began to idealize the Victorian family, when they thought that fathers were really fathers, mothers true mothers, and children respected their elders.

But at the turn of the century, the railroads, the telegraph and rapid urbanization were undermining traditional communities and ways of life. And everybody worried about a fast-spreading disease: neurasthenia. The idea was that the unnatural pace of life sapped people of energy, and gave them neurasthenia, which could express itself in anxiety, headaches, insomnia, back pain, constipation, impotence and chronic diarrhoea. The Victorian middle classes handled the transitions of the era by becoming the first generation to value the old as such; they started to care about antiques and covered their walls with portraits of ancestors. The historian John Gillis has shown that their fear of urbanization and work outside the household ruining family life led them to invent the notion of a traditional family life that has been lost – a time that was simpler, less problematic, more rooted in place and tradition.[9] They felt life before the Industrial Revolution was better.

In the US, many longed for the quiet, happier life in the days before the civil war.

Before the Industrial Revolution family life was indeed different. Around half of a birth cohort died before they were fifteen years old, and 27 per cent of those who survived were fatherless by the time they reached that age. The share of marriages broken up by death was similar to the share broken up by divorces today. Most families sent children away to live in other households as servants or apprentices.[10] After the French Revolution, Edmund Burke thought, 'The age of chivalry is gone; that of sophisters, economists and calculators has succeeded; and the glory of Europe is extinguished forever.'[11] In America, many worried the republic had somehow lost its way since the founders created it.

Jason Feifer and the scholars he talked to continued to look for the good old days, and kept wandering further back into the past, until they finally reached ancient Mesopotamia, five thousand years ago. After having invented civilization and writing, it didn't take more than two centuries before humans started writing about how difficult life is now and how it must have been so much easier in the past. It seems the first society was also the first nostalgic society.

The American scholar Samuel Noah Kramer found examples of the Sumerians in cuneiform script complaining about how their leaders abused them and the merchants cheated and, above all, how family life was not what it used to be. One clay tablet frets about 'the son who spoke hatefully to his mother, the younger brother who defied his older brother, who talked back to the father'.[12] On an almost four-thousand-year-old clay tablet, Kramer found the story of Enmerkar and the land of Aratta, and expression of the idea that there was once a golden age of peace and security, and that we had since fallen from this blessed state:

Once upon a time, there was no snake, there was no scorpion,
There was no hyena, there was no lion,
There was no wild dog, no wolf,
There was no fear, no terror,
Man had no rival. [...]
The whole world, the people in unison,
To Enlil in one tongue gave praise.[13]

In other words, if you happen to think we have uniquely difficult problems today, with a more rapid pace of life, corrupt rulers and unruly youngsters, don't trust your feelings. Every generation has thought the same. Every generation has interpreted its struggle with the human predicament and the difficulty of relationships as a sign that things have become worse since a supposedly more harmonious time in the past.

One important explanation for this historical nostalgia is that we know we survived these problems, so in retrospect they seem smaller. Otherwise we wouldn't be here. But we can never be certain we will be able to solve the problems we are facing today. That has been the predicament of every generation, and that is why we always look back at a simpler time. We know the radio didn't ruin the young, but we don't know if the smartphone will. We know we survived smallpox and polio, but we don't know about Ebola or the coronavirus. We know the planet didn't blow up during the Cold War, but who can say for sure that we won't do it this time around? And this also leads us to forget the terrible anguish our ancestors suffered when dealing with what were then the worst difficulties that they could imagine.

Another reason is that we often confuse personal nostalgia with the historical sort. When were the good old days? Was it by chance the one incredibly short period in mankind's history when you were alive and – more importantly – young? I can't say anything certain about you, of course, but whenever I ask people this question, that is the most common answer. And polls bear this out. A British study found that people in their thirties think life was better in the 1990s than today. Brits in their fifties prefer the 1980s, and those over sixty think life in the 1960s was the best. A US poll found that those born in the 1930s and 1940s thought the 1950s was America's best decade, while those born in the 1960s and 1970s preferred the 1980s.[14] (It is interesting that the great nostalgic 1980s television show was *Happy Days*, set in a glamorous version of the 1950s. And thirty years later, we had another influential, nostalgic television series, *Stranger Things*, now looking back fondly on the fashion and music of the 1980s.)

Perhaps that is why we have this great wave of nostalgia in the Western world right now. The big baby-boomer generation, born after World War II, is retiring and a suspiciously large share of them think the good old days were in their youth. Because when we are young, life for most people is kind of exciting: something new awaits around every corner, we scheme and dream, but we can also feel pretty safe because our parents are there to pick up our bills and take care of us. Eventually, we all grow older and learn about the horrors of the world. We take on more responsibility, and we have kids ourselves, so suddenly we have to pay attention to every kind of risk and problem in society. With time, some of our dreams are frustrated, a certain decay in physical capacity sets in, and what once seemed new and exciting is replaced by things the now-young think are new and exciting but seem strange and unsettling to us.

When thinking about memory in an abstract way, it's easy to assume we have a clearer memory of things that happened to us recently. That is not the case. Researchers have found that we encode more memories during adolescence and early adulthood than during any other period of our lives, and when we think back on our lives, this is the period we most often return to. We might have this 'reminiscence bump' because that was a period when we started forming our identity and experienced many firsts (first love, first job, first time we went to a Depeche Mode concert). It is a period of rapid change followed by stability, and so it figures prominently in our recollection of our lives.

Although strong, those memories are notoriously unreliable. When schoolchildren returning from summer holiday are asked to name good and bad things from the break, their lists are almost equally long. When the exercise is repeated a couple of months later, the list of good things grows longer and the bad list gets shorter. By the end of the year, the good things have pushed out the bad from their memories completely. They don't remember their holiday any more, just their idealized image of 'holiday'. It is difficult for any version of the present to compete with that.[15]

Nostalgia is a necessary human psychological trait, but it can't be a governing philosophy. We should beware of politicians, populists (and parents) who claim things were so much better in the past and that we should try to recreate that former world. Obviously some things were better and we should investigate and see what we can learn from that, but trusting our gut feeling is letting ourselves be deceived by our reminiscence bump.

Douglas Adams once came up with three rules to summarize how we react to technological innovation at different ages. I think they also sum up how most of us react to changes in behaviour, culture and neighbourhoods:

1. Anything that is in the world when you're born is normal and ordinary and is just a natural part of the way the world works.
2. Anything that's invented between when you're fifteen and thirty-five is new and exciting and revolutionary and you can probably get a career in it.
3. Anything invented after you're thirty-five is against the natural order of things.[16]

Technofear

The problem with politicized nostalgia is that progress, which creates the marvels the next generations will eventually feel nostalgic about, depends on the unforeseeable and unexpected, on experiments and innovations. Daniel Isenberg called his book on business successes *Worthless, Impossible, and Stupid* because every great new business model was first seen by most wise men as worthless, impossible or stupid, or all three. This goes for most new technologies as well. As the English economist and scientist-inventor William Petty observed in 1679:

> when a new invention is first propounded, in the beginning every man objects, and the poor inventor runs the gantloop of all petulant wits [...] not one of a hundred outlives this torture [...] and moreover, this commonly is so long a doing that the poor inventor is either dead or disabled by the debts contracted to pursue his design.[17]

The smallpox vaccine at first seemed impossible – the Royal Society told its inventor Edward Jenner in 1798 'not to risk his reputation by presenting to this learned body anything which appeared so much at variance with established knowledge and withal so incredible'. Since the source of the vaccine was infected cows, it was also stupid: clergy objected to the 'iniquity of transferring disease from the beasts of the field to Man'. Some even feared the vaccine would give them bovine traits, and one woman said her vaccinated daughter had begun to cough like a cow and grow hairy.[18] Nevertheless, it would go on to save hundreds of millions of lives. Likewise, the amazing invention of anaesthetics was resisted, especially for women during childbirth, since the Bible dictated that motherhood should be accompanied by suffering. Romantic objections were raised against steam engines, railways and gas lighting – to 'preserve the empire of darkness'. Electricity seemed too powerful to be handled by humans, and the *New York Times* feared that the light bulb could make the spectator blind.

The first railways in Britain were met with almost universal popular disapproval. People feared what the speed would do to the human body and news outlets reported widely on every accident. The monthly *The Household Narrative* had a special segment on 'accidents and disasters'. Landowners complained that the railways destroyed the landscape and the fox hunts, and farmers were concerned that they would ruin the hens' laying capacity and the cows' grazing habits. The Victorian literati described the railway as 'contamination'. Wordsworth claimed the influx of strangers would wreak moral havoc upon the English Lake District, and Ruskin objected that, 'A fool always wants to shorten space and time, a wise man wants to lengthen both.'[19]

Even the most innocent inventions were first seen as outrageous. *Pessimists Archive* – an invaluable resource on why we resist new things – documents that the bicycle was met with all the fears that usually face new technologies when it was new in the early twentieth century: they destroy our health, our morals and our jobs. They were dangerous, not just because of accidents, but also because the owner of the 'dandy horse' became intoxicated with power. Rumours were spread about cruel cyclists who ran over others and left them for dead. In addition, cyclists risked becoming physically deformed. Some thought the cycling generation would become hunchbacks from leaning forward all day, and women's reproductive ability would be destroyed by sitting in the bicycle saddle. Women who appreciated the freedom the bike gave them were warned they risked developing a 'bicycle face'; when they clenched their jaw and focused their eyes to balance on two wheels, their features risked getting caught in a deep, unflattering grimace. When everyone started cycling, they would also stop reading books, drinking beer and smoking cigars. Shoemakers would lose their jobs because no one walked. An American hat-maker demanded that Congress enact a law that cyclists must buy a hat, otherwise the industry would be destroyed.[20]

My favourite example of the fear of creative destruction is that infamous disturber of the peace, the umbrella. It came late to Europe, adopted from the Chinese, and at first was mostly carried by women to protect themselves from the sun. In the early 1750s, a British wool merchant, Jonas Hanway, brought it to the rainy streets of London. On paper it sounds like the best match since bangers met mash. But when Hanway protected himself from the rain with an umbrella, he incurred public ridicule. It looked silly and feminine, thought people, an evidence of weakness of charac-ter. The angriest were the coach drivers, who feared the umbrella would take their jobs. They hurled abuse at him, pelted him with rubbish and one even tried to run him over. Business was espe-cially good for two-wheeled horse-drawn carriages and sedan chairs when it rained, since they came equipped with canopies that kept passengers dry. Now no one would use transportation services any more.[21]

My ambition is not to show how silly previous generations are. If anything, it shows how silly we all are – these are universal reac-tions to things that are new and strange. In recent memory, similar anxiety has been widely felt about innovations like the internet, video games, genetically modified organisms and stem-cell research. Soon they too will end up in the *Pessimists Archive*.

Not all of these fears were unfounded. New technologies do result in accidents, they disturb traditional cultures and habits, and destroy old jobs while simultaneously creating new ones. But the only way to learn how to make the best use of them and reduce the risks is trial and error, not wild speculation. Only by being allowed to function and adapt do they prove their worth, and we get used to them. In 1969, a majority of Americans said that *in vitro* fertilization was 'against God's will'. The federal government imposed a moratorium on funding, and legislation to ban it was considered by Congress. Yet, less than a decade later, 60 per cent approved of it, and more than half said they would consider using it if they were infertile.[22]

If we had a plebiscite on new technologies the moment they were introduced, I am pretty sure we would have banned most innovations – from the vaccine and the bicycle to GMOs and the electric scooter. As Adam Thierer argues in his book *Permissionless Innovation*, public policy cannot be guided by fear of hypothetical worst-case scenarios as that halts all kinds of innovation and makes the best-case scenarios less likely. That is fine if we already live in utopia, but not if we still have problems to solve. And while new innovations are not perfect, wisdom is only born of experience, which involves risk, mistakes and failures and new adaptations and new innovations. Learning by doing does not just summarize learning, but also the human condition.

Unfortunately, this view of an open future has two strong enemies: conservatives – and progressives.

The future and its enemies

Most animals are programmed to know what to eat. Humans are not, we have to learn it. As omnivores we have to be curious but we also have to be a little bit worried because what we eat can kill us. This is the omnivore's dilemma – we must search for and explore potential foods, but meanwhile we have to be wary of them until they have been proven non-toxic. We have neophilia and neophobia. We are both attracted to and fear new things.[23]

Usually, we think this is reflected in two camps, one holding us back, the other one pushing us forward. On the one hand there are conservatives who ask us to slow down because innovation threatens traditions, old industries and social cohesion; on the other hand there are progressive idealists and technocrats who ask us to hurry up because they have seen something better in the future and want us all to speed towards it. But the world is more complicated than this. The question is not whether you like progress or not, it's whether you like open-ended progress – where you are open to giving people freedom to experiment and create even though you don't know what the final result will be. This is the kind of change that grows, not one that is imposed.

In his works spanning many different academic disciplines, Friedrich Hayek explained that progress can only come from this spontaneous order:

> Since the value of freedom rests on the opportunities it provides for unforeseeable and unpredictable actions, we will rarely know what we lose through a particular restriction of freedom. Any such restriction, any coercion other than the enforcement of general rules, will aim at the achievement of some foreseeable particular result, but what is prevented by it will usually not be known... And so, when we decide each issue solely on what appear to be its individual merits, we always over-estimate the advantages of central direction.[24]

Virginia Postrel's 1998 Hayekian book *The Future and Its Enemies* is still the best guide to the new conflicts over culture and technology, and the strange political realignments that are taking place right now. She argues that both status quo conservatives and progressive technocrats share a common element: the hostility to open-ended change, guided not by planners but by millions of experiments and trial and error. Whether it be the rejection of a new technology or the demand that it is imposed in the same way for everybody, this hostility represents an urge to control what cannot be controlled. For both, the goal is stasis, it's just that one group finds it in the past, the other one in the future. It is a bit like G. K. Chesterton's sardonic description of the progressive and the conservative: 'the advanced person who rushes us into ruin, and the retrospective person who admires the ruins'.[25]

The real divide, says Postrel, is between *dynamists* who think that the future is open, and *stasists*, of both the conservative and the progressive variety, who have a particular endgame in mind. She asks:

> Do we search for stasis – a regulated, engineered world? Or do we embrace dynamism – a world of constant creation, discovery and competition? Do we value stability and control, or evolution and learning? [...] Do we think that progress requires a blueprint, or do we see it as a decentralized, evolutionary process? Do we consider mistakes permanent disasters, or the correctable by-products of experimentation? Do we crave predictability, or relish surprise?[26]

None of these groups reflects traditional political divides. Just as dynamists can be classical liberals, free market conservatives, centrists, libertarian greens or pro-globalist leftists, the forces opposing them also come from all over the political spectrum. The conservatives who fear dynamism are strong both in the Left and the Right. As Brink Lindsey has phrased it, they are both pining for the 1950s – the Left wants to work there, and the Right wants to come home from work there. And after the Trump takeover of the Republican party, now it seems like the Right wants to work there as well. It is the reactionary Right that has historically been associated not just with resistance to new family constellations, new immigrants and secularization, but also with new technologies; however, in the conservative Left you also find a rejection of new technologies when they happen to dislike them, such as genetically modified crops, nuclear power and many of the platforms of the sharing economy.

Technocrats who reject dynamism are also of both the Left and the Right – those who want to control the future to ensure progress is equitable and doesn't hurt labour interests, and those who want to do so to protect culture and social cohesion. Leftist Democrats want to plan the economy to create the right jobs, like the Green New Deal (which 'wasn't originally a climate thing at all', but 'a how-do-you-change-the-entire-economy thing', as one of its originators has admitted).[27] National conservatives want to plan the economy and restrict foreign competition to create stable employment in traditional industries like manufacturing. Just as the Romans made a desert and called it peace, the stasists make a plan and call it progress.

Often the lines blur completely. Sometimes the grand plan for the future is entirely backwards-looking, trying to recreate an imagined better and more stable past, and is supported by both the stasist Left and Right. Bernie Sanders has said that he 'would be delighted to work with' Trump on implementing trade barriers to reduce the restructuring of the economy. Nationalist Fox TV host Tucker Carlson praises Elizabeth Warren's interventionist plan for the economy, saying 'she sounds like Donald Trump at his best'.[28] Their common enemy is 'market fundamentalists' and 'libertarian zealots', who don't know what the solution is but think the chance to find it increases if millions, not just a few people at the top, are looking for it. Not just the Industrial Revolution, but the computer revolution illustrates this.

Why didn't the Soviet Union invent the PC?

Why wasn't the personal computer invented by communists? Or why wasn't the PC at least widely produced and used in communist countries? An American study of the development of the computer in the Soviet Union from 1988 concluded: 'In many respects, the USSR is at square one.'[29] It was not for a lack of knowledge about what was going on in computing. A large network of industrial spies kept the Soviet leaders fully informed about all the new technologies, and they regularly laid their hands on Western computers, reverse-engineered them and produced clones. The communist leaders knew what was going on with personal computers. But they just couldn't see the point. And probably you wouldn't have either. Sure, they understood why those who launch missiles and manage factories need computing capabilities, but why would anyone want a computer in their home?

The general idea seemed to be that it was a novel way of sorting library cards and recipes. In fact, an early offering for the US consumer market was a 1969 kitchen computer from Honeywell, weighing over 45 kilograms. The user could program the computer with recipes, plan the dinner, and then read the recipes in blinking text on a monochrome screen while cooking. And all this for the neat sum of $10,000 (around $70,000 today), which included a built-in cutting board, and a two-week programming course to understand how to pull the levers.[30]

I don't know about you, but if I were in the Soviet Politburo and heard the news, I would also have said: '*Nyet*, let the decadent capitalists waste their resources on technological frivolity if they want, but we should devote those resources to important things. Possibly a bit more wheat and steel.' And that is exactly what they decided:

> little effort was made to produce large quantities of suitable computer hardware intended for widespread general-purpose use. No great need for this was perceived in the industrial or military sectors; the cost would have been a severe strain on the limited capabilities available, and would have been out of proportion to the short-term benefits.[31]

The leading producer of Soviet computers was the Ministry of Radio Technology, and they had come to the authoritative conclusion that the computer would never become personal.

Most people, and most committees around the world, would have made the same decision. That is why we need open economies with permissionless innovation, so that the small groups who believe in something can use a great diversity of decentralized funding sources and test it on the consumer market, to see if it is in fact worthless, impossible and stupid, or if it turns out to be the next big thing. It allowed Steve Jobs and Steve Wozniak to assemble the Apple I in Job's bedroom and garage in 1976, and sell the first copies to a small computer retailer and then start a company with the help of an angel investor.

The Soviets also had their eccentrics in garages. In 1979, three employees of the Moscow Institute of Electronic Engineering used Western technologies to build their own home computer called the Micro-80. But in the Soviet Union there were no private companies that could support them, no private stores or consumer classes to sell to and teach how to use it, and no venture capitalists to take a chance on them. They had to ask the responsible bureaucrats for the go-ahead to develop the computer. They were turned down.

It was not that these bureaucrats were more stupid than anyone else. 'There is no reason anyone would want a computer in their home,' as the founder of computer company Digital Equipment Corporation said in 1977, echoing the Soviet Ministry of Radio Technology. That was a reasonable assumption at the time. Atari was offered the Apple computer but said no. Wozniak asked Hewlett-Packard if they wanted it five times, and they turned it down five times. And in 1985 Wozniak himself thought they had oversold their product and that the 'home computer may be going the way of video games, which are a dying fad'. The president of Apple, John Sculley, agreed: 'People use computers in the home, of course, but for education and running a small business. There are not uses in the home itself.'[32] Jobs was himself ousted from Apple, before he returned in 1997 to save the faltering company.

He managed to turn it into the world's most valuable company, partly based on the success of a revolutionary smartphone in 2007, which was immediately met by the certain prediction 'Apple won't succeed with the iPhone' by the innovation guru (and I mean that in a non-ironic sense) Clayton Christensen, 'History speaks pretty loudly on that.'[33]

The simple truth is that no one can predict the future. Ironically, in the 1988 study that claimed the Soviet Union was at square one, the authors also added a few words about their own US: 'It would be optimistic to predict a rapid transition of personal computing to a phase 5 [a part of daily life] technology.' The reason for their prediction was that – just like the communists they passed judgment on – they simply didn't see the point:

> The utility of the telephone and television is clear, but only a small part of the U.S. population has an immediate need for personal computing, or would suffer greatly from its absence.[34]

The difference was that, in an open-access system like the US economy, computer enthusiasts could keep looking, just like Columbus could keep searching for a patron. And they could find customers that no plan would have taken into account. It could be the rich man who used it as a status symbol, the hobbyists and hackers who just wanted to tinker with it, the gamers and the businesses who suddenly found a use for it that the inventors had not thought of. IBM had not expected the large consumer demand for business processing services, but when they did, it changed its business model accordingly. When Windows didn't take off, Microsoft planned to replace it with an operative system it had developed with IBM in the late 1980s, and Window's support team was cut to virtually zero. No one was more surprised than Microsoft itself when Windows 3.0 sold two million copies in the first six months, and it quickly changed the whole company's focus accordingly. In his account of the story, Martin Eller, lead developer for graphics on Windows, wrote that it might seem to outsiders like the captains of industry steer their tanker gracefully through the straits, but from the inside it more closely resembles white-water rafting: 'Oh my God! Huge rock dead ahead! Everyone to the left! NO, NO, the *other* left!!!'[35]

The birth of the internet

The development of the internet, which made the personal computer and all digital devices much more interesting, was also the result of a complex, open process. There is an urban myth that the internet was invented by the US Department of Defense to ensure they would have a communications system that could survive a nuclear attack, and that the European Organization for Nuclear Research, CERN, created the world wide web. The internet is sometimes used as an example of incredible foresight by central authorities that managed to push their vision onto researchers and entrepreneurs with overwhelming resources. In reality, the reason you might have heard many different people presented as inventors of the internet is that many were working on similar ideas at the same time, at the Defense Research Agency ARPA, but also in universities, garages and private companies. As the science writer Steven Johnson writes: 'Like many of the bedrock technologies that have come to define the digital age, the internet was created by – and continues to be shaped by – decentralized groups of scientists and programmers and hobbyists (and more than a few entrepreneurs) freely sharing the fruits of their intellectual labor with the entire world.'[36]

What is true is that in 1969, ARPA had created ARPAnet, a network of computers in projects they were funding. But the story has two weaknesses, according to Robert Taylor, who led the project: ARPAnet was not a military project – it was built for the purpose of using many computers at the same time without having to walk between them – and it was not an internet, since that is a link between two or more data networks.[37]

In the early 1960s, J. C. R. Licklider at the company Bolt, Beranek and Newman (BBN) proposed an 'Intergalactic Computer Network' and described many of the aspects that would become the internet infrastructure. When Licklider started working at ARPA, he convinced his colleagues to work with network technology. The 'package-sharing' way of sending information was borrowed by American and British academics, and also suggested at the RAND Corporation. More networks were developed and there was a need for more efficient communication between them. ARPA's Robert Kahn, also from BBN, together with Vint Cerf at Stanford University created the TCP/IP protocol that linked the networks into an open architecture.

Since the pioneers primarily wanted to share processor time at mainframe computers, they could have made the decision to block other applications. But they had sufficient understanding of the limitations of their own imagination to make the platform open and unspecified so that others could later use it as they saw fit, for e-mail, the world wide web and other applications.

At the same time, the British computer consultant Tim Berners-Lee worked on a way to keep track of all his colleagues and their projects, and got the idea of a system organized through hyperlinks. He eventually developed this into an idea of a digital platform that could gather all information on the internet, based on a previous platform called SGML developed at IBM in the 1960s. After having received the official blessing to continue this research from CERN, where he then worked, it only took a year before he could present the first web server, web browser and website. But 'it was a side project that his superiors knew next to nothing about'.[38] As Berners-Lee himself has noted:

Inventing the World Wide Web involved my growing realization that there was a power in arranging ideas in an
unconstrained, weblike way. And that awareness came to me
through precisely that kind of process. The Web arose as the
answer to an open challenge, through the swirling together of
influences, ideas, and realizations from many sides.[39]

And nothing but the unconstrained swirling together of ideas
from all sides could fill this web with life. Glenn Reynolds once
asked us to imagine the digital economy being created top-down,
in an orderly fashion, the way that someone with a regimented
sense of order would do it.[40]

Let's imagine it is 1993, and the UN Secretary-General
gives you an assignment: in, say, twenty years, this world wide web
must be filled with all the information everyone may be interested in and will be able to access wherever they are. You have
twenty years to make sure there are websites with Catalan poetry,
information about nightclubs close to Cologne, facts about frog
diseases, video interviews with the Ugandan diaspora, guides to
urban myths, manuals for old power tools, databases with trade
statistics, historical temperature data from Pacific islands, and cute
pictures of cats. And everything else people might be interested
in. Go!

How would you do this? Who will lead the project? Who
will you put on the committee to assess what should be prioritized? How will you decide what to digitize of all the information
currently on paper? How many need to be employed to scan the
right books and newspapers? Who will pay the bill? How on
earth will we be able to afford it? How do we really know what's
important?

Today it is obvious the internet has become integral to business,
science and culture. But had I talked to some leading economists
a short time ago, I might have heard that communication online

is not that crucial. As late as 1998, the prominent economist Paul Krugman claimed the internet would soon stop growing so fast. It did not matter that more people were being linked, he said, because 'most have nothing to say to each other! [By] 2005 or so, it will be obvious that the Internet's impact on the economy has not been greater than the fax machine' (in an article with the perfect title 'Why most economists' predictions are wrong').[41] Perhaps it would have been better to spend our resources on developing a faster fax machine instead?

I might have concluded early on that there was no point in trying to get commercial interests on board, since even many of the pioneers did not understand its potential. In April 1994, a Microsoft board member brought up the topic of the internet, to which Bill Gates' response has been described: 'His view was that the Internet was free. There's no money to be made there. Why is that an interesting business?'[42]

I have no idea how I would have gone about creating a new online world. Among the few things I know is that if I had been on such a committee, I would hardly have prioritized another search engine in 1997 (Google) because we already had so many. Similarly, I would hardly have given the go-ahead to a page where Harvard students could rank each other's attractiveness (Face-Mash, which soon became Facebook). I would probably have been tempted to block Netflix to save the nice video rental store down the road. Creating such a flourishing online world would have been impossible. Even if you gathered the most brilliant minds in a committee and got so many resources that you could hire ten thousand librarians to search for books and scan the important sections, you'd never have got it ready for 2113, let alone 2013.

But we didn't have such a committee; we had no plan, no hierarchy, structure or coordination. We only had a platform open to all, and we had *everyone*. That's why it worked. For everybody had the freedom to write and create freely, based on their knowledge and their interests, irrespective of whether others thought it uninteresting, unimportant or even offensive. Those who were interested in frogs wrote about frog diseases, those who liked Catalan poetry published that, and the only filter was constant feedback. Netflix was allowed to compete, even though I still miss my local video retailer.

Those who did something that was appreciated by others received more attention and were inspired to do more. Some turned their ideas into business models and began to demand payment and could invest more heavily in them, meaning they did it better and better and more and more. At this point, the ideas could come from people anywhere, and not just from the centre. The way people's ideas developed often surprised themselves. Entrepreneurs, enthusiasts and eccentrics developed completely new and unexpected solutions and techniques; they could then benefit from the stacks of layers others had developed, and add their own layers on top of them. YouTube could be built in six months by three former PayPal employees because they could build it on top of web, but also Adobe's Flash platform for video, and the language of JavaScript to embed clips. Originally the idea was to create a video dating site, but since they did not receive enough dating videos, they decided to allow uploads of anything, which turned out to be quite popular.

Such feedback loops suddenly changed everybody's perception of what was possible. Bill Gates' genius was not prophecy but flexibility. The moment he saw what was happening when he browsed the web, he changed his mind and turned the whole company around to his vision. In May 1995, with the release date of Windows 95 just three months away, he wrote a new memo to his exhausted executive staff, turning 180 degrees away from his previous dismissal of the subject: assigning the internet 'the highest level of importance', he now wanted 'every product plan to try and go overboard on Internet features'.[43]

This is how it happens: experiments, feedback, learning, adaptation, steering clear of the huge rocks ahead, new experiments, more learning, new adaptations, and suddenly something special happens.

Governments can help this process along, not by giving directions or subsidizing particular solutions, but by more broadly supporting scientific research and its dissemination. More knowledge is always better and increases the chances of more unexpected insights. However, trying to tell people what to do with that knowledge will terminate the discovery process. Progress is by its nature unexpected and unforeseeable and cannot be commanded. It comes from strange places, unexpected people and weird combinations. You wouldn't get Silicon Valley if you didn't mix and blend hackers and hippies, Stanford and Berkeley, entrepreneurs and venture capitalists. Newspapers and online retailers learned safe methods of credit payments online and video streaming from porn sites. Advanced robotics companies solved the difficult problem of simultaneous localization and mapping by learning from the gaming industry (which turned out not to be a fad). Serious industries could fill all their products with cheap sensors just because kids kept buying new mobile phones all the time, which drove down the price of their production.

Today's giants, like Google, Apple and Tencent, prosper because they do not rely exclusively on their own creativity and ability. Instead they have created platforms for outsiders, App Store, Google Play and WeChat are ecosystems for millions of other innovators, so that their offerings evolve every second thanks to people they have never heard about or ever met. Third-party sellers account for half of Amazon's sales, and Alibaba even shares its data with outsiders to help them to improve their business and sell more via Alibaba. If you can't beat them, invite them over to your platform.

Present at the computer creation

Both the anti-dynamist forces that Virginia Postrel identified – the nostalgic conservatives and the impatient technocrats – were present at the creation of the digital world. Wherever you look, there are defenders of the status quo, of course. Some feared the computer threatened our humanity, and that it would leave no room for human creativity and imagination. In the early 1960s, a New York railroad man feared computers would lead to 'programmed mediocrity pervading all facets of life'.[44] In 1976, US federal authorities warned that computers posed a danger to air transportation by reducing oral communication between pilots and air traffic control. (The risk of dying in a crash has since declined by 95 per cent.) In the early 1990s, books with titles like *The Jobless Future* and *The End of Work* predicted computers would take our jobs and that we would soon see massive unemployment. (Since then the US economy has created 35 million new net jobs, and the employment rate before the COVID-19 pandemic was almost exactly the same.) In 1995 the flagship magazine of American conservatives, *Weekly Standard*, had the cover story 'Smash the Internet', featuring a sledgehammer destroying a screen.

Some of the predicted problems did come about, but we adapted to them in ways no one could have foreseen, because those adaptations were made by millions of people based on what they learned, not by a committee based on prophesies. For example, there was much restructuring, not because computers took our jobs but because workers with computers took jobs from workers without computers. Since 1980, occupations with above-average computer use have grown almost 1 per cent faster than other occupations every year.[45] So countries and institutions that delayed new technology hurt people, whereas those that facilitated the development of skills and business models that made man and machines complementary benefited from them.

Automation always seems more destructive than creative because it is easier to think of jobs that may disappear than new ones that might be created. McKinsey has calculated that one-third of new jobs created in the US in the past twenty-five years were in occupations that did not exist, or barely existed, twenty-five years ago. A survey in 2011 found the internet had destroyed 500,000 jobs in France in the previous fifteen years, but 2.4 new jobs were created for every job that was destroyed.[46]

This is our traditionalist, nostalgic impulse: better the devilish technology or the jobs you know. There were also those who saw salvation in the computer but thought they had to make everybody else see it as well. Technocrats always promise development, but one in which they control events, avoid nasty surprises and set standards for everybody. They want to bring order, pick winners and impose a single set of values.

Newt Gingrich, who would go on to become Republican Speaker of the House and a strong supporter of Donald Trump, worried in 1984 that the computer revolution was wild and chaotic. The government had to 'shape technology' into a 'coherent picture'. He praised Minitel, the French government's system of interactive home terminals, which he thought 'may make France the leading information-processing society in the world by the end of the century'. When he became Speaker in 1995, he suggested a $40 billion entitlement programme for laptops for poor Americans, sending the message: 'We're going into the 21st century, third-wave information age, and so are you, and we want to carry you with us.'[47]

In 1988, you could read in *Harvard Business Review* that the US Defense Department, the CIA, the National Security Agency, the National Science Foundation, US Defense Science Board, the White House Science Council, and most major US semiconductor, computer and electronic capital equipment producers agreed: US entrepreneurs were quickly losing clout in the global computer market because the US had no overarching plan and suffered from fragmentation, instability and 'extreme entrepreneurialism'. This chronically entrepreneurial market would not be able to sustain the large-scale investments needed, or be able to compete with Japanese and German 'huge, industrial complexes embedded in stable, strategically coordinated alliances often supported by protectionist governments'. In the context of global markets, then, US entrepreneurs were of 'minor and declining importance', concluded the author, Charles Ferguson, and 'only economists moved by the invisible hand have failed to apprehend the problem'.[48]

This is the technocratic impulse. We are in no mood for surprises because we know what the future is like, and we will carry you there. Such thinking usually fails because it is really the element of surprise that gives open societies the edge, as the American economist George Gilder argued in an exchange with Ferguson. America is still the home of tech, not France, and it happened because of chronic entrepreneurialism, not in spite of it.

The China paradox

Sometimes it sounds like market economies grew rich because they incentivized people to work and innovate, but that's not the point. Every society has incentives; the difference came with incentives generated by the market that constantly changed according to knowledge, demand and supply – and, of course, openness to different ways of reacting to them. Other countries before eighteenth-century Britain also had strongly incentivizing patent systems, but the rewards were set by experts, so it was just a way for a small number of people to make choices for everybody else, instead of everybody having the right to make choices themselves according to their local information and personal ambitions.

The North Korean dictator Kim Jong-il thought his movies were so much worse than South Korea's because 'film industry

people knew that the state would feed them even if they performed only minimally'. Yet, even when he killed crews who did
not create hits (it's difficult to think of a stronger incentive), the
Juche movie industry just didn't take off – not for a lack of incentives, but because it lacked openness to diversity, experimentation
and competition. (In desperation, Kim kidnapped a leading South
Korean director and actor to kick-start the industry.)[49]

When communist planners realized workers behaved according
to the 'we pretend to work and they pretend to pay us' principle,
they created bonuses and public recognition for those who worked
hard. Mostly this just led to people putting in time and producing
more shoddy and unwanted goods. But even in the best version
of this system imaginable, it only rewards what you already know
you want, so it might help you to get more steel and boots but it
doesn't give workers room to improvise according to their local
knowledge or to attempt the unexpected. It doesn't make them
tinker with micro-improvements and innovations that the leaders
don't know they are looking for, and that people might not even
know themselves they are capable of. As one of the last Soviet
leaders, Leonid Brezhnev, complained, their businesses shy away
from innovation and new products 'as the devil shies away from
incense'.[50]

This is the pivotal question for China's future economy. Popular
opinion has it that China's remarkable rise was engineered by wise
and prescient planners in the all-powerful Communist Party. This
is a fairy tale, as economists like Weiying Zhang and Nina Wang
have documented, and to the extent that the party believes its own
myth it will be detrimental to the future of China.[51]

The changes that began to dismantle the Maoist command
economy did not emerge from the heads of planners but from
the initiative of starving villagers. Peasants in Xiaogang in Anhui
province started to privatize their land in secret in December
1978, which increased production dramatically, and inspired

others to do the same. Private farming spread 'like a chicken pest', as one farmer put it. 'When one village has it, the whole country will be infected.'[52] Soon other villagers started small companies operating outside the plan, and developed a pricing system, while unemployed young Chinese began to demand the right to open small shops and businesses.

None of these changes were initiated by the rulers. Their important contribution was to acknowledge the development afterwards, once they saw the success of these initiatives, and not to punish the pioneers. The party gave the changes its official seal of approval under Deng Xiaoping, who famously said that opening China's windows might let some flies in, but that is better than expiring from lack of air. Under his policy of 'Reform and Opening-up', economic free zones were created, where entrepreneurs were allowed to experiment with private enterprise, foreign investments and international trade. After having seen the failure of the Maoist model, Chinese leaders and businessmen were unusually quick to pick up new ideas and methods from other places, even old enemies like Taiwan, Hong Kong and the US. In the 1990s, China began to actively recruit foreigners in order to harness their skills. Outsiders began to describe China as a closed society with an open mind.

These policies were responsible for China's economic rise and unprecedented reduction in poverty. Almost all 250 million jobs created in China's cities since 1978 have been created by private companies. These companies accounted for only one-third of exports in 1995 but almost 90 per cent today.[53]

Once China had acquired large economic muscles, it became possible to carry lots of old state capitalism along on the journey. But the fact that China is successful and these state companies are big does not mean they are the ones making China successful. On the contrary: through their privileged status, they have access to capital, land, technology and talent that more productive companies would have used otherwise, and they have had to be disciplined again and again to stop them from sinking massive wealth into prestige projects, laziness and corruption. Productivity growth in China has fallen steeply since the financial crisis. Growth rates steadily decline and debts are piling up. This is especially ominous for a party whose implicit bargain with the people is that they will make them rich in return for total power. A severe economic crisis would tear up this social contract.

Anyone can raise productivity by moving farmers to factories (even the Soviet Union could do that) but it is much more difficult to make sure that those factories constantly experiment and innovate. This is a particular problem in the service sector, which is not exposed to international competition. Therefore, there are reasons to doubt the future of the Chinese model if it doesn't open up further. Under Xi Jinping, China has instead gone backwards, towards more state control and a personality cult of almost Maoist proportions. No longer should the Chinese 'seek truth from facts', as Deng asked them, but through studying 'Xi Jinping thought', which is written into the constitution, with state employees and students forced to study it, even via specialized Xi phone apps. This is exactly how rulers make sure they only hear what they want to hear, and it is usually how they lose their grip on reality and their country.

Through industrial policy China has managed to indigenize foreign technologies, like high-speed trains and nuclear power, and deploy them on a large scale. They have also been world leaders in developing face recognition and other software dependent on large quantities of data and cheap labour to label it (sadly, in order to spy on its own population). But precisely because China's industrial policy neglects market demand and financial constraints, it also fosters subsidy-dependent, low-profit industries. It has created drastic overcapacity, for example in shipbuilding, and since it chases prestige rather than market share, it has often spent too much on trying to imitate high-end world leaders rather than developing innovative solutions for the home market, for example in semiconductors.

There is a paradox at the heart of the Chinese development model. When Chinese leaders know what they want, they often give businesses and innovators more freedom than Western countries that heap new small-scale regulations onto them all the time. But the problem is that Chinese leaders, like every authoritarian, don't like surprises. They want to control how people think, and if they succeed they undermine the contrarian creativity necessary for continuously emergent novelty.

This paradox was on unintended and somewhat comical display in two different articles in the same edition of *The Economist* in April 2018. In one of them, a businessman investing in both China and the US praised China's government for being 'much more open to innovators experimenting', while American innovators must slow down and negotiate with local officials to be able to operate.[54] Sounds like paradise for an entrepreneur – until you read the other article, about how Chinese authorities suddenly shut down the flagship app of the tech company ByteDance because it was seen as vulgar. The founder was even forced to apologize publicly. He was 'filled with guilt and remorse' for not understanding that 'technology must be led by socialist core values'.[55]

This is the China paradox: authorities are open to everything they like, but closed to everything they find worthless, impossible or stupid – and when they've exhausted innovations to imitate, that is the only place to find new ones.

Bureaucratic inertia

It is usually not ideology that hampers dynamism, but rather rigidity that stems from a sense of 'that's not the way we do things around here'. One reason innovations rarely come from big incumbents is that all their focus is devoted to making their business model work. Why cannibalize their own market? IBM lost the market for personal computers when it did not develop faster computers because it would hamper the sales of its slower ones. Sony should have developed the iPod and perhaps the iPhone, but didn't want to cannibalize the sales of its Walkman. Kodak did not want to develop the digital camera because it would threaten its film sales. This is why we depend on hungry upstarts with nothing to lose.

Our government often functions in the same way. We are so focused on optimizing the present system that we make it difficult for the surprises that come from outside, the ones that don't fit in and might threaten the old ways. 'A bureaucracy always tends to become a pedantocracy,' as John Stuart Mill observed.[56]

Often new business models only manage to slip through because there is a glitch in the regulatory matrix. According to a popular but unverifiable story, Yale student Fred Smith's economics paper, which suggested a new system for delivery based on a hub and spokes, only got a C because 'the idea must be feasible'. When Smith wanted to test the system in reality, the US Postal monopoly stopped the idea. But there was an exception to its monopoly for extremely urgent consignments, so Smith's company FedEx stamped 'Extremely Urgent' on every letter and parcel and went on to revolutionize delivery services.

Today, Uber is a prominent example of how innovation runs into old regulations. This smooth transportation service has not just made it possible to get a car when you need it and forced other taxi services to adapt, it has also inspired similar services in countless other services ('you can think of it as an Uber for X'). However, it crashed straight into regulatory structures. Some US cities only accept two kinds of car services: licensed cabs you catch on the streets, and black cabs that you have to order in advance. Booking a car via an app worked well in practice but not in theory.

Uber has faced a barrage of regulations in different cities. Sometimes it has been banned outright, in some places it has been forced to raise the minimum price to get closer to a traditional car service, while in others, like France and Barcelona, authorities imposed a fifteen-minute delay before passengers could be picked up. So if the car was two minutes away, the driver and the passenger had to sit still and wait for thirteen minutes before they could leave.

There were legitimate concerns about safety and transparency, but rules about this are rarely sufficiently general to be open to new technologies and business models, which illustrates the inherent conservatism of regulation. When Uber starts from scratch and builds the best possible solution to a problem based on the newest technology, it breaks the rules that were adapted to the solutions and technologies of yesterday. Uber only came as far as it has because it was willing to break those rules and had the resources and the popularity to enter into a long-term battle against them. In some places it is winning now. Most innovators and entrepreneurs would have had to give up much earlier.

In his book *Simple Rules for a Complex World*, legal scholar Richard Epstein takes aim at the ever-present temptation to make rules complex because society is growing in complexity. When that happens, more decisions are moved to legislators and authorities that are far from the events and have no knowledge of the kind of interactions that actually take place; as a result, they leave less room for surprises. Instead a complex society must decentralize more decisions to the actors themselves. We need few and predictable rules that leave as much room as possible open to unexpected innovations and social relations that would be still-born under more detailed regulations.[57]

The inherent vice of openness is that it cannot say in advance all the great things it will do for us. The inherent virtue of control is that it can promise us anything, and later find an excuse for why it didn't happen. The American political scientist Aaron Wildavsky pondered this glorious weakness when looking at markets, democracy and science – three spheres driven by incessant search, criticism and cooperation by many minds rather than a plan:

> In all three arenas, proof is retrospective rather than prospective. Looking back over past performance, adherents of free science, politics, and markets argue that on average their results are better than alternatives, but they cannot say what these will be. [...]
>
> The strength of spontaneity, its ability to seek out serendipity, is also its shortcoming – exactly what it will do as well as precisely how it will do it cannot be specified in advance.[58]

Coping with uncertainty

Uncertainty about the future feels wrong. We want to know where we'll end up if we walk in a particular direction, we need to know where our next meal is going to come from, and we have to understand where potential predators and enemies are hiding. Making a mental map of the world and our future makes it easier to navigate. When parts of that map are missing, we are uncomfortable because it is a signal that we have to look for something. That is why it would be unsettling for you if I started to stray away from the subject of this book now and wrote about entirely different things for a while. You would have to work hard to try to figure out the relevance and the context, and once you did (hopefully), you would get a sensation of reward. This is an explanation for the sometimes exaggerated 'information craving' we all get. When we can't figure out Trump or a new disease, we keep updating news sites to get more clues about what's going to happen.

Psychologists have noticed that people often react to bad news – even a cancer diagnosis – with something close to relief because waiting anxiously for a diagnosis is even worse. We prefer to know the worst than to suspect it, and this makes sense (at least in the cancer case; I'm not sure about Trump) because then we can start adapting to it. We change our behaviour and our attitudes, we find our bootstraps and tug. But we can't come to terms with terms we don't yet know. In one study, a group of volunteers were given twenty high-intensity shocks, and another group got three high-intensity and seventeen low-intensity shocks. Counter-intuitively, the low-intensity group rated themselves as more afraid, their hearts beat faster and they sweated more. It is more difficult to prepare mentally for shocks of varying intensity that you cannot foresee, and so they suffered more.[59]

That the world is to a certain extent unpredictable is deeply unsettling, and this is why many who don't feel in control themselves will settle for some form of what psychologists call 'compensatory control'. One that has given mankind comfort throughout the ages is to believe in a benevolent, interventionist god that assures us things happen for a reason or will turn out well in the end. Another is to believe that a strong man or government will save us.

But, as the psychologist Rob Brotherton explains in a book about conspiracy theories, another way to achieve compensatory control is to believe that we have powerful enemies scheming against us. This sounds strange – what could be worse than that? But remember, for many, not knowing whether they have cancer or not is worse than knowing they have it. Uncertainty is worse than even certainty about bad things. If something happens by chance, we have no way of comprehending or predicting it, much less controlling it. But if some shadowy group is in control, steering events – even if they do it in disastrous, evil ways – at least you can understand what happens and why. You might even be able to start a resistance.[60] It is telling that some people reject the idea that globalization is the result of new transportation and communication technologies and people and businesses eager to use them to improve their lives. Instead, they say it was engineered by a small cabal of rich cosmopolitans keen to enrich themselves or to destroy the nation state. Some claim it was all the work of a single Jewish billionaire, George Soros. This doesn't make any sense until you realize this is a case of compensatory control. If you believe this conspiracy theory, you don't have to try to understand the dynamics of an open world where the complex interactions of billions of people with free will decide what will happen next. The world suddenly seems comprehensible and, after all, one man can be stopped.

We all want certainty, but what makes sense for us in our micro world just doesn't work in the macro world of economics, technology and culture. This is because the only way to be certain of the result of millions of people interacting is to stop them coming to terms with their individual situation and adapting to it according to their own plans. The only way to stop the world so that I have time to adapt to it, is to stop you and everybody else from adapting to it, because change is just the aggregate combination of millions of small adaptations.

We have to keep moving, even if it sometimes makes us uncomfortable. Not just because we want a better life in general, but also because every solution we come up with also has unintended consequences that we then have to solve. People die of bacterial infections, so we discover antibiotics, but some bacteria develop resistance, so we have to keep working. More people survive longer, so we have to develop hip replacement and bypass surgery. We reduce hunger with artificial fertilizer, and poverty with a massive expansion of production, but this causes a surge of carbon dioxide in the atmosphere, and global warming, so then we need to create technologies to deal with that.

Progress is never progress towards an end goal, after which we will live happily ever after. If that is our vision of progress, we will always be disappointed and interpret any remaining problems as a sick society. Progress is always two steps forwards and one step back, because there is always push-back, and we have to push back against the push-back. Progress is less like utopia and more like a video game. We face immediate threats to our survival and well-being on this level, and if we succeed we move to the next level, where we face new problems that we also have to solve. We never reach utopia, but we constantly level up. Steven Pinker formulates it this way:

> progress does not mean that everything gets better for everyone everywhere all the time. That would not be progress. That would be a *miracle*. Progress is not a miracle; it's the result of solving problems. Problems are inevitable, and solutions create new problems that must be solved in their turn.[61]

However, the flip side is that, as more people in more places get more education and access to powerful technologies, the world becomes less predictable. Suddenly ideas, innovations and competition can come at us from more places. It becomes easier for people who never used to have a voice to congregate and mobilize digitally to defend their interests and protest present policies. In the online world, new thoughts and celebrities are born every day rather than going through a many-year vetting process by established gatekeepers.

Much of what has become known as the populist revolt is in fact a refusal to recognize this complexity. It can take the form of a longing for a simpler time, or an attempt to understand the world through conspiracy theories. It rejects the idea that problem-solving is complex and depends on time-consuming discovery processes, with many stakeholders and difficult trade-offs involved.

Instead it assumes there are simple solutions that would make life better for most people but they are blocked by a self-serving establishment. With the right person in charge, it would be easy to drain the swamp and turn things around.

This dissatisfaction with slow and unwieldy decision-making, with checks and balances and many different interests represented, has historically threatened liberal democracy – especially in times of crisis when it seems immediate action is required. In his classic book on the rise of totalitarianism, *The Road to Serfdom* from 1944, Friedrich Hayek wrote about this kind of moment, characterized by a general:

> dissatisfaction with the slow and cumbersome course of democratic procedure which makes action for action's sake the goal. It is then the man or the party who seems strong and resolute enough 'to get things done' who exercises the greatest appeal.[62]

This is far from an exclusive right-wing desire. When contemplating the threat from global warming, *New York Times* columnist Thomas L. Friedman echoes these sentiments by saying that China's one-party state 'can just impose the politically difficult but critically important policies' and that our slow and cumbersome democracy 'is worse'.[63] When Pär Holmgren, Member of the European Parliament for the Swedish Greens, was asked what he would do if he was prime minister, he responded: 'I would immediately abolish elections' because the environmental threat is like a third world war, so 'we don't have the time to squabble between the parties'.[64]

But it is precisely when problems are as severe as global warming, with such potential for disaster, that we need as many ideas and as much knowledge as possible, and so must resist the temptation to impose a single idea from the top. As H. L. Mencken warned us: 'there is always a well-known solution to every human problem – neat, plausible, and wrong'.[65]

Global warming

Postrel's two groups, the reactionaries and the technocrats, think they know exactly how to deal with global warming. Their solution is to reach stasis, in the past or in the future. For the most conservative group, the whole Industrial Revolution was a mistake because all the fossil fuel it released ended up warming the planet. We should roll things back or at least move to a zero-growth society.

This argument ignores that these problems, difficult though they are, are the result of us having levelled up. The problems they solved were also of the life-and-death variety: extreme poverty and underdevelopment. One of the worst environmental problems in the world is the *lack* of modern energy sources, which leads people in poor countries to use solid fuels for cooking and heating. This has declined rapidly but still results in respiratory diseases that kill more than two million people every year. Wealth and technology are the prerequisite for dealing with all the problems nature might throw at us, whether they are related to environmental degradation or not. The risk of dying in a climate-related disaster has decreased by more than 90 per cent since the 1950s, not because natural disasters have become fewer but because wealth, technology, construction and healthcare have improved.

The reactionary attitude reminds me of the old joke about the tourist in Ireland who asks a local about directions to Dublin, and is told: 'If I were you, I wouldn't start from here.' Well, we are here, with almost eight billion people dependent on modern technology for survival and well-being. The big disaster would be if our growing population built ever-larger economies with old and dirty technology. Poverty is the worst polluter, as India's prime minister Indira Gandhi used to say, since one can never get

people to prioritize long-term environmental values over immediate health and education of their children. The Environmental
Performance Index, which ranks the world's countries according to as many environmental indicators as possible – from clean
water to biological diversity – documents a strong relationship
between countries' GDP and a good environment. The researchers
summarize that 'income is a major determinant of environmental
success'. Another important determinant is political openness: the
first thirty-one countries in the ranking are democracies.[66]

In addition, zero growth would be completely insufficient to
achieve our climate goals. According to the UN Climate Panel
IPCC, emissions must be halved by 2030 and end completely by
2050 to limit the global temperature rise this century to below
two degrees Celsius above pre-industrial levels. Thus, if we retain
today's technology, we would first have to halve production and
transportation – and thus our incomes – and then eliminate them
completely. Few would accept this, which is why even the reactionary analysis often leads to technocratic conclusions.

The technocratic solution is to just fix the problem: come up
with the best solution and implement it everywhere. It sounds
great. But we've seen this movie before, and trying to pick winners
is just as difficult in green technology as it is in any other technology. Giving public funds to particular projects is a way of replacing
the knowledge, evaluations and trial-and-error discipline supplied
by millions of actors with the guesses of a small group of politicians and bureaucrats.

In the 1960s, many governments were sure nuclear power was
the future, and they pushed a massive expansion of a premature,
expensive technology onto the market in a very short time. Had
they accepted a more cautious approach, building and mainte-
nance might have become a routine business, which would have
reduced both costs and safety hazards. We might also have seen
the development of better reactors. 'This is a risk we are running if

politicians decide they know the answers, they know the winners and they're going to pick them,' says Dieter Helm, Professor of Energy Policy at Oxford.[67]

In 2006, President George W. Bush was certain that corn-based ethanol was the right way to reduce CO_2 emissions. 'It's coming, and government can help,' with billions in subsidies and mandates to blend it into gasoline. Many farmers switched from soybean to corn, which resulted in much higher grain prices. But ethanol turned out to pull less of a punch than gasoline and be very energy-intensive to produce. And since it's corrosive it would need an entire pipeline system of its own; in the absence of such a pipeline, it was transported by truck. 'Once you put all that together, you're actually using more energy by using ethanol than you are saving,' says Lynne Kiesling, an economist specializing in energy issues. She argues that, without the strong governmental push, ethanol would have had greater potential:

> In the absence of government intervention, experimentation would have gone on, but in a smaller scale and would be much more trial and error. We would have learned some of these physical properties and we would have learned about its energy cost and that it's really hydrophilic and corrosive.[68]

European governments recently decided to promote solar and wind power. But again, since they wanted to scale up massively, they spent billions on spreading early versions of solar arrays and wind turbines over the continent. Of all available sources, including nuclear and natural gas, this was the most expensive way of reducing greenhouse gases. Had just a tiny share of that been spent on research into better energy conversion and using applications and materials in radically new ways, it could have made a much bigger difference to the future of renewables. But doing that would not have allowed European politicians to create jobs and photo opportunities, or as many chances to brag about how they are solving the problem.

This is one reason technocratic solutions often come up short. It's not just that it's difficult to predict the future, it's also that the process is distorted for political reasons – and because special interests influence the process. Between 2007 and 2013, corn ethanol interests, especially Archer Daniels Midland Company, spent $158 million on lobbying, and in return the US government spent almost $30 billion on corn ethanol tax credits alone. That is a pretty good return on investment. The process is also distorted for ideological reasons. For example, the political Left often loves wind power whereas the Right cheers on nuclear power, and both want to subsidize their pet projects above all else. 'While that is good for us, I can't imagine it's a good way for the government to use taxpayer money,' said one investor in the California solar company Solyndra, describing a very favourable government loan in 2009. Government favours also change companies' priorities, from making customers happy to making politicians happy. One board member claimed Solyndra's company founder survived only because of his close relationship with the Obama administration. Within a week of getting the first loan, Solyndra applied for another, worth $400 million.

Those who don't risk their own money don't devote the same efforts to make sure the investment pays off. One Management and Budget official complained the Department of Energy's loan process for Solyndra had 'barely any review of materials submitted, no synthesis for program management and inherent conflicts in origination of team members monitoring the deals they structured'. As President Obama's chief economic adviser Larry Summers summed it up: 'Government is a crappy venture capitalist.' In 2011, Solyndra filed for bankruptcy.[69]

Everything is a knowledge problem

The dynamist response to global warming and every other problem starts with the Socratic insight that the beginning of wisdom
is to be aware of our own ignorance. I don't know the solution,
and neither do you, and our politicians certainly don't. Instead,
we need a system that makes everybody take their contribution to
global warming seriously and incentivizes everybody to volunteer
their best ideas about how to deal with it. The best way would be
a carbon tax on all sorts of carbon-based fuels at the wholesale
stage, which would be passed on to all consumers downstream. In
this way, we would all pay for the damage we are doing, and we all
get an incentive to steer our consumption to goods and services
that make less use of carbon sources.

The genius of this system is that it would free us of the need
for a crystal ball. We would not have to predict what the best way
of reducing greenhouse gases is, and we would not second-guess
scientists, innovators, companies and consumers. It wouldn't tell
people how to decarbonize, it would leave it to millions of innovators, consumers and businesses to find the most efficient and
cheapest way to minimize CO_2 emissions. It would remove the
subsidies and regulatory help rewarded to particular companies. It
would relieve politicians and bureaucrats of the impossible task of
evaluating technologies, and remove their opportunity to benefit
companies they know privately, believe in personally, like for ideological reasons, reflect well on them, create jobs in their districts, or
whom they depend upon for campaign funds. Companies would
only benefit to the extent that they reduced emissions.

The difficulty is to get people to vote for a tax that would make
them worse off, and to implement it globally. No perfect international coordination is required, but the more countries that
implement the tax the better, so that carbon-intensive production does not simply move elsewhere. Since the top ten emitters

account for nearly three-quarters of global emissions, an agreement just between them would go a long way. Environmental movements are growing fastest in rich, Western countries, which indicates that support might be rising for such policies. Poor countries could be encouraged to participate by being allowed to phase in the tax as their average income surpassed a certain threshold.

As to the material well-being of citizens, there is no reason why a carbon tax would take away more money in total from them. It is supposed to be an incentive, not a source of revenue. The revenue could be used to cut income taxes, so people don't suffer from it materially, and capital and corporate taxes if we are afraid that it will hurt business competitiveness. Another way to build popular support for a carbon tax has been suggested. What if all the revenue was returned to every citizen's bank account in an equal lump sum every year? It would give the tax an egalitarian profile, and the poorest would receive more than they pay extra in carbon taxes.

In a statement supporting a carbon tax, twenty-seven Nobel laureate economists wrote: 'Substituting a price signal for cumbersome regulations will promote economic growth and provide the regulatory certainty companies need for long-term investment in clean-energy alternatives.'[70] The energy expert Dieter Helm thinks this is the way to reduce emissions most efficiently: 'in the market, reality is reality. You pay the cost. You're not there to be lobbied. You're not there because you got subsidies. You know that if you get it wrong, you pay.'[71]

New solutions would come from both the demand and the supply side, in ways that politicians and bureaucrats could never foresee. Consumers would conserve energy, switch from coal to natural gas, from natural gas to solar, and would demand production processes that are as clean as possible. The market would look for better solutions all the time, and innovators and entrepreneurs would have a powerful and predictable incentive to put strange new ideas about energy sources, fuels, materials, storage and distribution solutions into practice.

Personally, I would be surprised if solar is not the long-term future of energy, considering that the sun beams more than enough energy onto earth every hour to satisfy global energy needs for an entire year. But perhaps generation-IV nuclear will be even cheaper, and many scientists and innovators believe they can achieve the breakthrough in fusion power that would give us unlimited, cheap, clean power. Perhaps cars will run on clean energy or on ethanol made from algae. We might see a breakthrough in designer algae, where we change the DNA to make gasoline or jet fuel at a cheap cost.

Possibly the best way to deal with global warming is to suck CO_2 out of the air. We can do it with trees, of course, but if we don't have the patience or the room to grow enormous, new forests, we can do it with technology adapted from known industrial processes. One negative emissions plant from the company Carbon Engineering is said to be the equivalent of planting 40 million trees, and might be able to capture a tonne of CO_2 for less than $100.

We just don't know what is going to work best, so we have to be open to surprises that might come from a laboratory or a garage anywhere in the world. In *The Beginning of Infinity*, David Deutsch writes: 'If something is permitted by the laws of physics, then the only thing that can prevent it from being technologically possible is not knowing how.'[72] In other words, everything is a knowledge problem and the way to attain more knowledge is openness to trial and error.

And we sure need new solutions. Even though all generations have faced their own existential threats, at the moment there is a confluence of different such threats. We experience the first consequences of global warming at the precise moment of undergoing a geopolitical shift that almost seems like a Copernican revolution for the West: we are no longer the centre of the universe. We appear to be surrounded by chaos and enemies, and mass immigration and terrorist groups seem to be threatening our culture and our very societies. And suddenly a brand new coronavirus pandemic harms and kills on a massive scale. All this in an era when the financial crisis has just made us doubt the sustainability of our economy and the rationality of our leaders.

This has increased our sense of danger, which increases zero-sum thinking and groupishness. This then risks creating a feedback loop. We attack outgroups and start trade wars, and they respond in kind, so we conjure up the very enemies we are afraid of. And when we retreat from established trade relations it hurts the economy and makes it seem even more like a zero-sum game.

If chaos and foes are all around us, we have to protect ourselves, we have to flee – or we have to man the barricades and fight back.

8

FIGHT OR FLIGHT

'Quite an experience to live in fear, isn't it? That's what it
is to be a slave.'

Roy Batty in *Blade Runner*, 1982

'You know what a conservative is?' Philadelphia's mayor
Frank Rizzo once asked rhetorically, 'That's a liberal who
got mugged the night before.'

Rizzo, a blue-collar Democrat and a previous police commissioner, did not have any kind of tolerant, limited-government
conservatism in mind, but his own racially tinted, big-government
conservatism ('Vote white,' he urged his constituency in 1978).
His point was that it's all fine and dandy to talk about rule of law
and rights of the minority until you meet the harsh reality of a
very dangerous world. Then you want a strong government that
shoots first and ask questions later.

This is understandable. When we are under attack we have to
defend ourselves, and when that is inadequate we want the collective or the government to rush to our defence. If individual rights
and division of power restrain government action, it seems like
abetting the enemy, and we want stronger, immediate action. As

the Justice of the US Supreme Court, Thurgood Marshall, put it in 1989 when he worried about how the war on drugs justified erosions of privacy: 'History teaches that grave threats to liberty often come in times of urgency, when constitutional rights seem too extravagant to endure.'[1] He had episodes like the Japanese internment camps during World War II and the McCarthy era in mind.

We don't have to go to such extremes as world war or even armed robbery. Our fear of the unknown is so powerful that we only have to dial up the level of insecurity a little bit to spark anxiety about openness. According to an experiment published in *Psychological Science*, we might even say that a liberal is a conservative who hasn't washed his hands. In this experiment, they asked participants about attitudes to various groups, but first they reminded them that it was flu season. They also mentioned that washing one's hands frequently could protect you against transmission. Then one randomly assigned group got the chance to use hand sanitizer before answering questions, and one group did not. Afterwards, those who had not cleaned their hands expressed more negative attitudes to outgroups than those who had.[2]

Fear does powerful things to us, as revealed by an experiment with television ads. Some people got to watch the horror classic *The Shining*, and during a particularly scary moment there was a commercial break. Some of the adverts included information about how popular a product was, some didn't. It turned out that the viewers who had been scared rated products that had been presented as common and popular more highly than products presented as different and unique, for example a 'limited edition'. An ad about a museum 'visited by over a million people a year' was preferred over the same museum, when a visit was presented as a way of standing out from the crowd.

People who had seen the same ads during a romantic film had the opposite preference. They preferred different and unique offerings and wanted to stand out from the crowd rather than do what a million people a year do. The same individuals can be conformists or individualists, depending on their frame of mind. 'Like wildebeests in the presence of a leopard, people who are feeling threatened want to be part of a larger group,' as the researchers conclude.[3]

Other studies have documented that feelings of fear or disgust make attitudes more socially conservative on issues like immigration, gender roles, gay rights, premarital sex and pornography. For example, just being faced with moral dilemmas in a dirty and disorderly room will make you more judgmental than if you face them in a tidy room.[4] Liberally minded students who are asked to consider their own death become less sympathetic to equal treatment of homosexuals soon thereafter.[5] US students are less willing to recommend a strong woman for a professorship if they have read a story about America in decline just before. (Those who read an article about a rising America became more willing to hire her than the group that did not read an article.)[6]

But it is not simply a matter of social conservatism. It has also been found that induced feelings of disgust lead people to endorse more interventionist attitudes in economics – for example, they'll be more willing to say that businesses exploit workers and that we need more government redistribution.[7] Many Anglo-Saxons assume there is such a thing as a conservative personality type, who is social conservative and also in favour of free markets, and a progressive personality type, who wants to tax and spend and live and let live. However, this seems to be a consequence of people aligning themselves to the two traditional political packages on offer in the US and Britain. Worldwide it's more likely that we find free market liberals and big-government conservatives. A study of 70,000 people from fifty-one countries shows that, on average, those who prefer control and conformity are conservative culturally but also more to the left economically.[8]

In 1794, the American Founding Father James Madison warned us about 'the old trick of turning every contingency into a resource for accumulating force in government', but since then we have fallen for it again and again. In the modern classic *Crisis and Leviathan*, the American economic historian Robert Higgs documented that governments usually attain more power and grow in times of crisis such as depressions and wars. After the crisis has passed, governments rarely yield all those new powers, so they remain on a higher growth path.[9]

The main effect of feelings of vulnerability, disorder and disgust is that they make us less individualistic both culturally and economically, less tolerant of dissent and more willing to say that the government should enforce collective norms. We circle the wagons. This has had tremendous survival value for us historically. When the hyenas close in on us, we have to stand our ground collectively. There is no room for disagreements and nonconformism. We all have to throw stones at the hyenas collectively if any of us are to survive. When a hostile tribe attacks us, the old disagreements with our brother or our neighbour must be put on hold, so that we can fight back together. Those suspected of being disloyal to our group have to be pushed out. And when the dam bursts or the village is on fire, the eccentric and the dissenter are absolutely useless. We have to fight the common threat, without critical questions about our priorities or ways of doing things.

The potential to react strongly to a threat is incredibly important, much like we need our immune system to defend our bodies. But just like the immune system can react to a false alarm and react aggressively to dust or pollen or even mistake part of your body as foreign so it starts to attack yourself, so our sense of collective threat is oversensitive. It was, after all, developed in a situation where we regularly faced lethal threats from predators and neighbouring bands and it would have been much worse to underreact than to overreact.

Usually it works out well, in everyday life, when we engage with people on a person-to-person rather than group-to-group basis. Despite the way disasters often appear in the media, people normally react to them in a relatively mature manner. The pioneer of disaster research, Enrico Quarantelli, employed the simple method of going to every disaster zone he could get to, and documenting behaviour. 'Overall, the research evidence is that mythical beliefs to the contrary, disaster victims do not panic, they are not passive, they do not become caught up in antisocial behaviour, and they are not behaviourally traumatized.'[10] Usually, people do what they can to help the sufferers, share supplies and evacuate buildings peacefully. And old divisions of class and race are momentarily forgotten as they fight the common calamity.

But that is how we act spontaneously, as individuals, not how we act collectively when we decide on a unified, political approach to the horrors that affect our society. As the research has been summarized:

> The literature suggests that insecurity is conducive to in-group solidarity, rigid conformity to group norms, and rejection of outsiders, leading people to seek strong, authoritarian leaders to protect them from the dangerous outsiders seen as threatening people's jobs and personal safety.[11]

The silent revolution

If you can wash away some of your fear of a dangerous world, what would happen if you didn't just get a hand sanitizer or a vaccine but a full-blown protection that made you invulnerable? One study tested this by asking students to imagine they were suddenly endowed with a superpower, and then querying them about attitudes to social change. Those who got the gift of flying didn't change their attitudes. However, those who were told to imagine they were invulnerable to physical harm did. Conservatives who felt like Superman were suddenly just as open to social change as liberals were.[12]

In a way, this sounds like a caricature of comfortable globalist elites, feeling invulnerable to creative destruction and yet lecturing the more unfortunate about how they must welcome techno- logical change and cultural transformation. It's the proverbial liberal who does not have to fear being mugged because he lives in a posh neighbourhood and has money in the bank to cover all eventualities. But seen from another perspective, this is exactly the transition the whole Western world has gone through over the past century: from poverty, violence and a great risk of an early death, to relative wealth and security. A life expectancy of around eighty years is not the same as invulnerability, of course, but com- pared to previous generations, who averaged thirty or thirty-five years, it certainly seems like we're getting much closer. And now- adays we rarely die suddenly because of an unexpected threat, but in most cases at an advanced age, in a hospital bed, due to cancer or heart disease. If we could only die from sudden accidents and violence, life expectancy in the US – the country of firearms and heavy traffic – would increase from seventy-eight years to an aver- age of 8938 years![13]

We also picked up more emancipatory, libertarian values along the way, as Abraham Maslow's hierarchy of needs suggested, and which has been documented by Ronald Inglehart and the World Values Survey project. Once we had food, warmth and physical safety, the need for self-esteem and self-actualization took up more of our thinking. The Industrial Revolution, modern technology, mass education and urbanization made it possible for most people to take physical and material survival for granted for the first time in history. Because of this sense of security, they could tolerate more ambiguity than in a society facing more dangers, where the margin for error is smaller and therefore social norms are stricter.

This was reinforced after World War II, with rapid economic growth and peace between the major powers. There was a major inter-generational shift in values, from an emphasis on conformity and security to one on individualism and openness to new ideas. For every generation, the emphasis on individual autonomy and equal rights grew stronger – baby boomers more than the interwar generation, generation X more than the baby boomers. Millennials more than generation X. Not just because they were younger. Every generation was more liberal at the same age than the previous generation. The picture is the same in all countries studied, it's only that the process started later in some countries.

Our values began to be more aligned with the world we lived in – a more peaceful world with economic and technological progress and more non-zero-sumness. But unfortunately, we are not invulnerable. Once in a while, a whole country is robbed and sometimes it feels like the whole society forgot to wash its hands. If we are more judgmental when we answer questions in a messy room where researchers have prepared a used plastic cup on the table and rigged the rubbish bin with greasy pizza boxes and dirty tissues, what happens to our values when the whole world feels a bit untidy?

9/11 vs 11/9

I grew up in an era where the defining event was the fall of the Berlin Wall on 9 November 1989. Watching old videos of East and West Germans joyfully smashing and hacking the hated wall to pieces, and hugging old friends and strangers, still moves me to tears every time. It summarized all the hopes of that time, the idea that we are all fellow humans, with the same yearning for love and freedom, only separated by walls that will be torn down.

The defining image of the present era also brings me to tears, but for the opposite reason. It's the collapse of the World Trade

Center in New York on 11 September 2001. Where 11/9 symbolized liberty and love, the terror attacks of 9/11 symbolized war and hate. Where 11/9 expressed the unity of mankind, 9/11 gave us the impression that some just want to watch the world burn, and we might need higher walls to keep them away. In Europe, a series of terrorist attacks, starting with the 2004 Madrid train bombings and the 2005 London bombings, had a similar effect on the public psyche.

Large majorities of all generations of Americans think 9/11 is the event that had the biggest effect on their country during their lifetime, even those who experienced World War II, the Cold War, the civil rights revolution and the moon landing.[14] This affects our worldview just like the fall of the Berlin Wall did, but in the opposite direction. Uncertainty and fear make us more suspicious about the world and outgroups. You would expect uncertainty to result in openness to different perspectives on a problem, but combined with a threat it actually makes us more rigid in our thinking and less tolerant of political opponents. Whatever you thought before you got frightened, the more you know it to be true once you are scared.[15]

After 9/11, surveys showed that Americans attached less importance to self-actualization values – like accomplishment, pleasure and wisdom – and more to survival and security values.[16] As their survival was perceived to be threatened, they slipped down Maslow's hierarchy of needs, and started to prioritize collective safety over individual liberty. This makes us more hostile to outgroups, but there is also a warm, fuzzy side to this collectivism. Many have never felt as much one with strangers and neighbours as they did when disaster struck or war was declared. In the light of the external threat, we forget our everyday differences and stand together.

One vivid example of this can be witnessed in a trivial everyday setting by a young man named Paul, who delivered bagels to company employees in New York based on an honour system. Since he had also been a research analyst, he kept close track of when people took bagels without paying for them, which sadly happened a lot. Immediately after 9/11, the non-payment rate declined by 15 per cent, and it stayed low.[17]

In the early 2010s, brave uprisings against corrupt Middle Eastern dictatorships during the Arab Spring ended in a night-marish combination of terror, civil wars and new tyrannies. This was a severe blow to our hopeful views of political liberation. The lesson of 1989 was that the oppressed seemed just like 'us'; they just had to tear down the walls and then they would immediately get to work to build stable, democratic societies. After the Arab Spring, it seemed to many like the walls that collapsed in the Middle East had held back Islamists, extremists and warlords, and some observers even welcomed the return of authoritarian rule to restore order. Liberty, which used to be considered a univer-sal value that we wished to see everywhere, started to be seen as something threatening. Especially when those who suffered began washing up on our shores.

During 2015, more than a million refugees from Syria and other countries reached Europe. This refugee crisis put a serious strain on public services, especially in receiving countries like Germany, Austria and Sweden. Worse still, masses of migrants marching along highways and railway tracks in search of refuge created a sense of chaos and disorder that incited fear far outside these countries. As pointed out before, people adapt to migrants, but they tend to dislike rapid ethnic change, and it doesn't get more rapid than this. To many native-born, the large number of migrants sadly conjured up an old image of a barbarian horde storming the gates.

The Bulgarian political scientist Ivan Krastev has called the refugee crisis 'Europe's 9/11', posing the same kind of questions about identity and security as the terror attacks on the US did in 2001. Interestingly, the reaction was fiercest in former communist countries in Central and Eastern Europe, even though they received very few refugees. Krastev explains this by the memory these countries have of political fragility. The seemingly stable can suddenly collapse. This is what they thought they saw during the refugee crisis. Angela Merkel's decision to throw the borders open, without some kind of plan for what would happen next, further fanned the flames. It was a temporary decision to stop other countries from being overwhelmed, and was supposed to be handled by an improvised plan to force other countries to share the burden, but it failed. It was a mess, and made the hitherto broadly popular free movement of citizens between EU countries seem menacing.

The authoritarian predisposition

In her 2005 book *The Authoritarian Dynamic*, the political psychologist Karen Stenner warned that intolerance 'is not a thing of the past, it is very much a thing of the future'. It would come back to haunt us, again and again, she thought, and she specifically wanted to understand episodes of intense and sometimes violent expressions of intolerance that seem to come out of nowhere.[18]

Stenner's research led her to conclude that authoritarianism is not a stable personality trait, as some scholars of the 'authoritarian personality' suggested after World War II, but more of a predisposition. It is a low-level generalized tendency to prefer oneness and sameness over freedom and diversity (held by around a third of the population in Western democracies, according to Stenner), which does not express itself in any particular way during normal times. When those with this predisposition sense a threat to societal unity, though, they react explosively. They become intolerant of diversity and dissent and willing to restore unity by government control, even if it wrecks rule of law and free speech.

Not every threat has the same explosive effect on the groupish. This was tested by letting subjects read fabricated stories about different threats, ranging from metaphysical threats such as the insight that life is cruel and unjust and evidence that there is no afterlife, to normative threats about how the population is becoming increasingly separated and divided, and political leaders let the people down. You might expect the metaphysical threats to have a bigger impact on us, and perhaps that is true, but they are not politically potent. Yet the normative threats, even when modest (such as a more diverse population and unworthy leaders), triggered a strong authoritarian impulse. As Jonathan Haidt summarizes the finding:

> It's as though some people have a button on their foreheads, and when the button is pushed, they suddenly become intensely focused on defending their in-group, kicking out foreigners and nonconformists, and stamping out dissent within the group. At those times they are more attracted to strongmen and the use of force.[19]

This explains how waves of intolerance can appear seemingly out of nowhere, and old friends and family are shocked to see a completely new, aggressive political side from a normally centrist person. The attitude of the groupish does not diverge from others in control conditions, or when they face non-normative threats, but when they get the sense that society is coming apart they suddenly demand enforcement of conformity and obedience. Once this happens, there is a risk that the dynamic becomes self-fuelling. The group that values individual autonomy over social conformity tends to be unmoved by normative threats, and many of them become even more libertarian in times of risk. Since groups react so differently, this intensifies the perception of polarization in society and exacerbates the sense of a normative threat.

This kind of authoritarianism is not the same as conservatism. People with a groupish predisposition don't mind change as long as all groups change together. It's not respect for tradition and institutions as such that motivates them, but social cohesion. They are not averse to transformations but to complexity. They are willing to break even revered traditions and upend important institutions if they think it helps reinforce oneness and sameness, and they can be found both on the Left and on the Right politically. Many of them don't even care much about which policies are implemented, as long as someone does it forcefully from the top and makes it all-encompassing. For example, it is not unusual to see populist parties that used to be the main detractors of gay rights or women's rights today say that a major problem with immigrants is that they are not as gay-friendly or supportive of equality for women as we are now all supposed to be in this society.

One underrated factor behind the authoritarian reflex is the perception that our political leaders might not be worthy of our trust, that they are incompetent and/or are only looking after themselves and their wealthy friends. Many react to such insights by advocating a more limited government with less power and more checks and balances, but paradoxically the groupish react by demanding even more power for a strongman who can solve the problem. Perhaps they have higher expectations of leaders and so are more bitterly disappointed.

While Stenner was writing, this faith in leaders was bruised in America and the UK by the wars in Afghanistan and especially Iraq (which was supposed to be a short war that would reveal Saddam Hussein's stock of weapons of mass destruction and would create a stable democracy in the Middle East). Petty corruption, like British MPs' extravagant expenses or French politicians who include their immediate family on the public payroll, added to this. This is nothing new, of course. The Vietnam War and Watergate also tested our trust in officials. But it is probable that greater transparency in itself makes us doubt the behaviour and sincerity of our leaders more than before. Everything looks unappetizing if you look closely enough.

Breaking news

Society doesn't even need to descend into bedlam for groupishness to increase. As the experiments at the beginning of this chapter show, it is enough to remind people of a particular problem to make them react defensively. If we zoom in and spread the word about everything that goes wrong in the world, it can be enough to provoke us into a political fight-or-flight reaction. Violent crime in the US has been reduced by around half since the early 1990s, but except for a single year (2001, when they worried more about terrorism), most Americans told pollsters that they thought crime increased every year. On average 66 per cent thought crime increased every year between 1990 and 2018.[20]

The role of the media is to tell us the most shocking things that have happened since last we tuned in. Don't blame the journalists: this is because humanity is a problem-seeking species. That is why bad is stronger than good – psychologists have documented that we are more likely to remember and feel strongly about losing money, being abandoned by friends or receiving criticism than making money, gaining friends or receiving praise. Bad is stronger than good everywhere but in our nostalgic memories, which make the present seem even worse.

As long as we only had knowledge about risks that could actually threaten our personal well-being, this orientation was a useful evolutionary tool for survival. However, this genetic default setting wasn't prepared for global twenty-four-hour cable news. Suddenly journalists had a whole planet of horrors to pick and choose from. And even though war fatalities and homicide rates have halved in the last three decades, there is always a war and a serial killer somewhere in the world, and then that will top the news cycle everywhere and give us the impression that it's becoming more frequent. The problem is not fake news, it's real news without context or reflection.

Ironically, this thirst for drama also makes us blind to some of the worst ongoing tragedies on the planet, like chronic undernourishment or deaths from indoor air pollution, because they are not sudden and explosive, they are just there all the time in the background.

And then came social media, which further exposes us to new threats every second. As someone put it (I don't remember who, I saw it somewhere on social media), human horrors are not new but the mobile phone camera is. Suddenly there is a citizen journalist close to everything that goes wrong in the world, who can broadcast it to the rest of humanity, and now we all share the scariest and nastiest things that have been done by people we have never heard of. This exaggerates the extent of horrors, so we wake up every morning and think the world is falling apart.

Our methods of consuming social media contribute to this sense. Once upon a time we watched the evening news on television, or opened the newspaper in the morning, prepared for our daily dose of crime and war. We were mentally prepared for bad news. Now it's mixed in with everything else, since we haven't yet organized our personal consumption of news online. In our social media feeds we see someone's concert pictures, and then a terrorist attack, we see pictures of funny cats, a comedy clip, and then a teenager saying that everyone who votes like you do is demented, someone checks in at the beach, and someone else is stabbed to death on a street corner. We are mentally unprepared when disaster strikes. It gives us the sense that bad things come at us from all angles, all the time, and it never ends. So it makes total sense for dictatorships like Russia, that want to destabilize open societies, to create fake websites and bots and plant fictional stories about

crime, terrorism, conspiracies and racial tensions to stoke fear
and conflict.

Stenner and Haidt talked about a metaphorical button on our
foreheads. The one that makes us want to build walls and silence
dissenters. When is that button pushed? When people feel their
society or their group is under threat. Stenner focuses on threats
to the moral order and domestic diversity running amok, but even
more dramatic is the fear that the whole world is falling apart, that
everything outside your neighbourhood is on fire. If I wanted to
invent something to push this button, repeatedly, I would invent
a communications technology where people instantly share awful
news with their friends, the biggest tragedies they experience, the
worst crimes they read about, and the most hateful expressions
they hear from the other political side, even though it comes from
a nobody in a city you've never heard of. In short, I would invent
social media.

Social media represents an unprecedented democratization of
the media, both on the production side and the consumption side,
and it has improved our lives in countless ways. It has made it
possible to connect with more people and learn more about what
interests us, and it has enabled an explosion of creativity in all
the arts, where people can now experiment and learn from one
another without a gatekeeper telling us what is good taste.

The truth is that the overall global trend has been a remarkable
rise in our well-being. But our psychology is still the same. If we
let this control us, and we just devour all the breaking news without thinking about context, statistics and risk analysis, our media
feeds will form misleading impressions about the state of the
world. In this sense, the media functions like an accelerator of all
the other things we have looked at in this part of the book: it reinforces our tribalism, our sense that the present is uniquely difficult
and scary, and our tendency to see the world as a zero-sum game.
It makes us afraid and it triggers our fight-or-flight instinct – we

want to fight the scapegoats, whether they are foreign countries, Wall Street or immigrants, and we want to flee and hide behind walls and tariffs.

The terrible irony is that our misunderstandings of the world can make us seek desperate solutions that undermine progress, and turn life into the hellhole we already mistakenly believe it to be. It is a self-fulfilling prophecy of doom.

Is it the stupid economy?

Many assume the rise of nativism is a reaction of the economically left-behind. This would be convenient because all of us think we have a solution to socioeconomic problems (and would flatter the nativists, since they only fight for the forgotten), but it has been surprisingly difficult to pin down the evidence.

Trump's victory in 2016 took place in the midst of a rapid economic recovery with declining unemployment. Since 2010, manufacturing employment had increased slightly. States like Georgia and Maryland abandoned the Democrats in the tough times of 2012, but came back in the recovery of 2016. Trump won the Rust Belt, but voters there did not attribute their votes to the economy more in 2016 than in 2012.

Neither is it simple to find socioeconomic factors behind Brexit. Just 5 per cent of Brexiteers say that inequality is the most important question facing the country (compared to 20 per cent of Remainers). More than a quarter of two-person households in England and Wales split their votes in the referendum, which suggests it is more related to values than household economy. And in fact, supporting the death penalty – a question no one raised in the campaign – is a stronger predictor of a Brexit vote than either income, age, education, party support or geography.[21]

The one correlation that is strong and reliable between economics and voting regards the assessment of current economic conditions. Right before the election in November 2016, Republicans had an average negative assessment of the economy at -23, so not strange that they voted for Trump, right? But this is a hopeless indicator, since many decide what they think about the economy based on what they think about the current government. After November 2016, the Republican assessment of the economy increased from -23 to +18 in just two months. And this can't be explained by Trump's policies, since he only took office in January 2017. Meanwhile, Democrats' assessment declined from 30 to 16.[22]

Political psychologist Karen Stenner's explanation for the difficulty of pinning down socioeconomic causes of the populist revolt is that there is none. When those of an authoritarian disposition suffer from personal problems, like financial distress, they counter-intuitively express more tolerant and inclusive values. Stenner's explanation is that personal threats distract them from their concern for collective threats. (In fact, being long-term unemployed makes you *less* likely to vote for authoritarian populist parties.)[23]

However, economic conditions do have an effect; otherwise it would be difficult to explain why nativist revolts often follow recessions. But the links of transmission are a bit more complex. People might not attribute a particular vote to economic conditions but to a new insight into the corruption of elites or the problems associated with immigration. The fact that they suddenly find those issues much more important might in its turn be related to the recession.

Stenner's results suggest personal problems do not predict a populist vote, but they do not rule out that economic and societal problems for 'people like me' do. A sense of a personal threat does not trigger tribal beliefs, but a threat against your group does. An economic downturn can seem like such a threat, especially if it feels like other groups are prospering while your group is struggling. Much has been made of the fact that populist votes tend to come from the working class and from rural areas, but perhaps that is not because of some sort of innate authoritarianism, but the simple fact that they are more vulnerable to rapid social and economic change.[24] We have many historical examples of support for authoritarian policies from the middle class and from the elites when they have felt that particular policies or societal changes threatened their position in society.

Revolts against openness

Disorientation and uncertainty are common conditions for nativist, nostalgic revolts. Difficulties are interpreted as a sign that we have somehow strayed from the right path, we have lost ourselves, or someone has led us astray. As a result, we must return to traditional beliefs, those things that used to give us strength but have been diluted by selfishness, decadence and foreign influences, and because the young are weak and too consumer-oriented.

Today this sort of reactionary nostalgia emanates from white supremacists in Europe and the US, and from religious extremists like Al-Qaeda and the Islamic State. All of them are oblivious to the fact that those past cultures had been magnificent only because they were innovative and inquisitive, open to ideas and people from all cultures. They have a glorious past to look back on only because their reactionary predecessors did not manage to do what they are trying to accomplish now.

But the reaction speaks to something primordial. It is similar to the idea of order/disorder/order that we find in most of our legends and fairy tales, according to the folklorist Max Lüthi.[25] Once upon a time there is a state of happiness, then there is mischief, but then order is restored. It is a reflection of the human predicament of dealing with difficulties and solving problems and moving on with our lives. But in the political sphere, the mischief is other people, and the fairy-tale hero is the strongman who can put them in their place. And once he is there, 'he begins to stir up one war after another in order to keep the public in need of a general', as Plato prophesized in *The Republic*.[26]

The An Lushan Rebellion (755–63) was one of the bloodiest wars in history. It was started by an ambitious and disgruntled general and wreaked havoc on Tang China. The frontiers collapsed and China lost control of the Silk Road to the west. Anti-globalist Confucian scholars and bureaucrats argued that China had lost its way by opening up. The elite had become Buddhists, fallen in love with foreign products, wore Persian dresses and played polo – the game of nomads from the steppe. Now was the time to purge foreigners and return to 'pure', traditional values. The government soon banned foreign envoys and stopped foreigners from wearing Chinese clothes. Massacres of thousands of foreign merchants and settlers took place in Yangzhou in 760 and in Guangzhou in 878. Foreign religions were persecuted.

In the same way, the relatively open Mongol Empire in the thirteenth century was destroyed by intolerance and insulation. After violent disputes over succession, the empire broke up into four khanates, and as they sometimes fought and developed their separate identities, they sought legitimacy by allying themselves with powerful local groups to stamp out others. When the bubonic plague began to spread in the 1330s, the khanates were cut off from each other, trade collapsed and they started searching for scapegoats.

The Mongols of Russia converted to Islam and attacked Christians and the Mongols of Persia, who were seen as oppressing Muslims, until the Persian Mongols converted to Islam themselves and started attacking other religions, including their own original shamanism and Buddhism. In China, Kublai Khan's successors instead promoted Buddhism above other religions. Facing the fallout of the plague and rebellions, some in the ruling class thought the problem was that they had become 'too Chinese' and had to return to their 'pure' Mongol roots. They began to isolate themselves and oppress their subjects, which only resulted in more anti-Mongol revolts and soon the collapse of their rule.

Likewise, the dogmatic religious forces opposed to science and innovation in the Arab world got the upper hand after Christians closed in from the north and Mongols from the east. After the destruction of Baghdad in 1258, conservatives restored what they thought to be a more traditional Islam. As we saw in chapter 3, confusing the consequences of a colder climate with modern decadence and collective sin, many of the great empires reacted to the series of rebellions and state breakdowns in the late 1500s to mid-1600s by trying to reimpose traditional beliefs and past glories. In his history of this chaotic period, Jack Goldstone wrote: 'after 1650 the Ottoman and Chinese empires became more rigidly orthodox and conservative than they had been earlier; they eschewed novelties, while rewarding conformity to past habits'.[27]

The demagogue's strategy, as H. L. Mencken once described it, is to 'keep the populace alarmed (and hence clamorous to be led to safety) by an endless series of hobgoblins, most of them imaginary'.[28]

Adolf Hitler could come to power promising to restore German might because of the sad state the Treaty of Versailles and economic crisis had left the country in. In May 1928, his National Socialist Party did not get more than 2.6 per cent of the votes. Just four years later, during the Depression and amidst political violence on the streets, it got 37.3 per cent. Hitler attained the power to erect the dictatorship after whipping up panic about a potential communist coup after the Reichstag fire on 27 February 1933. The next day, the 'Reichstag Fire Decree' suspended most civil liberties in Germany, and within a month Hitler got the right to rule by decree.

More recently, Vladimir Putin convinced Russians that the only way to escape the chaos of the 1990s was to give him total control and restore some sort of mythological blend of Imperial,

OPEN

Orthodox Russia and Stalinism. He got some assistance by a few suspiciously well-timed apartment bombings in Moscow, probably with FSB involvement, that stoked fear and created popular support for a second Chechen war. His approval rating increased from 2 to 45 per cent in three months. When Chechnya was defeated (in 2012 he got 99.8 of the votes in the region), he needed a new enemy, and created the narrative that a sinful West was trying to destroy Russia.[29]

Many modern demagogues are borrowing from this familiar order/disorder/order playbook. It is Venezuela's Chávez and Maduro claiming that treacherous elites and foreigners ruined the once-proud Bolivarian Republic, and that the independent judiciary and free media has to be dismantled to restore it. It is the neo-Ottomanism of Turkey's Recep Tayyip Erdogan demolishing democratic institutions to build a unified society based on political Islam and create regional hegemony instead of Westernization. It is the Hindu nationalists of India, rocking the delicate balance between groups in a vast, multicultural country by stoking hostility against Muslims. It is Hungary's Viktor Orban's yearning for a Great Hungary before the Treaty of Trianon in 1920, and building a 100-metre monument of black granite close to parliament, which has the names of more than 12,000 places lost at the peace engraved into it.

Yet we also hear echoes of such promises of restoration in the Brexit campaign's promise to 'Take *back* control' and the ambition to 'Make America great *again*'. As Donald Trump said in February 2014 before being a presidential contender, when complaining about the state of the country on a Fox News show:

> You know what solves it? When the economy crashes, when the country goes to total hell and everything is a disaster. Then you'll have riots, to go back to where we used to be when we were great.[30]

Scapegoats

A sense of threat regularly makes us distinguish 'us' and 'them' more strongly, which can readily be exploited by the authoritarian. In one study, Christian students were asked to think of two individuals who were very similar in most respects but for the fact that one of them was Christian and the other Jewish. Under normal circumstances, they rated them fairly similarly. But when the students were reminded of their own mortality, they suddenly found the Christian more attractive and the Jew less attractive.[31] Combined with humanity's propensity for reactive violence and tendency to overestimate the pain we suffer while underestimating the pain we inflict on others, this often spirals out of control.

As we have seen, people are more likely to believe in conspiracy theories in times of trouble, and one tried-and-tested strategy to justify harsh rule is to summon up a devious, mighty group working in the shadows to bring misfortune to us all. They are called 'scapegoats' because of the ancient ritual of designating a goat to carry our collective sins and driving it away. Since the animal didn't have anything to do with it, it didn't have to be a goat. Sometimes it was a bull, sometimes a convict or a slave. In similar fashion, the modern scapegoat can be any group, since it is not about them but about ourselves. Jews, Muslims, EU bureaucrats, the wealthiest 1 per cent, kulaks, leftists, globalists, class enemies, the fake media or any of the nine black categories during Mao's Cultural Revolution: landlords, wealthy farmers, anti-revolutionaries, bad influences, right-wingers, traitors, spies, capitalist roaders and 'the stinking old ninth' – intellectuals.

A necessary condition is difference – real or perceived – since it is about forming and protecting our ingroup identity, and directing anger and frustration towards an outgroup. Preferably there should be something strange about them that creates suspicion. Jews did not die at the same rate as other Europeans during the

Black Death in the mid-1300s. Perhaps this was because they were often isolated in ghettos, buried their dead quickly in separate cemeteries, or washed their hands after bathroom visits and before eating. But combined with lingering anti-Semitism, this convinced many the Jews had poisoned the wells to kill Christians. Church leaders initiated pogroms from Barcelona to the Baltic coast that killed thousands.

'In its periods of introversion and intolerance Christian society, like any society, looks for scapegoats,' wrote historian Hugh Trevor-Roper. 'Either the Jew or the witch will do, but society will settle for the nearest.'[32] During the wars of religion of the 1500s and 1600s the universal scapegoat was the witch. Where orthodoxy won out, the church worried about those who had retained certain old beliefs and differed in customs. They persecuted them and made up stories of complex international conspiracies with the devil (and tortured them until they confessed). What was started by the Dominicans was escalated by Luther and Calvin, who claimed that even witches who did no harm had to be burned. As pogroms, witch-crazes, red scares or cultural revolutions get going, they take on their own logic, partly for individual motives. People joined attacks on minorities to steal from them, informed that the neighbour they held a grudge against had bourgeois tendencies, and quite often it just so happened that people found out their difficult in-laws were witches.

Trevor-Roper thought of the witch-craze as the way for a society in fear to give an apparent objective identity to its subjective anxiety. It is easier to torture and kill flesh and blood than your own inner demons, just like it paradoxically can feel better to believe in a global conspiracy that creates mischief than just to experience an amorphous and inexplicable mess. In times of prosperity the whole subject of witches could be ignored, and the whole craze died down after the religious wars.

Will it happen again?

Are we doomed to experience such a backlash again? And might we even have ourselves to blame, since openness devours itself, by provoking a forceful authoritarian reaction? Political psychologist Karen Stenner seems to think so, writing that 'freedom feeds fear that undermines freedom, and democracy is its own undoing. The overall lesson is clear: when it comes to democracy, less is often more, or at least more secure.'[33] In her essay with Jonathan Haidt, they are even more unambiguous in their pessimism: 'Western liberal democracies have now exceeded many people's capacity to tolerate them – to live with them, and in them.'[34]

This, however, would only hold if the groupish are more authoritarian in liberal democracies than in non-liberal societies. That is a possibility, since a more pluralistic society might offer more normative threats to react against than a static autocracy that keeps everybody in line. On the other hand, there is good reason to suspect that populations in democracies can adapt to a higher everyday level of difference and that it takes more to get them to think society is coming apart.

This empirical question has been studied by Kris Dunn at the University of Leeds, and he finds there are not just fewer authoritarians in democratic regimes than in autocratic regimes, but also that authoritarians are more tolerant in democracies.[35] One reason might be that the conformists are more norm-adherent, and adjust their attitudes to the group norms in different societies. So vibrant democracies with long traditions of pluralism are not at the greatest risk of authoritarian reversals. On the other hand, young, unstable democracies that are still in the process of opening up might be, since they experience rapidly increasing pluralism while societal norms might not yet be supportive of individualism and democracy. Recent experiences in countries like Turkey and Hungary spring to mind.

This is consistent with a common argument, recently made by Fareed Zakaria, that liberal democracy is rarely the result of a dictatorship quickly granting general suffrage, without first having gone through a period of rule of law, division of powers and a thriving civil society with independent organization and a free media. If people are not used to a free society, the result might just be a majoritarian democracy, where the 50 per cent + 1 oppresses everybody else.[36]

So the strong pessimism about liberal democracy's ability to survive seems unwarranted. However, Stenner's analysis might still have a strong, explanatory value in assessing particular outbursts of authoritarianism. Unfortunately, in the years after her book was published, a series of crises created a large-scale test of her thesis: large-scale terrorism, chaos in the Middle East, the migration crisis, and growing geopolitical uncertainty where Western countries lose in relative economic clout to rapidly growing countries to the East and South. And then came the financial crisis of 2008 and the ensuing global recession. This ticked an uncomfortably large number of boxes that predict authoritarian and nativist reactions. As we have seen, it is almost a law of economic history that major economic downturns are followed by a surge of zero-sum thinking, conspiracy theories and persecution of scapegoats. Businesses and jobs were destroyed on a colossal scale and those who kept their jobs saw their incomes stagnate over a long period. It contributed to a whole generation getting lower incomes than their parents did at a similar age, and undermined the core assumption that each generation will be better off than the previous one.

More people began to see the world as a zero-sum game, not just trade relations with other countries, but the domestic economic and political situation as well. In a 2011 study, American whites said they thought many steps had been made towards racial equality in the US, but that this was now linked to a new 'inequality' at their expense. The less anti-black bias that whites perceive in society in a given decade, the greater they thought the anti-white bias was. In the very title of the paper, the two psychologists warned that, 'Whites see racism as a zero-sum game that they are now losing.'[37] If the world is a zero-sum game, and people perceive they are losing it, they will begin to man the barricades and fight back.

Historically, economic threats create a demand for conformity, rigid rules and strong leaders. For example, US Christian denominations that enforce obedience and threaten excommunication grow in membership during times of economic hardship, whereas more liberal denominations grow during economic expansion. During times of economic insecurity, comic-strip heroes become more tough, more TV characters enforce conformity, people want harsher punishment for crime, and they want stronger, more powerful political leaders.[38]

The Great Recession did not just hit our wallets, it also undermined trust in our leaders and institutions. The crisis exposed how little our governments, our politicians and even bankers understood about what had happened on the financial markets they had praised during the previous decade. And their nonplussed reaction and often very public bickering about causes and responses did not show them from their most impressive side. The official response to the crisis was even more problematic. To prevent a collapse of the banking system, decision-makers found no better solution than bailing out the most vulnerable financial institutions. So after having taken risks and making mistakes of a magnitude that created the worst crisis since the 1930s, bankers and speculators were saved by taxpayers – while millions of people who had no part in creating the crisis lost their jobs and homes.

Central banks all over the world quickly opened the monetary taps and reduced interest rates to record lows, in some instances even going into negative territory. This is what central banks regularly do to try to unleash animal spirits, but this time the policy was more aggressive and longer-lasting than usual. It did not lead to a rapid recovery for the real economy, but it did for the stock market, which disproportionately benefited the wealthy who already owned assets. It helped housing prices to bounce back and even surpass pre-crisis levels, which made life in dynamic metropolitan areas even more unaffordable for people who were already struggling with their household economy.

This all meant that the general economic malaise was accompanied by a sense that the rich and well-connected got away with everything and that the elites don't care about the little guy. Such a breakdown in respect for our leaders led many voters to withdraw their support for the system, and demand stronger leaders who could 'get things done'. And then a pandemic shut down economies all over the world.

So you can see why now is the perfect time for demagogues to tell people that the country is falling apart and the world is dangerous, to peddle conspiracy theories and parade scapegoats. And to restore the good old days we had before the chaos and corruption of today.

We are the monsters we fear

There is a 1960s episode of the old anthology TV series *The Twilight Zone* that starts on a late Saturday afternoon in an idyllic small town somewhere in America. People greet each other, children are playing and the bell can be heard from an ice cream vendor. 'Maple Street in the last calm and reflective moment – before the monsters came.' The people on Maple Street hear a strange sound from the sky, and a boy says it might be a UFO. Strange things start happening. There is a general power failure and cars don't start. The lights go on and off in different houses. The increasingly fearful townspeople begin to air suspicions that one of their own might be an alien, intent on hurting them all. Any sign of eccentricity, staying up late at night or being a radio hobbyist, is suddenly interpreted as a sign of malevolence.

One of them warns that this search for scapegoats will make them 'eat each other alive', but that only makes him seem more suspicious. The neighbours in this tightly-knit community begin to turn on each other, they start attacking the homes of suspects and they fight in the street. Soon Maple Street is in complete chaos.

The scene then cuts to a nearby hilltop. It is revealed that the town has indeed been visited by an alien spaceship. Its leader tells his subordinate that this proves how easy the procedure of conquest is. No weapons are needed, they just have to stop a few machines and throw humans into darkness for a few hours. The humans will be so sure that monsters lurk around the corner that they will create them if they can't find them, and so start to destroy themselves.

'There are weapons that are simply thoughts, attitudes, prejudices to be found only in the minds of men,' as the closing narration has it, 'prejudices can kill, and suspicion can destroy and a thoughtless, frightened search for a scapegoat has a fallout all of its own – for the children and the children yet unborn. And the pity of it is that these things cannot be confined to the Twilight Zone.'[39]

The good news is that there are no hidden extraterrestrials manipulating us to instil paranoia and panic. The bad news is that it doesn't take extraterrestrials.

This doesn't mean there is no hope for openness. It just means that it will continue to find itself under attack. As the novelist Mario Vargas Llosa has warned us, we can never decisively win the battle against the tribe, but we can lose it.[40]

9

OPEN OR CLOSED?

'[C]ivilization has not yet fully recovered from the shock
of its birth – the transition from the tribal or "enclosed
society", with its submission to magical forces, to the
"open society" which sets free the critical powers of man.
The shock of this transition is one of the factors that have
made possible the rise of those reactionary movements
which have tried, and still try, to overthrow civilization
and to return to tribalism.'

Karl Popper, 1945

Around the time of the fall of communism, two essays that
would later be extended to book format captured the interest of the chattering classes. The first one was Francis Fukuyama's
'The End of History?' from 1989, arguing that liberal capitalist
democracies were the final form of government and that history
had in effect ended. The other essay, in many ways a response, was
'The Clash of Civilizations?' by Fukuyama's old teacher Samuel
Huntington. Huntington thought a new phase of history was
starting after the Cold War, one that would be defined by traditional civilizations, which would set the pattern for collaborations

and conflicts. Ideology and commercial interests would mean less for the formation of alliances and association, as countries with similar traditions would grow closer. Tensions would appear and war be waged along the borders of the different civilizations, like the West, Eastern Orthodox, Chinese, Islam, Hindu, Japan, Latin America and Africa.

Ever since then – and especially after 9/11 – the popular verdict has been that Huntington was quickly proven right whereas Fukuyama's thesis was just an extreme example of the exaggerated hopes around the fall of the Berlin Wall. History did not end, Russia and China did not become democracies, and we got new, violent conflicts, often along the 'bloody borders' of Islam, as Huntington had talked about.

The popular verdict is wrong. A closer look at what the two gentlemen actually wrote reveals that it is Huntington who has been proven wrong, and that Fukuyama was more insightful.

Of course Fukuyama did not argue that history would end in any kind of literal sense, that all political battles would end or nothing more would happen. His point was that the ideological and political battles during the twentieth century had shown that no system was able to produce wealth better than free market capitalism and no political system was better at giving citizens a sense of recognition and dignity than liberal democracy. This does not mean these systems can't be defeated or that there can be no backsliding, but it does mean it is not possible to create a system with fewer internal contradictions than liberal democratic capitalism.

As I have made clear, this is also my belief. There is no lack of problems and difficulties in free market democracies but, unlike authoritarian systems, they are open to improvements because they are full of experiments, feedback loops and mechanisms for self-correction. Free markets and an open civil society are constantly changing according to the needs, interests and demands of people. Open societies are more stable than closed societies because disaffection can be channelled into complaints, arguments, new groups and political organizations and so modify the system peacefully rather than overthrow it. The system does not seem to be threatened with extinction.

There were some exaggerated hopes swirling around at the time the Berlin Wall came down, but since Fukuyama wrote his article in 1989 the share of countries that are electoral democracies has actually increased from 41 to 64 per cent.[1] The fact that most governments in the world pledge allegiance to democracy, some form of rule of law and a relatively open economy seems almost banal today, but this represents an astonishing turn of events, not just compared to the ancient past but even to 1974, when the German chancellor Willy Brandt thought that 'Western Europe has only 20 or 30 years more of democracy left in it; after that it will slide, engineless and rudderless, under the surrounding sea of dictatorship.'[2]

But just because we can't go forwards and replace liberal capitalism with an even more responsive and open system, it doesn't mean we can't go backwards. Fukuyama recognized that we live in a 'world still full of authoritarianisms, theocracies, intolerant nationalisms' and thought we could very well 'drag the world back into history with all its wars, injustices, and revolution'.[3]

Far from being a triumphalist, Fukuyama feared that freedom and wealth would not be enough, as people fought for something more important: recognition and respect. He thought we might see a new radical Left, dressing up as liberals and handing out so many new rights that the traditional individual rights became meaningless. But he feared even more an assault from a reactionary Right, yearning for heroism and hierarchies that are lost in an egalitarian, consumerist world populated by the last men 'without chests'. Therefore, there is a constant temptation to 'return to being first men engaged in bloody and pointless prestige battles, only this time with modern weapons'. When he discussed whether the status-seeking and power-hungry would in the long run be satisfied with the comfortable life at the end of history, he just happened to mention 'a developer like Donald Trump'.[4]

I don't agree with all of Fukuyama's analysis, and I do think he overdosed on Hegel and Nietzsche. But he was perceptive in his historical positioning of liberal capitalism and of the cultural and psychological factors that make us uncomfortable with it, and which therefore threaten to undermine it.

Meanwhile, history has not been as kind to Samuel Huntington's predictions as popular perception would have it. We did not experience global chaos after the Cold War; instead it has been the most peaceful era yet.[5] Despite the Syrian civil war, the rate of battle deaths in 2018 was a quarter of what it was during the 1980s. And except for the wars in Afghanistan and Iraq, which represented America's attempts to prevent chaos and terrorism, almost all major wars in recent decades have been fought *within* Huntington's civilizations rather than between them: Sri Lanka, Congo, Sierra Leone, Syria, Darfur, South Sudan, Yemen, the Lord's Resistance Army insurgency in Uganda. Somalia is one of the few African countries where most people belong to the same ethnic group, have the same religion and speak the same language. It is also a country that has been plagued more than others by divisions and war.

Russia invaded Georgia and Ukraine, even though they share orthodox traditions (*because* they do, some would say). No one looking at the current relationship between Saudi Arabia, Iran and Turkey would say that a common Muslim front against the rest of the world is in the making. In their rivalry with each other, they enlist supporters far from their civilization. Saudi Arabia works closely with the US and even Israel. Iran coordinates with the orthodox Russians and supports Hamas, even though they are Sunni Muslims. It looks much more like traditional power politics than a civilizational struggle. The bloodthirsty Islamic State primarily killed other Muslims, especially Shia Muslims, and internal divisions in countries like Syria, Libya and Yemen have been so large that the countries have fallen apart. Other Muslim countries have supported different sides in these internal conflicts.

While there are dangerous rifts between countries from different civilizations, like India and Pakistan (though Pakistan's war with Islamic terrorists in the north-west has been deadlier), many of the most dangerous tensions exist between countries that are historically as close as it gets, like North and South Korea, and China and Taiwan.

If that is not enough to convince you that Huntington's vision of the future does not bear much resemblance to our own, I'd recommend you consider his bizarre attempt to provide a scenario of what a future war along civilization lines could look like. The year is 2010, China and Taiwan attack US facilities in East Asia to get the Yankees out of their Sinic backyard, and enlist the support of Japan and what seems to be a united Islamist Iran-Iraq-Saudi-Egypt-Turkey alliance. An Orthodox alliance of Bulgaria and Greece responds by invading Turkey, and Russia extends its control of Muslim countries to the south and is rewarded by being invited to become a NATO member. After a war that is devastating for all sides (before it is over, Algeria has attacked Marseilles with nuclear weapons), the way is open for India to reshape the world along Hindu lines. The American public blames the weakening of the US on the Western orientation of the Anglo-Saxon elites, and Hispanic leaders take over the country, boosted by the promise of a Marshall Plan from the booming Latin American countries.[6]

Of course, predicting the future is a fool's game, but in one way Huntington was right. There is a major, global conflict brewing, yet it is not a clash of civilizations but a clash within each civilization – between those who want to keep their cultures open and those who want to close them. On the one hand, there are those

who think the world is non-zero-sum and that we can all prosper
if we keep societies and markets open and cooperate across borders. On the other hand, there are those who think the world is
zero-sum and that their only way to prosper is to protect markets
and societies from outsiders and to make the others lose.

They are represented in every society. Wherever I have travelled
in the world, I have met liberals and cosmopolitans who want
their societies to be free and their countries open, not because they
don't care about their country but because they love it so much
that they want it to benefit from the ideas and creativity of other
people as well. They are not necessarily rootless 'anywheres'. Many
of them are firmly rooted in place, family and tradition. But, unlike
cultural chauvinists, they understand that others also have places,
families and traditions that give meaning to them, and that a good
society and a decent government doesn't take sides but gives equal
freedom to all. They know there are many problems, headaches
and injustices in modern, open societies, but also that the worst
way of dealing with them is to shut down our system of discovery by implementing a one-size-fits-all solution from the top.
The only way to find better solutions is to allow millions to keep
looking.

Their opponents are not other countries and civilizations, but
dictators, fundamentalists and protectionists trying to control
their lives and steal their future. And despite aggressive nationalist
agitation from these groups, they also join hands across borders.
White supremacists adore Russia's kleptocrats, who in turn support
the populist Right and Left with money, fake news and attacks on
voting systems. China's communist party provides lesser dictators
with surveillance technology and generous funding. As proven
by their harsh measures against any attempt to organize criticism
and opposition, their real enemy is not the West but their own
people. Populist leaders in the West, like Donald Trump, do their
utmost to upend alliances with other open societies, which makes

them – and the US – more divided and weaker. Nevertheless, they never seem to have anything but praise for despots on other continents.

They stoke fear of other countries and groups to trigger our authoritarian reflex because if we insist on conformity to group norms and unravel checks and balances on executive power, we voluntarily hand them power over our lives. We give up our freedoms, and in return we get our daily Two Minutes of Hate, the daily public event in George Orwell's *Nineteen Eighty-Four*, where loyal subjects vent all their anxiety and frustrations against convenient public enemies.

This is the major threat to our civilization – not outsiders and rivals, but those who would suffocate it from within.

How do we break the cycle?

A cycle has already begun, with a rise in fear and tribalism, with feedback loops that perpetuate more zero-sum thinking and anxiety about the future, and so even more groupishness. How do we break it?

First, count to ten. It is easy to get carried away and to become a part of the problem rather than the solution. If you just want to yell at the enemy and call them names, remember that people are never as certain of their own righteousness as when they are under attack.

You might think you are less affected by the biases that distort worldviews and decision-making processes. We all do. After having heard about different biases in judgment, people could easily spot them in others but not in themselves. Just one adult out of 661 thinks they are more biased than the average person. We all have our evolutionary wiring, and some of those wires are trying to convince us that we don't have it. And the more of a bias blind spot we have, the more likely we are to ignore advice and avoid examining and testing our preconceptions. To overcome our biases, we have to recognize them and understand them.[7]

I did not intend this, but some readers might have come away from the second half of this book concluding that all is hopeless. If we are evolutionarily hardwired to be tribalists, we have no choice about it, and this entire book is superfluous. I have written a book warning people about a behaviour they can do nothing about. We will always succumb to zero-sum thinking and group-war, whatever we do.

But having a default setting does not mean that there is no way to change the setting. Being prewired does not mean being hardwired. If the doctor hits the correct spot on my knee, my calf jerks upwards. That response is hardwired. The psychological wiring I have written about is not like that. There are tendencies that push us in a certain direction, and if we don't reflect we might fall for them, but we can decide to take measures to lean against them. Our psychological predispositions cannot be removed, but they can be consciously overridden.

We have other default settings that aren't always helpful in the modern world. Just as evolution made us fear strangers, it made us crave energy-rich foods. And just like this fear of strangers becomes problematic in a world where they are all around us, it is bad for our health to be constantly peckish in a world where food is everywhere. That doesn't mean we are hardwired to eat it all. We can learn about nutrition and health, we can adapt principles of when, what and how much to eat, and we can exercise.

If we let our emotions control us, 'us vs them' will sometimes win out, but we don't have to do that; we can think things through and question our prejudices and decide to find out more. When we are tempted to succumb to groupishness, we can remind ourselves about the reasons why such temptations are the default, and about how inapplicable they are to modern life. We can learn about our tribalism, we can understand it, and we can question our prejudices, as long as our reflective selves are not drowned out by the shouting from demagogues and cheerleaders. 'Default is not destiny', as my friend Stuart Hayashi puts it.

We can study history and learn that the good old days aren't there, and about how openness created human progress. We can study economics and learn about how production and trade are not zero-sum. And we can learn about our default psychologies that tempt us to gloss over such facts. We can choose to apply our knowledge to create institutions that make positive-sum outcomes possible, and we can inform ourselves about how previous civilizations were lost because people didn't do this enough.

It is also crucial to reflect on how we learn about the world. In the last decade we have gone from the information scarcity that mankind always suffered from, where we lapped up anything we could get hold of, to a world of information surplus. This is a monumental shift, and we have not even begun to adapt to it. It is similar to when we moved from a world of famine to one of food surplus. This forced us to watch our food consumption. For the same reason and in the same way, we now have to watch our media consumption.

We look for the most dramatic and shocking information because it used to be the most important for our survival, and now with the whole world at our fingertips, we find it everywhere and conclude that the world is falling apart. We also find lethal foes in our social media feeds all the time. Have you noticed that nowadays you spend a lot of time being angry with someone you didn't even know existed five minutes ago? That unknown French author who said something terribly sexist, or that anonymous college kid who declared that anyone with your views is retarded. Nothing triggers our tribalism as much as facing the enemy, and suddenly we conclude that everybody on the other side is like that. But look, the idiots were always there (on your own side as well), they had just never entered your field of vision.

We must understand that journalists, tech companies and politicians thrive on our rage. Not because they are bad, but because your emotional reaction makes you engage and give them your time and energy. Don't fall for it. Don't let them hack your brain.

It is important to remember that tribalism is just one side of *Homo sapiens*. We are tribalists but also traders. We have a tendency to close ourselves off but also to open up. We craved safety, but we also became more safe by getting out of the cave and exploring the unknown, finding something new to eat. We feared strangers, but we also prospered because we met strangers who could become a new partner to live with, trade with or learn from.

When explaining our groupishness, I also showed how flexible it is, and that no group distinction is given by nature. We regularly expand our circles of respect, turn outgroups into ingroups by shifting perspective, and turn enemy into friend when focusing on the individual or a cross-cutting identity. Remember that the psychological researchers who wanted to study conflict at Robbers Cave had to work hard to separate the boys and stop them from accidentally becoming friends. You don't have to do the researchers' work for them by shutting yourself off from everybody who is different or doesn't share your perspective.

Humans are good at discriminating, but also experts at realizing that old cues are no longer relevant, at adapting to changing circumstances and learning that different customs are not the same as immoral behaviour. Just being aware that our prejudices or group-formations are flexible, and talking about them, helps us override automatic bigotry. It is even possible to control the disgust and fear of disease (which has been linked to xenophobia), as proven by all the nurses who regularly encounter and are repelled by a patient's rash or cough but quickly learn to override that reaction.

Just as there are studies showing that vulnerability and insecurity triggers tribalism, there are studies documenting that it is possible to activate individualism and tolerance. As we have seen, people who consider themselves extra vulnerable fall back on primal herding behaviour for protection, but those who imagine having extra powers become more individualistic and tolerant. When we have more self-esteem we are more likely to make independent judgments and not cave in to the group. When people watch a horror movie, they want to conform, but when they watch a romantic movie, they want to stand out from the crowd.

This does not mean we should all watch more romantic comedies (though as a last resort, I'd be willing to do even that), but it speaks to how we contain multitudes. We are wired for both tribalism and tolerance, and the intellectual atmosphere reinforces different parts of this complex personality. A culture that says the collective is everything and the individual nothing will get the individuals it asks for.

There is some promising evidence that self-esteem helps us overcome tribalism. One reason why we stick to old ideas is that they are part of our identity and that has to be defended at all costs. In one study, researchers provided one group with an alternative source of self-worth, for example by asking them to write about a personally valuable trait or giving them positive feedback on an important skill. The subjects who got some sort of affirmation were more open to facts and views that contradicted their own views.[8]

Perhaps it's possible to override our groupishness when we remind ourselves that we are competent and worthy of acting on our own judgment, independent of what our group might think. This effect is contested, but the line of research is important. We know which buttons to push to make us more groupish; now we have to search for the buttons that make us more independent.

In the introduction I explained that this book is about open institutions, not about openness as a nice, warm, fuzzy personality trait. But they are related. And to save the open world there may be an area where it *is* important for individuals to be nice and warm and fuzzy, and to possess the psychological trait of openness to experience, to learning, to continuing to grow. If this civilization is to go on, we must open our hearts to openness itself.

What can we do?

There are also political conclusions to be drawn from this analysis. If we want openness to survive, support for it has to be broad-based. If a large part of the population thinks they are nothing but collateral damage of globalization and technological innovation, rather than beneficiaries, they will always be tempted to tear it all up.

It can't be repeated enough that global exchange is most important for low- and middle-income households. Tariffs are regressive taxes that most hurt the poor and protect big businesses against competitors and consumers. But even though the benefits of free trade are twenty times larger than the costs, the costs are concentrated to a small group that takes a big hit. We free traders have been a little too happy with the average improvement, but no one enthusiastically takes a loss because the profits of everyone else in the country are twenty times greater than their loss. When unemployment hits you, the unemployment rate is not 5 per cent, but 100 per cent.

Too often governments have handled this transformation by removing those affected from the labour force. Of a dollar spent by the US federal government to manage a job lost, about 99 cents is spent to remove the person from the workforce and just a cent to help them get a new job. Those who lose a job may receive unemployment benefits, early retirement and disability benefits, which mitigate the blow in the short term but create long-term exclusion and bitterness. Fewer people take another job, retrain or move to where the jobs are; instead they stay in areas abandoned by industry.

One reason for declining labour mobility is declining geographic mobility. This is a trend all over the Western world, but is on starkest display in America, since it used to be the country where people moved to opportunity. In the 1950s, 20 per cent of the population moved every year. Since then the share has steadily declined. In the late 2010s, the share fell under 10 per cent for the first time since the Census Bureau started tracking it in 1947.[9]

More imagination is needed in education, labour market and social policy to provide people with what Swedish trade unions used to call 'the safety of wings' – not the safety of staying put, but of moving to where the new opportunities are. Instead of generous unemployment benefits, we could provide wage insurance that compensates people if they take a job with a lower wage than previously. Instead of paying them for staying where they are, we could pay them to move to where the jobs are. This has the obvious drawback that it would depopulate left-behind communities even more, but perhaps we should focus less on saving communities and more on saving people.

One of the most destructive parts of our welfare system is that those who start working again lose most of their benefits. Almost 40 per cent of the unemployed in the OECD countries face a marginal rate higher than 80 per cent if they take a job.[10] Replacing the welfare system with a universal basic income (UBI), often proposed to deal with technology-induced unemployment, could get us out of this welfare trap. Since it is paid out no matter how much the wage increases, it doesn't discourage work. It would also go some way to dealing with the fear of losing jobs and incomes due to recessions or restructuring. However, if the UBI is set at a high level it would be a very expensive way of sending tax money to the middle class. If it is set at a low level, it might not help much in creating a sense of security.

A better alternative would be to replace welfare schemes with a 'negative income tax'. Below a guaranteed minimum, the government tops up your income with a share of your shortfall, and if you make more than that, you start paying tax. Just like a UBI, it would remove administrative overheads and government snooping on the poor – but, unlike a UBI, it would not hand out money to the middle classes and the rich, and so would be much cheaper.

There is a case to be made that technology will be even more disruptive to old industries in the future, but the same technology gives us better tools than ever to facilitate transitions. With new educational platforms online, the conditions should be greater than ever to constantly upgrade the skills of the workforce. In the private sector we now see the creation of custom-built software, like Accenture's Job Buddy, which tells employees about the risk that their jobs will be automated and points them in the direction of the training they would benefit from. This helps employees to future-proof themselves by constantly upgrading their skills for a changing labour market. Governments should be more like a job buddy than a welfare buddy. Instead of focusing all efforts on an education in the beginning of life, which will in many ways soon be obsolete, it should make constant retraining easily accessible.

A dynamic economy also presupposes the removal of barriers to change, for example prohibitive housing costs that stop people from moving to where the jobs are. For several decades, governments have supported home ownership over renting, often for ideological purposes. Many had the impression that owners were more responsible citizens and would be a force for stability in society. Governments started subsidizing mortgages and down payments, and supporting ownership over renting through the tax code, for example via generous deductions. Deeper mortgage markets and declining interest rates have made it possible for the wealthy to bid up the price of housing in central locations. On a functioning market, this would result in the building of more homes, but the housing market is broken. Strict land-use restrictions and building regulations have made it increasingly difficult to build anywhere people might want to live. And once a permit is given, it can be appealed by local residents whose primary motivation is often to protect the view from their windows and the value of their homes. The rate of housing construction in the rich world is half of what it was in the 1960s. And rent control – supposedly to benefit renters – incentivizes renters to hold on to their contracts, and so also reduces mobility and the incentive to build more rental apartments.

One study showed that a doubling of a US state's home-ownership rate is followed in the long run by a doubling of the unemployment rate.[11] So many are left in places with little opportunity, and can only watch dynamic, urban areas with growing opportunities from a distance. Obviously this can breed resentment and a sense of being left behind. It doesn't help when urban intellectuals wax lyrically about your condition, and explain that you are there because you are a 'somewhere', firmly rooted in place and community, with a more natural identity than the rootless 'anywheres'. Many of them are not proud somewheres, they are just stuck.[12]

Japan showed in the early 2000s that it is possible to loosen the planning system substantially, and so increase building and reduce the cost of housing even in Tokyo. Interestingly, Japan is one of the few industrialized countries without a populist movement.

Another barrier to movement is occupational licensing. The share of the American workforce covered by state-licensing laws has risen from less than 5 per cent to more than 25 per cent since the 1950s.[13] More than 1100 occupations are regulated in at least one state, from nurses and opticians to make-up artists and florists. The stated intent is to ensure the capacity and quality of work done, but it has turned into a way for insiders to keep others out of their job market. A 2012 study showed that cosmetologists and truck drivers need licences in fifty-one states (including

Washington, DC), barbers and manicurists in fifty states and pre-school teachers in forty-nine. To work as a bartender you need a license in thirteen states. On average, obtaining a licence for a job requires paying $209, almost nine months of education and training, and passing one exam.[14] This makes it much more difficult to enter a new sector, and hampers social mobility and employment. Since many states stop anyone with a felony conviction from obtaining a licence, it makes it difficult for those people to readjust.

The situation is similar in other Western countries, but America makes it worse since many of the licences are state-specific. If you are a licensed schoolteacher or pharmacist who loses your job, you might not be allowed to pick up a similar position in another state without going through the whole process of coursework and apprenticeships again. The between-state migration for individuals in occupations with state-specific licences is 36 per cent lower than for other workers.[15] Abolishing licence requirements or turning them into voluntary accreditations – or at least making them portable across state lines – would do much to help people.

Many critics claim that politicians in the West have only concerned themselves with the creative, cosmopolitan classes in urban areas, and that people in smaller cities and rural areas, facing unemployment and crime, have been left to fend for themselves. This creates a sense of vulnerability and a willingness to strike back. After recent populist reactions we risk ending up with politicians taking the other side, fulminating against rootless urban globalists, which will only reinforce the split between young/old, urban/rural, white collar/blue collar. The solution is not to take another side, but to talk to the hopes and ambitions that cross-cut these divides.

Many writers and politicians emphasize the need for an inclusive, civic nationalism, strengthening common symbols and rituals that make us feel like we have a common project. By all means, try that. Sometimes words speak louder than actions, but most often they don't. A sense of inclusion is not created through flag-waving or exotic inclusion projects, but by making sure that we get the basics right: that the infrastructure is not falling apart, that the schools are decent and that there is a local police station. A sense of physical insecurity makes for a fearful population, and if liberals ignore crime because they think it is something just right-wing politicians care about, they will find that voters agree, and move in that direction.

An open society can experiment with different institutions and continue to adapt them piecemeal in the light of experiences and discontent. Our version of democracy is never finished. If people feel the present version of representative democracy is not very representative we should continue to tinker with it. Once upon a time, before governments were supposed to be involved in everything, we didn't have professional politicians working full-time in a capital far away, but teachers, farmers, workers, business-men and journalists who worked part-time as politicians and only went away to the capital for the few months when parliament was in session. They were firmly rooted in the local community and in a workplace and constantly met their voters, so they came to be seen as the people's voice in the centre of power, rather than the other way around. Digital technology could give us an opportunity to restore something similar.

Referendums arouse emotion and tribalism, but it is worth exploring platforms for deliberative democracy, where ordinary cit-izens meet and discuss the merits of particular decisions. Debates among the like-minded often make a group more extreme in their views, but a structured discussion with people with other views has been shown to make people more open to new arguments. Civic organizations have been founded to accomplish precisely this, to bridge divides and reduce polarization.

Such bodies can also get a formal status. For example, in 2016,

Ireland created a Citizens' Assembly made up of ninety-nine Irish citizens randomly selected to represent the electorate. They were tasked with discussing sensitive and complicated issues with the help of expert witnesses and coming up with recommendations for elected representatives. This creates another dynamic than ordinary day-to-day politics. The citizens are not there to incite their own, to attract donations or to win an election. They have nothing to gain by using a controversial issue as a stick with which to beat the other side. They are there to solve such issues. The assembly has been credited with raising the level of debate and reducing tensions ahead of referendums on abortion and same-sex marriage. It would have been interesting to see what a deliberative body would have done on the Brexit issue or for US immigration policy.

Don't let it go

The simplest thing we can do politically is to refuse to support the authoritarians who try to turn us against one another, and stoke fear of outgroups and minorities, even if they offer you self-esteem, tax cuts or state help. It sounds easy, though what if that helps the other guy to get in with his lousy policies? But the one thing that is worse than bad policies is the attempt to short-circuit the (more or less) rational, open debate about pros and cons and costs and benefits with various policy positions, and replace it with a tribal shouting match if not a civil war.

The insight that even established democracies are vulnerable to populist revolts and authoritarian takeovers should also inject new energy to the debate over rule of law and constitutional restraints on government power. And rules have to be written down, with control mechanisms. Gentlemen's agreements and established practice cannot be certain to hold in an era of tribal politics. Liberal democracy is not the idea that whoever gets 51 per cent of the votes is allowed to do anything against the 49 per cent. It is the idea that minorities – even the smallest minority, the individual – has inalienable rights and that power is always a threat and must therefore always be controlled by the people, by a strong constitution and by independent courts. In many democracies, a powerful executive with support from parliament can quickly upend many of the freedoms that we take for granted, and can shield themselves from control.

Most people agree – when their party is out of power. But the moment their own side is in charge, they always push for more executive power. Hopefully, this era of political turbulence will teach people that hypocrisy is costly. If you are not comfortable with handing a particular authority to a Donald Trump or a Nicolás Maduro or a Viktor Orbán, perhaps you shouldn't entrust anyone with it, because now we know that people like that can very well make it to the top. Should leaders have, for example, the power to appoint judges, offer amnesty, make law by signing executive orders, or launch nuclear weapons without anyone else's consent?

Populists who talk about a one, true people, and everybody else as an obstacle to the general will, are often good at pointing out flaws in our political system. But whatever the problem, these people are never the solution because their lack of patience for the rule of law and division of powers makes such problems even worse. No matter how much the populist seems to share your worries about the system, he will not be responsible to you and the other voters. He will be his own boss and use that position for his own interest.

A database of forty-six governing populist leaders and parties in democratic countries between 1990 and 2018 shows that half of them rewrote or amended the constitution. On average there was a 7 per cent decline in freedom of the press on their watch, an 8 per cent decline in civil liberties and a 13 per cent decline in political rights.[16] While rallying against corruption was often their way to power, their countries fall an average of five places on Transparency International's Corruption Perceptions Index under their rule. Often they lead the way personally. Four in ten populist leaders are eventually indicted for corruption. And this is an underestimate, since many populists erode their country's independent judiciary to ensure they are never charged. Partly because they hurt independent institutions, they hold on to power twice as long as non-populists.

In the end, if this strongman takeover is to be stopped, it's down to you and me. Few things are more dangerous right now than excessive self-criticism on behalf of believers in openness. Constantly examining and adjusting your beliefs is necessary, but after the rise of populism there has been a bizarrely long line of intellectuals and politicians waiting for their turn to apologize that globalization has gone too far. It seems they confuse the fact that many resist their ideas with there being something wrong with those ideas.

This is fraught with danger. As we have seen, backlashes against openness occur regularly throughout history but, for a number of reasons, they don't always win. Sometimes the hostility dies down when threats dissipate and growth returns, other issues come to the fore, populist leaders discredit themselves or more liberal movements and politicians manage to inspire new support for the open society. However, the reaction wins every time fence-sitters come to agree with it and advocates of openness fall silent. So that is the one thing we must not do.

People want to conform, especially in times of trouble. That is why continued opposition to a popular reaction is hard, but that's also why it is so important. People often disguise their preferences to fit in, and they often go with the flow – not because it is right but because it is the flow. But we have also learned from psychological tests that sometimes a single person speaking up is enough to break this conformist spell and give others the courage to also reject the perceived consensus. So we need intellectuals and grassroots movements, brave politicians and independent journalists to defend the open society. But more than anything, we need private citizens to explain to friends and colleagues what is at stake, and to speak up whenever someone is trying to strengthen the tribe by peddling conspiracy theories and attacking outgroups. Remember that a single dissenting point of view can open minds.

The legendary British historian Arnold Toynbee, who studied the rise and fall of civilizations, always objected to simplified comparison between societies and biological life. A living organism has its lifespan determined by its nature, but societies don't have an inherent limit to their lifespan. So they don't die of age or natural causes. Societies die of suicide or murder, Toynbee concluded – and nearly always suicide.

The end of openness brought every previous efflorescence in history down. This one may yet be saved.

ACKNOWLEDGEMENTS

Homo sapiens innovate and imitate, and since every idea is a new combination of old insights, hunches and experiences, this list of gratitude should really go on and on – all the way from Thales, Anaximander and Anaximenes on the island of Miletus, to the equally creative and inspiring Alicia, Alexander and Nils-Erik who, two and a half millennia later, help me see things from a new perspective every day. However, my editor, Mike Harpley, would object to extending the book even further and I have learned that it's worth listening to him if I want a better book. (By the way, thanks for noticing I confused 'mammoth' and 'mummy'. That would have been embarrassing.) I am also grateful to my copy-editor, Charlotte Atyeo, for making me sound fluent in English.

Thanks to Tom G. Palmer, not just for helping me realize what's at stake when openness is threatened, but also for always going first into every battle about it. As usual, Mattias Bengtsson helped me sort through my ideas and provided me with treasured input.

I am especially grateful to Stuart Hayashi for a never-ending stream of research, input, support and advice. This book would not have been the same without all the time and energy you devoted to it. The only way I can think of to pay you back in full is to save civilization. I'll see what I can do.

The usual suspects, Fredrik Segerfeldt and Mattias Svensson, read early drafts of the book, supported me when I needed it and scorned me when I needed that. I do appreciate it. Thanks also to Alex Nowrasteh for sorting out some important things under severe time constraints.

Once again, my equally patient and encouraging agent, Andrew Gordon, helped me explain what I wanted to say and get this book into print.

Sansa was there for me every step of the way. She is our Cornish Rex, and kept me company when I did the research, and slept in my lap when I wrote. The cat, as Albert Jay Nock once pointed out, is nature's arch-individualist and opponent of servitude, so Sansa knows what's at stake.

Frida was not there physically to the same extent but was no less supportive. Thanks for your love, inspiration and patience. Anywhere, with you.

NOTES

Introduction: Traders and tribalists

1   U. Wierer, S. Arrighi, S. Bertola, G. Kaufmann, B. Baumgarten, A. Pedrotti et al., 'The Iceman's lithic toolkit: Raw material, technology, typology and use', *PLoS ONE 13*(6), 2018. G. Artioli, I. Angelini, G. Kaufmann, C. Canovaro, G. Dal Sasso and I. M. Villa, 'Longdistance connections in the Copper Age: New evidence from the Alpine iceman's copper axe', *PLoS ONE 12*(7), 2017.

2   'Ebola: Economic impact already serious; Could be "catastrophic" without swift response', World Bank [press release], 17 September 2014.

3   K. A. Appiah, *The Lies That Bind: Rethinking Identity*. London, Profile Books, 2018, pp. 195 ff.

4   K. Popper, *The Open Society and Its Enemies*. London, Routledge, 1966, vols. 1 and 2.

5   F. A. Hayek, *The Constitution of Liberty*. London, Routledge, 2011, p. 81.

6   J. Mokyr, 'Cardwell's Law and the political economy of technological progress', *Research Policy, 23*(5), 1994.

7   C. Lakatos, D. Laborde and W. Martin, 'Reacting to food price spikes: Commodity of errors' [Let's Talk Development blog], World Bank, 5 February 2019, https://blogs.worldbank. org/developmenttalk/ reacting-food-price-spikes-commodity-errors (accessed 9 March 2020).

8   R. Bailey, *Liberation Biology*. New York, Prometheus Books, 2005. R. Bailey, 'No more pandemics?', *Reason Magazine*, 17 January 2020, https://reason. com/2020/01/17/no-more-pandemics/ (accessed 9 March 2020).

9   T. Snyder, *The Road to*

Unfreedom: Russia, Europe, America. New York, Tim Duggan Books, 2018, p. 236.
10 T. G. Palmer, 'A new, old

challenge: Global anti-libertarianism', Cato Policy Report, November/December 2016.

1

Open exchange

1 B. Woodward, *Fear: Trump in the White House*. New York, Simon & Schuster, 2018, p. 208.
2 M. Ridley, *The Rational Optimist: How Prosperity Evolves*. London, Fourth Estate, 2010, p. 91.
3 C. Wheelan, *Naked Economics: Undressing the Dismal Science*. New York, W. W. Norton & Company, 2002, p. 187.
4 A. Smith, *An Inquiry Into the Nature and Causes of the Wealth of Nations* in *The Glasgow Edition of the Works and Correspondence of Adam Smith*. Indianapolis, Liberty Fund, 1776/1981, p. 29.
5 A. S. Brooks et al., 'Long-distance stone transport and pigment use in the earliest Middle Stone Age', *Science*, 360(6384), 2018.
6 P. Farb, *Man's Rise to Civilization: As Shown by the Indians of North America From Primeval Times to the Coming of the Industrial State*. New

York, Dutton, 1968, p. 43.
7 A postmodern Swedish etiquette book says that if you accept a trip or a car you have to sleep with the giver, and possibly help him to bury a dead body in the forest. N. Espinoza and J. Holmström, *Protokoll: Grundkurs I Normalt Beteende*. Stockholm, Hydra, 2009.
8 S. Pinker, 'The cognitive niche: Coevolution of intelligence, sociality, and language', *Proceedings of the National Academy of Sciences*, 107(2), 2010.
9 W. von Hippel, *The Social Leap: The New Evolutionary Science of Who We Are, Where We Come From, and What Makes Us Happy*. New York, Harper Wave, 2018.
10 M. Tomasello, M. Carpenter, J. Call, T. Behne and H. Moll, 'Understanding and sharing intentions: The origins of cultural cognition', *Behavioral and Brain Sciences*, 28(5), 2005.

11 K. Popper and J. C. Eccles, *The Self and Its Brain*. London, Routledge, 1984, p. 48.

12 J. Henrich, *The Secret of Our Success: How Culture is Driving Human Evolution, Domesticating Our Species and Making Us Smarter*. Princeton, Princeton University Press, 2016, p. 20.

13 Ibid, p. 41.

14 M. Wollstonecraft, *A Vindication of the Rights of Women*. New York, Cosimo, 2008, p. 157.

15 A. Powell, S. Shennan and M. G. Thomas, 'Late Pleistocene demography and the appearance of modern human behavior', *Science, 324*(5932), 2009.

16 C. Darwin, *The Descent of Man, and Selection in Relation to Sex*. New York, D. Appleton, 1878, p. 50.

17 F. A. Hayek, *Law, Legislation and Liberty: A New Statement of the Liberal Principles of Justice and Political Economy*. London, Routledge, 1982, p. 15.

18 F. de Waal, 'Food sharing and reciprocal obligations among chimpanzees', *Journal of Human Evolution, 18*(5), 1989.

19 von Hippel, 2018.

20 R. Horan, E. Bulte and J. Shogren, 'How trade saved humanity from biological exclusion: An economic theory of Neanderthal extinction', *Journal of Economic Behavior & Organisation, 58*(1), 2005. S. Kuhn and M. Stiner, 'What's a mother to do? The division of labor among Neandertals and modern humans in Eurasia', *Current Anthropology, 47*(6), 2006. Henrich, 2016.

21 R. Wrangham, *The Goodness Paradox: How Evolution Made Us More and Less Violent*. London, Profile Books, 2009.

22 D. Sandgathe, H. Dibble, P. Goldberg, S. J. P. McPherron, A. Turq, L. Niven and J. Hodgkins, 'On the role of fire in Neanderthal adaptations in Western Europe: Evidence from Pech de L'Aze and Roc de Marsal, France', *PaleoAnthropology*, 2011. D. Sandgathe, H. Dibble, P. Goldberg, S. J. P. McPherron, A. Turq, L. Niven and J. Hodgkins, 'Timing of the appearance of habitual fire use', *Proceedings of the National Academy of Sciences, 108*(29), 2011.

23 K. Marx and F. Engels, *Manifesto of the Communist Party*. 1848, https://www.marxists.org/archive/marx/works/1848/communist-manifesto/cho1.htm (accessed 9 March 2020).

24 J. Henrich et al., '"Economic

man" in cross-cultural perspective: Behavioral experiments in 15 small-scale societies', *Behavioral and Brain Sciences*, *28*(6), 2005. J. Henrich et al., 'Markets, religion, community size, and the evolution of fairness and punishment', *Science*, *327*(5972), 2010.

25 R. Bailey, 'Do markets make people more generous?', *Reason Magazine*, 27 February 2002, https://reason.com/2002/02/27/do-markets-make-people-more-ge/ (accessed 9 March 2020).

26 Henrich, 2016.

27 S. Hejeebu and D. McCloskey, 'The reproving of Karl Polanyi', *Critical Review*, *13*(3–4), 1999.

28 Y. N. Harari, *Sapiens: A Brief History of Humankind*. New York, Harper, 2015, p. 123.

29 R. Wright, *Nonzero: History, Evolution & Human Cooperation*. London, Abacus, 2001, p. 93.

30 P. Watson, *Ideas: A History of Thought and Invention, From Fire to Freud*. New York, Harper, 2006, ch. 4.

31 J. Jacobs, *The Economy of Cities*. New York, Knopf Doubleday, 2016, p. 36.

32 N. Crafts, 'The "death of distance"', *World Economics*, *3*, 2005. S. Johnson, *Where Good Ideas Come From: The Seven Patterns of Innovation*. London, Penguin Books, 2011, Introduction. L. Bettencourt, J. Lobo, D. Helbing, C. Kühnert and G. B. West, 'Growth, innovation, scaling, and the pace of life in cities', *Proceedings of the National Academy of Sciences*, *104*(17), 2007.

33 J. Diamond, *The World Until Yesterday*. London, Penguin Books, 2013, p. 280.

34 Watson, 2006, p. 90.

35 D. Wengrow, *What Makes Civilization? The Ancient Near East and the Future of the West*. Oxford, Oxford University Press, 2018, ch. 4.

36 W. J. Bernstein, *A Splendid Exchange: How Trade Shaped the World*. New York, Grove Press, 2008, p. 28.

37 P. Kriwaczek, *Babylon: Mesopotamia and the Birth of Civilization*. London, Atlantic Books, 2012, p. 140. See also N. Sanandaji, *The Birthplace of Capitalism – the Middle East*. Stockholm, Timbro, 2018.

38 M. A. Edey, *The Sea Traders*. New York, Time-Life Books, 1974, p. 7.

39 D. Jacoby, 'Silk economics and cross-cultural artistic interaction: Byzantium, the Muslim world, and the Christian west', *Dumbarton Oaks Papers*, *58*(210), 2004.

40 P. D. Smith, *City: A Guidebook*

for the Urban Age. London, Bloomsbury, 2012, p. 217.

41 D. A. Irwin, *Against the Tide: An Intellectual History of Free Trade.* Princeton, Princeton University Press, 1998, p. 11.

42 Wright, 2010, ch. 6.

43 Smith, 2012, p. 209.

44 I. Morris, *Why the West Rules – For Now: The Patterns of History, and What They Reveal About the Future.* London, Profile Books, 2010, p. 288f.

45 B. Ward-Perkins, *The Fall of Rome and the End of Civilization.* Oxford, Oxford University Press, 2006, ch. 5.

46 A. Chua, *Day of Empire: How Hyperpowers Rise to Global Dominance and Why They Fall.* New York, Anchor Books, 2007, p. 39.

47 Irwin, 1998, p. 15f.

48 J. R. McConnell et al., 'Lead pollution recorded in Greenland ice indicates European emissions tracked plagues, wars, and imperial expansion during antiquity', *Proceedings of the National Academy of Sciences, 115*(22), 2018.

49 Ward-Perkins, 2006.

50 Henrich, 2004.

51 R. Jones, 'The Tasmanian paradox: Change, evolution and complexity', in R. Wright (ed.), *Stone Tools As Cultural Markers: Change, Evolution And Complexity.* Australian Institute of Aboriginal Studies, Canberra, 1977, p. 194.

52 R. Boyd, P. Richerson and J. Henrich, 'The cultural niche: Why social learning is essential for human adaptation', *Proceedings of the National Academy of Sciences, 108*(2), 2011.

53 Henrich, 2004.

54 Wright, 2001, p. 102.

55 S. Redding and A. Venables, 'Economic geography and international inequality', *Journal of International Economics, 62*(1), 2004.

56 T. Paine, *The Writings of Thomas Paine.* Altenmünster, Jazzybee Verlag, 1967, p. 218f.

57 J. Norberg, *Progress: Ten Reasons to Look Forward to the Future.* London, Oneworld, 2016.

58 W. R. Cline, *Trade Policy and Global Poverty.* Washington, DC, Peterson Institute for International Economics, 2004.

59 D. J. Trump, Inaugural address, 20 January 2017, https://www.whitehouse.gov/briefings-statements/the-inaugural-address (accessed 9 March 2020).

60 D. Ben-Atar, *Trade Secrets: Intellectual Piracy and the Origins of American Industrial Power.* New Haven, Yale University Press, 2004.

61 US-China Business Council, 'Member survey', August 2019.

62 W. Beveridge, *Tariffs: The Case Examined*. London, Longmans, Green & Cooo, 1931, p. 110.

63 S. C. Bradford, P. L. E. Grieco and G. C. Hufbauer, 'The payoff to America from global integration', *The World Economy*, *29*(7), 2005.

64 M. Perry, 'Three charts based on today's census report show that the US middle-class is shrinking… because they're moving up' [Carpe Diem blog], American Enterprise Institute, 10 September 2019, https://www.aei.org/carpe-diem/three-charts-based-on-todays-census-report-show-that-the-us-middle-class-is-shrinking-because-theyre-moving-up/ (accessed 9 March 2020).

65 'Wages with benefits' [blog], FRED Economic Data, 19 September 2016, https://fredblog.stlouisfed.org/2016/09/wages-with-benefits/ (accessed 9 March 2020).

66 Z. Wang, S. J. Wei, X. Yu and K. Zhu, 'Re-examining the effects of trading with china on local labor markets: A supply chain perspective', Working Paper 24886, National Bureau of Economic Research, 2018.

67 D. Boudreaux, 'Trump's trade cluelessness' [blog], Cafe Hayek, 12 February 2019, https://cafehayek.com/2019/02/trumps-trade-cluelessness.html (accessed 9 March 2020). 'Manufacturing sector: Real output', FRED Economic Data, https://fred.stlouisfed.org/series/OUTMS (accessed 9 March 2020).

68 M. Hicks and S. Devaraj, 'The myth and reality of manufacturing in America', Center for Business and Economic Research, Ball State University, 2015.

69 P. D. Fajgelbaum and A. K. Khandelwal, 'Measuring the unequal gains from trade', *The Quarterly Journal of Economics*, *131*(3), 2016.

70 S. Alder, D. Lagakos and L. Ohanian, 'Competitive pressure and the decline of the Rust Belt: A macroeconomic analysis', Working Paper 20538, National Bureau of Economic Research, 2014.

71 'Automotive industry: Employment, earnings, and hours', US Bureau of Labor Statistsics, https://www.bls.gov/iag/tgs/iagauto.htm (data extracted 6 March 2020).

72 L. Ohanian, 'Competition and the decline of the Rust Belt', Federal Reserve

Bank of Minneapolis, 20
December 2014, https://
www.minneapolisfed.
org/article/2014/
competition-and-the-decline-
of-the-rust-belt (accessed
9 March 2020).

73 G. C. Hufbauer and S. Lowry,
'US tire tariffs: Saving a few

jobs at high cost', Policy
brief, Peterson Institute for
International Economics,
2012.

74 M. Peters, 'Trump wants
to restrict trade and
immigration. Here's why he
can't do both', *Washington
Post*, 11 September 2017.

2

Open doors

1 M. A. Clemens, 'Economics
and emigration: Trillion-
dollar bills on the sidewalk?',
*Journal of Economic
Perspectives*, 25(3), 2011.
Obviously, there are costs
associated with moving as
well, but the economic costs
of lower wages in destination
countries are factored into
this model.

2 Wengrow, 2018.

3 S. Rushdie, *Imaginary
Homelands: Essays and
Criticism 1981–1991*.
London, Granta Books, 1992,
p. 394.

4 'ASHG denounces attempts
to link genetics and racial
supremacy', *The American
Journal of Human Genetics*,
103, 2018, https://www.cell.
com/ajhg/fulltext/S0002-
9297(18)30363-X (accessed
9 March 2020).

5 R. N. Thompson, C.P.
Thompson, O. Pelerman,
S. Gupta and U. Obolski,
'Increased frequency of travel
may act to decrease the
chance of a global pandemic',
*Philosophical Transactions of
The Royal Society of London*,
374 (1775), 2019. C. Wilson,
'Why air travel makes deadly
disease pandemics less likely',
New Scientist, 2018, https://
www.newscientist.com/
article/2184266-why-air-
travel-makes-deadly-disease-
pandemics-less-likely/
(accessed 9 March 2020).

6 M. Sikora et al., 'Ancient
genomes show social and
reproductive behaviour
of early upper Paleolithic
foragers', *Science*, *358*(6363),
2017.

7 J. Jacobs, *The Death and Life
of Great American Cities*. New

York, Vintage Books, 1961, p. 30.

8 Watson, 2006, pp. 73 and 96.

9 Ridley, 2010, p. 6.

10 M. Nielsen, *Reinventing Discovery: The New Era of Networked Science*. Princeton, Princeton University Press, 2012, pp. 1534ff.

11 J. L. Simon, *The Ultimate Resource 2*. Princeton, Princeton Univerity Press, 1998, p. 7.

12 J. L. Simon, *The Economic Consequences of Immigration*. Ann Arbor, The University of Michigan Press, 1999, p. 175.

13 S. Kerr and W. Kerr, 'Economic impacts of immigration: A survey', NBER Working Paper 16736, 2011.

14 K. Boyle, I. Goldin, B. Nabarro and A. Pitt, 'Migration and the economy: Economic realities, social impacts & political choices', Citi Global Perspectives and Solutions, September 2018.

15 T. Carlson, *Ship of Fools: How a Selfish Ruling Class Is Bringing America to the Brink of Revolution*. New York, Simon & Schuster, 2019, p. 11.

16 21st Century Fox, Annual report, 2017.

17 C. Nemeth, *In Defence of Troublemakers*. London, Hachette, 2018.

18 P. Legrain, *Immigrants: Your Country Needs Them*. London, Little, Brown, 2007, p. 117. See also R. Guest, *Borderless Economics: Chinese Sea Turtles, Indian Fridges and the New Fruits of Global Capitalism*. New York, Palgrave Macmillan, 2011.

19 Chua, 2007, p. xxi.

20 P. Briant, *Alexander and His Empire: A Short Introduction*. Princeton, Princeton University Press, 2010, p. 183.

21 Montesquieu, *Considerations on the Causes of the Greatness of the Romans and their Decline*, 1734/1965, https://constitution.org/cm/ccgrd_1.htm (accessed 9 March 2020).

22 C. Freeman, *The Closing of the Western Mind: The Rise of Faith and the Fall of Reason*. New York, Vintage Books, 2005, p. 68.

23 E. Gibbon, *The History of the Decline and Fall of the Roman Empire*. Philadelphia, Claxton, Remsen & Haffelfinger, 1875, p. 34.

24 Chua, 2007, p. 33.

25 Chua, 2007, p. 47.

26 V. Traverso, 'How pants went from banned to required in the Roman Empire', Atlas Obscura, 19 September 2017, https://www.atlasobscura.com/articles/

trousers-pants-roman-history-banned-trajan (accessed 9 March 2020).

27 P. J. Geary, *The Myth of Nations: The Medieval Origins of Europe*. Princeton, Princeton University Press, 2002, p. 85.

28 Montesquieu, 1965.

29 J. Weatherford, *Genghis Khan and the Making of the Modern World*. New York, Broadway Books, 2004, p. 233.

30 Ibid, p. 157f.

31 Ibid, p. 172f.

32 C. M. Reinhart and K. S. Rogoff, *This Time is Different: Eight Centuries of Financial Folly*. Princeton, Princeton University Press, 2011, ch. 6. Historical GDP numbers are from the Maddison Project, https://www.rug.nl/ggdc/historicaldevelopment/maddison/releases/maddison-project-database-2018 (accessed 9 March 2020).

33 J. M. Anderson, *Daily Life During the Spanish Inquisition*. Westport, Greenwood Publishing, 2002, p. 98.

34 Chua, 2007, p. 170.

35 H. Hitchings, *The Secret Life of Words: How English Became English*. New York, Farrar, Straus and Giroux, 2009, p. 197.

36 J. de Vries and A. van der Woude, *The First Modern Economy: Success, Failure, and Perseverance of the Dutch Economy, 1500–1815*. Cambridge, Cambridge University Press, 1997.

37 G. J. Tellis and S. Rosenzweig, *How Transformative Innovations Shaped the Rise of Nations*. London, Anthem Press, 2018, ch. 8.

38 I. Kramnick and R. L. Moore, *The Godless Constitution: A Moral Defence of the Secular State*. New York, W. W. Norton & Company, 2005, ch. 2.

39 P. Schrag, *Not Fit For Our Society: Immigration and Nativism in America*. Berkeley, University of California Press, 2010, p. 23.

40 T. Jefferson, *The Life and Selected Writings of Thomas Jefferson*, edited by A. Koch and W. Peden. New York, The Modern Library, 1993, pp. 273f and 488f.

41 T. West, *Vindicating the Founders: Race, Sex, Class, and Justice in the Origins of America*. Lanham, Rowman & Littlefield, 1997, p. 149.

42 Kramnick and Moore, 2005, p. 38.

43 Ibid, p. 40f.

44 F. Waldinger, 'Bombs, brains, and science: The Role of human and physical capital for the creation of scientific knowledge', *Review of*

Economics and Statistics, 98(5), 2016.

45 P. Offit, *Pandora's Lab: Seven Stories of Science Gone Wrong*. Washington, DC, National Geographic Books, 2017, p. 90.

46 C. P. Snow, *The Physicists*. Loee, House of Stratus, 2010, p. 42.

47 K. Hentschel, *Physics and National Socialism: An Anthology of Primary Sources*. Basel, Springer Science & Business Media, 2011, p. 307.

48 B. Franklin, *The Political Thought of Banjamin Franklin*. Indianapolis, Hackett Publishing, p. 71.

49 Jefferson, 1993, p. 204.

50 Schrag, 2010, p. 31f.

51 Ibid, p. 60.

52 T. Sowell, *Race and Culture: A World View*. New York, Basic Books, 1995.

53 A. Nowrasteh and A. Forrester, 'Immigrants recognize American greatness: Immigrants and their descendants are patriotic and trust America's governing institutions', Immigration Research and Policy Brief no. 10, The Cato Institute, 4 February 2019.

54 R. Rumbaut, D. Massey and F. Bean, 'Linguistic life expectancies: Immigrant language retention in Southern California',

Population and Development Review, 32(3), 2006.

55 A. Nowrasteh, 'Ethnic attrition: Why measuring assimilation is hard' [blog], The Cato Institute, 8 December 2015, https://www.cato.org/blog/ethnic-attrition-why-measuring-assimilation-hard (accessed 9 March 2020).

56 'Remarks at the presentation ceremony for the Presidential Medal of Freedom', Ronald Reagan Presidential Library and Museum, 19 January 1989, https://www.reaganlibrary.gov/011989b (accessed 9 March 2020).

57 Legrain, 2007, p. 317.

58 S. Pinker, *Enlightenment Now: The Case for Reason, Science, Humanism and Progress*. London, Allen Lane, 2018, p. 227. C. Welzel, *Freedom Rising: Human Empowerment and the Quest for Emancipation*. Cambridge, Cambridge University Press, 2013, ch. 4.

59 Pew, 2017.

60 D. Sanders, *The Myth of the Muslim Tide: Do Immigrants Threaten the West?* New York, Vintage Books, 2012.

61 'A review of survey research on Muslims in Britain', Ipsos Mori Social Research Institute, 21 March 2016, https://www.ipsos.com/sites/

default/files/ct/publication/
documents/2018-03/a-
review-of-survey-research-
on-muslims-in-great-britain-
ipsos-mori_0.pdf (accessed 9
March 2020).
62 'Migrant WVS', Insitute for
Future Studies, https://www.
iffs.se/world-values-survey/
migrant-wvs/ (accessed 9
March 2020).
63 E. Kaufmann, *White Shift:
Populism, Immigration and
the Future of White Majorities.*
London, Allen Lane, 2018.
64 B. Duffy, *Why We're Wrong
About Nearly Everything:
A Theory of Human
Misunderstanding.* New York,
Basic Books, 2019, ch. 4.
65 G. Borjas, *Immigration
Economics.* Cambridge,
Harvard University Press,
2014, p. 120. A. Nowrasteh,
'Wage effects of immigration
are small' [blog], The Cato
Institute, 10 April 2017,
https://www.cato.org/blog/
wage-effects-immigration-
are-small (accessed 9 March
2020). R. Lowenstein, 'The
immigration equation',
interview with George Borjas,
New York Times, 6 July 2006.
66 F. Jaumotte, K. Koloskova
and S. C. Saxena, 'Impact of
migration on income levels
in advanced economies', The
International Monetary Fund,
24 October 2016.

67 Kerr and Kerr, 2011.
68 'The way forward for
immigration to the West',
The Economist, 25 August
2018.
69 'EEA migration in the UK:
Final report', Migration
Advisory Committee,
September 2018.
70 L. Ku and B. Bruen, 'Poor
immigrants use public
benefits at a lower rate than
poor native-born citizens',
Economic Development
Bulletin no. 17, The Cato
Institute, 4 March 2013.
71 M. Landgrave and A.
Nowrasteh, 'Criminal
immigrants in 2017: Their
numbers, demographics,
and countries of origin',
Immigration Research and
Policy Brief no. 11, The Cato
Institute, March 2017.
72 Duffy, 2019, ch. 4.
73 B. Bell, F. Fasani, and
S. Machin, 'Crime and
immigration: Evidence from
large immigrant waves',
*Review of Economics and
Statistics*, 21(3), 2013.
L, Nunziata, 'Immigration
and crime: Evidence from
victimization data', *Journal of
Population Economics*, 28(3),
2015.
74 R. Putnam, '*E Pluribus Unum*:
Diversity and community in
the twenty-first century –
The 2006 Johan Skytte Prize

lecture', *Scandinavian Political Studies*, *30*(2), 2007.

75 T. Van der Meer and J. Tolsma, 'Ethnic diversity and its effects on social cohesion', *The Annual Review of Sociology*, *40*(1), 2014.

76 'Political scientist: Does diversity really work?', Transcript of interview with Robert Putnam, 'Tell me more', National Public Radio, 15 August 2007, https://www.npr.org/templates/story/story.php?storyId=12802663 (accessed 9 March 2020).

77 R. D. Enos, 'Causal effect of intergroup contact on exclusionary attitudes', *Proceedings of the National Academy of Sciences*, *111*(10), 2014.

3

Open minds

1 A. Freeborn, 'How a seaweed scientist helped win the war', Natural History Museum, 26 March 2014, https://www.nhm.ac.uk/natureplus/blogs/behind-the-scenes/2014/03/26/how-a-seaweed-scientist-helped-win-the-war.html (accesed 9 March 2020).

2 K. R. Lakhani, L. B. Jeppesen, P. A. Lohse and J. A. Panatta, 'The value of openness in scientific problem solving', Harvard Business School Working Paper 07-050, 2007. See also Nielsen, 2012.

3 K. Popper, *Conjectures and Refutations: The Growth of Scientific Knowledge*. London, Routledge, 2014, p. 66.

4 E. Schrödinger, *Nature and the Greeks and Science and Humanism*. Cambridge, Cambridge University Press, 1996, ch. 4.

5 Popper, 1966, vol. 1, p. 177.

6 A. Gregory, *Eureka! The Birth of Science*. London, Icon Books, 2017, p. 11f.

7 Popper, 1966, vol. 1, p. 177.

8 Aristotle, *Nicomachean Ethics*, 1096a, 11–15.

9 Thucydides, *The Landmark Thucydides*. New York, Simon & Schuster, 2008, p. 113.

10 J. Goldstone, *Why Europe? The Rise of the West in World History, 1500–1850,*. New York, McGraw-Hill, 2009, p. 48.

11 St. Augustine of Hippo, *The City of God*, Altenmünster, Jazzybee Verlag, 2015, ch. 41.

12 They hated the Persian culture, however, and soon wanted to return home. In a sign of his feelings for them, the Persian king inserted a clause in a peace treaty with Justinian that the philosophers should be allowed to return and live in peace. C. Nixey, *The Darkening Age: The Christian Destruction of the Classical World*. London, Macmillan, 2017, ch. 16.

13 S. Greenblatt, *The Swerve: How the World Became Modern*. New York, W. W. Norton & Company, 2011, ch. 4.

14 Nixey, 2017, p. 165f.

15 The classic *Monty Python* shows only survived because they were bought by the more fragmented US television market, which preserved copies. J. Rossen, 'Wipe out: When the BBC kept erasing its own history', *Mental Floss*, 8 August 2017, https://www.mentalfloss.com/article/501607/wipe-out-when-bbc-kept-erasing-its-own-history (accessed 9 March 2020).

16 A. Gottlieb, *The Dream of Reason: A History of Philosophy from the Greeks to the Renaissance*. London, Penguin Books, 2016, p. 363.

17 P. Athanassiadi, *Mutations of Hellenism in Late Antiquity*. Oxford, Routledge, 2017, p. 28.

18 J. Marozzi, *Islamic Empires: The Cities that Shaped Civilization: From Mecca to Dubai*. New York, Pegasus Books, 2019, ch. 3.

19 D. Landes, *The Wealth and Poverty of Nations: Why Some are so Rich and Some so Poor*. New York, W. W. Norton & Company, 1999, p. 54.

20 For the strange detours Aristotle's texts took to reach us, see B. Laughlin, *The Aristotle Adventure*. Flagstaff, Albert Hale Publishing, 1995.

21 E. Chaney, 'Religion and the rise and fall of Islamic science', Harvard University, May 2016, https://scholar.harvard.edu/files/chaney/files/paper.pdf (accessed 9 March 2020). See also T. Kuran, *The Long Divergence: How Islamic Law Held Back the Middle East*. Princeton, Princeton University Press, 2011.

22 *The Letters of St Augustine*. Altenmünster, Jazzybee Verlag, 2015, p. 228.

23 Chaney, 2016.

24 Lord Acton, *The History of Freedom*. Altenmünster, The Acton Institute, 1993, p. 60.

25 D. L. Lewis, *God's Crucible: Islam and the Making of Europe, 570–1215*. New York, Liveright Publishing, 2018, p. 369.

26 Goldstone, 2009, p. 171.

27 Brother Azarias, *Aristotle and the Church*. New York, Kegan, Paul & Trench, 1888, ch. 7.

28 R. B. Rubenstein, *Aristotle's Children: How Christians, Muslims, and Jews Rediscovered Ancient Wisdom and Illuminated the Middle Ages*. Orlando, Harvest, 2004, p. 184.

29 Laughlin, 1995.

30 A. Magnus, *Book of Minerals*. Oxford, Clarendon Press, 1967, book II; tractate II, ch. 1, p. 69.

31 Landes, 1999, p. 201.

32 K. Devlin, *Logic and Information*. Cambridge, Cambridge University Press, 1995, p. 7.

33 Aristotle, *Nicomachean Ethics*, 1179a.

34 Gottlieb, 2016, p. 430.

35 Landes, 1999, p. 202.

36 H. J. Cook, *Matters of Exchange*. New Haven, Yale University Press, 2007, p. 41.

37 A. Chafuen, *Christians for Freedom: Late-Scholastic Economics*. San Francisco, Ignatius Press, 1986.

38 Goldstone, 2009, p. 117. J. Goldstone, *Revolution and Rebellion in the Early Modern Period*. New York, Routledge, 2016, pp. 452ff.

39 M. Koyama and M. Meng Xue, 'The literary inquisition: The persecution of intellectuals and human capital accumulation in China', George Mason University Working Paper in Economics 15-12, 14 February 2015.

40 Greenblatt, 2011, p. 239.

41 J. Mokyr, *A Culture of Growth: The Origins of the Modern Economy*. Princeton, Princeton University Press, 2017, p. 156.

42 H. F. Cohen, *How Modern Science Came Into the World: Four Civilizations, One 17th-Century Breakthrough*. Amsterdam, Amsterdam University Press, 2010, p. 439.

43 D. Hume, *Essays: Moral, Political and Literary*. Indianapolis, Liberty Fund, 1987, pp. 119ff.

44 P. T. Hoffman, *Why Did Europe Conquer the World?* Princeton, Princeton University Press, 2015, p. 108.

45 E. L. Jones, *The European Miracle: Environments, Economies and Geopolitics in the History of Europe and Asia*. Cambridge, Cambridge University Press, 1987, p. 111.

46 J. B. DeLong and A. Shleifer, 'Princes and merchants', in A. Shleifer and R. W. Vishny, *The Grabbing Hand: Government Pathologies and Their Cures*. Cambridge, Harvard University Press, 1998.

47 Mokyr, 2017, p. 167.

48 Ibid, p. 178.

49 Ibid, p. 189.

50 T. Ferris, *The Science of Liberty: Democracy, Reason, and the Laws of Nature*. New York, Harper Perennial 2010, p. 83.

51 P. Bayle, *Historical and Critical Dictionary*. London, J. J. and P. Knapton, 1735, p. 389.

52 Mokyr, 2017, p. 108.

53 Mokyr, 2017, p. 199.

54 D. S. Chawla, 'Hyperauthorship: Global projects spark surge in thousand-author papers', *Nature*, *13*, 2019.

55 Mill, 1868, p. 25.

56 P. E. Tetlock, *Expert Political Judgement: How Good is It? How Can We Know?* Princeton, Princeton University Press, 2006. Just to be clear, confirmation bias doesn't just affect our opponents, even though our own confirmation bias makes us remember their mistakes more. Personally, I have predicted runaway inflation and a housing bust in Stockholm so many times that I don't trust myself any more. (I just write it down here so that my confirmation bias will not make me forget that I ever did.)

57 Ferris, 2010, p. 211.

58 G. Shih, E. Rauhala and L. H. Sun, 'Early missteps and state secrecy in China probably allowed the coronavirus to spread farther and faster', *Washington Post*, 1 February 2020.

59 Y. Inbar and J. Lammers, 'Political diversity in social and personality psychology', *Perspectives on Psychological Science*, *7*(5), 2012.

60 J. M. Jones, 'More U.S. college students say campus climate deters speech', Gallup, 12 March 2018, https://news.gallup.com/poll/229085/college-students-say-campus-climate-deters-speech.aspx (accessed 9 March 2020).

61 J. S. Mill, *On Liberty*. London, Savill and Edwards, 1868, p. 25.

62 J. Boyer, *The University of Chicago: A History*. Chicago, The University of Chicago Press, 2015, pp. 263–8.

63 H. Spencer, *The Man Versus the State: With Six Essays on Government, Society and Freedom*. Indianapolis, Liberty Classics, 1982, p. 230.

64 T. Standage, *A History of the World in 6 Glasses*. New York, Walker & Company, 2006, ch. 8.

4

Open societies

1   D. McCloskey, *Bourgeois Equality: How Ideas, Not Capital or Institutions, Enriched the World*. Chicago, The University of Chicago Press, 2016, p. 7.

2   If you like what you're hearing, I've got a book on it: Norberg, 2016.

3   See, for example, J. Goldstone, 'Efflorescences and economic growth in world history: Rethinking the "rise of the West" and the Industrial Revolution', *Journal of World History*, *13*(2), 2002.

4   S. Davies, *The Wealth Explosion: The Nature and Origins of Modernity*. Brighton, Edward Everett Root, 2019, p. 85.

5   M. Elvin, *The Pattern of the Chinese Past*. California, Stanford University Press, 1973, p. 167.

6   T. G. Palmer, *Realizing Freedom: Libertarian Theory, History, and Practice*. Washington, DC, The Cato Institute, 2009, p. 351.

7   B. McKnight and H. Kuklick, *Law and Order in Sung China*. Cambridge, Cambridge University Press, 1992, pp. 53ff.

8   Elvin, 1973, p. 198.

9   Palmer, 2009, p. 351.

10 Davies, 2019, p. 95.

11 Mill, 1868, p. 42.

12 Chua, 2007, p. 75f.

13 D. Acemoglu and J. A. Robinson, *Why Nations Fail: The Origins of Power, Prosperity, and Poverty*. New York, Crown Business, p. 223.

14 L. White, *Modern Capitalist Culture*. London, Routledge, 2016, p. 77.

15 S. Ogilvie, *The European Guilds: An Economic Analysis*. Princeton, Princeton University Press, 2019, p. 462f.

16 Ogilvie, 2019, pp. 470ff.

17 Acton, 1993, p. 62.

18 Jones, 1987, p. 91f.

19 C. Hill, *The Century of Revolution: 1603–1714*. London, Routledge, 2002, p. 31f.

20 Popper, 1966, vol. 1, p. 176.

21 A. Sharp (ed.), *The English Levellers*. Cambridge, Cambridge University Press, 1998, pp. 153, 173, 136ff.

22 H. N. Brailsford, *The Levellers and the English Revolution*. Manchester, C. Nicholls & Company Ltd, 1976, p. 624.

23 S. Pincus, *1688: The First Modern Revolution*. New Haven, Yale University Press, 2009, p. 51.

24 McCloskey, 2016, p. 291.

25 Pincus, 2009, p. 369f.

26 R. Aschcraft, *Revolutionary Politics & Locke's Two Treatises of Government*. Princeton, Princeton University Press, 1986, ch. 6. For the connection between Levellers and Whigs, see also G. De Krey, *Following the Levellers, vol. 2: English Political and Religious Radicals from the Commonwealth to the Glorious Revolution, 1649–1688*. London, Palgrave Macmillan, 2018.

27 J. Locke, *Two Treatises of Government*, edited by P. Laslett. Cambridge, Cambridge University Press, 1690/1988, p. 297.

28 Acemoglu and Robinson, 2012, p. 102.

29 W. Röpke, *The Social Crisis of Our Time*. Chicago, The University of Chicago Press, 1950, p. 39.

30 Acemoglu and Robinson, 2012, pp. 305ff.

31 R. Dowden, *Africa: Altered States, Ordinary Miracles*. London, Granta Books, 2014, p. 367.

32 J. Mokyr, *The Enlightened Economy: Britain and the Industrial Revolution 1700–1850*. London, Penguin Books, 2011, p. 111.

33 This was in itself enough to lift the country, thought Adam Smith almost a century later: 'That security which the laws of Great Britain give to every man that he shall enjoy the fruits of his own labour, is alone sufficient to make any country flourish', Smith, 1981, p. 540.

34 Landes, 1999, p. 222.

35 Mokyr, 2011, p. 410.

36 Goldstone, 2009, p. 129.

37 Mokyr, 2005, p. 268. Many Luddite riots were not really anti-machine, but just a way to destroy something valuable as a negotiating tactic. The famous story that the inventor of the flying shuttle, John Kay, had to flee to France because of angry workers is apocryphal. He fled because of financial difficulties.

38 Pincus, 2009, p. 485.

39 G. H. Smith, *The System of Liberty: Themes in the History of Classica Liberalism*. Cambridge, Cambridge University Press, p. 193.

40 Mokyr, 2011, p. 397f.

41 Smith, 1981, p. 898.

42 A. Cobban, *A History of Modern France*. Middlesex, Penguin Books, 1957, p. 15.

43 D. Ormrod, *The Rise of Commercial Empires: England and the Netherlands in the Age of Mercantilism, 1650–1770*. Cambridge, Cambridge University Press, 2003, p. 92f.

44 Voltaire, *Letters on England*.

London, Penguin Books, 2005, p. 41.

45 For a critique of the outdated view that empire and slavery made Britain rich, see F. Segerfeldt, *Den Svarte Mannens Börda*. Stockholm, Timbro, 2018.

46 Mokyr, 2011, p. 389, p. 122.

47 D. Defoe, *A Plan of the English Commerce*. London, Charles Rivington, 1728, p. 300.

48 A. P. Usher, 'The industrialisation of modern Britain', *Technology and Culture*, *1*(2), 1960.

49 J. Mokyr, 'The knowledge society: Theoretical and historical underpinnings', Presented to the Ad Hoc Expert Group on Knowledge Systems, United Nations, New York, 4–5 September 2005.

50 J. Boswell, *The Life of Samuel Johnson*. London, John Murray, 1831, vol. 5, p. 67.

51 R. C. Allen, 'The great divergence in European wages and prices from the Middle Ages to the First World War', *Explorations in Economic History, 3 8*(4), 2001.

52 D. McCloskey, *Bourgeois Virtues: Ethics for an Age of Commerce*. Chicago, The University of Chicago Press, 2006, p. 25.

53 S. Coontz, *Marriage: A History*. London, Penguin Books, 2006, p. 146.

54 Acemoglu and Robinson, 2012, p. 26.

55 Jefferson, 1993, pp. 456, 558.

56 B. Bailyn, *The Ideological Origins of the American Revolution*. Cambridge, The Belknapp Press, 1967, p. 28.

57 A. Greenspan and A. Wooldridge, *Capitalism in America: A History*. New York, Penguin Press, 2018, p. 10.

58 Goldstone, 2009, p. 129. Greenspan and Wooldridge, 2018, p. 8. See also H. Evans, *They Made America*. New York, Little, Brown and Company, 2004.

59 A. Lincoln, *Speeches and Writings 1859–1865: Speeches, Letters, and Miscellaneous Writings, Presidential Messages and Proclamations*. New York, Library of America, 1989, p. 3f.

60 M. Weber, *The Protestant Ethic and the Spirit of Capitalism*. Mineola, Dover Publications, 2003, p. 17.

61 D. M. Levy, *How the Dismal Science Got its Name*. Ann Arbor, The University of Michigan Press, 2002, p. 41.

62 A. Smith, *The Theory of Moral Sentiments*, in *The Glasgow Edition of the Works and Correspondence of Adam Smith*. Indianapolis, Liberty Fund, 1759/1979, p. 206f.

63 Levy, 2002.
64 T. L. Haskell, 'Capitalism and the origins of the humanitarian sensibility', parts I and II, *The American Historical Review*, 90(2 and 3), 1985.
65 F. Engels, 'Outlines of a critique of political economy', Deutsch-Französische Jahrbücher, 1844, https://www.marxists.org/archive/marx/works/1844/df-jahrbucher/outlines.htm (accessed 9 March 2020).
66 P. Cone, *Pre-Industrial Societies: Anatomy of the Pre-Modern World*. London, Oneworld, 2015.
67 T. Bisson, *Cultures of Power: Lordship, Status, and Process in Twelfth-Century Europe*. Philadelphia, University of Pennsylvania Press, 1995, p. 153.

5

Us and them

1 S. Zweig, *The World of Yesterday*. London, Cassel & Company Ltd, 4th edition, 1947, ch. 1.
2 H. Spencer, *Herbert Spencer: Structure, Function and Evolution*, edited by S. Andreski. London, Nelson, 1972, p. 213.
3 H. Trevor-Roper, *The Crisis of the Seventeenth Century: Religion, The Reformation, and Social Change*. Indianapolis, Liberty Fund, 1967, p. 83f.
4 S. Connor, 'War, what is it good for? It made us less selfish', *Independent*, 5 June 2009.
5 J.-K. Choi and S. Bowles, 'The coevolution of parochial altruism and war', *Science*, 318(5850), 2007. S. Bowles, 'Did warfare among ancestral hunter-gatherers affect the evolution of human social behaviors?' *Science*, 324(5932), 2009.
6 J. Greene, *Moral Tribes: Emotion, Reason, and the Gap Between Us and Them*. London, Atlantic Books, 2015, p. 23.
7 D. E. Brown, *Human Universals*. New York, McGraw-Hill, 1991.
8 E. Simas, S. Clifford and J. Kirkland, 'How empathic concern fuels political polarization', *American Political Science Review*, 114(1), 2019.

9 C. Magris, *Danube*. London, Harvill Press, 2011, p. 45f.

10 H. Tajfel, 'Experiments in intergroup discrimination', *Scientific American*, 223(5), 1970.

11 M. Billig and H. Tajfel, 'Social categorization and similarity in intergroup behaviour', *European Journal of Social Psychology*, 3(1), 1973.

12 Words like 'tribes' and 'tribalism' must be thought of in an adjectival sense, not as literal nouns. Tribes only appeared some 10,000 years ago, with agriculture. During most of mankind's existence we lived in bands. But those bands were 'tribal'.

13 J. Sidanius, H. Haley, L. Molina and F. Pratto, 'Vladimir's choice and the distribution of social resources', *Group Processes Intergroup Relations*, 10(2), 2007.

14 C. Stangor, *Social Groups in Action and Interaction*. New York, Psychology Press, 2004, ch. 5. See also M. Klintman, T. Lunderquist and A. Olsson, *Gruppens Grepp*. Stockholm, Natur & Kultur, 2018.

15 R. Chillot, 'Do I make you uncomfortable?', *Psychology Today*, 5 November 2013. L. Aarøe, M. B. Petersen and K. Arceneaux, 'The behavioral immune system shapes political intuitions', *American Political Science Review*, 111(2), 2017.

16 Vasey et al., 'It was as big as my head, I swear!: Biased spider size estimation in spider phobia', *Journal of Anxiety Disorders*, 26(1), 2012. J. H. Riskind, R. Moore and L. Bowley, 'The looming of spiders: The fearful perceptual distortion of movement and menace', *Behaviour Research and Therapy*, 33(2), 1995.

17 Y. J. Xiao and J. J. Van Bavel, 'See your friends close and your enemies closer', *Personality and Social Psychology Bulletin*, 38(7), 2012.

18 J. K. Hamlin, N. Mahajan, Z. Liberman and K. Wynn, 'Not like me = bad: Infants prefer those who harm dissimilar others', *Psychological Science*, 24(4), 2013.

19 G. Hein, G. Silani, K. Preuschoff, C. D. Batson and T. Singer, 'Neural responses to ingroup and outgroup members' suffering predict individual differences in costly helping', *Neuron*, 68(1), 2010.

20 D. Berreby, *Us & Them: The Science of Identity*. Chicago, The University of Chicago Press, 2008, p. 25.

21 G. Cohen, 'Party over policy: The dominating impact of

group influence on political beliefs', *Journal of Personality and Social Psychology*, *85*(5), 2003. If you are looking for a real-world example, look at how Republican voters quickly switched from being free traders to being protectionists the moment protectionist Donald Trump became their president.

22 R. Wrangham, *The Goodness Paradox: How Evolution Made Us More and Less Violent*. London, Profile Books, 2019, p. 3.

23 Wrangham, 2019. See also C. Boehm, *Moral Origins, The Evolution of Virtue, Altruism, and Shame*. New York, Basic Books, 2012.

24 S. Shergill, P. Bays, C. Frith and D. Wolpert, 'Two eyes for an eye: The neuroscience of force escalation', *Science*, *301*(5630), 2003.

25 J. Haidt, 'The new synthesis in moral psychology', *Science*, *316*(5827), 2007.

26 W. von Hippel, interview on *The Wright Show*, https://www.youtube.com/watch?v=bhChHOWI2Mw (accessed 9 March 2020).

27 M. Simons, 'Mother Superior's role in Rwanda horror is weighed', *New York Times*, 6 June 2001.

28 A. Sen, *Identity & Violence: The Illusion of Destiny*.

London, Penguin Books, 2007, p. 4.

29 R. Kurzban, J. Tooby and L. Cosmides, 'Can race be erased? Coalitional computation and social categorisation', *Proceedings of the National Academy of Sciences*, *98*(26), 2001.

30 Medieval Sourcebook: Twelfth Ecumenical Council: Lateran IV 1215, Fordham University, http://www.fordham.edu/halsall/basis/lateran4.asp (accessed 9 March 2020).

31 J. van Bavel and W. Cunningham, 'When "They" become part of "Us", "They" don't all look alike', *Personality and Social Psychology, Connections*, 25 February 2013, https://spsptalks.wordpress.com/2013/02/25/socialidandpersonmemory/ (accessed 9 March 2020).

32 E. O. Wilson, *On Human Nature: Twenty-Fifth Anniversary Edition*. Cambridge, Harvard University Press, 2004, p. 163.

33 A. Terracciano et al., 'National character does not reflect mean personality trait levels in 49 cultures', *Science*, *310*(5745), 2005. R. McCrae and A. Terracciano, 'National character and personality', *Current Directions in Psychological Science*, *15*(4),

2006. R. McCrae et al.,
'The inaccuracy of national
character stereotypes', *Journal
of Research in Personality*,
47(6), 2013.

34 Berreby, 2008, p. 178.

35 Berreby, 2008, p. 163.

36 K. Popper, *In Search of a Better
World: Lectures and Essays
From Thirty Years*. London,
Routledge, 2012, p. 189.

37 Appiah, 2018, p. 198. See
also D. Herbjørnsrud, 'The
real battle of Vienna', Aeon
Essays, 24 July 2018, https://
aeon.co/essays/the-battle-
of-vienna-was-not-a-fight-
between-cross-and-crescent
(accessed 9 March 2020).

38 'Trump supporters need not
apply', *The Economist*, 18 July
2019.

39 J. Martherus, A. Martinez,
P. Piff and A. Theodoridis,
'Party animals? Extreme
partisan polarization and
dehumanization', *Political
Behavior*, 2019, https://
www.researchgate.net/
publication/334206437_
Party_Animals_Extreme_
Partisan_Polarization_and_
Dehumanization (accessed
9 March 2020).

40 M. Gentzkov and J. Shapiro,
'Ideological segregation
online and offline', *The
Quarterly Journal of Economics*,
126(4), 2011.

41 A. Strindberg, *En Blå Bok III*.

Stockholm, Bonniers, p. 1031.

42 YouGov Survey, 24–26
August 2015, https://
d25d2506sfb94s.cloudfront.
net/cumulus_uploads/
document/ldqd85v3ie/
tabs_HP_Presidential_
Policy_20150826.pdf
(accessed 9 March 2020).

43 'How Brexit made Britain
a country of Remainers and
Leavers', *The Economist*,
20 June 2019.

44 Martherus et al., 2019.

45 F. Elliott, 'Brexit: Remainers
"more bothered" by differing
views in family, poll shows',
The Times, 19 January 2019.

46 K. Stenner, *The Authoritarian
Dynamic*. Cambridge, Cam-
bridge University Press, 2005.

47 C. Bodenner, 'If you want
identity politics, identity
politics is what you get', *The
Atlantic*, 11 November 2016.

48 S. Pinker, *The Better Angels
of Our Nature: The Decline
of Violence in History and Its
Causes*. London, Allen Lane,
2011.

49 E. Paluck, S. Green and
D. Green, 'The contact
hypothesis re-evaluated',
Behavioural Public Policy,
3(2), 2018, https://papers.
ssrn.com/sol3/papers.
cfm?abstract_id=2973474
(accessed 9 March 2020).

50 M. Levine , A. Prosser,
D. Evans and S. Reicher,

'Identity and emergency intervention: How social group membership and inclusiveness of group boundaries shape helping behavior', *Personality and Social Psychology Bulletin*, *31*(4), 2005.

51 Berreby, 2008, p. 17f.

52 Paine, 1967, p. 218. See also Pinker, 2011.

53 M. B. Brewer, 'Ingroup identification and intergroup conflict: When does ingroup love become outgroup hate?', in R. D. Ashmore, L. Jussim and D. Wilder (eds.), *Social Identity, Intergroup Conflict, and Conflict Reduction*. New York, Oxford University Press, 2001.

6

Zero-sum

1 R. Wright, *The Evolution of God*. New York, Back Bay Books, 2010.

2 Sidanius et al., 2007.

3 R. Niebuhr, *Moral Man and Immoral Society, A Study in Ethics and Politics*. Louisville, Westminster John Knox Press, 2001, pp. xxv and 22.

4 B. M. Friedman, *The Moral Consequences of Growth*. New York, Alfred A. Knopf, 2005.

5 Letter from Marx to Engels, 15 August 1857, Marx–Engels Correspondence 1857, https://marxists.catbull.com/archive/marx/works/1857/letters/57_08_15.htm (accessed 9 March 2020).

6 V. Lenin, *Imperialism: The Highest Stage of Capitalism*. London, Penguin Books, 2010.

7 T. Cowen, *Stubborn Attachments*. San Francisco, Stripe, 2018, p. 40.

8 P. H. Rubin, 'Folk economics', *Southern Economic Journal*, 70(1), 2003.

9 B. Caplan, *The Myth of the Rational Voter: Why Democracies Choose Bad Policies*. Princeton, Princeton University Press, 2006, ch. 2.

10 Greene, 2015, p. 12.

11 D. Deutsch, *The Beginning of Infinity: Explanations That Transform the World*. London, Penguin Books, 2012, p. vii.

12 The manager solved the problem by offering the workers high-quality meals

onsite instead. von Hippel, 2018.

13 A. P. Fiske, 'The four elementary forms of sociality: Framework for a unified theory of social relations', *Psychological Review*, 99(4), 1992. L. Cosmides and J. Tooby, 'Adaptations for reasoning about social exchange', in D. M. Buss (ed.), *The Handbook of Evolutionary Psychology, vol. 2: Integrations*. Hoboken, John Wiley & Sons, 2015.

14 J. Jacobs, *Systems of Survival*. New York, Vintage Books, 1994, p. 57.

15 For a wonderful illustration of the complexity of the coffee industry, see A. J. Jacobs, *Thanks a Thousand: A Gratitude Journey from Bean to Cup*. London, Simon & Schuster, 2018.

16 McCloskey, 2016, p. 60.

17 S. Pinker, *The Blank Slate: The Modern Denial of Human Nature*. London, Penguin Books, 2003, p. 234.

18 M. Rice, *The Archaeology of the Arabian Gulf*. London, Routledge, 2002, p. 137f.

19 T. Sowell, *Knowledge and Decisions*. New York, Basic Books, 1996.

20 D. Boudreaux, Facebook post, 2 August 2019.

21 D. Mutz and E. Kim, 'The impact of ingroup favoritism on trade preferences', *International Organization*, 71(4), 2017. The number of jobs is not the best way to measure the effect of trade, since the major benefit of trade is specialization, which creates more wealth and better jobs, not more jobs. But as a proxy for popular attitudes to trade I can live with it.

22 E. Mansfield and D. Mutz, 'Support for free trade: Self-interest, sociotropic politics, and out-group anxiety', *International Organization*, 63(3), 2009.

23 Mutz and Kim, 2017.

24 Even though it is possible to cherish both values and embrace growth but still be critical of, for example, the household registration system that gives urban residents benefits, at the expense of the rural population.

25 W. D. Nordhaus, 'Schumpeterian profits in the American economy: Theory and measurement', NBER Working Paper w10433, 2004, https://ssrn.com/abstract=532992 (accessed 9 March 2020).

26 R. Fogel, *The Escape from Hunger and Premature Death, 1700–2100*. Cambridge, Cambridge University Press, 2004, p. 40.

27 Fogel, 2004, p. 40.

28 J. Schumpeter, *Capitalism, Socialism and Democracy*. New York, Harper Torchbooks, 1962, p. 67.

29 C. Jarrett, 'Survey results: What would you give up for the internet?', Highspeedinternet.com, 30 November 2015, https://www.highspeedinternet.com/resources/new-hsi-survey-reveals-where-americans-values-lie (accessed 9 March 2020).

30 E. Brynjolfsson, F. Eggers and A. Gannamaneni, 'Using massive online choice experiments to measure changes in well-being', NBER Working Paper 24514, 2018.

31 'Have billionaires accumulated their wealth illegitimately?' *The Economist*, 7 November 2019.

32 L. Zingales, *A Capitalism for the People: Recapturing the Lost Genius of American Prosperity*. New York, Basic Books, 2014, p. 59.

33 J. Fernández-Albertos and D. Manzano, 'Dualism and support for the welfare state', *Comparative European Politics*, *14*(3), 2014.

34 K. Simler and R. Hanson, *The Elephant in the Brain: Hidden Motives in Everyday Life*. New York, Oxford University Press, 2018.

35 Wright, 2001, p. 37.

36 The Inuit hunter who makes the first strike on the bear with his spear gets the prized upper half of the skin, and that's important because the long mane hairs of the bear skin are used to line women's boots. M. Shermer, *The Mind of the Market*. New York, Time Books, 2008, p. 16f.

37 D. Friedman, 'The economics of status' [blog], 18 October 2006, http://daviddfriedman.blogspot.com/2006/10/economics-of-status.html (accessed 9 March 2020).

38 von Hippel, 2018.

7

Anticipatory anxiety

1 J. Poushter, 'Worldwide, people divided on whether life today is better than in the past', Pew Research Center, 5 December 2017, https://www.pewresearch.org/global/2017/12/05/worldwide-people-divided-

on-whether-life-today-is-better-than-in-the-past/ (accessed 9 March 2020).

2 W. Rybczynski, *Home: A Short History of an Idea*. New York, Penguin, 1987, p. 9.

3 S. Boym, *The Future of Nostalgia*. New York, Basic Books, 2002.

4 Popper, 1966, vol. 2, p. 50.

5 Geary, 2002, ch. 1.

6 A. J. Levinovitz, 'It never was golden', Aeon Essays, 17 August 2016, https://aeon.co/essays/nostalgia-exerts-a-strong-allure-and-extracts-a-steep-price (accessed 9 March 2020).

7 'The good ol' days', Pessimists Archive, https://pessimists.co/the-good-ol-days/ (accessed 9 March 2020).

8 "American life is too fast', *New York Times*, 21 October 1923.

9 J. R. Gillis, *A World of Their Own Making: Myth, Ritual, and the Quest for Family Values*. Cambridge, Harvard University Press, 1997. See also S. Coontz, *The Way We Never Were: American Families and the Nostalgia Trap*. New York, Basic Books, 2016.

10 Gillis , 1997, pp. 9 and 18.

11 C. A. Goodrich, *Select British Eloquence*. New York, Harper & Brothers, 1853, p. 366.

12 S. N. Kramer, *History Begins at Sumer: Thirty-Nine Firsts in Recorded History*. Philadelphia, University of Pennsylvania Press, 1981, ch. 28.

13 Kramer, 1981, ch. 27.

14 'When, exactly, were the "good old days"?', YouGov, 6 June 2019, https://yougov.co.uk/topics/lifestyle/articles-reports/2019/06/05/when-exactly-were-good-old-days (accessed 9 March 2020). A. McGill, 'Just when was America great?', *The Atlantic*, 4 May 2016, https://www.theatlantic.com/politics/archive/2016/05/make-the-sixties-great-again/481167/ (accessed 9 March 2020).

15 Coontz, 2016, p. xiv.

16 D. Adams, *The Salmon of Doubt*. New York, Del Rey, 2005, p. 95.

17 J. Mokyr, *The Gifts of Athena: Historical Origins of the Knowledge Economy*. Princeton, Princeton University Press, 2005, p. 218.

18 Ibid, p. 266.

19 L. Denault and J. Landis, 'Motion and means: Mapping opposition to railways in Victorian Britain', Mount Holyoke College: History 256, December 1999, https://www.mtholyoke.edu/courses/rschwart/rail/workingcopiesmmla/railfinals/motionandmeans.html (accessed 9 March

2020). See also C. Juma, *Innovation and its Enemies*. New York, Oxford University Press, 2016.

20 'The bicycle', Pessimists Archive, https://pessimists.co/bicycle-archive/ (accessed 9 March 2020).

21 M. Waters, 'The public shaming of England's first umbrella user', Atlas Obscura, 27 July 2016, http://www.atlasobscura.com/articles/the-public-shaming-of-englands-first-umbrella-user (accessed 9 March 2020).

22 Bailey, 2005, p. 242.

23 J. Haidt, *The Righteous Mind: Why Good People are Divided by Politics and Religion*. London, Penguin Books, 2013, p. 172.

24 Hayek, 1982, pp. 56–7.

25 G. K. Chesterton, *The Collected Works of G. K. Chesterton*. San Francisco, Ignatius, 1990, vol. 33, p. 313.

26 V. Postrel, *The Future and Its Enemies: The Growing Conflict Over Creativity, Enterprise and Progress*. New York, Touchstone, 1999, p. xiv.

27 D. Montgomery, 'AOC's Chief of Change', *Washington Post*, 10 July 2019.

28 Matthew Choi, 'Fox News host says Warren "sounds like Donald Trump at his best"', Politico.com, 5 June 2019, https://www.politico.com/

story/2019/06/05/tucker-carlson-elizabeth-warren-donald-trump-1355871 (accessed 9 March 2020).

29 R. A. Stapleton and S. E. Goodman, 'The Soviet Union and the personal computer "revolution"', Report to National Council for Soviet and East European Research, June 1988.

30 'If she can only cook as well as Honeywell can compute', as the ad had it.

31 S. Goodman, 'Soviet computing and technology transfer: An overview', *World Politics*, 31(4), July 1979, p. 544.

32 'Apple wizard says computer "fad" dying', *The Pantagraph*, 20 January 1985. D. Sanger, 'Computers for the home', *The Day*, 5 May 1985.

33 J. McGregor, 'Clayton Christensen's innovation brain', *Bloomberg*, 18 June 2007.

34 Stapleton and Goodman, 1988.

35 J. Edstrom and M. Eller, *Barbarians Led by Bill Gates*. New York, Henry Holt & Company, 1998, p. xii.

36 S. Johnson, 'The internet? We built that', *New York Times*, 21 September 2012.

37 In an email exchange documented here: http://www.nethistory.info/

Archives/origins.html (accessed 9 March 2020).

38 Johnson, 2011, p. 221.

39 Ibid, p. 89.

40 G. Reynolds, *An Army of Davids*. Nashville, Thomas Nelson Inc., 2006, p. 123f.

41 P. Krugman, 'Why most economists' predictions are wrong', *The Red Herring*, June 1998.

42 Edstrom and Eller, 1998, p. 10.

43 Ibid, p. 200.

44 'Some believe computers can have evil effects', *Daytona Beach Morning Journal*, 15 December 1962.

45 J. Bessen, 'The automation paradox', *The Atlantic*, January 2016.

46 'Technology, jobs, and the future of work', McKinsey Global Institute, briefing note, February 2017.

47 Postrel, 1998, p. 19. T. Murphy, 'Your daily newt: A $40 billion entitlement for laptops', Mother Jones, 20 December 2011, https://www.motherjones.com/politics/2011/12/your-daily-newt-nutty-idea-im-just-tossing-out/ (accessed 9 March 2020).

48 C. Ferguson, 'From the people who brought you Voodoo Economics', *Harvard Business Review*, 66(3), 1988.

49 B. Martin, *Under the Loving Care of the Fatherly Leader*. New York, St Martin's Press, 2006, p. 333.

50 T. Sowell, *Basic Economics: A Citizens Guide to the Economy*. New York, Basic Books, p. 74.

51 W. Zhang, 'The logic of the market: An insider's view of Chinese economic reform', Washington, DC, The Cato Institute, 2015. R. Coase and N. Wang, *How China Became Capitalist*. Houndmills, Palgrave Macmillan, 2013.

52 K. X. Zhou, *How the Farmers Changed China: Power of the People*. Boulder, Westview Press, 1996.

53 N. R. Lardy, *Markets over Mao: The Rise of Private Business in China*. Washington, DC, Institute for International Economics, 2014.

54 'Some American startups are borrowing ideas from China', *The Economist*, 19 April 2018.

55 'China wages war on apps offering news and jokes', *The Economist*, 19 April 2018.

56 J. S. Mill, *On Representative Government*. London, Longmans, Green & Co, 1872, p. 46.

57 R. Epstein, *Simple Rules for a Complex World*. Cambridge, Harvard University Press, 1995.

58 A. Wildavsky, 'Progress and public policy', in G. Almond, M. Chodorw and R. H.

Pearce (eds.), *Progress and Its Discontents*. California, University of Californa Press, 1985, p. 366.

59 D. Gilbert, *Stumbling on Happiness*. New York, Vintage Books, 2007, ch. 1.

60 R. Brotherton, *Suspicious Minds: Why We Believe Conspiracy Theories*. London, Bloomsbury Sigma, 2015, p. 110.

61 S. Pinker, 'Enlightenment wars: Some reflections on "Enlightenment Now," one year later', Quilette, 14 January 2009, https://quillette.com/2019/01/14/enlightenment-wars-some-reflections-on-enlightenment-now-one-year-later/ (accessed 9 March 2020).

62 F. A. Hayek, *The Road to Serfdom*. Chicago, The University of Chicago Press, 1994, p. 150.

63 T. Friedman, 'Our one-party democracy', *New York Times*, 8 September 2009.

64 M. Svensson, 'Det viktigaste

för klimatet är att avskaffa demokratin', *Neo*, 10 December 2009.

65 H. L. Mencken, *Prejudices, Second Series*. Timeless Wisdom Collection, 2015, p. 216

66 '2018 Environmental Performance Index: Air quality top public health threat', Yale News, 23 January 2018, https://news.yale.edu/2018/01/23/2018-environmental-performance-index-air-quality-top-public-health-threat (accessed 9 March 2020).

67 Interview, 28 April 2014.

68 Interview, 27 March 2014.

69 This description is based on J. Norberg, *Power to the People*. Hermosa Beach, Sumner Books, 2015.

70 'Economists' statement on carbon dividends', organized by the Climate Leadership Council, https://www.econstatement.org (accessed 9 March 2020).

71 Interview, 28 April 2014.

72 Deutsch, 2012, p. 213.

8

Fight or flight

1 'Skinner v. Railway Labor Executives' Association', no. 87–1555, Argued 2 November 1988, https://www.

law.cornell.edu/supremecourt/text/489/602 (accessed 9 March 2020).

2 J. Huang, A. Sedlovskaya,

J. Ackerman and J. Bargh, 'Immunizing against prejudice: Effects of disease protection on attitudes toward out-groups', *Psychological Science*, *22*(12), 2011.

3 D. Kenrick and V. Griskevicius, *The Rational Animal: How Evolution Made Us Smarter Than We Think.* New York, Basic Books, 2013, p. 28f.

4 S. Schnall, J. Haidt, G. Clore and A. Jordan, 'Disgust as embodied moral judgment', *Journal of Personality and Social Psychology*, *34*(8), 2008.

5 P. Nail, I. McGregor, A. Drinkwater, G. Steele and A. Thompson, 'Threat causes Liberals to think like Conservatives', *Journal of Experimental Psychology*, *45*(4), 2009.

6 L. Rudman, C. Moss-Racusin, J. Phelan and S. Nauts, 'Status incongruity and backlash effects: Defending the gender hierarchy motivates prejudice against female leaders', *Journal of Experimental Social Psychology*, *48*(1), 2012.

7 D. Petrescu and B. Parkinson, 'Incidental disgust increases adherence to left-wing economic attitudes', *Social Justice Research*, *27*(4), 2014.

8 A. Malka, Y. Lelkes and C. Soto, 'Are cultural and economic Conservatism positively correlated? A large-scale cross-national test', *British Journal of Political Science*, *49*(3), 2019.

9 J. Madison, *Letters and Other Writings of James Madison.* Philadelphia, J. B. Lippincott & Co, 1867, vol. 2, p. 7. R. Higgs, *Crisis and Leviathan: Critical Episodes in the Growth of American Government.* New York, Oxford University Press, 1987.

10 E. Quarantelli, 'Human and group behavior in the emergency period of disasters: Now and in the future', Preliminary Paper 36, Disaster Research Center, University of Delaware, 1993.

11 P. Norris and R. Inglehart, *Cultural Backlash: Trump, Brexit and Authoritarian Populism.* Cambridge, Cambridge University Press, 2019, p. 145.

12 J. Napier, J. Huang, A. Vonasch and J. Bargh, 'Superheroes for change: Physical safety promotes socially (but not economically) progressive attitudes among conservatives', *European Journal of Social Psychology*, *48*(2), 2018.

13 'We suck at driving', Polstats, http://polstats.com/#!/life (accessed 9 March 2020).

14 C. Deane, M. Duggan and R. Morin, 'Americans name the 10 most significant historic events of their lifetimes', Pew Research Center, 15 December 2016.

15 I. Haas and W. Cunningham, 'The uncertainty paradox: Perceived threat moderates the impact of uncertainty on political tolerance', *Political Psychology*, *35*(2), 2014.

16 E. Murphy, J. Gordon and A. Mullen, 'A preliminary study exploring the value changes taking place in the United States since the September 11, 2001 terrorist attack on the World Trade Center in New York', *Journal of Business Ethics*, *50*(1), 2004. E. Murphy, W. Teeple and M. Woodhull, '9/11 impact on teenage values', *Journal of Business Ethics*, *69*(4), 2006.

17 S. D. Levitt and S. J. Dubner, *Freakonomics*. London, Allen Lane, 2005, p. 48.

18 Stenner, 2005, p. 137.

19 J. Haidt, 'When and why nationalism beats globalism', *The American Interest*, *12*(1), 2016.

20 'Crime', Gallup, https://news.gallup.com/poll/1603/crime.aspx (accessed 9 March 2020).

21 Kaufmann, 2018. E. Kaufmann, 'Levels or changes?: Ethnic context, immigration and the UK Independence Party vote 2016', *Electoral Studies*, *48*, 2017. D. Mutz, 'Status threat, not economic hardship, explains the 2016 presidential vote', *Proceedings of the National Academy of Sciences*, *115*(19), 2018. Norris and Inglehart, 2019.

22 J. Jones, 'Democrats' confidence in economy steadily eroding', Gallup, 31 May 2017, https://news.gallup.com/poll/211583/democrats-confidence-economy-steadily-eroding-post-obama.aspx (accessed 9 March 2020).

23 Stenner, 2005, p. 58. Norris and Inglehart, 2019, p. 280.

24 See S. M. Lipset, 'Democracy and working-class authoritarianism', *American Sociological Review*, *24*(4), 1959.

25 M. Lüthi, *The Fairytale: As Art Form and Portrait of Man*. Bloomington, Indiana University Press, 1984, p. 55.

26 Plato, *Republic*, in J. Cooper (ed.), *Complete Works*. Indianapolis, Hackett Publishing, 1997, p. 1177.

27 Goldstone, 2016, p. 452.

28 H. L. Mencken, *In Defense of Women*. Mineola, Dover Publications, 2004, p. 29.

29 Snyder, 2018, p. 50f.

30 'Fox & Friends' [video], Fox News, 10 February 2014.

31 J. Greenberg, T. Pyszczynski, S. Solomon et al., 'Evidence for terror management theory II,' *Journal of Personality and Social Psychology*, *5*8(2), 1990.

32 Trevor-Roper, 1967, p. 74.

33 Stenner, 2005, p. 335.

34 J. Haidt and K. Stenner, 'Authoritarianism is not a momentary madness', in C. R. Sunstein (ed.), *Can It Happen Here?* New York, HarperCollins, 2018, p. 209.

35 K. Dunn, 'Authoritarianism and intolerance under autocratic and democratic regimes', *Journal of Social and Political Psychology*, 2(1), 2014.

36 F. Zakaria, *The Future of Freedom: Illiberal Democracy at Home and Abroad*. New York, W. W. Norton & Company, 2004.

37 M. Norton and S. Sommers, 'Whites see racism as a zero-sum game that they are now losing', *Perspectives on Psychological Science*, 6(3), 2011.

38 S. Sales, 'Threat as a factor in authoritarianism: An analysis of archival data', *Journal of Personality and Social Psychology*, 28(1), 1973. D. K. Simonton, *Greatness: Who Makes History and Why*. New York, The Guilford Press, 1994.

39 'The monsters are due on Maple Street', *The Twilight Zone*, season 1, ep. 22, first aired 4 March 1960 on CBS.

40 M. Vargas Llosa, *Lockrop*. Stockholm, Timbro, 2019.

9

Open or closed?

1 'Freedom in the world: Electoral democracies 1989–2016', Freedom House, https://freedomhouse. org/sites/default/files/ Electoral%20Democracy%20 Numbers%2C%20FIW%20 1989-2016.pdf (accessed 9 March 2020).

2 G. Ward, *The Politics of Discipleship*. Grand Rapids, Baker Academic, 2009, p. 49.

3 F. Fukuyama, *The End of History and the Last Man*. London, Penguin Books, 2012, pp. 288 and 312.

4 Fukuyama, 2012, p. 328. See also P. Sagar, 'The last hollow laugh', Aeon Essays, 21 March 2017, https://aeon.co/ essays/was-francis-fukuyama- the-first-man-to-see-trump-

coming (accessed 9 March 2020).

5 Pinker, 2011.

6 S. Huntington, *The Clash of Civilizations and the Remaking of World Order*. New York, Simon & Schuster, 2007, ch. 12.

7 I. Scopelliti, C. Morewedge, E. McCormick, H. L. Min, S. Lebrecht and K. Kassam, 'Bias blind spot: Structure, measurement, and consequences', *Management Science*, 61(10), 2015.

8 G. Cohen, J. Aronson and C. Steele, 'When beliefs yield to evidence: Reducing biased evaluation by affirming the self', *Personality and Social Psychology Bulletin*, 26(9), 2000. The same effect was not found in B. Nyhan and J. Reifler, 'The roles of information deficits and identity threat in the prevalence of misperceptions', *Journal of Elections, Public Opinion and Parties*, 29(2), 2019.

9 'CPS historical migration/geopgraphic mobility tables', United States Census Bureau, November 2019, https://www.census.gov/data/tables/time-series/demo/geographic-mobility/historic.html (accessed 9 March 2020).

10 'The welfare state needs updating', *The Economist*, 12 July 2018.

11 D. Blanchflower and A. Oswald, 'Does high home-ownership impair the labor market?' NBER Working Paper 19079, 2013.

12 D. Goodhart, *The Road to Somewhere: The New Tribes Shaping British Politics*. London, Penguin Books, 2017.

13 'Occupational licensing: A framework for policymakers', The White House, July 2015.

14 D. Carpenter II, L. Knepper, A. Erickson and J. Ross, 'License to work: A national study of burdens from occupational licensing', Institute for Justice, 2012.

15 J. Johnson and M. Kleiner, 'Is occupational licensing a barrier to interstate migration?', Federal Reserve Bank of Minneapolis, Staff report 561, December 2017.

16 J. Kyle and Y. Mounk, 'The populist harm to democracy: An empirical assessment', Tony Blair Institute for Global Change, 26 December 2018, http://institute.global/insight/renewing-centre/populist-harm-democracy (accessed 9 March 2020).

INDEX

physical fallacy, 268
race and, 232
trade, 265
tyranny of cousins, 230
Huntington, Samuel, 110, 362–3, 365–6
Hussein, Saddam, 345
Hussey, Edward, 287
Hutchins, Robert Maynard, 165
Hutus, 230–31
Hypatia, 134
hyper-fast stars, 80

IBM, 305, 307, 319
Ibn al-Haytham, 156
Ibn Hayyan, Jabir, 156
Ibn Rushd, 137–8, 143, 144, 145
ice core drilling, 49
Identity & Violence (Sen), 231
identity politics, 241
al-Idrisi, Muhammad, 137
immigration
    birth rates and, 115
    crime and, 110, 119
    culture and, 69–73, 116, 119, 120–23
    disgust and, 336, 371
    division of labour and, 117
    empires and, 84–106
    European migration crisis (2015–), 10,
        114, 115, 118, 342–3
    exoticism, 84
    GDP and, 68
    innovation and, 81–4
    Islam and, 112–14, 255
    labour market and, 115, 116–19
    opposition to, 69, 70, 114–23, 223,
        254–5
    productivity and, 68, 81, 117, 204
    protectionism and, 66–7
    self-selection and, 107, 112
    skilled vs unskilled, 66, 82, 102, 116,
        117
    trade and, 35, 66–7, 234–5
    tribalism and, 223, 235–6, 240, 243
    urban vs rural areas, 114
    welfare and, 118, 281
    zero-sum thinking and, 254–5, 259
immigration in United States, 102–14
    crime and, 110, 119
    innovation and, 81–2, 202

overestimation of, 115, 223
tribalism and, 223, 240
zero-sum thinking and, 254–5, 259
In Defence of Global Capitalism (Norberg),
    270
in vitro fertilization, 298–9
inbreeding, 78
India, 42, 45, 46, 56, 75, 129, 136, 140,
    146, 270
    Arabic numerals, 70, 137
    engineering in, 269
    Hindu nationalism, 354
    industrialization, 207
    Maurya Empire (323–184 BC), 53
    Mughal Empire (1526–1857), 98, 148,
        149, 215
    national stereotypes, 235
    Pakistan, relations with, 366
    pollution in, 326
    poverty in, 276, 326
Indo-European language, 75
Indonesia, 41
Industrial Revolution; industrialization, 5,
    6, 13, 54, 132, 180, 339
    in Britain, 182, 188–99, 202
    in China, 169, 172–3, 207
    climate change and, 326
    in Dutch Republic, 101
    in India, 207
    in Japan, 71
    in United States, 202, 291–2
    in Vietnam, 207
inequality, 273, 349
Inglehart, Ronald, 339
ingroups and outgroups, 217–47
    fluidity, 230–38
    political, 224–5, 238–42
    zero-sum relationships and, 252–5
Innocent III, Pope, 233
InnoCentive, 126–7
innovation, 4, 6, 10, 27, 80
    ancient world, 32, 42, 44, 46
    authoritarianism and, 318
    bureaucratic inertia and, 318–21
    canon and, 195
    cities and, 40, 53, 79
    creative destruction, 57, 179, 182, 190
    cultural evolution, 28
    immigration and 81–4